NEITHER BELIEVER NOR INFIDEL

NEITHER BELIEVER NOR INFIDEL

SKEPTICISM AND FAITH IN MELVILLE'S SHORTER FICTION AND POETRY

JONATHAN A. COOK

NORTHERN ILLINOIS UNIVERSITY PRESS
an imprint of

CORNELL UNIVERSITY PRESS
Ithaca and London

First published 2023 by Cornell University Press

Library of Congress Cataloging-in-Publication Data

Names: Cook, Jonathan A. (Jonathan Alexander), 1953- author.
Title: Neither believer nor infidel : skepticism and faith in Melville's shorter fiction and poetry / Jonathan A. Cook.
Description: Ithaca [New York] : Northern Illinois University Press, an imprint of Cornell University Press, 2023. | Includes bibliographical references and index.
Identifiers: LCCN 2022051736 (print) | LCCN 2022051737 (ebook) | ISBN 9781501770968 (hardcover) | ISBN 9781501770975 (epub) | ISBN 9781501770982 (pdf)
Subjects: LCSH: Melville, Herman, 1819–1891—Criticism and interpretation. | Faith in literature. | Skepticism in literature.
Classification: LCC PS2387 .C67 2023 (print) | LCC PS2387 (ebook) | DDC 813/.3—dc23/eng/20230125
LC record available at https://lccn.loc.gov/2022051736
LC ebook record available at https://lccn.loc.gov/2022051737

Contents

Preface

Over the last few decades, academic study of the concept of "secularization" in the West has been transformed. According to an older paradigm, a zero-sum conflict was thought to exist between religion and modernity, so that steady advances in scientific rationalism, industrialization, urbanization, and communications media (among other factors) over the last two centuries inevitably led to a retreat of religious faith. Yet the idea of a simple linearity of development from a religious to a secular mind-set has now yielded to more contested and complex designs, including the recognition of the often codependent relationship between religion and science. A growing body of scholarship has thus significantly complicated the idea of a steady progress of secularization in the West; indeed, some commentators have even disputed whether the word and its congeners could still be useful tools for analysis. For if the terms "secularist" and "secularism" as variations on the traditional idea of the "secular" were first introduced in the early 1850s by a leading Victorian freethinker, George Jacob Holyoake, as positive-sounding substitutes for the more pejorative "atheist" and "infidelity," by the early twenty-first century the same terms were newly controversial in connection with whether modern societies were in fact losing their capacity for religious faith, and if so, how the process was unfolding.[1]

Just as the historical idea of secularization has become more problematic, the study of religious doubt in nineteenth-century England and the United States has become more nuanced, with boundary lines between belief and unbelief now recognized as permeable. For it is increasingly clear that previous notions of a uniform transformation of Christian believers into unbelievers following exposure to new scientific and historical knowledge undermining their faith are overly simplistic. Examples of leading Victorian intellectuals confirm the complex intermixtures of faith and doubt in their life histories. Consider the case of the novelist George Eliot, who lost her faith in the freethinking milieu of her young adulthood and went on to translate the German texts of both David F. Strauss's *Life of Jesus* and Ludwig Feuerbach's *Essence of Christianity*; yet in her fiction she nevertheless created a kind of "secular scripture" dramatizing some of the basic moral tenets of Christianity using an array of redemptive Christlike protagonists. So, too, even as he acted throughout his career as Darwin's combative scientific "bulldog," Thomas Henry Huxley also scattered biblical phrases throughout his voluminous writings, likely borrowed from the New Testament (Acts 17:23) for his coinage of the word "agnostic," sought to keep the text of the King James Bible in school curricula, and spent the last decade of his life writing essays on the text of the Bible.[2]

A similarly complex picture emerges with regard to the relationship of Christian faith and doubt in the nineteenth-century United States. For in addition to its vast numbers of evangelical Protestants and tiny population of freethinkers, the nation exhibited comparable patterns of individuals developing from believers into skeptics, or shedding and then resuming their Christian faith, or remaining stuck in a limbo of doubt-ridden belief or anxious unbelief. In *Skepticism and American Faith: From the Revolution to the Civil War*, Charles Grasso presents a rich panorama of notable religious, political, legal, and educational figures in the early national and antebellum eras—including Thomas Cooper, George Bethune English, Frances Wright, Robert Dale Owen, Richard Hildreth, William Alcott, Abner Kneeland, Orestes Brownson, Horace Mann, and John Russell Kelso—whose varied case histories reveal a broad and often fluctuating spectrum of Christian belief and doubt. So, too, in *The Church of Saint Thomas Paine: A Religious History of American Secularism*, Eric Leigh Schmidt has highlighted the tendency among mid- and later nineteenth-century freethinkers to inadvertently mimic Christian traditions, as seen in their unabashed sanctification of the iconic figure of Thomas Paine, their attempt to create secularized funerary rituals, and their organization of secular "churches" for Sunday lectures and fellowship.[3]

By recognizing the shifting and permeable dividing line between Christian belief and unbelief, and the complex nature of secularization in the nineteenth-century Anglo-American world, we can better understand the literary career of Herman Melville, the American author whose writings illustrate many of the era's disruptive religious trends associated with secularization and cultural modernity. For in Melville we see a writer who engaged in a lifelong scrutiny of the truth claims of

Christianity in both his fiction and poetry. Often relying on the Bible as a template for his moral imagination, Melville's writings recurrently negotiate between representations of traditional Christian faith and doubt about its legitimacy—a doubt enhanced by his intellectual engagement with the traditions of classical and modern skepticism.

In a famous 1856 journal entry written in Liverpool, Nathaniel Hawthorne astutely commented that Melville "will never rest until he gets hold of a definite belief," for he "can neither believe nor be comfortable in his unbelief; and he is too honest and courageous not to try to do one or the other." Hawthorne's remarks here encapsulate an essential truth about Melville's ambivalent—and often ambiguous—attitude toward Christianity; for he habitually suspended judgment over its ultimate truth claims, in keeping with the tenets of classical skepticism as articulated by its modern interpreters such as Montaigne and Bayle. In fact, Hawthorne's characterization of Melville's dilemma of endlessly oscillating between belief and unbelief is anticipated by Melville's own earlier assertion, via Ishmael in *Moby-Dick*, of the desirability of such an uncommitted attitude toward religious faith: "Doubts of all things earthly, and intuitions of some things heavenly; this combination makes neither believer nor infidel, but makes a man who regards them both with equal eye." Neither rational doubt nor intuitive faith thus has ultimate sway in Ishmael's view, for both are equal means in an ongoing quest for truth. But these confident and affirmative claims by the narrator of *Moby-Dick*, as spokesman for the author, offer a stark contrast to Hawthorne's more somber evocation of Melville's mood five years later, when the latter's professional literary career was becoming increasingly problematic and would in fact soon come to a premature end.[4]

The subject of Melville and religion—including the shaping influence of religious skepticism—is increasingly recognized as a vital critical approach to his writings. In *Melville's Wisdom: Religion, Skepticism, and Literature in Nineteenth-Century America*, for example, Damien B. Schlarb has provided a detailed investigation into the impact on Melville's literary imagination of the biblical wisdom tradition found in the books of Job, Proverbs, and Ecclesiastes, with their varied messages of skepticism in matters of divine justice and human morality. The present study may be seen to complement the more theoretically driven approach of Schlarb, for while I also examine the impact of Job and Ecclesiastes on two of Melville's fictions from the mid-1850s, my critical aims and findings are significantly different; moreover, I draw on both Old and

New Testament textual referents as they continually shaped Melville's writing. In keeping with arguments for a "post-secular" approach to Melville, as advocated by Schlarb and others, the present study, taking its title from Ishmael's assertions quoted above, seeks to demonstrate that religious concerns—especially the fraught conflict of belief with unbelief—decisively shaped his literary imagination throughout much of his career.[5]

The aim of the present study, then, is to explore the varied dimensions of the religious skepticism and residual faith that informed a significant portion of Melville's writings beginning in the early 1850s, when he began composing his shorter fiction, to his death in 1891, when he left his last work of prose fiction, *Billy Budd*, in manuscript after publishing four volumes of poetry in the last three decades of his life. Chapter 1 accordingly offers, in a biographical overview of the first four decades of his life, an introductory survey of Melville's development as a religious skeptic. Chapters 2 and 3 focus on Melville's fictional subversion of two leading tenets of Christian faith in his first two short stories. Chapter 2 examines Melville's "Bartleby, the Scrivener" as a sustained critique of Christian ideals of charity in which a host of New Testament texts relating to its teachings are ironically inverted within the scrivener's oblique modern reenactment of the career of Christ; for if the depiction of the story's narrator was intended to show his failure fully to embrace New Testament teachings on charity, the impracticability of these same ideals is similarly dramatized in the narrator's efforts to deal with the impassive behavior of his unworldly employee—both factors suggesting a contemporary terminus to the Christian faith. Chapter 3 analyzes the depiction of evangelical Christian ideals of conversion and spiritual resurrection in "Cock-a-Doodle-Doo!," showing Melville's demonstration of the close relationship between self-delusional folly and transformative belief in the seemingly miraculous salvation symbolized by the story's charismatic rooster.

Chapters 4 and 5 survey narratives in which Melville evoked Old Testament–related ideas of earthly injustice and divine indifference to human suffering. Chapter 4 examines the depiction of the female Job figure in the eighth sketch of "The Encantadas, or Enchanted Isles" ("Norfolk Island and the Chola Widow"), as mediated through the cultural type of the "patient Griselda" originally found in Chaucer—a type of uncomplaining female suffering that characterized the story of Agatha Robertson that Melville learned about during a visit to Cape Cod with his father-in-law in July 1852 and then offered to Hawthorne as a subject of fiction, based on a similar theme in Hawthorne's "Wake-field." Chapter 5 traces the influence of the book of Ecclesiastes on *Israel Potter*, Melville's narrative of a Revolutionary War soldier whose transatlantic career illustrates the pessimistic import of this biblical book and its exemplary wisdom of universal "vanity" that Melville singled out for praise in a letter to Hawthorne and highlighted in parts of *Moby-Dick*.

Chapters 6, 7, and 8 examine Melville's ambivalent attitude toward Christian faith in the wake of his initial literary career as a novelist and short story writer when he published only poetry but then resumed writing prose fiction with *Billy Budd* near the end of his life. Chapter 6 focuses on Melville's adaptations of Christian faith and the classical culture of mourning within his first volume of poetry, *Battle-Pieces and Aspects of the War*, in order to perform the civic duty of memorializing the dead in the Civil War. Chapter 7 traces a thematics of doubt in Melville's last published volume of poetry, *Timoleon, Etc.*, in which he explored a range of historical religious traditions while dramatizing Christianity's apparent retreat in the later nineteenth-century Anglo-American world. Finally, chapter 8 reviews Melville's last work of prose fiction, *Billy Budd*, in which Melville seamlessly blended history and myth in his representation of the Fall and the related problem of evil, as derived from source texts in the Bible and Milton's *Paradise Lost*—subjects also examined in the writings of Arthur Schopenhauer in which he immersed himself shortly before his death. As the capstone to his literary career, *Billy Budd* illustrates the hybrid form of "secular scripture" that was symptomatic of the skeptical oscillations between faith and doubt that characterized his career as a writer.

I am grateful to the friends and colleagues who have read parts of this study or offered other forms of assistance. Special thanks are due to Steve Olsen-Smith, Brian Yothers, Dawn Coleman, Richard Kopley, David Diamond, Monika Elbert, Anita Barrett of the Loudoun County Interlibrary Loan office, and Amy Ferranto of NIU Press. An earlier version of chapter 7 was published at *EAPSU Online: A Journal of Critical and Creative Work* (2011): 6–53, and a version of chapter 8 appeared in Brian Yothers, ed., *Critical Insights: Billy Budd* (Ipswich, MA: Salem Press, 2017), 178–96.

.

NEITHER BELIEVER NOR INFIDEL

CHAPTER 1

The Making of a Skeptic

Biographical Considerations

As manifested by his fiction and poetry, Herman Melville was a tireless religious seeker whose lifelong spiritual quest was motivated by a recurrent skepticism toward the truth claims of Christianity, mediated by an equally tenacious devotion to the Bible, with its foundational myth of the Fall providing grounds for his lifelong preoccupation in his writings with the problem of evil. Melville's religious vision was accordingly conditioned by a constant oscillation between faith and doubt, heart and head, typical of many Victorian intellectuals. Coming of age in a distinctly evangelical era of American history marked by ongoing religious revivalism, Melville was exposed to alternative belief systems during his life as a sailor in the Pacific, and then during his early career as a novelist in New York City and then Pittsfield, Massachusetts, when his skeptical mind-set was notably enhanced by his extensive reading. The present chapter will survey the biographical background to the development of Melville's religious skepticism, which made a prominent appearance in his fiction in *Mardi* and then reached mature expression in *Moby-Dick*, while continuing to shape his writings throughout the 1850s and beyond.[1]

By the middle of the nineteenth century, systematic doubt about the supernatural origins of Christianity and the Bible had been fostered by the higher criticism pioneered by German biblical scholars, which sought to analyze the various books of the Old and New Testament in relation to authorship and historical setting. David F. Strauss's *The Life of Jesus, Historically Considered*, published in England in 1846 in a translation by George Eliot, had initiated the process of "demythologizing" the text of the New Testament, legitimated by the new Hegelian philosophy; while Ludwig Feuerbach's *Essence of Christianity*, published in a translation by Eliot in 1854, argued for Christianity as an idealized reflection of human nature. In the realm of British science, Charles Lyell's *Principles of Geology* (1830–33), Robert Chambers's *Vestiges of the Natural History of Creation* (1844), and Charles Darwin's *Origin of Species* (1859) successively undercut the mythical account of the creation outlined in Genesis and generally discredited Christian supernaturalism and dogma. These and other contemporary challenges to Christianity were reflected in the troubled faith or intractable doubt of such leading English authors and intellectuals as Carlyle, Eliot, Mill, Tennyson, Ruskin, Clough, and Arnold, whose writings variously reflected the pervasive mid-nineteenth-century climate of anxiety about the legitimacy and future of Christianity. Moreover, as A. N. Wilson has noted, the religious skepticism of many eminent Victorians was often associated not only with personal depression over loss of faith but also with a wider sense of cultural disintegration: "Nineteenth-century unbelief seldom limits itself to an expression of specific uncertainty about, let us say, the literal truth of the Bible, or the existence of angels. It accompanies wider symptoms of disturbance, a deep sense (personal, political, social) of dissolution."[2]

In the United States, skepticism toward Christianity was often denominated "infidelity," with its most influential text being Thomas Paine's *The Age of Reason* (1794), an outspoken deist attack on the doubtful authority and alleged immorality of the Christian Bible that threatened to derail the country's development as an evangelical Protestant nation in the generation of the Founders. As a result, Paine was demonized by the Federalist political and clerical establishment both before and after he returned to the United States in 1802. Paine's probing critique of the Bible questioned the widely assumed truth of the sacred text and cast doubt on the adequacy of human language to represent supreme religious realities, highlighting the unreliability of the Bible's supernatural truth claims veiled in mystery, miracle, and prophecy. Most shocking to Paine was the apparent immorality of the Bible: "Whenever we read the obscene stories, the voluptuous debaucheries, the cruel and torturous executions, the unrelenting vindictiveness with which more than half the Bible is filled, it would be more consistent that we called it the word of a demon than the word of God. It is a history of wickedness that has served to corrupt and brutalize mankind; and, for my own part, I sincerely detest it, as I detest everything that is cruel." According to Paine, not the unreliable written text of the Christian Bible but the infinitely various "bible" of nature should be the object of human reverence and study. Decrying the influence of Christian priestcraft in alliance with oppressive political regimes, Paine embraced the idea of a rationalized religion to replace the pious frauds propping up Christianity. As Paine concluded, "Of all the systems of religion that ever were invented, there is none more derogatory to the Almighty, more unedifying to man, more repugnant to reason, and more contradictory in itself, than this thing called Christianity. Too absurd for belief, too impossible to convince, and too inconsistent for practice, it renders the heart torpid or produces only atheists and fanatics."[3]

Along with other leading texts promoting deism, notably Ethan Allen's *Reason: The Only Oracle of Man* (1785) and Elihu Palmer's *The Principles of Nature* (1801), Paine's controversial tract provided an ideological counterweight to the incipient forces of the Second Great Awakening and served as a bugaboo for evangelical critics of "infidelity" well into the nineteenth century. The perceived threat to the whole frame of American legal and moral culture from questioning the truth of the Bible and Christianity was famously expressed by President George Washington in his 1796 Farewell Address while responding to the rise of infidelity in revolutionary France: "Let it simply be asked: Where is the security for property, for reputation, for life, if the sense of the religious obligation desert the oaths which are the instruments of investigation in courts of justice? And let us with caution indulge the supposition that morality can be maintained without religion. Whatever may be conceded to the influence of refined education on minds of peculiar [i.e., uncommon] structure, reason and experience both forbid us to expect that national morality can prevail in exclusion of religious principle." Washington thus endorsed the Christian faith as a moral bulwark for the new nation even though in his personal beliefs he was, as David L. Holmes notes, a "Deistic Episcopalian," as were several other Founding Fathers.[4]

Despite this warning from the iconic figure of Washington in his 1796 address, in the second quarter of the nineteenth century the skeptical mind-set toward Christianity that eventually came to be known as "freethought" in America resulted in a proliferation of societies scattered throughout New England, the mid-Atlantic states, and the Old Northwest. While freethinkers could warn about the threat of an increasingly oppressive "Christian" party in the nation's politics, evangelical Christians could use the specter of the "infidel" to scare Christians into orthodox conformity. Freethought lectures and debates nevertheless took place in small but growing numbers from the late 1820s to the mid-1840s, with a grand three-day "Convention of the Infidels of the United States" being held in New York City in May 1845, with five hundred in attendance.[5]

An important influence on the development of freethought in America was the arrival in the 1820s of a number of English immigrants—Robert Owen, Robert Dale Owen, Frances Wright, Gilbert Vale, George Houston, Benjamin Offen, and George Henry Evans—dedicated to various reforms in religion, workingmen's rights, women's rights, education, and abolition. Following his move to the United States in 1824 and his founding of the New Harmony utopian community in Indiana a year later, Robert Owen engaged in frequent proselytizing of his ideas about a revolutionary new economic, moral, and religious model for society. For four days in April 1829, for example, Owen debated Alexander Campbell, founder of the Disciples of Christ, on the validity of the Christian religion, an event chronicled in a two-volume tome, *Debate on the Evidences of Christianity* (Cincinnati, 1831). His son Robert Dale Owen, aided by the outspoken and convention-breaking Frances ("Fanny") Wright, published the reformist and freethought *New Harmony Gazette* and then launched the *Free Enquirer* in New York City in 1829, which they coedited until 1832. Assuming leadership in the Working Men's Party in 1829–30 and producing an early pamphlet on birth control, *Moral Physiology* (1830), Robert Dale Owen set forth his ideas on freethought in various publications, and in 1831 engaged in an extended debate with Origen Bacheler, a defender of Christian orthodoxy, later published as the two-volume *Discussion of the Existence of God and the Authenticity of the Bible* (New York, 1833). For her part, as a popular lecturer advocating a potent mix of social reforms including abolitionism, women's rights, public education, economic equality, and free thought, Fanny Wright—dubbed the "High Priestess of Infidelity"—attained national notoriety with her lecture series in New York, Philadelphia, Boston, and elsewhere on her travels in 1829–30. With her ideas appearing in print as a *Course of Popular Lectures* and

Lectures on Free Inquiry (1829), she established a Hall of Science offering freethought literature and lectures in New York City.[6]

In Boston, the ex-Universalist minister and freethought agitator Abner Kneeland published the *Boston Investigator* beginning in 1831 but was arrested for blasphemy in early 1834 and put on trial five times before he was finally convicted in 1838 and sentenced to serve sixty days in jail—the judge at his final trial being Melville's future father-in-law, Lemuel Shaw. In a two-part article decrying Kneeland and his subversive movement in "Atheism in New-England," published in December 1834 and January 1835 in the *New-England Magazine*, the Unitarian reformer Samuel Gridley Howe estimated the population of "infidels" in the country at fifty thousand—still a very small group compared to the ever-growing host of evangelical Protestants, but a perceived threat to the nation's moral well-being. While evangelicals pointed to the rise of "infidelity" as an alarming sign of cultural decline, freethought inquirers pointed to the existence of a potential "Christian" party in politics as a warning sign that religion was controlling the country, violating the Constitution's separation of church and state.[7]

Symptomatic of the orthodox alarm at the simultaneous liberalization of Christianity and growing spread of freethought was Lyman Beecher's *Lectures on Scepticism* (1835), first delivered in Boston beginning in late 1829 and 1830 at a time when Fanny Wright, Robert Dale Owen, and Abner Kneeland were appealing to audiences and readers in the city where Beecher presided over the Congregational Hanover Street Church from 1826 to 1832; he would repeat the lectures in 1833 in Cincinnati, where he moved to take charge of the Lane Theological Seminary. As an outspoken opponent of dueling, intemperance, Sabbath-breaking, Unitarianism, and Catholicism, Beecher now launched a frontal attack on infidelity of all sorts, saving his harshest denunciations, in his lecture "Political Atheism," for the small contemporary movement of freethought, which he considered a potential threat capable of unleashing the horrors of another French Revolution: "It is not, then, by a numerical majority at the polls only that this atheistic minority may destroy us. They may create a pestilent atmosphere, and send out moral contagion, and blow blasting and mildew from between their shriveled lips. They may poison the fountains, and fever the heart, and madden the brain of the nation. . . . Let the belief and feeling of accountability fail from the public mind, and poverty, and envy, and ambition, and lust, be summoned to a crusade against religion, and purity, and property, and law, and how long would the police of our cities protect us?" Like Samson belaboring the Philistines with the jawbone of an ass, Beecher used a rhetorical bludgeon to go after a host of contemporary foes—the higher criticism, Unitarian rationalism, spiritual backsliding—but saved his most hyperbolic blows for the freethought radicals (whose names were never mentioned) working to subvert the authority of Christianity as the moral basis of American society.[8]

The development of Herman Melville's religious faith and ensuing disenchantment with Christianity mirrored many of the larger cultural trends of the day. During his childhood in New York City in the 1820s and then boyhood in Albany in 1830–37, Melville was initially exposed to elements of his father's liberal Unitarianism and then, more copiously, his mother's Dutch Reformed Calvinism, both denominations providing the basis for an antithetical theological mix that shaped his ideas of Christianity for much of his later life. During his brief stint at the Albany Academy in 1830–31, Melville's studies included classical biography and Jewish antiquities, and he would later be enrolled at the Albany Classical School in 1835, where he developed his writing skills in English, and then at the Albany Academy in the fall of 1836 to improve his Latin. Both institutions offered training in a range of practical business skills as well as the inculcation of Christian virtues. Following his father's premature death in January 1832, Melville was thoroughly exposed to the Calvinist belief system of his mother's well-established Albany family, the Gansevoorts, attending church twice on Sundays and becoming steeped in the stern ideas of original sin, predestination, and divine sovereignty in keeping with the tenets of the Heidelberg Confession; and throughout his youth he would be developing a deep familiarity with the text of the Christian Bible at church, at school, and at home.[9]

Although immersed as a teenager in the forbidding theological world of his mother's family in the early 1830s, in the latter part of the decade Melville would also have been exposed to the strains of freethought found in the *Albany Microscope* (1819–48), a satirical muckraking weekly newspaper edited and published by Joel Munsell, in which Melville first appeared in print during the floridly vituperative exchange of letters in early 1838 in connection with leadership of the Philo Logos Society. Successor to the Ciceronian Debating Society, this new debating group was also affiliated with the Albany Young Men's Society for Mutual Improvement, which Melville joined in 1836 following the lead of his older brother Gansevoort. As part of his response in 1838 to Charles Van Loon, who was studying to become a Baptist minister and had denounced Herman as a *"Ciceronian baboon"* and "moral Ethiopian," Melville sarcastically attacked his opponent's hostility and rancor: "May these truly christian attributes cling around the sacred lawn with which you are hereafter to be invested, and your angelic nature be a fit illustration of the peaceful spirit of the gospel you profess." Such a critical defrocking of a morally fallible Christian would be a regular feature of Melville's future fiction and was also eminently appropriate for the organ in which he was publishing. The *Albany Microscope*'s editor, Joel Munsell, an admirer of Thomas Paine, regularly skewered the local ministry while favoring the interests of enlightened artisans, mechanics, and tradesmen. The historian David G. Hackett notes the opposition of Munsell and his allies to the growing influence of evangelical Protestants in Albany in the 1830s: "To counter this threat, the freethinkers supported their own liberal educational institutions, which they saw as alternatives to the evangelicals' churches and Sabbath schools. In this way they hoped to hasten the arrival of their own rationalist kingdom. This was a world free of religious tyranny, where men would truly be able to think and act for themselves."[10]

Necessitated by his family's decline into genteel poverty after the onset of the Panic of 1837 and the bankruptcy of the family fur business, followed by a move north in 1838 to the town of Lansingburgh near the eastern terminus of the Erie Canal, Melville tried his hand at school teaching, first in Pittsfield, Massachusetts, in the fall of 1837, and then in Greenbush, New York, from late 1839 to mid-1840. He had signed on as a common sailor in the merchant marine with a voyage from New York to Liverpool and back during the late spring and summer of 1839, and the following summer he traveled west with his friend Eli James Murdoch Fly to Galena, Illinois, to visit his uncle Thomas Melvill, in the process becoming familiar with the waterways of the Erie Canal, Great Lakes, and the Mississippi and Ohio Rivers. Failing to find work on land, Melville decided to try his luck in the dangerous profession of whaling and signed on to a whaling voyage to the South Seas in January 1841, jumping ship in the Marquesas in mid-1842 and subsequently spending time on the islands of Tahiti and Hawaii before returning home in October 1844 as a common sailor in the United States Navy. His experiences of domestic and international travel added enlightening real-world knowledge to his limited formal education, which he continually supplemented by voracious reading. His Pacific travels in particular would also expose him to the contrast between civilized and "savage" societies, in the process revealing the pernicious meddling of Christian missionaries in the region while challenging his overall faith in evangelical Christianity and perhaps the beneficence of the Judeo-Christian god. Such experiences would inform the sustained anti-missionary thrust of his two semiautobiographical South Seas narratives, *Typee* and *Omoo*, and the incipient religious skepticism of the epic-length encyclopedic *Mardi*; while his ensuing novels of the sea based on his experience of the merchant marine and United States Navy, *Redburn* and *White-Jacket*, dramatized a social reform agenda based on Christian ideals of moral philanthropy that were largely ignored in the real world. Following his marriage to Elizabeth Shaw in August 1847, Melville's life in New York City in the late 1840s involved formal church attendance at the Unitarian Church of the Divine Unity, with Henry W. Bellows as pastor. But Melville's extensive reading during this period, aided by his access to well-stocked libraries, increasingly put him at odds with the Protestant beliefs of his age.[11]

Setting the stage for Melville's writing of *Moby-Dick* in 1850–51 was his reading in the late 1840s of Renaissance and Baroque writers, many of them grounded in traditions of philosophical and religious skepticism originating in the classical world. Codified by the second-century philosopher Sextus Empiricus (c. 160–210 CE), classical skepticism was historically denominated Pyrrhonism after one of its original practitioners, Pyrrho of Elis (c. 360–275 BCE), who pioneered the technique of questioning the finality of truth claims and the logical methods by which truth could be discovered. In his *Outlines of Pyrrhonism*, Sextus set forth various skeptical arguments based on the unreliability of human perceptions and the relativity of human judgment. The basis for his ten traditional "modes" of skepticism thus included the differences in human perceptions as opposed to those of animals; human perceptions contrasted with other humans; the contrast in human sense modalities; the varied circumstances surrounding these sense modalities; the varying physical positions of things, their admixtures, and frequency of occurrence; and the contrasting customs, laws, and beliefs among human societies. Encouraging suspended judgment (*epoche*) and systematic doubt of sense impressions because of their possible distortion or fallibility, proponents of early skepticism—coined from the Greek verb for "examine" or "consider"—taught that reaching absolute truth on any subject was impossible, for only relativistic and approximate forms of truth were obtainable. By doubting absolute claims to truth, the skeptical thinker could potentially reach a condition of *ataraxia*, or equanimity, free from the stresses of conflicting ideas and beliefs. According to Sextus, "in order to form a conception of God one must necessarily—so far as depends on the dogmatists—suspend judgment as to his existence or nonexistence. For the existence of God is not pre-evident. For if God impressed us automatically, the dogmatists would have agreed together regarding his essence, his character, and his place; whereas their interminable disagreement has made him seem to us nonevident and needing demonstration."[12]

Melville's first extended encounter with the traditions of classical skepticism came from his reading of the essays of Montaigne (1533–1592), a copy of which he purchased in New York in January 1848 while in the middle of writing *Mardi*. Montaigne wrote his essays in order to examine a broad range of subject matter using the lens of classical skepticism, all according to his general rubric of *Que sais-je?* (What do I know?). As a student of both Greek and Latin antiquity (he knew the text of many Latin authors by heart), as well as a reader of recent writings about newly discovered peoples in the Americas, Montaigne embraced a relativistic scheme of knowledge and morality, thereby shunning the religious dogmatism that had led to lethal conflicts in France and Germany under the impact of the Reformation. In his essay "On the Cannibals," for example, Montaigne thus famously argued that a tribe of Brazilian Indians' practice of eating their enemies was no more morally abhorrent than many barbarous European practices of the day—a message of cultural relativism that likely resonated with the author of *Typee*.[13]

Witnessing the rise of Protestantism in France, Montaigne remained a moderate Catholic who sought a philosophic means of undercutting dogma through systematic doubt concerning the powers of human reason; in his view, only faith could provide a sure grounding in Christianity. In his longest essay, "An Apology for Raymond Sebond," Montaigne used Pyrrhonian skepticism to cast doubt on Sebond's theological rationalism, which argued that the main principles of Christianity can be proven by natural reason; on the contrary, for Montaigne, Christianity can only be based on faith because of the unreliability of human reason. Vigorously attacking human vanity, pride, and arrogance, Montaigne suggested that human beings were merely clever animals with an exalted sense of their own rational powers. On the contrary, our minds are prey to the passions and to our bodily functions, and our sense data is often unreliable. For Montaigne, the words of Saint Paul served as a reminder of the fallibility of human reason: "For it is written, I will destroy the wisdom of the wise, and will bring to nothing the understanding of the prudent [see Isa. 29:14]. Where is the wise? Where is the scribe? Where is the disputer of this world? Hath not God made foolish the wisdom of this world?" (1 Cor. 1:19–20).

Melville's next major milestone in his self-education in skepticism came from his immersion in the encyclopedic writings of Pierre Bayle (1647–1706). While staying in Boston with his wife's family in April 1849 for the birth of his first child, Melville reported to his friend Evert Duyckinck in New York that he had bought a four-volume set of Bayle's *Historical and Critical Dictionary*. He had clearly read through many articles in the four volumes by the time he began writing *Moby-Dick*, which bears the implicit impact of Bayle's thought. A Protestant philosopher who fled France for the Netherlands during the autocratic reign of Louis XIV, Bayle was trained as a Calvinist and devoted himself to attacking the pretenses of human reason. As a massive storehouse of Pyrrhonian skepticism in the form of essays on philosophers, theologians, biblical figures, and other significant historical individuals, and offering voluminous footnotes, the *Dictionary* has been called the "arsenal of the Enlightenment" for its wealth of articles ostensibly undermining Christian dogma. In his article on David, for example, Bayle performed an outspoken exposure of the plethora of crimes, notably adultery and murder, that marked the life of the legendary biblical king, showing that the divine favor given him was inexplicable according to human reason. Bayle famously argued that a society of atheists could be more moral than a comparable group of modern Christians, according to any reasonable measure. In his articles on the ancient Manicheans and Gnostics, Bayle showed that the moral inversion of traditional Judeo-Christian beliefs found in the Gnostic demonization of the creator god was plausible based on evidence for the apparent divine malignity adduced by Gnostic writers.[14]

As Richard H. Popkin notes, "No matter what the context of his remarks, whether sacred or secular, Bayle makes it clear that reason fails to make the real world intelligible. The revealed world, he insists, is in direct opposition to the most evident maxims of reason and morality. From Genesis onward, faith involves claims that reason cannot understand, endorse, or live with." Bayle's sustained undermining of the faculty of reason, undergirded by an alleged commitment to Christian belief, has left many readers of Bayle, both then and now, wondering whether he was really a committed Christian, especially since he left no record of such personal faith. For as Popkin has remarked, "Until we can actually decide what Bayle did in fact believe and adhere to, we cannot ascertain the degree to which he was sincere, and the degree to which the next generation, the *philosophes*, understood or misunderstood him. The avowed, the constant, and the continual statement of Bayle's message was that of the inadequacy and incoherence of man's intellectual endeavors, of the need for a different guide—faith and revelation—and of the picture of the Christian life in terms of the Erasmian goal of pious study."[15]

Melville's intellectual growth in the late 1840s and early 1850s was significantly influenced by his assimilation of the encyclopedic writings of Montaigne and Bayle, supplemented by a number of other Renaissance and Baroque authors exploring the intersection of faith and reason such as Rabelais, Sir Thomas Browne, and Robert Burton. A concurrent reading of Shakespeare would expose him to the dramatist's profound knowledge of human nature as well as insights into the "power of blackness" framed within a Montaigne-like religious skepticism, as Melville's essay on Hawthorne's *Mosses from an Old Manse* would attest. Melville might have read the leading eighteenth-century English religious skeptics, Hume and Paine, but evidence for this is indirect. More assuredly, his reading of the dialogues of Plato in the later 1840s also heightened his awareness of the fallibility of human reason, while his apparent acquaintance with other classical writers on religion and morals such as Plutarch, Cicero, Seneca, and Lucian likely challenged his commitment to traditional Christian beliefs. Finally, Melville's reading of Byron and Shelley among the English Romantic poets would also expose him to their subversive religious skepticism, while an exposure to Emerson as a lecturer and his subsequent reading of the Transcendentalist's essays introduced him to a contemporary form of philosophical idealism that adopted a demythologized view of Christ and Christianity.[16]

Salient indications of religious and philosophical skepticism pervade *Moby-Dick*, but they explicitly dominate three chapters that we will briefly examine. Early in the narrative Melville depicted a potentially heroic model for a rigorous skepticism when he paused in chapter 23 ("The Lee Shore") to describe the figure of Bulkington, who had signed onto the crew of the *Pequod* immediately after arriving back in Nantucket on the *Grampus* after a four-year voyage. Discovering Bulkington at the wheel of the *Pequod* as it sails out from port for a prolonged whaling voyage, Ishmael salutes the fearless and impressive-looking mariner and his willingness to face further physical hardship while shunning the seductive comforts of the land, or the "lee shore" toward which the wind is directed. Ishmael uses the occasion to present the "mortally intolerable truth; that all deep, earnest thinking is but the intrepid effort of the soul to keep the open independence of her sea; while the wildest winds of heaven and earth conspire to cast her on the treacherous, slavish shore." Using the analogy of the soul as a ship, Ishmael allegorizes the quest for truth as navigating the open seas of thought to avoid a wreck. As a lapsed Presbyterian, Ishmael is implicitly subverting the constraints of Christianity in this declaration of mental independence from any form of dogma or social convention. Ishmael ends his salute to Bulkington by envisioning the search for ultimate truth as a potentially self-destructive quest that is redeemed by its implicit moral courage: "better is it to perish in that howling infinite, than be ingloriously dashed upon the lee, even if that were safety! For worm-like, then, oh! who would craven crawl to land! Terrors of the terrible! is all this agony so vain? Take heart, take heart, O Bulkington! Bear thee grimly demigod! Up from the spray of thy ocean-perishing—straight up, leaps thy apotheosis!" In Ishmael's philosophical vision, then, Bulkington is an emblematic embodiment of skeptical inquiry.[17]

Later in the narrative, in the midst of an extended examination of sperm whale anatomy in chapter 85 of *Moby-Dick* ("The Fountain"), Ishmael discusses the anatomical features of the whale that provide a basis for its respiratory system, with its regular exhalations leading to its mist-laden spoutings—a discussion partly based on Melville's own experience at sea as well as his recent reading in whaling books by Thomas Beale and Frederick Debell Bennet. Near the end of the chapter, Ishmael presents the nautical belief that such mist was potentially corrosive to the skin and might even blind one in the eyes. In a seriocomic turn, he hypothesizes that the whale's "fountain" is merely harmless water vapor, based on the decidedly nonscientific theory that "from the heads of all ponderous profound beings, such as Plato, Pyrrho, the Devil, Jupiter, Dante and so on, there always goes up a certain semi-visible steam, while in the act of thinking deep thoughts"—an argument allegedly confirmed by Ishmael himself based on his experience of seeing steam rising from his head after drinking hot tea on a hot August day while writing a metaphysical treatise on Eternity in his attic. Ishmael's idiosyncratic Shandean catalog of "ponderous profound" beings, both human and divine, is notable for its inclusion of the founder of classical skepticism (Pyrrho) as well as the main classical proponent of philosophical idealism (Plato); on the other hand, the Devil, Jupiter (a stand-in for the Christian god), and Dante all have knowledge of both heaven and hell, theoretically giving them a profundity of knowledge of the cosmos and its relation to human society.[18]

In order to show that he is not merely joking here, Ishmael returns to his discussion of the sperm whale's vaporous spout by noting how fitting it is that such a ponderous and profound creature while swimming through "a calm tropical sea" should have its head "overhung by a canopy of vapor"; moreover, that vapor could sometimes be "glorified by a rainbow, as if Heaven itself had put its seal upon his thoughts." Drawing on the biblical symbolism of the rainbow as a sign of God's new covenant from the story of Noah (Gen. 9:12–17), Ishmael finishes the chapter by using all his previous observations on the sperm whale "fountain" to comment on his own particular form of religious skepticism, which involved an acceptance of both intuitive faith and doubt, but embraced neither as a final answer: "For, d-ye see, rainbows do not visit the clear air; they only irradiate vapor. And so, through all the thick mists of the dim doubts in my mind, divine intuitions now and then shoot, enkindling my fog with a heavenly ray. And for this I thank God; for all have doubts; many deny; but doubts or denials, few along with them, have intuitions. Doubts of all things earthly, and intuitions of some things heavenly; this combination makes neither believer nor infidel, but makes a man who regards them both with equal eye." On the subject of Christian faith, Ishmael was thus "neither believer nor infidel" but looked at both positions "with an equal eye," meaning he accepted the skeptical position that no knowledge—especially that of metaphysical realities—was final; for if heavenly "intuitions" were a welcome alternative to the vaporous doubt that all Christian believers might sometimes experience, these intuitions did not lead him to a reliable religious faith. Instead, he embraced a skeptical condition of suspended judgment (*epoche*) in the interest of mental equanimity (*ataraxia*), or an "equal eye." By positioning himself outside the dominant religious orthodoxies of the day, Ishmael was covertly posing a radical theological challenge to his readers.[19]

The debate on religious skepticism continues in chapter 114 ("The Gilder"), as the *Pequod* enters the Japanese cruising ground and the crew enjoys the smooth swells and beautiful calm scene of the Pacific Ocean, inspiring Ahab to enjoy a temporary respite from his fevered hunt for the white whale. Ishmael evokes the golden glow of the tranquil scene, which provides an illusory reprieve from the savage predation occurring beneath the surface of the ocean, while the "high rolling waves" convey a pastoral feeling of "rolling prairie" as "fact and fancy, halfway meeting, interpenetrate." It is left to Ishmael to extract a moral from the scene while lamenting the transience of such magical calms in the course of life, which he views as inevitably blended with periodic storms to create the characteristic "warp and woof" of life comparable to the continual fluctuations in religious faith in the human life cycle: "There is no steady, unretracing progress in this life; we do not advance through fixed gradations, and at the last one pause:—through infancy's unconscious spell, boyhood's thoughtless faith, adolescence' doubt (the common doom), then scepticism, then disbelief, resting at last in manhood's pondering repose of If. But once gone through, we trace the round again; and are infants, boys, and men, and Ifs eternally." Just as Ishmael oscillated between earthly doubts and heavenly intuitions in 'The Fountain," he now posits the idea that religious faith evolves in a perpetual cycle temporarily ending in manhood's "pondering repose of If"—classical skepticism's suspended judgment and associated mental equanimity.[20]

In addition to his reading and his composition of *Moby-Dick*, Melville's literary friendships in the late 1840s and early 1850s provide a key index to his developing religious skepticism. Melville's most important literary friendship in the later 1840s was with journalist, editor, and publisher Evert Duyckinck, who oversaw the American appearance of *Typee* with the New York publisher Wiley and Putnam and later served as editor of the weekly *Literary World*, to which Melville contributed several book reviews. Melville's rapid intellectual growth at this time was facilitated by his frequent borrowing of books from Duyckinck's vast private library, conveniently located a few blocks from the Melville family residence in lower Manhattan. Melville's letters to Duyckinck, a devout Episcopalian, reveal both the good-natured fellowship he enjoyed with this friend and the other members of Duyckinck's literary circle, as well as his awareness that his friend was not as broadminded as he himself was on the matters of Christian faith. While visiting Boston in February 1849 during his wife's delivery of their first child, Melville thus apparently offended Duyckinck's orthodox sensibilities by writing of his recent experience of first reading Shakespeare in a concentrated manner in a newly purchased edition of the plays. Calling Shakespeare "the divine William" whose works were "full of sermons-on-the mount, and gentle, aye, almost as Jesus," Melville stretched the limits of propriety by envisaging the English playwright as ranking with archangels and messiahs: "I fancy that this moment Shakspeare in heaven ranks with Gabriel Raphael and Michael. And if another Messiah ever comes twill be in Shakspeare's person."[21]

In a now lost letter to Melville in Boston, Duyckinck apparently expressed his discomfort with such potentially sacrilegious language, so in his next letter to his friend in early March, Melville sought to qualify his earlier remarks on Shakespeare by noting, "To one of your habits of thought, I confess that in my last, I seemed, but only *seemed*, irreverent. And do not think, my boy, that because I, impulsively broke forth in jubilations over Shakspeare, that, therefore, I am of the number of the *snobs* who burn their tuns of rancid fat at his shrine." Taking Shakespeare out of heaven, Melville subsequently put him firmly back on earth in human form for Duyckinck's benefit, with an added compliment to his friend, by writing, "I would to God Shakspeare had lived later, & promenaded in Broadway. Not that I might have had the pleasure of leaving my card for him at the Astor [hotel], or made merry with him over a bowl of the fine Duyckinck punch; but that the muzzle which all men wore on their souls in the Elizebethan day, might not have intercepted Shakspere's full articulations." Melville himself would also increasingly feel a "muzzle" on his soul regarding the full range of his religious speculations and doubts—a muzzle he would have to maintain with Duyckinck himself—but in the composition of his great whaling novel, he would nevertheless give expression to many of them.[22]

Further indication of Melville's evolving religious skepticism and his attraction to metaphysical questions can be found in the journal he kept on his four-month trip to England and the Continent beginning in October 1849, with the practical goal of placing his most recent novel, *White-Jacket*, with an English publisher. Near the start of his voyage, Melville met George Adler, a professor of German at New York University and the compiler of a recently completed German-English dictionary. As Melville remarked of Adler in his travel journal on October 12, 1849, "He is full of German metaphysics, & discourses of Kant, Swedenborg &c. He has been my principal companion thus far." In his notation for the next day, Melville elaborated on the kind of conversation he was having with Adler: "Walked the deck with the German, Mr Adler till a late hour, talking of 'Fixed Fate, Free-will, foreknowledge absolute' &c. His philosophy is *Colredegian*: he accepts the Scriptures as divine, & yet leaves himself free to inquire into Nature. He does not take it, that the Bible is absolutely infallible, & that anything opposed to it in Science must be wrong. He believes that there are things *out* of God and independant of him,—things that would have existed were there no God:—such as that two & two make four; for it is not that God so decrees mathematically, but that in the very nature of things, the fact is thus." Beginning his remarks with a well-known quotation from the scene of Satan's conversation with the fallen angels in Hell in book II of Milton's *Paradise Lost*, Melville notes here his new friend's belief, following the writings of Coleridge, that a metaphysical reality existed independently of God's creation; moreover, the Bible was not infallible and thus could be contradicted by new scientific truths.[23]

On October 22, Melville wrote of more late-night conversations with Adler: "We talked metaphysics continually, & Hegel, Schlegel, Kant &c were discussed under influence of the whiskey. I shall not forget Adler's look when he quoted La Place the French astronomer—'it is not necessary, gentlemen, to account for these worlds by the hypothesis' &c." The truncated quotation refers to Laplace's notorious assertion that the hypothesis of a god was not necessary to understand the workings of celestial mechanics. Melville spent much of his first few weeks in England in Adler's company, and their conversations continued even after Adler's departure for Paris, where Melville again met up with him in early December. Melville's multiple encounters with Adler at this time undoubtedly provided him with a strong catalyst for his interest in the basics of German philosophy and for his growing alienation from Christian orthodoxy.[24]

While Melville revealed some of the early warning signs of his growing religious skepticism both in his correspondence with his New York literary friend Duyckinck and in his transatlantic conversations with the philosophically informed Adler, it was only when he had moved to the Berkshires of western Massachusetts in the fall of 1850 that he found the friend to whom he could speak his whole heart and mind on religious matters. Evidence of Melville's recurrent religious preoccupations is thus noticeably evident in his close literary friendship with Nathaniel Hawthorne, with whom he shared a youthful exposure to the rigors of Calvinist theology and then marriage into a Unitarian family. Melville's letters to Hawthorne show that recurrent metaphysical speculation was an integral part of their conversations; indeed, it dominates the content of most of his longer letters. In his long letter of mid-April 1851 following his reading of *The House of the*

Seven Gables, for example, Melville praised Hawthorne as being someone unafraid to report the "absolute condition of present things as they strike the eye of the man who fears them not, though they do their worst to him." He goes on to speculate on the possible existence or nonexistence of certain divine secrets in a heterodox manner that recalls his earlier shipboard conversations with George Adler: "And perhaps, after all, there is *no* secret. We incline to think that the Problem of the Universe is like the Freemason's mighty secret, so terrible to all children. It turns out, at last, to consist in a triangle, a mallet, and an apron,—nothing more! We incline to think that God cannot explain His own secrets, and that He would like a little information upon certain points Himself. We mortals astonish Him as much as He us."[25]

Beginning with the premise that certain divine "Powers" harbor deep metaphysical secrets from humanity, Melville whimsically suggests that such grand secrets of the universe might be as simple as the closely guarded knowledge surrounding three symbolic tools of Freemasonry. He then makes the humorously heretical suggestion, evocative of his interest in ancient Gnosticism likely gained from reading Bayle's *Dictionary*, that God might not be omniscient and thus would need to ask humans about certain aspects of the creation. Melville continues his quasi-Gnostic exploration of the limits of God's knowledge of the creation by directing his focus to the problem of human knowledge of the divine, asserting, "But it is this *Being* of the matter; there lies the knot with which we choke ourselves." Invoking the ontological concept of Being as terminally problematic, Melville implies that the mystery of transcendence invites people to hang themselves in despair: "As soon as you say *Me*, a *God*, a *Nature*, so soon you jump off from your stool and hang from the beam. Yes, that word [i.e., 'Being'] is the hangman." Making the claim that the individual subject (me) could be both a god and a created being within time (i.e., a "nature") risks self-annihilation. Paradoxically, God would still be a tangible presence even if removed from all lexicons, as though an ineluctable part of human consciousness: "Take God out of the dictionary, and you would have him in the street."[26]

Melville's skeptical explorations here were likely shaped by his reading of the essays of Montaigne during the later 1840s, notably the "Apology for Raymond de Sebond," the French writer's most influential expression of doubt in relation to the presumed knowledge of God. Near the conclusion of this essay, Montaigne incorporated an extended passage from Plutarch's essay "On the *Ei* at Delphi," a key part of which reads, in the Charles Cotton translation that Melville owned,

> We have no communication with being, by reason that all human nature is ever in the midst, betwixt being born and dying, giving but an obscure appearance and shadow, a weak and uncertain opinion, of itself: and if, perhaps, you fix your thought to apprehend your being, it would be but like grasping water; for the more you clutch your hand to squeeze and hold what is in its own nature flowing, so much the more you lose what you would grasp and hold. So, seeing that all things are subject to pass from one change to another, reason, that there looks for a real substance, finds itself deceived, not being able to apprehend any thing that is subsistent and permanent, because that every thing is either entering into being, and is not yet arrived at it, or begins to die before it is born.[27]

In the French philosopher's view (as confirmed by Plutarch), humans are trapped in the world of becoming and so have no access to the true ontological "Being" that would allow them direct knowledge of the divine. It should be noted that Plutarch's essay on the meaning of the inscription of the letter epsilon ("ei") at Delphi—the better known inscriptions there being "Know Thyself" and "Nothing Too Much"—discusses whether the fifth letter of Greek alphabet here refers to the number 5, or the word "if," or the phrase "thou art" (among other possibilities). This ambiguity would later help inspire Melville's formulation in his novel *Pierre; or, the Ambiguities* of Plotinus Plinlimmon's provocative fragmentary pamphlet titled "Ei," on the nature of God and Christian faith in the modern world. In general, Melville's consciousness of the inaccessibility of the divine by human reason, reinforced by his fundamental agreement with Montaigne's religious skepticism, is in keeping with the basic tenor of his ongoing dialogue with Hawthorne on religious matters. In accordance with such ideas, near the end of his April 1851 letter Melville claims that his Berkshire friend rejects conventional wisdom about divine matters by saying "NO! in thunder" and thus attaining the "happy condition of judicious, unincumbered travelers in Europe; they cross the frontiers into Eternity with nothing but a carpet-bag,—that is to say, the Ego." Imputing to Hawthorne his own refusal to carry unexamined cultural and theological baggage both in this life and the next, Melville celebrates his Berkshire friend as being a fellow skeptic, projecting his own rebellious mind-set onto his more conventionally Christian friend.[28]

In another revealing letter to Hawthorne in early May 1851, Melville shared his sense of exhaustion after the enormous labor involved in completing his new whaling novel, reflecting pessimistically that trying to tell the "truth" in his writing was an unpopular and even dangerous activity: "Try to get a living by the Truth—and go to the Soup Societies. Heavens! Let any clergyman try to preach the Truth from its very stronghold, the pulpit, and they would ride him out of his church on his own pulpit bannister." Telling the truth within the precincts of a Christian church was thus perilous even for a minister, reflecting the church's firm commitment to religious dogma and society's intolerance for unconventional verities. Going on to reflect on his reading of Hawthorne's recently published story "Ethan Brand," narrating the title character's ultimately suicidal quest to find evidences of human sin, Melville comments on the need for honoring the dictates of the heart over those of the head: "To the dogs with the head! I had rather be a fool with a heart, than Jupiter Olympus with his head. The reason the mass of men fear God, and *at bottom dislike* Him, is because they rather distrust His heart, and fancy Him all brain like a watch." Rejecting the heartless retributive god of the Old Testament as well as the modern watchmaker god of William Paley's natural theology, Melville sets himself, as a champion of the heart, against the Christians who fear and dislike the punitive God they ostensibly worship. In his letter to Hawthorne, Melville also acknowledges the ephemerality of literary fame while noting the biblical basis for this belief: "I have come to regard this matter of Fame as the most transparent of all vanities. I read Solomon more and more, and every time see deeper and deeper and unspeakable meanings in him." By invoking of the idea of "vanity" and the name Solomon, Melville was clearly revealing his appreciation for the wisdom of the book of Ecclesiastes, a text containing the Bible's best-known teachings on skepticism, which called into question the goodness of God, the workings of providence, and the immortality of the soul.[29]

Based on several encounters with Melville in Lenox, Hawthorne's wife Sophia recorded a number of insightful remarks about her husband's new friend in letters to her older sister Elizabeth, some of which confirm the unsettled nature of Melville's thinking on many theological questions while evidencing his skeptical mind-set. So in her letter to Elizabeth of May 7, 1851, written after she had read Melville's aforementioned letter to her husband about *The House of the Seven Gables*, Sophia commented, "The fresh, sincere, glowing mind that utters it is in a state of 'fluid consciousness,' & to Mr Hawthorne speaks his innermost about GOD, the Devil & Life if so be he can get at the Truth—for he is a boy in opinion—having settled nothing as yet—informe [shapeless]—ingens [vast]— & and it would betray him to make public his confessions & efforts to grasp,—because they would be considered perhaps impious, if one did not take in the whole scope of the case." As Sophia noted, Melville prioritized the quest for truth over religious dogma, making him liable to accusations of impiety for those who did not know the earnest nature of his thought.[30]

In another letter of October 24, 1852, Sophia repeated her claims about Melville's unconventional habits of mind, using a metaphor from chemistry to explain his experimental thinking: "He is an incalculable person, full of daring & questions, & with all momentous considerations afloat in the crucible of his mind. He tosses them in, & heats his furnace sevenfold & burns & stirs, & waits for the crystallization with a royal indifference as to what may turn up, only eager for truth, without previous prejudice. His ocean-experience has given sea-room to his intellect, & he is in the mere boyhood of his possibilities." Sophia is clearly admiring of Melville in her comments on her husband's literary friend, whose fluid state of consciousness and religious beliefs offered a dramatic contrast to her husband's more settled convictions; her remarks also inadvertently recall Melville's own confession to Hawthorne in a letter of May 1851: "From my twenty-fifth year, I date my life. Three weeks have scarcely passed, at any time between then and now, when I have not unfolded within myself."[31]

Hawthorne's journal entries on his encounters with Melville similarly depict his friend's recurrent intellectual preoccupation with intractable philosophical and theological doubts. On August 1, 1851, for example, on the occasion of Melville's thirty-second birthday, the two literary friends spent the day together and conversed long into the evening at the Hawthorne family cottage in Lenox, as Hawthorne noted: "Melville and I had a talk about time and eternity, things of this world and of the next, and books, and publishers, and all possible and impossible matters, that lasted pretty deep into the night; and if the truth must be told, we smoked cigars even within the sacred precincts of the sitting room." With his wife absent visiting her relatives in Boston, Hawthorne was unusually free to engage with his younger friend's irresolvable metaphysical questions on the contrast between temporal and eternal matters, becoming and being, that would preoccupy many New Englanders in the twilight of Calvinist theology.[32]

Melville's unfettered freedom to share his religious speculations with Hawthorne in the Berkshires abruptly ended when his friend moved back to the Boston area in late November 1851. Meanwhile, the dangers of Melville's religious skepticism to his career as a novelist came out in full force in the critical reactions to his epic whaling novel *Moby-Dick*, published in the fall of 1851, and in its more subversive domestic sequel *Pierre*, published in the summer of 1852. The measure of Melville's violation of the religious norms of his evangelical Protestant culture can be seen in the critical reaction to these morally and metaphysically provocative novels. Writing in his weekly magazine, the *Literary World*, Melville's friend Evert Duyckinck produced a two-part review of *Moby-Dick* that applauded the literary plenitude of Melville's Faustian drama, but he nevertheless rebuked the breezy skeptical mind-set of Melville's narrator, who engaged in what the reviewer called the "piratical running down of creeds and opinions," which Duyckinck piously considered "out of place and uncomfortable. We do not like to see what, under any view, must be to the world the most sacred associations of life violated and defaced." This observation was less outraged than the opinion of professional religious reviewers such as the Congregational New York *Independent*, which opined of the author of *Moby-Dick*, "The Judgment day will hold him liable for not turning his talents to better account, when, too, both authors and publishers of injurious books will be conjointly answerable for the influence of those books upon the wide circle of immortal minds on which they have written their mark."[33]

Such attacks on the author's irreverence helped make *Moby-Dick* a commercial failure, thereby fueling the skeptical and satirical animus of Melville's subsequent novel *Pierre*, which proved an unmitigated commercial and critical disaster for its scandalous depiction of a young man breaking off his engagement to a conventionally genteel young woman to embrace a pretended marriage with his socially outcast half sister in order to protect the posthumous reputation of his philandering father—all while allegedly following the exalted precepts of the Sermon on the Mount. Not surprisingly, a sanctimonious Evert Duyckinck protested in his review of the novel that it devilishly undermined the idea of a Christian model of behavior: "The most immoral *moral* of the story, if it has any moral at all, seems to be the impracticability of virtue; a leering demoniacal spectre of an idea seems to be speering [sneering] at us through the dim obscure of this dark book, and mocking us with this dismal falsehood." The critic for the New York *Day Book*, on the other hand, repeated the general consensus that *Pierre* constituted "the ravings and reveries of a madman," while the editor of the *American Whig Review*, George Washington Peck, noted of *Pierre*'s author, "When he dares to outrage every principle of virtue; when he strikes with an impious, though, happily, weak hand, at the very foundations of society, we feel it our duty to tear off the veil with which he has thought to soften the hideous features of the idea, and warn the public against the reception of such atrocious doctrines."[34]

Given the public outrage over the apparent moral and religious enormities evident in *Pierre*, and its near-lethal cost to his literary reputation, it is appropriate that the novel seemed to echo at least two passages from the conclusion to Thomas Paine's *Age of Reason*. At the start of the chapter in which Pierre Glendinning reads the subversive pamphlet of Plotinus Plinlimmon on his journey to New York City, the narrator begins by claiming "all profound things, and emotions of things are preceded and attended by Silence. . . . Yea, in silence the child Christ was born into the world. Silence is the general consecration of the universe. Silence is the invisible laying on of the Divine Pontiff's hands upon the world. Silence is at once the most harmless and the most awful thing in all nature. It speaks of the Reserved Forces of Fate. Silence is the only Voice of our God." In the *Age of Reason*, Paine similarly claimed that silence characterized the noncommunicative identity of the deistic God: "But though, speaking for myself, I thus admit the possibility of revelation, I totally disbelieve that the Almighty ever did communicate anything to man by any mode of speech, in any language, or by any kind of vision or appearance, or by any means which ourselves are capable of receiving, otherwise than by the universal display of himself in the works of the creation, and by that repugnance we feel in ourselves to bad actions, and disposition to good ones."[35]

Then, in the pamphlet concerning the contrast between heavenly and worldly ethical values, or what he denominates in navigational terms "chronometricals" versus "horologicals," the enigmatic philosopher in *Pierre* notes that any attempt to live out Christ's ideal precepts is apt to lead to egregious and unholy acts: "Though Christ encountered woe in both the precept and the practice of his chronometricals, yet did he remain throughout entirely without folly or sin. Whereas, almost invariably, with inferior beings, the absolute effort to live in this world according to the strict letter of the chronometricals is, somehow, apt to involve those inferior beings eventually in strange, *unique* follies and sins, unimagined before." Pursuing the same point, Paine wrote of Christianity, "Morality is injured by prescribing to it duties that, in the first place, are impossible to be performed, and if they could be would be productive of evil; or, as before said, be premiums for crime." Melville's Pierre necessarily fails to heed the advice of the philosopher, whom he later observes in New York City at the Church of Apostles, and proceeds to carry out his misguided plan to redeem his father's sexual sins while enacting his own unique follies and sins, ultimately leading to the deaths of his mother, cousin, fiancée, alleged half sister, and ultimately himself (by suicide). Although the overlapping passages from Paine's *Age of Reason* and Melville's *Pierre* may be merely coincidental, they share a common thread of "infidel" thought and hint at the reasons for the authors' shared cultural ostracism.[36]

Following the scandalous publication of *Pierre* in 1852, Melville's literary career hung by a thread, and he only kept it going by turning to the form of short fiction for two new monthly magazines, *Putnam's* and *Harper's*, even as he now increasingly hid his religious skepticism under multiple layers of irony and indirection. Indicative of Melville's increasing sense of the obsolescence of Christianity in the modern Anglo-American world at this time was his response to his reading of an essay, "The Cessation of the Oracles," in Plutarch's *Moralia*, at some point in later 1853 or early 1854, as indicated by a May 1854 letter recommending the essay to his older sister Helen. In this essay, Plutarch recounts a long conversation on the general subject of the decline in the number of oracles in first-century Greece, but the essay is most famous for containing an account of the reported death of the nature god Pan, which Christian apologists such as the early church historian Eusebius (c. 260/65–339) linked to the advent of Jesus and the end of classical paganism. The idea of considering classical paganism to have died with the death of the god Pan was echoed by Milton's well-known ode "On the Morning of Christ's Nativity" (1629), in which the poet describes the various pre-Christian gods who are now forced into silence or threatened with extinction. The idea that paganism died with the simultaneous death of Pan and advent of Christ seems to have struck a chord in Melville's imagination, suggesting the idea of a sudden cessation of the operability of Christian doctrine and an inevitable decline in the credibility of Christianity in the mid-nineteenth century.[37]

By the same token, at some point in later 1855 while rereading *Don Quixote*, Melville annotated Cervantes's assertion that "a knight-errant without a mistress is like a tree without leaves, a building without cement, a shadow without a body that causes it" by noting, "or as Confucius said, 'a dog without a master' or to drop both Cervantes and Confucius parables—a god-like mind without a God." Identifying himself here as possessing a religious nature but lacking a god to believe in, Melville maintained his quest for religious truth during the years in which he produced his shorter fiction, despite being chastened by his increasing inability to make a living from this writing and estrangement from his two closest literary confidants, Duyckinck and Hawthorne. Yet in the fall of 1856 after completion of *The Confidence-Man*—a virtual summa of religious and philosophical skepticism—Melville had significant encounters with these two friends while showing that his taste for metaphysical discussion was as active as ever. Before he left on his trip to Europe and the Holy Land in mid-October, he renewed his friendship with Duyckinck while dropping by the latter's New York City residence; Duyckinck thus noted in his journal at this time Melville's continuing propensity for "metaphysics": "Herman Melville passed the evening with me—fresh from his mountain charged to the muzzle with his sailor metaphysics and jargon of all things unknowable—a good stirring evening ploughing deep and bringing to the surface some rich fruits of thought and experience."[38]

However, the most revealing report of Melville's frame of mind at this time came in his friend Hawthorne's journal account of their meeting in early November 1856 in Liverpool, England, where Hawthorne had been serving as the American consul and Melville was on his way to visit the Levant and Holy Land. Describing Melville's visit, Hawthorne noted their conversation as they sat near the beach at Southport, sixteen miles north of Liverpool, where the Hawthornes had recently moved:

> Melville, as he always does, began to reason of Providence and futurity, and of everything that lies beyond human ken, and informed me that he has "pretty much made up his mind to be annihilated"; but still does not seem to rest in that anticipation; and, I think, will never rest until he gets hold of a definite belief. It is strange how he persists—and has persisted ever since I knew him, and probably long before—in wandering to-and fro over these deserts, as dismal and monotonous as the sand hills amid which we were sitting. He can neither believe, nor be comfortable in his unbelief; and he is too honest and courageous not to try to do one or the other.

Melville's well-known confession at Southport that he was ready to be "annihilated" does not imply that he was ready to commit suicide or end his career as a writer; his use of this contemporary theological term meant that he was resigned to physical and spiritual extinction at his death, as he had given up any belief in the doctrine of the resurrection that Saint Paul made the basis for Christian faith (1 Cor. 15:15). However, Melville still didn't feel satisfied with such a position, because he was not temperamentally prepared to consider himself an atheist or infidel (the term "agnostic" wouldn't be coined by Thomas Huxley for another dozen years). In effect, Melville did not make a final decision on the question of belief, thereby practicing what classical skepticism characterized as suspended judgment or *epoche*. Hawthorne's famous summation of his friend's religious mind-set shows Melville's habitual oscillation between the unsuccessful will to believe and the inability to be comfortable in his unbelief—evidence of a skeptical irresolution that characterized his mature thought. The many critics who note the importance of Hawthorne's characterization of Melville's loss of faith often neglect to mention that such expressions of religious skepticism constituted a dominant theme in Melville's extant communications with his Berkshire friend.[39]

In his journal notation, Hawthorne in fact remarks on how throughout their friendship Melville had always turned to such metaphysical topics for discussion, which Hawthorne personally considered monotonous and sterile, having long decided to put his own faith in a nondoctrinal form of Protestant Christianity. Hawthorne similarly noted Melville's somber mood, showing that his Berkshire friend had not in fact attained the mental equanimity that was supposed to emerge from skeptical inquiry according to the tenets of classical skepticism. Melville's depression stemming from his loss of religious faith was in fact a condition he shared with many of his Victorian literary contemporaries. For as Richard D. Altick notes, "It was no light matter to renounce the faith in which one had been reared, and to which one's family had subscribed without questions for many generations. Only after long and agonized soul-searching did many later Victorians commit themselves to various kinds of anti-religious stands—free thought, skepticism, rationalism, agnosticism, secularism, humanism." Melville had additional reason to be depressed over the precipitous decline of his literary career by late 1856, resulting in a disastrous loss of income partly stemming from the increasingly subversive philosophical and theological content of his fiction beginning with *Moby-Dick*.[40]

Melville's record of his travels to Europe and the Levant would provide ample testimony to his deep ambivalence concerning Christianity
and his inability to summon the will be believe, as confirmed by Hawthorne in November 1856. For if Melville had hoped for a renewal of
his Christian faith by visiting the Holy Land in early 1857, he would
be cruelly disappointed, as he was now hard-pressed to experience any
rainbow-hued divine intuitions to accompany his many doubts about
Christianity in the cotemporary world. Such doubts would make him
more receptive to the secular and aesthetic values of classical culture,
which he would study and increasingly appreciate during his travels to
Greece and Italy after visiting the Holy Land. The revealing journal of
his travels thus presents a grim account of touring the sacred sites in
Jerusalem and its environs after his visits to Constantinople and Egypt,
both of which primed him for his disillusioned evaluation of Ottoman-
controlled Palestine.[41]

Of his visit to the Great Pyramid in Egypt, Melville thus wrote of the
historical provenance of the baleful Old Testament god: "I shudder at
idea of ancient Egyptians. It was in these pyramids that was conceived
the idea of Jehovah. Terrible mixture of the cunning and awful. Moses
learned in all the lore of the Egyptians." After arriving in Palestine,
he commented under the heading *Barrenness of Judea* on the "whit-
ish mildew pervading whole tracts of landscape—bleached—leprosy—
encrustation of curses." In the Church of the Holy Sepulcher in Jerusalem, he noted after entering the room designated Christ's tomb, "All
is glitter & nothing is gold. A sickening cheat." He confessed himself
almost literally afflicted with disillusionment: "No country will more
quickly dissipate romantic expectations than Palestine—particularly Jerusalem. To some the disappointment is heart sickening." In keeping
with the idea of divine malice that had earlier shaped his characterization of Ahab, he suggests a supernatural explanation for the desolation
of Judea: "Is the desolation of the land the result of the fatal embrace of
the Deity? Hapless are the favorites of heaven." Finally, of the attempts
of various Americans to advance the arrival of the Second Coming by
helping the Jews resettle Palestine, in keeping with a prophesy of Saint
Paul in Romans 11, Melville noted, "The whole thing is half melancholy, half farcical—like all the rest of the world."[42]

If his account of visiting Palestine, with its dense associations of biblical history, was marked by a persistent sense of disenchantment and
disillusionment, the same mood informed his reaction, on February 5,

1857, while sailing by the bleak island of Patmos, where Saint John the Divine allegedly received his influential revelation:

> Steered out from intricasies & saw Samos ahead, and Patmos—quite lonely looking. Patmos stands in fact quite isolated—the more so, apparently from so suddenly coming upon it after the apple-like clusterings of the other isles. Patmos is pretty high, & peculiarly barren looking. No inhabitants.—Was here again afflicted with the great curse of modern travel—skepticism. Could no more realize that St: John had ever had revelations here, than when off Juan Fernandez, could believe in Robinson Crusoe according to De Foe. When my eye rested on arid heigth, spirit partook of the barreness.—Heartily wish Niebuhr & Strauss to the dogs.—The deuce take their penetration and acumen. They have robbed us of the bloom. If they have undeceived any one—no thanks to them.[43]

While Melville identifies his religious skepticism here as a common mid-Victorian affliction, his bitterness at his inability to believe in the reality of Saint John's visionary experience on Patmos—a symptom of his loss of Christian faith—represents a kind of delayed climax to all the disillusionment he had recorded during his ten-day visit to Jerusalem and its environs. Experiencing both intense physical and psychological discomfort at the "sickening cheat" of what he had seen, Melville was ready to blame the historical criticism of Barthold Niebuhr's *Roman History* (1827–28) and David F. Strauss's *Life of Jesus* (1835), both of which authors helped revolutionize the study of ancient Rome and the New Testament, respectively, by exposing their pervasive mythical elements. Melville is accordingly unable to summon any intuition of heavenly things while viewing the island residence of Saint John the Divine, and he lashes out at Niebuhr and Strauss for having destroyed the beauty of Christian faith, leaving only a desolate and sterile religious landscape. Melville's bitter comments were uncannily anticipated a dozen years earlier by the Unitarian minister Stephen G. Bulfinch in a review of Strauss's *Life of Jesus* in the July 1845 issue of the *Christian Examiner*: "Truly, if the *caput mortuum* of Christianity which mythicism leaves us, be all that is true of our religion, our feelings would tempt us to forgive the Evangelists who have so beautifully deceived, rather than the critics who so coldly disenchant us." As expressed in his travel journal, Melville's reaction to seeing Patmos is almost a textbook example of the well-known "disenchantment of the world," or the retreat of religious faith under the pressures of rationalism and modernity, as notably articulated by Max Weber in the early twentieth century.[44]

Fortunately, Melville's disenchantment with the Holy Land and the "cheat" of Christian faith was soon balanced by a re-enchanted view of the classical art and culture of Greece and Italy, as he sought compensation for lost faith in an appreciation of art—a phenomenon typical of several mid- and later nineteenth-century English and American writers such as John Ruskin, Algernon Swinburne, Walter Pater, Charles Eliot Norton, Henry Adams, and Henry James. For as historian James Turner remarks, "As avatar of human spiritual values, art ascended the throne abdicated by God. An ideal worthy of reverence, it gave consolation in sorrow, hope in dark times, strength in adversity. For Henry Adams or Charles Eliot Norton, the sanctuary lamp had long since flickered and died in Chartres and San Marco; but venerating the cathedrals themselves remained truly meet and just, right and helpful unto salvation." During his brief stop in Athens, Melville accordingly admired the Acropolis and Parthenon while noting of the Temple of Theseus, "resurrection—figure of Victory tying her sandal—grace & loveliness of the whole conception." In Naples, he noted the "magnificence of the city" and visited Pompeii as well as the "beautiful promontory of villas—along the sea" at Posillipo west of the city. In Rome, where he suffered from exhaustion, loneliness, and neuralgic pains, Melville nevertheless spent more than three weeks assiduously surveying the vast array of ancient ruins, churches, gardens, and galleries—study that would inform his lecture "Statues in Rome" in the coming fall. Melville thus wrote after visiting the Vatican and its museum, with its famous artworks by Raphael and Michelangelo, "Fagged out completely, & sat long time by the obelisk, recovering from the stunning effect of a first visit to the Vatican." Describing the grounds of the Villa Borghese, he noted: "Great beauty of them. Fine rich odours of bushes & trees. The laurel & c. The closed villa, statues seen thro' railing. Silence & enchantment." At the Villa Doria Pamphili, he remarked: "Great extent—rich green—Paridise within Paridise. Yellow villa.—long vista of green & green water. The cedars & pines. Avenues of olives." Like many of his countrymen, Melville would perceive the landscape and art of Italy as paradisiacal, and the experience would decisively shape some of his later poetry.[45]

Moving on to Florence, where he spent a week, he noted that "Florence is a lovely city even on a cold rainy day" and then remarked, "To the Duomo & Campanile. Came upon them unexpectedly, Amazed at their magnificence." At the Uffizi gallery he was "very much astonished at the Wrestlers & charmed with Titian's Venus. The Portraits of painters interesting." In Venice, where he spent a subsequent week, he was ready to be re-enchanted by the aesthetic appeal of religious services while visiting an Armenian convent: "Chapel. 8 worshippers, & 8 priests. Superb vestments, blended with supurb light streaming in from shining lagoon through windows draped with rosy silks, chaunting, swinging silver censers—puff of incense at each worshipper. Great gorgeousness of effect." On the Rialto, he remarked: "Numbers of beautiful women. The rich brown complexions of Titian's women drawn from nature, after all." In Milan he noted of its famous cathedral: "Glorious. More satisfactory to me than St. Peters. A wonderful grandure." After the bleakness of the stones of Judea, the beauty of Italy was clearly something of a restorative to Melville's mood. Indeed, it is not too much to say that Melville's prolonged artistic pilgrimage through Greece and Italy helped to make up for his disenchantment with the Holy Land by enriching his knowledge of classical, medieval, Renaissance, and Baroque art and architecture that would become a new subject of intellectual devotion.[46]

Melville's return to the United States in late May 1857 coincided with a downturn in the national economy and the bankruptcy of his most recent publisher, which was partly responsible for making him go on the lecture circuit to help earn a living; he dutifully produced a lecture on "Statues in Rome" in the fall and winter of 1857–58, followed by lectures on "The South Seas" and "Travel" in subsequent lecture seasons. But he did not enjoy being a professional lecturer like Emerson, and his general disillusionment with Christianity and concurrent turn toward classical civilization was much in evidence when he was visited on his Pittsfield farm by two students from nearby Williams College, Titus Munson Coan and John Thomas Gulick, on April 19, 1859. Both students wrote admiring accounts of their visit with the former literary celebrity, but it is Gulick who provides the most revealing insight into Melville's state of mind at this time:

Though it was apparent that he possessed a mind of an aspiring, ambitious order, full of elastic energy, and illumined with the rich colors of a poetic fancy, he was evidently a disappointed man, soured by criticism, & disgusted with the civilized world & with Christendom in general and in particular. The ancient dignity of Homeric times afforded the only state of humanity individual or social to which he could turn with any complacency. What little there was of meaning in the religions of the present day had come down from Plato.—All our philosophy and all our art & poetry was either derived or imitated from the ancient Greeks.[47]

Gulick's account shows that Melville's attitude to Christianity had seemingly reached its nadir, as he expressed a preference for classical Greek civilization, with its cultural and artistic foundations in the epics of Homer and one of its great philosophical achievements in the dialogues of Plato. Although Melville's expression of a decisive preference for the world of classical antiquity may have been partly exacerbated by the evangelical heritage of Coan, who had grown up as the son of a Hawaiian missionary, Melville at this time was clearly a confirmed and deeply disillusioned critic of his country's largely Protestant religion. In his critical stance of unapologetic unbeliever, he was staking a position that became more common in the nation following the publication of Darwin's *Origin of Species* in 1859, followed by the massive physical and cultural disruptions of the Civil War in the next decade and beyond.[48]

In the foregoing biographical survey, we have seen that in his reading, correspondence, journals, and recorded remarks in the later 1840s and throughout the 1850s, Melville was preoccupied with recurrent doubts regarding Christianity, repeatedly examining its truth claims in the light of skeptical inquiry. (In the ensuing three decades of his life, Melville left little personal record of his thought on these matters.) Yet it should be noted that despite his disenchantment with Christianity during his early literary career, Melville did not stop using the Bible as a template for his literary imagination, as he had done throughout his career as a writer. Indeed, given his early immersion in this foundational text of Western and American culture, it would have been impossible to separate himself from a work to which he had been repeatedly exposed from childhood and which he continued to reread throughout his life. Although there is no tangible proof that Melville was familiar with the contemporary higher criticism of the Bible, he knew that the Bible's claim to be divinely inspired truth was increasingly untenable by the mid-nineteenth century. Rejecting its dogmatic elements as obsolete, Melville nevertheless turned to Christian scripture as a sourcebook of narrative design and moral instruction, thereby forming one of the deep structures of his fiction and poetry. For as William H. Shurr notes, "Melville consistently took the best—the richest and the most beautiful—that the Christian tradition had to offer; in each of his works the ideal was subjected to the test of fictional reality and found wanting. This pattern is significant because it is consistent and pervasive."[49]

As is abundantly evident from his writings, Melville was intimately familiar with the texts of both testaments and the traditional reading of the Old Testament as a typological model for the New. While interpreting the life of Christ as exemplary of a sublime ethical idealism, Melville turned to the letters of Saint Paul for more conventional examples of Christian moral practice and belief. In his incorporation of the Bible into his fiction and later his poetry, Melville was in effect highlighting the ultimate textual basis for the Christian religion while avoiding reference to specific denominational divisions of contemporary Christianity, even as the fault line between orthodox Calvinist and liberal Unitarianism that had shaped his early life continued to influence his thought. As we will see in the next chapter, in his first published short story in the fall of 1853, "Bartleby, the Scrivener," he would frame the narrative in New Testament language and ideas of charity in order to illustrate the potential obsolescence of this central moral tenet of Christianity and the seeming obsolescence of Christianity itself, while employing techniques of irony and indirection to hide his subversive messaging. As he had earlier claimed in his 1850 review of Hawthorne's *Mosses from an Old Manse*, the same use of irony and indirection was characteristic of the work of both Shakespeare and Hawthorne: "For in this world of lies, Truth is forced to fly like a sacred white doe in the woodlands; and only by cunning glimpses will she reveal herself, as in Shakespeare and other masters of the great Art of Telling the Truth,— even though it be covertly, and by snatches." In his ensuing fiction of the 1850s and beyond, Melville would be attempting to tell the truth covertly and by snatches, much of it having to do with the problematic status of modern Christianity.[50]

CHAPTER 2

Biblical Inversion and the Ends of Christianity

"Bartleby, the Scrivener"

Given the widely acknowledged presence of Christian symbolism in "Bartleby, the Scrivener," it is not surprising that one long-standing branch of criticism of the story has focused on its incorporation of themes and motifs from the New Testament, and the Bible more generally. Such criticism has identified the elusive character of Bartleby as a suggestively messianic figure whose mysterious advent, arrest, and death obliquely dramatize an enactment of Christ's New Testament career and anticipated Second Coming. In addition, several critics have found connections between "Bartleby" and various biblical texts in relation to ideas of Christian charity, beginning with Bruce Franklin's argument over half a century ago that a basis for the scrivener's symbolic identity could be found in the Olivet Discourse in which Christ warned of the damning consequences of not extending charity to the "least" of one's brethren when Christ returned to judge the world (Matt. 25:31–46), a key text for antebellum moral and social reformers. Since that time many other biblical texts have been found relevant to "Bartleby," but so far there has been no definitive attempt to provide an overarching unity to the religious themes of the story.[1]

Among notable examples of religious approaches to the story, William Bysshe Stein interprets Bartleby as taking on the role of the narrator's Christian conscience, while "his ability to suppress this influence reflects the waning authority of Christianity in the ordering of life—the degeneration of the collective conscience." Donald M. Fiene has identified a host of covert biblical references associating Bartleby with the New Testament image of Christ, including his promised Second Coming, with the story revealing that "when Christ returns as the Messiah we shall deny him and betray him and crucify him again—even those of us who are Christians and assume ourselves to be of the elect." Stanley Brodwin notes the pervasive death imagery in the story, interpreting it as dramatizing a "loss of faith in resurrection, the Christian faith that in Christ there is the promise of eternal life. This is the question or belief which Melville agonized over within himself and which he saw disintegrating his society." Graham Nicol Forst sees the relationship between the narrator and Bartleby as comparable to that of the un-comprehending rich Pharisee Nicodemus who asks Jesus how he can be "reborn" at an advanced age, but who later defends Jesus from the Jews and eventually assists in Jesus's entombment, as described in the Gospel of John. In a linguistic and structural analysis of the story using a neglected manuscript fragment, Richard Kopley identifies the circle and center as key structural paradigms in which both the lawyer's office and the Tombs prison suggest elements of the ancient Jewish Temple in Jerusalem, while at the center of the story is the figure of Bartleby as Christ. Steven Doloff identifies Jesus's parable of the Good Samaritan in the Gospel of Luke, chapter 10, as a key proof text for the story, noting that the parable is told in answer to a lawyer's question about who exactly is one's "neighbor" whom God enjoins one to love: "Indeed, Melville's story would seem to be a parody of the parable, as we see a self-professed 'saved' Christian attempt the good deeds of the Biblical Samaritan but, ironically, still fall short of Christ's 'divine' injunction, spiritually hampered by his self-justifying, earthbound prudence." Noting the mix of classical and Christian motifs in the story, Thomas Dilworth critiques the rationalistic lawyer for his inability to feel Christian love for Bartleby, pointing out that the narrator's employment as a master in chancery likely involved him in foreclosing on leaseholds held by John Jacob Astor, whose fortune in Manhattan real estate grew from having leased properties at low rates from Trinity Church and the Protestant Episcopal Trinity Corporation; some of the legal documents Bartleby copied thus might have been related to eviction notices. Finally, Damien B. Schlarb interprets Melville's story as strategically shaped by the book of Job and the biblical wisdom tradition: "'Bartleby' emblemizes the transformation of knowledge into wisdom in the Solomonic sapiential tradition, just as Bartleby, the person, signals forth that same transformation to the lawyer."[2]

The goal of the present chapter is to demonstrate that many of the acknowledged and unrecognized allusions to the Bible found in the story are ironically inverted so as to call into question the biblical teachings on charity to which many of them refer. In keeping with Melville's skeptical mind-set throughout the 1850s and beyond, "Bartleby" ostensibly faults the narrator for not living up to his tepid Christian faith through his ultimate failure to exercise a life-saving charity toward his troublesome employee, but it also implicitly demonstrates the impossibility of adhering to New Testament ethical standards within a newly urbanized industrial economy based on rationalized self-interest. By the same token, the character of Bartleby subversively embodies the Christian ideal of ascetic withdrawal from the world, demonstrating the absurdist and potentially suicidal consequences of such an ideal. The present reading of "Bartleby" will show how Melville's story ironically—and often comically—critiques the Protestant culture of his era by revealing that the central doctrines of Christianity promoting social responsibility and nonmaterial values are cultural relics in a world of competitive individualism and a rapidly developing market economy. For as John F. Kasson remarks, "In the rapid transition to an industrial economy and a burgeoning urban society, the traditional modes by which individuals defined themselves and recognized one another, always particularly fluid in America, seemed to contemporaries to fall apart." Melville's parable of Bartleby and the lawyer-narrator is a prime example of such a dissolution of moral ties between individuals, portending a potential end to the Christian dispensation as an obsolete "dead letter."[3]

Published in two installments in *Putnam's Monthly Magazine* in November and December 1853, the story of problematic employee relations told in "Bartleby" was symptomatic of an era that saw the development of vast new wealth powered by financial and legal interests increasingly concentrated in New York City. Such economic expansion took place in tandem with the continued promotion of Protestant Christianity as providing the moral foundation of American society, manifested in the ongoing revivalism of the Second Great Awakening— culminating in the so-called Businessmen's Revival of 1857–58—as well as the host of religious publications and reform organizations based in New York City. As a result, by the later 1840s the dramatic increase in national wealth created a sense of uneasiness in the more respectable press, as the pursuit of profit and the embrace the capitalistic values seemed to fly in the face of the teachings of the nation's Protestant faith, with its emphasis on charity and equality before God, and with a moral stigma on selfishness and excess wealth. Such cultural cognitive dissonance provided an opportunity for skeptically inclined individuals to question the modern practicability of Christian faith. For as James Turner has noted, "Capitalist organization, technological change, and urbanization had subtly dissociated God from ordinary verities. And this subliminal disjunction more often pushed belief in God up from the dim layer of unexamined assumptions that form the background of thought into the full light of consciousness. There God lay exposed to reflection and questioning."[4]

As the premier commercial city of a rapidly expanding national economy based on faster and more efficient new modes of transportation, communication, and production, New York in the 1840s was increasingly characterized by a dramatic contrast between its ostentatious wealth and its shocking poverty, both of which might coexist a few blocks from each other. Beginning in 1842, Moses Beach, publisher of the city's leading penny newspaper, *The Sun*, began to publish a roster titled *Wealth and Wealthy Citizens of New York*, the so-called "Rich List," indicating all inhabitants of the city worth more than $100,000; and in 1844 the journalist Nathaniel P. Willis of the *Evening Mirror* famously dubbed the wealthy elite of the city the "Upper Ten Thousand." During this period the city was also home to notorious slum neighborhoods such as the Five Points, while widespread poverty, prostitution, intemperance, and crime haunted the physical and economic expansion of the city. Such a phenomenon led to a class of publications exposing the permeable barrier between the respectable and criminal cultures in the genre of "city mystery" writing such as George G. Foster's *New York in Slices* (1849) and *New York by Gaslight* (1850). The decade of the 1840s also saw the massive influx of new immigrants, first from Ireland and then from Germany, as the lower portions of Manhattan filled with overcrowded tenements, increasing the overall population of Manhattan to a half million by mid-century.[5]

The rise of New York City to the position of premier commercial center of the nation, together with the advent of the new market economy, meant that the inhabitants were increasingly strangers to one another, being chiefly focused on pursuing their own economic advantage or attempting to survive as members of working-class or impoverished communities. Edward K. Spann has described the social atomization that increasingly characterized New York City in the 1840s among both native-born citizens and recent immigrants:

> Most New Yorkers, like humans elsewhere, sought and found commitments which gave them a stake in some kind of collective life, but their society involved special discouragements against the development of a strong sense of community: Moving day [May 1, when leases expired], the inadequacy and high cost of housing, the common practice of residing in boarding houses as well as rented rooms and houses, the diversity and anonymity of life in a large metropolis, and the necessary disruptions of life and home associated with a fast-growing, transforming commercial city. Perhaps in no other city were even citizens so much strangers to each other.

Such a condition is suggestive of the radically isolated condition of Bartleby in Melville's story, for the impecunious scrivener is explicitly identified by the narrator as a victim of breakdown of communal life in the nation's largest city. For as the narrator notes of his employee, "If he would but have named a single relative or friend, I would instantly have written, and urged their taking the poor fellow away to some convenient retreat. But he seemed alone, absolutely alone in the universe."[6]

It is important to note that "Bartleby" not only depicts the urban anomie typical of New York City at the time but also reflects the dehumanizing popular impressions of its Wall Street location. For given the setting of Melville's story in an office at the epicenter of New York's—and the nation's—new market economy, as mentioned in its original subtitle ("A Story of Wall Street"), it is imperative to understand the contemporary reputation of the great financial center in lower Manhattan, where stocks in the nation's burgeoning enterprises were traded while banks and law offices facilitated the nation's unprecedented new economic growth. By the mid-1840s, the temporal setting of Melville's story, New York had some ten "millionaires" (a word coined in this decade), whose fortunes were based in trade, real estate, manufacturing, insurance, banking, and transportation. Already Wall Street had become a legendary domain of mysterious enrichment and ruination, with George G. Foster describing it in *New York in Slices* as a place of deadening corruption: "Wall-street! Who shall fathom the depth and the rottenness of thy mysteries? Has Gorgon passed through thy winding labyrinth, turning with his smile every thing to stone—hearts as well as houses?" Foster went on to highlight the worship of the "almighty dollar" by the denizens of finance: "It would seem as if we had found an avenue of temples—and so we have: only they are all erected to one divinity and devoted to the worship of one god—Mammon." The presence of Episcopalian Trinity Church at the end of the famous street provided an iconic contrast to Foster's idolatrous temples of "Mammon"; for as a modern financial historian has remarked, "Alexander McKay, the era's architect to the rich and powerful, noted the incongruity of Trinity Church, standing at the axial head of the Street, 'as if perpetually to remind the busy throngs that they cannot serve two masters.'" Both Foster and McKay thus echoed Christ's well-known warning in the Sermon on the Mount: "No man can serve two masters: for either he will hate the one and love the other; or else he will hold to the one, and despise the other. Ye cannot serve God and mammon" (Matt. 6:24).[7]

Melville's "Bartleby" accordingly takes place in a morally polarized realm pitting the antithetical influences of God and Mammon as an implicit thematic backdrop to its action. For one of the key ideas evoked by the beginning of the story through its setting on Wall Street and the narrator's early mention of his high esteem for John Jacob Astor, the nation's richest American in the 1840s, is the fact that the narrative takes place in a realm of narrowly monetary and materialistic values. The contest of God and Mammon forms an implicit feature of the narrator's dealings with his increasingly useless employee, and whether he can make the shift in his relation to Bartleby by embracing New Testament values in the form of Christian charity over his dedication to Mammon, following the narrator's comically rationalized conversion experience.[8]

In writing a story about a Wall Street lawyer's office, Melville was dealing with a subject involving both close family experience and topical interest. His lawyer brothers Gansevoort and Allan had both been examiners in chancery in the mid-1840s, and as a resident of Manhattan in the later 1840s Melville shared a house with Allan, who had an office at 14 Wall Street. The mysteries of the law were also the frequent subject of contemporary fiction, and it would seem likely that "Bartleby" was initially suggested by a first-person reminiscence of a peculiar legal copyist evoked in the first chapter of James A. Maitland's novel *The Lawyer's Story*, as it appeared on February 18, 1853, in the *New York Tribune* and *New York Times*. Yet while drawing on the humorous, sentimental, and melodramatic conventions of such narratives illustrating the changing realities of the legal profession, "Bartleby" clearly reaches beyond a mundane evocation of legal practice to evoke larger moral and metaphysical elements informing the parabolic world of the tale and the crisis of values on which it is based.[9]

The beginning of "Bartleby" makes it clear that the lawyer-narrator is fully immersed in the materialistic values of Mammon suitable for his Wall Street legal practice. In his introductory remarks, the lawyer thus notes that it is his "profound conviction that the easiest way of life is the best," and his ideal work environment is to "do a snug business among rich men's bonds and mortgages and title-deeds" (14). He accordingly expresses his indignation that his position as a master in chancery was ended by the "new Constitution" passed by the New York legislature in 1846 because he "had counted upon a life-lease of the profits" (14). The lawyer's assertions comically contradict the Christian ideals of spiritual striving, self-sacrifice, and voluntary poverty, for Christ had affirmed "how hard it is for them that trust in riches to enter into the kingdom of God!" (Mark 10:24) and claimed that the path to spiritual redemption is full of difficulty: "Wide is the gate, and broad is the way, that leadeth to destruction, and many there be which go in thereat: Because strait is the gate, and narrow is the way, which leadeth unto life, and few there be that find it" (Matt. 7:13–14).[10]

The narrator similarly demonstrates his faith in the values of the modern market economy when he sets forth an obsequious description of his professional association with John Jacob Astor, the personification of contemporary Mammon, beginning with his creation of a vast network of fur and China trading, later enhanced by a steadily increasing empire of land speculation and real estate holdings in Manhattan and elsewhere; Astor was, in short, a financial titan worth over twenty million dollars at his death in March 1848 (equal to half a billion dollars today). The pride the lawyer expresses in his association with Astor thus demonstrates his approving admiration for the richest American of the age, who was notorious for his single-minded pursuit of wealth. As Astor's nineteenth-century biographer, James Parton, noted, "To get all that he could, and to keep nearly all that he got—those were the laws of his being. He had a vast genius for making money, and that was all that he had." In the same vein, this biographer remarked of Astor, "He enjoyed keenly the consciousness, the feeling of being rich. The roll-book of his possessions was his Bible. He scanned it fondly, and saw with quiet but deep delight the catalogue of his property lengthening month to month. The love of accumulation grew with his years until it ruled him like a tyrant. If at fifty he possessed his millions, at sixty-five his millions possessed him."[11]

The lawyer in Melville's story reinforces his allusion to Astor as a capitalist icon with the self-deprecatory claim that he relished the sound of John Jacob Astor's name, "which, I admit, I love to repeat because it hath a rounded and orbicular sound to it, and rings like unto bullion" (14). The use of the word "hath" here demonstrates the narrator's self-consciously comic reversion to biblical archaism; yet the relevant biblical allusion is only recognized with his subsequent use of the ensuing simile. For while the phrase "like unto" is found over seventy times in the King James Bible, the addition of the word "bullion" in the narrator's language manifestly plays on Saint Paul's statement to the Athenian philosophers during his famous sermon on Mars Hill, as recorded in the book of Acts, regarding the new religion of Christ: "God that made the world and all things therein, seeing that he is Lord of heaven and earth, dwelleth not in temples made with hands; . . . Forasmuch as we are the offspring of God, *we ought not to think that the Godhead is like unto gold, or silver*, or stone, graven by art and man's device" (Acts 17:24, 29; emphasis added). By proposing the sound of John Jacob Astor's name as ringing "like unto bullion," the narrator is inverting Saint Paul's deliberate denial that the Christian God can be compared to an idol of gold or silver, the two precious metals that were officially designated "bullion." As a Wall Street lawyer, the narrator implicitly makes a god of Mammon in his sycophantic attitude toward the nation's most celebrated contemporary capitalist. The narrator's phrasing here additionally suggests a parodic inversion of another familiar New Testament passage, namely Saint Paul's characterization of the hollowness of those lacking in authentic "charity," or love for one's neighbor: "Though I speak with the tongues of men and of angels and have not charity, I am become as sounding brass or a tinkling cymbal" (1 Cor. 13:1). In Melville's Wall Street story, the lawyer's love of the "rounded and orbicular sound" of John Jacob Astor's name, which "rings like unto bullion," implicitly evokes Saint Paul's critique of uncharitable individuals who may speak elegantly but in reality sound like empty percussive noises.

At the start of the story, then, the narrator in his Wall Street office is implicitly associated with the modern capitalist anti-Christian powers of Mammon, but we nevertheless resist seeing any deep moral fault in him here because of his engaging personality, self-deprecating humor, and surprisingly humane attitude toward the eccentric employees of his law office. Indeed, when we read of his broad tolerance for his three established employees, we can hardly convict him of utterly lacking in compassion or charity. The elderly, shabbily dressed Englishman Turkey is thus severely limited in the quality of his copying in the afternoon by his consumption of wine at lunch, and the narrator unsuccessfully encourages him to take the afternoons off; he also generously gives him a better overcoat, which doesn't improve Turkey's obstreperous afternoon behavior. By the same token, the irritable young clerk named Nippers is hopelessly restless and unfocused throughout the morning hours and is involved in sketchy political and legal dealings outside the office, which the narrator deliberately overlooks. The twelve-year-old office boy, Ginger Nut, who goes on errands for cakes and apples for the two copyists, is similarly notable for the messy collection of nutshells he keeps in his desk drawer. The comic Dickensian descriptions of these three office assistants demonstrate that the narrator is in fact enormously tolerant of the irregular work habits and personal weaknesses in his three employees, so when Bartleby arrives at his door he has already shown himself accommodating to virtually any peculiar behavior or irregular productivity, despite his self-confessed affinity for the financial values of his capitalist idol, John Jacob Astor.[12]

Just as the narrator of "Bartleby" from the first is satirically identified with the values of Mammon, the character of the scrivener is implicitly identified with various facets of the depiction of Christ in the New Testament. In the first paragraph of the story, the narrator notes that except for one "vague report" that he will mention at the end of the story, the original sources of information about Bartleby are severely limited: "What my own astonished eyes saw of Bartleby, *that* is all I know of him" (13). The lawyer's use of the word "astonished" here is of particular significance because of its biblical resonances, being used nineteen times in the New Testament largely in connection with the impact of Christ on his audience. In the description of Christ's ministry, for example, people are thus repeatedly "astonished at his doctrine" (Matt. 7:28; 22:33; Mark 1:22, 11:18; Luke 4:32), or "astonished at his understanding and answers" (Luke 2:47), while during the visionary experience of his conversion, Saint Paul was "trembling and astonished" when Christ spoke to him (Acts 9:6). In "Bartleby," the lawyer implicitly asserts his "astonished" sense of wonder and amazement at the history of his former employee whose life mimics Christ's mythic identity, including his voluntary poverty, arrest and incarceration, and premature death as an accused criminal.

The reader's early introduction to Bartleby reveals him to be a character partially modeled on the well-known Old Testament image of the "suffering servant" in Isaiah 53, traditionally taken to be a typological anticipation of Christ as a figure of vicarious atonement. As the narrator notes, "I can see that figure now—pallidly neat, pitiably respectable, incurably forlorn! It was Bartleby" (19). The biblical "suffering servant" is similarly introduced as an object of sorrow and pity: "He is despised and rejected of men; a man of sorrows, and acquainted with grief. . . . Surely he hath borne our griefs, and carried our sorrows; yet we did esteem him stricken, smitten of God, and afflicted" (Isa. 53:3–4). Bartleby's persistent habit of silence and his eventual preference not to assist his employer in the latter's worldly affairs also matches the suffering servant's reticence and resistance: "He was oppressed, and he was afflicted, yet he opened not his mouth" (Isa. 53:7). In a typological parallel, in the scene of his interrogation before the Jewish high priest Caiaphas, Jesus "held his peace" (Matt. 26:63), while during his trial before Pilate, Jesus similarly "answered nothing" to the question whether he was King of the Jews (Matt. 27:12), and "answered him to never a word" when asked to respond to his accusers (Matt. 27:14). As a symbolic figure, Bartleby thus plays the role of a mock Christ whose arrival at the narrator's office is revealingly described as an "advent" (15), and who takes up an invisible, emaciated residence in the inner sanctum of the lawyer's office as one of the "least" of one's brethren whom Christ made a test case of charitable action (Matt. 25:40, 44).

While the narrator of "Bartleby" is impressed by his new employee's early application to the task of copying, he nevertheless faults his drone-like demeanor: "I should have been quite delighted with his application, had he been cheerfully industrious. But he wrote on silently, palely, mechanically" (19–20). Bartleby's industrious copying at the start of his employment, together with his self-effacing habits and the narrator's confinement of him behind a screen in his office—all these suggest that the new scrivener has inadvertently assumed a kind of monastic identity suitable for a practitioner of religious asceticism, an identity enhanced by the narrator's repeated reference to Bartleby's cubicle as his "hermitage" (21, 23, 25, 36) and his observation that Bartleby only gets nourishment by eating a few ginger cakes obtained by the office boy. Like a monk, too, Bartleby is initially an assiduous copyist of documents who strictly limits his interactions with humanity but nevertheless maintains a "wonderful mildness" (27) of demeanor. Indeed, from his first appearance in Melville's story, Bartleby's behavior shows him to be virtually dead to the world, inadvertently imitating Christ's repeated devaluation of the material interests of human life, as set forth in the Sermon on the Mount: "Take no thought for your life, what ye shall eat, or what ye shall drink; nor yet for your body, what ye shall put on. Is not the life more than meat, and the body than raiment?" (Matt. 6:25). Equally clear in emphasizing the stark opposition between the demands of the flesh and spirit was the apostle Paul: "For the flesh lusteth against the Spirit, and the Spirit against the flesh: and these are contrary the one to the other" (Gal. 5:17). Later in Melville's story, when the lawyer drops by his office one Sunday on his way to church, he unexpectedly finds Bartleby there, looking like an "apparition" (26) and presenting a "cadaverously gentlemanly *nonchalance*" (27). Not surprisingly, the scrivener eventually appears as a kind of "ghost" (38) haunting the lobby of the narrator's office building and ultimately expires in prison from starvation after earlier telling the grub-man, in a telling understatement, "I am unused to dinners" (44). The impenetrable nature of Bartleby's personality and his withdrawal from human engagement create an absurdist example of modern Christian asceticism.[13]

While performing an initial stint of rapid copying work, perhaps to boost his meager compensation of "four cents a folio (one hundred words)" (25), Bartleby confounds the narrator by refusing to do any other related tasks in the office besides his assigned copying. Thus when asked to assist the narrator to briefly "examine a small paper" with him, Bartleby inexplicably replies with the politely phrased rejoinder, "I would prefer not to" (20)—the polite negation he subsequently repeats in response to the narrator's startled inquiries about the reason for his answer. Yet following a period of puzzled exasperation, the narrator slowly reconciles himself to his employee's dereliction of clerkly duty by rationalizing Bartleby's refusal as a harmless oddity that would ultimately spiritually benefit him (the narrator) by eliciting his indulgence toward this unusual employee: "Poor fellow! thought I, he means no mischief; it is plain he intends no insolence; his aspect sufficiently evinces that his eccentricities are involuntary. He is useful to me. I can get along with him. If I turn him away, the chances are he will fall in with some less indulgent employer, and then he will be rudely treated, and perhaps driven forth miserably to starve. Yes. Here I can cheaply purchase a delicious self-approval. To befriend Bartleby; to humor him in his strange willfulness, will cost me little or nothing, while I lay up in my soul what will eventually prove a sweet morsel for my conscience" (23–24). The narrator's revealing thought process shows the implicit self-interest and materialistic values that initially guide his actions, for humoring Bartleby can be done with little or no "cost" and it will presumably "lay up" a "sweet morsel" for his conscience, ironically reminding the reader of Christ's injunction to accumulate moral, not material, things of value for salvation: "Lay not up for yourselves treasures upon earth, where moth and rust doth corrupt, and where thieves break through and steal: But lay up for yourselves treasures in heaven" (Matt. 6:19–20). The narrator is ironically laying up a psychological "treasure" here on earth in his assumption that his treatment of Bartleby will provide a "sweet morsel" for his conscience to make him feel better about his actions, or lack thereof. His self-conscious acts of altruism will effectively give a boost to his self-esteem. The narrator's rationalizations here expose his misapplication of Christ's moral message, but the reader feels an obvious kinship with the narrator as someone whose tolerance and compassionate nature are being stretched to the limit and who finds it impossible to be charitable without calculating its ultimate cost to his own interest.

The narrator's struggle to decide how to respond to Bartleby's willfully uncooperative behavior provides ample material for comedy as the narrator helplessly turns to his other employees for advice about how to deal with the recalcitrant new clerk. Turkey and Nippers thus alternately tell him to deal harshly or gently with Bartleby, depending on whether they are in their morning or afternoon moods, while Ginger Nut makes the percipient observation that Bartleby is likely "a little *luny*" (22). In any case, the narrator does not treat Bartleby as someone afflicted with insanity, despite what would likely be judged today as symptoms of mental illness, with modern critics pointing to signs of melancholy (clinical depression), schizophrenia, and autism in Bartleby's behavior.[14] Instead, the narrator eventually accepts the fact that Bartleby will be allowed to work exclusively as a copyist without having to help out with other tasks such as proofreading. Indeed, the narrator even strives to rationalize Bartleby's unusual behavior by deciding that his "steadiness, his freedom from all dissipation, his incessant industry (except when he chose to throw himself into a standing revery behind his screen), his great stillness, his unalterableness of demeanor under all circumstances, made him a valuable acquisition" (25–26). Bartleby is thus an industrious worker but one whose impenetrable nature increasingly unsettles the narrator's social and professional expectations.

The narrator's hard-won acceptance of his eccentric employee soon changes, however, when he unexpectedly discovers the clerk living in his office, making the mystery of his elusive identity and personal history even more challenging. Thus, when the narrator stops by his office on his way to attend a Sunday morning service at nearby Trinity Church, he finds that Bartleby is in occupancy when his scrivener meets the surprised narrator at the door in his shirtsleeves. Returning later that morning when Bartleby has vacated the premises, the narrator can now appreciate the absolute isolation of his clerk's life: "What miserable friendlessness and loneliness are here revealed! His poverty is great; but his solitude, how horrible!" (27). The pathos of Bartleby's homeless condition suggests Christ's pathos-laden assertion of ultimate homelessness: "The foxes have holes, and the birds of the air have nests; but the Son of man hath not where to lay his head" (Matt. 8:20). Like Christ, Bartleby now begins to have a redemptive spiritual influence on the narrator, for realizing the scrivener's unworldly isolation, the narrator claims that for the first time in his life he feels a deep melancholy in discovering the full extent of a fellow mortal's narrow life: "The bond of common humanity now drew me irresistibly to gloom. A fraternal melancholy! For both I and Bartleby were sons of Adam" (28). Recognizing his spiritual kinship with Bartleby, the narrator duly notes how the comfortable middle- and upper-class portions of the urban population fail to acknowledge the human misery in their midst because they deliberately blind themselves to its reality: "I remembered the bright silks and sparkling faces I had seen that day, in gala trim, swan-like sailing down the Mississippi of Broadway; and I contrasted them with the pallid copyist, and thought to myself, Ah, happiness courts the light, so we deem the world is gay; but misery hides aloof, so we deem that misery there is none" (28).

Such remarks on the human propensity for avoiding the painful realities of urban poverty were in keeping with similar observations by Horace Greeley in a Christmas Day 1845 editorial in the *New York Tribune* contrasting the well-dressed mirthful crowds of the city's affluent residents with the hidden misery of the poor: "But beneath this flashing surge of joyous and happy life slowly beats the agonized heart of the suffering poor":

> Oh, we could wring the heart with real and living pictures of
> such misery and destitution as seem to belie the noble destiny of

humanity and disprove the goodness of Omnipotence! We could take you, oh most comfortable reader, a five minutes' walk from the crowded and brilliant throng in Broadway, to the dens of crime and starvation, where man seems a brute, woman a fiend, and childhood—the season of joy and smiles—a wretched and bitter mockery, without hope or heart. The gorgeous rainbow that spans the whirling torrent of metropolitan life rests its bases on such dark depths of misery and crime as it makes one shudder but to think of.[15]

Like Greeley's Christmas editorial pointing out hidden urban scenes to wring the reader's heart, the narrator's perception of "common humanity" with Bartleby in Melville's tale provides a powerful sermonic message of human sympathy to supersede the famous preacher he has failed to hear at nearby Trinity Church.

Based on such sentiments, the narrator is now inspired to accept Bartleby's full-time residency in his workplace despite the unusual nature of such an arrangement, noting that Bartleby henceforth "made my office his constant abiding place and home" (29). The narrator's assertion that his office was now Bartleby's "abiding place" is linguistically and thematically in keeping with Christ's telling the wealthy publican Zacchaeus that "to day I must abide at thy house" (Luke 19:5) and his assertion to his disciples that "the servant abideth not in the house for ever: but the Son abideth ever" (John 8:35; see also 15:4). Yet just as the narrator is beginning to gain insight into Bartleby's isolation during his accidental Sunday encounter with the scrivener at his office, a lawyerly "prudential feeling" overcomes him regarding his inability to remedy Bartleby's condition: "What I saw that morning persuaded me that the scrivener was the victim of innate and incurable disorder. I might give alms to his body; but his body did not pain him; it was his soul that suffered, and his soul I could not reach" (29). Having just realized his "common humanity" with Bartleby as two "sons of Adam" (28), the narrator now ironically begins to plan how he can dismiss Bartleby with the least trouble, seeking to find out more about the personal life of his clerk and offering any necessary monetary assistance for him "to return to his native place" (29).

In changing his attitude, the narrator has become prudentially concerned with Bartleby's unsettling influence after his employees begin inadvertently mimicking the scrivener in their unconscious use of the word "prefer," precipitating the narrator's final resolution that he must get rid of a man who has somehow gained proselytes in his seeming madness: "I thought to myself, surely I must get rid of a demented man, who already has in some degree turned the tongues, if not the heads of myself and clerks. But I thought it prudent not to break the dismission at once" (31). When the next day Bartleby tells the narrator that he will no longer copy documents, making him totally useless as an employee, the narrator doesn't fire him on the spot but calmly asks Bartleby the reason for his decision. "'Do you not see the reason for yourself,' he indifferently replied" (32). The narrator thinks that Bartleby must have hurt his vision because "his eyes looked dull and glazed," and he feels "touched" (32) by the assumed injury to his clerk's vision; but in reality he cannot see into Bartleby's unworldly soul or understand his condition of radical alienation from the world, as though illustrating Christ's challenge to his disciples: "Having eyes, see ye not?" (Mark 8:18).

When the narrator finally gives Bartleby an ultimatum of six days to leave the office, and he still finds the scrivener there after the designated time, claiming that he "prefers not" to depart, the narrator must comically resort to a face-saving scheme of leaving the office himself after trying to give the scrivener his remaining wages together with a twenty-dollar severance payment. The lawyer's premature self-congratulation over his avoidance of an ugly confrontation with Bartleby over the clerk's continued presence provides grounds for further comedy, as does his astounded discovery the next day that Bartleby was still living in his office, even telling his employer with insouciant aplomb not to come in because he was currently "occupied" (34). In Luke's version of the Parable of the Talents, the three servants are told by their nobleman-master to "Occupy till I come" (Luke 19:13; see also Matt. 25:14–30), implying that they should be using their monetary gifts of talents (or pounds) to increase his wealth. Bartleby's use of the word is a comically reductive formulation in keeping with the narrator's earlier discovery of Bartleby's "old bandanna handkerchief, heavy and knotted" that served as a "savings' bank" (28)—the meager financial resources of this "unprofitable servant" (Matt. 25:30).[16]

The continued presence of Bartleby after the narrator has done everything he thought necessary to ensure the clerk's departure inadvertently leads to the narrator's ostensible conversion to Christian principles of charity after he has previously tried to act in the role of a more practical-minded man of affairs. The narrator's description of his self-interested decision to accept Bartleby's increasingly burdensome presence in his office is surely one of the most amusingly ironic descriptions of the conversion experience in this era of mass evangelical conversions. For the decision comes after the narrator is so filled with "nervous resentment" (36) that he is ready to kill Bartleby, in the manner of the sensational murder of Samuel Adams by John C. Colt in a lower Manhattan office on September 24, 1841, the result of a dispute over the bill for Adams's printing of Colt's textbook on double-digit bookkeeping. Eschewing the cautionary example of Colt, whose shocking murder and dismemberment of his victim the narrator ascribes to the pernicious influence of a "solitary office, up stairs, of a building entire unhallowed by humanizing domestic associations" (36), the narrator uses a metaphor of wrestling to describe how, as an improbable spiritual athlete, he was "saved" from a violent impulse toward Bartleby latent within the "old Adam" and embraced Christ's "new commandment" of love as famously expressed in John 13:34: "But when this old Adam of resentment rose in me and tempted me concerning Bartleby, I grappled him and threw him. How? Simply by recalling the divine injunction: 'A new commandment give I unto you, that ye love one another.' Yes, this it was that saved me" (36). The "old Adam" tempting the narrator—with a likely allusion to the name of Colt's murder victim—is a stand-in for the sinful, devil-ridden self in the traditional Protestant conversion narrative, while the wrestling metaphor used by the narrator likely derives from the injunctions in Saint Paul's Letter to the Ephesians: "For we wrestle not against flesh and blood, but against principalities, against powers, against the rulers of the darkness of this world, against spiritual wickedness in high places" (Eph. 6:12).[17]

The narrator's ability to "save" himself from a diabolical act of murder thus hinges on an embrace of Christ's teachings that is unabashedly self-interested. It is thus not done out of a newfound love of God, or of Christ's mercy, or of settled conviction of penitence for one's sins, but simply out of the law of self-preservation. Indeed, the narrator's meditation on the remarkable usefulness of charity makes it sound more like a practical policy for business success rather than an expression of love based on the example of Christ's injunctions and subsequent atonement for the sins of humanity: "Aside from higher considerations, charity often operates as a vastly wise and prudent principle—a great safeguard to its possessor. Men have committed murder for jealousy's sake, and anger's sake, and hatred's sake, and selfishness' sake, and spiritual pride's sake; but no man that ever I heard of, ever committed a diabolical murder for sweet charity's sake. Mere self-interest, then, if no better motive can be enlisted, should, especially with high-tempered

men, prompt all beings to charity and philanthropy" (36). The narrator's candid confession of the ultimate reason for showing Christian
charity to Bartleby thus offers a hint of comic self-deprecation along
with the rhetorical force of a reductio ad absurdum.

Another way to view the narrator's comic "conversion" in Bartleby is
to compare it with the most famous conversion in the history of Christianity, Saint Paul's experience on the road to Damascus. In a scene that
was retold three times in the New Testament, the former persecutor
of the new Christian faith saw a "light from heaven: And he fell to the
earth, and heard a voice saying unto him, Saul, Saul, why persecutes
thou me?" (Acts 9:3–4); the visionary Christ then told him to go into
the city for further instructions. A temporarily blinded Saul/Paul is
then led into Damascus, where, after remaining blind for three days,
he is visited by Ananias, who has been instructed by Christ to seek out
Saul/Paul as a "chosen vessel unto me" (Acts 9:15). Laying hands on
the new apostle, Ananias tells him he will receive his sight back and be
filled with the Holy Ghost, after which "there immediately fell from
his eyes as it had been scales: and he received sight forthwith" (Acts
9:18). In comic contrast to Paul, the narrator of "Bartleby" does not
experience a heavenly vision, a fall to the ground, a direct address from
Christ, temporary blindness, miraculous healing, or radical change
from murderous persecutor to promoter of Christianity. Although the
narrator's change of heart involves a remembered injunction from the
Gospel of John to love his neighbor, his conversion experience contrasts
with Paul's in being eminently rational and "prudent." Indeed, his eventual abandonment of Bartleby when he proves to be a threat to the
narrator's legal business demonstrates that his alleged conversion to
Christian principles of charity was only a transparent rationalization
of self-interest—a prototype for the self-serving motivations for many
such religious conversions of his professional class.

Incongruous as it may seem to the reader today, the lawyer's self-
interested exercise of charity toward his employee conformed to the
practical teachings promoted by a number of religious-minded writers
on mid-nineteenth-century political economy, who attempted to reconcile the selfless motives of traditional Christian charity with the self-
interested motives of modern business. As Stewart Davenport notes,

> The followers of Jesus, on the one hand, were obliged to love their
> neighbors out of obedience to the commands of their savior and
> out of a Christ-like disregard for themselves and their own interests.

The followers of political economy, on the other hand, were similarly commanded to love their neighbors (or at least not to make war on them), but were told to do so for exactly the opposite reasons. Instead of appealing to the Christian ethic of selflessness and the potential sacrifice of one's personal interests, political economists argued that loving one's neighbor would actually help further one's interests, either individually or corporately.

Following Adam Smith's demonstration of the benefits of free market economics in *The Wealth of Nations*, many Anglo-American writers on political economy argued that individual pursuit of monetary gain ultimately benefited the whole of society and did not undermine its ethical norms grounded in its Protestant faith. Melville's example of the lawyer in "Bartleby" thus mimics the contemporary theory that Christian charity could actually serve the material interests of its proponent, as though God and Mammon were somehow practically reconcilable.[18]

With Bartleby still exasperatingly occupying his monastic "hermitage" (36), the lawyer nevertheless seeks intellectual support in a reading of Jonathan Edwards's *The Freedom of the Will* (1754) and Joseph Priestley's *The Doctrine of Philosophical Necessity Illustrated* (1777) for the idea that dealing with his recalcitrant scrivener "had been all predestinated from eternity, and Bartleby was billeted upon me for some mysterious purpose of an all-wise Providence, which it was not for a mere mortal like me to fathom" (37).[19] Becoming reconciled to Bartleby's presence through this reading in two classics of philosophical determinism, the narrator thinks he has found a possible vocation in being his scrivener's protector: "At last I see it, I feel it; I penetrate to the predestinated purpose of my life. I am content" (37). In viewing Bartleby as fated to be his "predestinated" charge in life, the narrator is asserting a permanent spiritual bond to his employee by using the language of Saint Paul: "According as he [God] hath chosen us in him before the foundation of the world, that we should be holy and without blame before him in love: Having predestinated us unto the adoption of children by Jesus Christ to himself, according to the good pleasure of his will" (Eph. 1:4–5).

Yet the ironic twist here is that despite his alleged "conversion" experience and his determined embrace of Christian doctrine, the narrator soon realizes that keeping Bartleby as an unemployed inhabitant of his office has begun to undermine his professional reputation because of the many visitors who question the anomalous presence of an employee disengaged from any productive work; the argument for commercial self-preservation thus comes into effect, negating his recent personal commitment to Christian ideals of behavior. The lawyer thus finally decides that rather than forcing Bartleby to leave during an unpleasant scene, he himself must move his office to get rid of his employee. Telling Bartleby that he will soon be vacating the premises, the lawyer tries to hand the copyist some money, but the latter lets it drop to the floor, showing his utter indifference to the commercial interests that govern the narrator's professional life—the realm of Mammon. Once established in his new office, the narrator is still comically anxious that Bartleby will somehow reappear, and this does indeed happen when the lawyer is contacted about the continuing presence of the scrivener in the entry-way of the lawyer's old building, inadvertently proving the lawyer's responsibility for his former employee as his "brother's keeper" (Gen. 4:9) and a fellow son of Adam.

As Bruce Franklin first pointed out, the lawyer's thrice-repeated rejection of responsibility for Bartleby covertly recalls Peter's three rejections of knowledge of Jesus to the Roman authorities following the latter's arrest—a rejection that Jesus had predicted the night before but that Peter denied he would do (Matt. 26:34–35).[20] Having moved his offices to get away from the troublesome copyist, the narrator is thus comically unnerved when the lawyer occupying his former office comes to tell him "you are responsible for the man you left there" (39), to which the narrator replies, "the man you allude to is nothing to me—he is no relation or apprentice of mine, that you should hold me responsible for him" (39). When the visiting lawyer asks who Bartleby is, the narrator honestly reiterates, "I know nothing about him. Formerly I employed him as a copyist; but he has done nothing for me now for some time past" (40). Finally, about ten days later, a group of men, including the lawyer he previously encountered and the landlord of his former office, come to tell him to do something about Bartleby because clients are leaving the building and a mob action is threatened against the seemingly deranged man. Resisting the urge to lock himself in his office, the narrator futilely remarks: "In vain I persisted that Bartleby was nothing to me—no more than to anyone else. In vain:—I was the last person known to have anything to do with him, and they held me to the terrible account" (40). The narrator's paranoid fear of responsibility for Bartleby is reflected in his final mention of the "terrible account" he faces in assuming ultimate responsibility for his former employee, a seemingly exaggerated fear that suggests the narrator is aware of the warning of Saint Paul on human accountability for one's fellow man at the Last Judgment: "But why does thou judge thy brother? or why dost thou set at nought thy brother? for we shall all stand before the judgment seat of Christ. For it is written, As I live, saith the Lord, every knee shall bow to me, and every tongue shall confess to God. So then every one of us shall give account of himself to God" (Rom. 14:10–12). The narrator's denials of direct responsibility for Bartleby are legitimate in terms of legal liability, and it is likely only because of his intimate knowledge of his former employee's utter helplessness that he is finally persuaded to try to assist him again.

If the narrator's repeated denials of responsibility for Bartleby undoubtedly make him comparable to Peter in the latter's denial of Christ, the comparison is more notable for its comic incongruities than its demonstration of moral inadequacies in the narrator. For unlike the poor uneducated Peter, who was an intimate associate and designated moral successor to Christ, the narrator is a privileged legal representative of Wall Street whose clerk is a laconic, unprepossessing man of mysterious motivations and origins. Moreover, rather than doing nothing to avoid Bartleby's arrest for vagrancy, the narrator ultimately does everything he can to save his former employee from incarceration as a public nuisance. Thus, the narrator's final interview with Bartleby before he is taken away to the Tombs for imprisonment gives him the chance to make a last offer of various professional opportunities for the scrivener, including copyist in another office, clerk in a dry goods store, bar-tender, bill collector, or even traveling companion on a trip to Europe "to entertain some young gentleman with your conversation" (41). Regarding the last offer, Bartleby predictably replies in the negative, now with a comically disarming excuse: "I like to be stationary. But I am not particular" (41). The narrator thus bends over backward to help a man whom he well knows to be incapable of leading a normal working life. But after adducing various improbable excuses, Bartleby inevitably finds fault in all these positions and even rejects a final offer from the narrator, who after briefly losing his temper over his former clerk's obstinacy, offers Bartleby the chance to reside at his house with him until they can secure the clerk's professional future. Bartleby rejects even this remarkably generous offer on the grounds that he "would prefer not to make any change at all" (41). In the end, Bartleby's unworldly behavior negates the narrator's last attempts to "save" his employee from impending disaster through his last-ditch charitable actions.

Exasperated by this final show of Bartleby's lack of rational self-interest, the narrator precipitously flees the site of his former office in fear of being further troubled with his former employee's fate; for as he notes, "I had distinctly perceived that I had now done all that I possibly could, both in respect to the demand of the landlord and his tenants, and with regard to my own desire and sense of duty, to benefit Bartleby, and shield him from rude persecution" (42). The narrator is thus caught between his consciousness of having exhausted all possibilities of helping Bartleby and his irrational sense of continuing emotional concern for a harmless individual who was innocent of wrongdoing but was nevertheless liable for arrest for vagrancy. The latter event inevitably happens, as the narrator discovers after he spends several days purposefully avoiding his new office because of his pained reluctance to hear the news of Bartleby's apprehension. When the narrator finally hears from his former landlord that Bartleby has been arrested for vagrancy and brought in for arraignment, he learns that "the poor scrivener, when told that he must be conducted to the Tombs, offered not the slightest obstacle, but in his pale unmoving way, silently acquiesced" (42).

As Marvin Fisher notes, "In a scene that must be an ironic reversal of Christ driving the money-men from the Temple, Wall Street landlords and city authorities . . . remove Bartleby from the Wall Street office, arrest him as a vagrant, and lock him in the Tombs."[21] The manner of Bartleby's unresisting and silent arrest also suggests the typological basis for his identity in the ordeal of the "suffering servant" as an Old Testament model for Christ, the former being "brought as a lamb to the slaughter, and as a sheep before her shearers is dumb, so he openeth not his mouth" (Isa. 53:7). Like Christ, too, Bartleby after his arrest will inadvertently be "numbered with the transgressors" (Mark 15:28). But despite being a modern Christ-like "man of sorrows," the representation of Bartleby in his last days suggests several ironic reversals of Christ's Passion. Thus, when Bartleby is imprisoned in the Tombs, or Halls of Justice, he is not taunted or tortured as was Christ on his way to trial and then crucifixion, but instead, being "under no disgraceful charge" (43), Bartleby is allowed by the authorities to roam the grass of the prison yard. It is here that the narrator finds him, noting that "from the narrow slits of the jail window, I thought I saw peering out upon him the eyes of murderers and thieves" (43). Rather than being crucified between two thieves, Bartleby is insulated from these dangerous criminals.

When the narrator greets his former employee in prison, Bartleby is unexpectedly dismissive and rude: "'I know you,' he said, without looking round,—'and I want nothing to say to you'" (43). Bartleby's surprisingly harsh condemnation of the narrator makes it seem as though the latter, like another Judas, has betrayed the scrivener by ultimately sanctioning his removal from the narrator's former office building, and in fact Bartleby's dismissal mimics Christ's scathing remark to the Jews who refused to learn from him: "But I know you, that ye have not the love of God in you" (John 5:42). The narrator receives a similarly rude response ("I know where I am") when trying to cheer Bartleby up about his new surroundings by claiming "it is not so sad a place as one might think. Look, there is the sky, and here is the grass" (43). The narrator's attempt to distract Bartleby's attention away from the surrounding misery of the Tombs is in fact transparently contrived, given that this famous New York jail and police court, constructed in the later 1830s over swampy landfill, had the reputation for being a sinkhole of corruption, with guards, policemen, lawyers, clerks, bail bondsmen, judges, and other functionaries pitted against an overcrowded mass of inmates. As the journalist George Foster described the prison in the late 1840s in *New York in Slices*, imagining a polluted wind blowing through it: "What unsightly labyrinths of filth and abomination—what heaped-up cells of iniquity and unrepentant crime—what dens of drunken madness, howling over the graves of Reason—what dark recesses, sacred to the orgies of a corrupt and abominable Justice—hast thou not passed over! No wonder that thou art tainted with a poison that strikes to the very soul but to breathe. No wonder that in such a redhot furnace of corruption, bribery, theft, burglary, murder, prostitution, and delirium tremens, the very air is rarefied with crime." In such an environment, liberal payment to guards and other attendants was the only means to procure meals and other privileges, and the narrator of "Bartleby" accordingly accosts the "grub-man" to arrange for his former employee to be fed. When introducing "Mr. Cutlets" to the copyist, however, he receives only Bartleby's reply that he prefers not to dine: "It would disagree with me; I am unused to dinners" (44). These are in fact Bartleby's last words before the narrator finds him dead in the yard a few days later. Not having benefited from a "last supper" like his typological model, Bartleby dies in the prison yard where, the narrator notes, "a soft imprisoned turf grew under foot. The heart of the eternal pyramids, it seemed, wherein, by some strange magic, through the clefts, grass-seed, dropped by birds, had sprung" (44).[22]

While Bartleby's silent death in the Tombs gives no indication of ultimate spiritual redemption, the unexpected presence of the grass in the yard gives assurance of natural life reborn in the midst of the desolate Egyptian-styled "Tombs." The narrator nevertheless claims, quoting from the book of Job, that Bartleby is now in heaven, "with kings and counsellors" (45), ignoring the fact that the Old Testament patriarch used these words in connection with a despairing death wish after losing all his possessions in a divine test: "Why died I not from the womb? why did I not give up the ghost when I came out of the belly? Why did the knees prevent me? or why the breasts that I should suck? For now should I have lain still and been quiet, I should have slept: then had I been at rest, With kings and counsellors of the earth, which built desolate places for themselves" (Job 3:11–14). The narrator's discovery of Bartleby's emaciated body in fetal position suggests that Bartleby has reverted to the stillborn child of Job's wishes rather than filling the role of the dead Christ, with the lawyer assuming the place of Joseph of Arimathea, who, along with the rich Pharisee Nicodemus, claimed Christ's body for burial (Matt. 27:57; Mark 15:42; Luke 23:50; John 19:38–39). There will be no sign of resurrection except in the story the narrator is writing of his mysterious charge.

In the narrator's final attempts to help Bartleby we may see an implicit ironic inversion of several key New Testament parables of the relations of rich and poor and demonstrating the necessity for Christian charity to one's fellows. Thus, in the parable of the Good Samaritan, the narrator inadvertently tries to act the role of the provincial Samaritan, who binds the wounds of the "half dead" man who was assaulted by thieves and was found lying by the road, in contrast to the priest and Levite who callously pass him on the other side (Luke 10:30–37). Yet like the priest and Levite, the narrator had earlier attempted to avoid dealing with Bartleby by moving his law office away from his troublesome employee; and like the injured man in Christ's parable, Melville's Bartleby is seemingly half dead, but in this case from psychological, not bodily, injuries. So, too, after taking him to an inn to recover, the Samaritan gives the innkeeper "two pence" to take care of the injured man and promises more assistance when he returns—actions that the narrator in "Bartleby" duplicates when he gives the "grub-man" in the Tombs money to feed Bartleby on his first visit to his former clerk, and then promises him more money when he returns on his second and last visit. However, the reversal of the parable of the Good Samaritan couldn't be more plain, for even though his charity arrives late, the narrator of "Bartleby" ends up struggling to find ways to help his former clerk, who resolutely shows himself opposed to any proffered assistance.[23]

By the same token, the narrator reverses the terms of the well-known parable of Lazarus and Dives (Luke 16:19–31), a key New Testament commentary on the moral corruptions of the rich and the virtues of the poor. As a critique of the selfish rich, Christ's parable shows two scenes, the first of the sickly beggar Lazarus asking for the crumbs from the rich man's table, the second showing the rich man in hell asking for a drink of water to ease his thirst and being refused. Like the biblical "Dives" of the parable, the narrator confesses, as we recall, that he likes to associate himself with the wealthiest New Yorker of the era, John Jacob Astor, whose name he enjoys pronouncing because it "rings like unto bullion." Yet unlike the biblical Lazarus, it is Bartleby himself who insists on feeding on "crumbs" in the form of ginger cakes in the lawyer's office, rather than seeking crumbs from the rich man's (his employer's) table. Moreover, rather than dying and going to hell and begging Lazarus in heaven for a drop of water to cool his thirst, the narrator remains alive to witness the scrivener's unexpected death through starvation. Bartleby in the end is not "comforted" by a heavenly reward for suffering, as is Lazarus, nor is the narrator "tormented" by the fires of hell, as is the rich Dives. Instead, the narrator merely waxes melancholy over the scrivener's lonely death and his ultimate moral mystery.

Finally, in keeping with Christ's teachings in the Parable of the Sheep and the Goats in the apocalyptic Olivet Discourse, the narrator treats his clerk—who may be considered as "one of the least of these my brethren" (Matt. 25:40)—in the manner that Christ instructs for favorable treatment at the Last Judgment: "For I was an hungred, and ye gave me meat: I was thirsty, and ye gave me drink: I was a stranger, and ye took me in: Naked, and ye clothed me: I was sick, and ye visited me: I was in prison, and ye came unto me" (Matt. 25:35–36). Following this rubric, the narrator twice visits his former employee in prison and attempts to obtain "meat" for him; earlier in the story he took him in when he was a "stranger" and let him live in his office and even invited him to live at home with him. The narrator thus eventually fulfills Christ's mandate in this apocalyptic parable, but he has nevertheless failed to redeem his problematic employee because of the latter's adamant refusal to be aided. By the end of the dramatic action of "Bartleby," we have witnessed a consistent pattern of ironic inversion in Melville's use of the New Testament teachings on Christian charity as a moral blueprint for the action of the story. For as James Turner has noted, "As the nation grew more urban, Bible stories, built from the metaphors and folkways of a pastoral and agrarian people, lost their immediate emotional resonance, became a touch alien. The Lord as Shepherd did not directly chime with the experience of a commercial lawyer or mercantile clerk."[24]

In the conclusion to "Bartleby," the narrator, still baffled by the life history of his former employee, repeats a rumor he thinks worth sharing with the reader. Confessing that this "vague report has not been without a certain strange suggestive interest to me, however sad" (45), the narrator reports that Bartleby apparently once worked in the Postal Service's Dead Letter Office in Washington, DC, and lost his job through a change of administration, thus pointing to the election of Polk to the presidency in 1844, since the story takes place before the revised New York State Constitution eliminated the lawyer's job as a master in chancery after 1846. After being held in local post offices for three months and their addressees' names being listed in newspapers during that time, unclaimed, or "dead," letters were sent to a central facility in the nation's capital for opening and then burning, four times a year, with over a million missives going up in flames by 1837; letters containing money or valuables would, however, be returned to the sender. In Melville's story, the narrator remarks on how depressing it must have been for a naturally melancholy individual like Bartleby to work in such a position, repeatedly examining the contents of letters that will never reach their intended recipients: "Dead letters! does it not sound like dead men? Conceive a man by nature and misfortune prone to a pallid hopelessness, can any business seem more fitted to heighten it than that of continually handling these dead letters, and assorting them for the flames?" (45).[25]

The idea of "dead letters" would have had both personal and larger symbolic resonances for Melville, as manifested in the conclusion to "Bartleby." Early and mid-nineteenth-century letter writers often expressed anxiety that death would intervene before the writer and recipient saw each other again, and, indeed, Melville wrote such a "dead letter" to his older brother Gansevoort on May 29, 1846, expressing concern for his reported ill health, little knowing that his brother had already died in England earlier that month. Commenting on the function of the Dead Letter Office in "Bartleby," the narrator observes that although on "errands of life, these letters speed to death" (45), and such might Melville have considered his own letter to his deceased older brother. The hidden dramas associated with the nation's Dead Letter Office had become the subject of a spate of articles and stories by the early 1850s, for as historian David M. Henkin writes, "By mid-century, accounts of the dead letter operation had begun to comprise a genre of sensationalist literature, laying bare dark and concealed worlds along the lines pursued profitably by the popular urban guides and city-mysteries fiction of the era. Much as sensationalist journalism led its readers on tours of the urban demimonde, accounts of the dead letter office exposed the mysterious workings of the major bureaucracy of the nineteenth century, while at the same time uncovering the idiosyncratic practices and human dramas that lay buried under reams of traceless and errant pieces of paper." Yet within the larger frame of "Bartleby," with its depiction of the narrator's inability to assist his enigmatic clerk, the lawyer's final emphasis on the depressing effect of "dead letters" also highlights a phrase with other relevant meanings.[26]

For the original phrase "dead letter" has biblical resonances originating in two of Saint Paul's letters arguing the idea that with the advent of Christianity, the "letter" of the Mosaic law was superseded and in effect "dead." In his Letter to the Romans, Saint Paul thus argued that "now we are delivered from the law, that being dead wherein we were held; that we should serve in newness of spirit, and not in the oldness of the letter" (Rom. 7:6); and in his Second Letter to the Corinthians, Paul similarly claimed to be undertaking his ministry because God "also hath made us able ministers of the new testament; not of the letter, but of the spirit: for the letter killeth, but the spirit giveth life" (2 Cor. 3:6). The phrase "dead letter," meaning an agreement or law that has become obsolete even though not formally annulled, dates from the early seventeenth century, the same time as the appearance of the King James Bible. The fact that Melville included the narrator's brief coda on the problematic life history of his scrivener, with its emphasis on the negative impact of "dead letters," suggests that Melville is hinting at a larger allegorical meaning for the Dead Letter Office. Indeed, given the failure of the narrator's attempt to extend meaningful Christian charity to his unworldly clerk despite his growing sense of responsibility for the latter, Melville is likely implying that the whole of the New Testament, with its central message of charity and love toward one's fellows, has now become a "dead letter," just as the Mosaic law and Old Testament dispensation allegedly became a "dead letter" following the advent of Christianity.[27]

Thus, as the narrator notes the depressing circumstances of Bartleby's work in the Dead Letter Office while pondering the failure of vital human assistance that the destruction of such letters implies, the narrator evokes the pathos of Bartleby's participating in such scenes: "Sometimes from out the folded paper the pale clerk takes a ring:—the finger it was meant for, perhaps, moulders in the grave; a bank-note sent in swiftest charity:—he whom it would relieve nor eats nor hungers any more; pardon for those who died despairing; hope for those who died unhoping; good tidings for those who died stifled by unrelieved calamities. On errands of life, these letters speed to death" (45). The imagined failure of life-giving "charity," "pardon," "hope," and "good tidings" posited by the narrator suggests the death of the redemptive messages found in the epistolary "letters" of the New Testament, the majority of which were written by, or ascribed to, Saint Paul and established the moral framework of Christ's teachings for the incipient Christian community. Of particular relevance here is Paul's statement that among the Christian cardinal virtues of faith, hope, charity, "the greatest of these is charity" (1 Cor. 13:13). The phrase "good tidings" used by the lawyer occurs only twice in the New Testament, first in the Nativity narrative of Luke when an angel of the Lord tells the fearful shepherds the good news of Christ's birth ("And the angel said unto them, fear not: for, behold, I bring you good tidings of great joy, which shall be to all people" [Luke 2:10]); and subsequently in Paul's First Letter to the Thessalonians, in which the apostle has received "good tidings of your faith and charity" (1 Thess. 3:6) from one of his messengers. The "good tidings" mentioned by the lawyer in "Bartleby" are thus implicitly comparable to the evangelical "good news" that constitutes the basic message of Christianity. In Melville's story, the futile "good tidings" mentioned by the lawyer are useless because their recipient is no longer alive, just as the person receiving the bank-note "nor eats nor hungers"—both being ironic fulfillments of Christ's assurance to his disciples in the Gospel of John that "I am the bread of life: he that cometh to me shall never hunger; and he that believeth on me shall never thirst" (John 6:35).[28]

As in much of Melville's fiction of the 1850s, Saint Paul's hymn to charity in 1 Corinthians 13 provides an implicit moral benchmark for "Bartleby, the Scrivener." Just as the beginning of the story included covert verbal play on 1 Corinthians 13:1 in the narrator's self-confessed love for pronouncing John Jacob's Astor's "orbicular" name that "rings like unto bullion" (14), the end of the story implicitly invokes Saint

Paul's insistence that if one lacks basic "charity," or love, in one's heart for a fellow human being, all one's allegedly charitable deeds amount to nothing. In his incremental tolerance for his clerk's eccentricities, growing compassion for his pitiable existence, and forbearance from violent words of condemnation, the narrator would seem to clearly pass the test of Saint Paul's stringent requirements for Christian charity: "Charity suffereth long, and is kind; charity envieth not; charity vaunteth not itself, is not puffed up. Doth not behave itself unseemly, seeketh not her own, is not easily provoked, thinketh no evil" (1 Cor. 13:4–5). But contrary to all of his efforts, the narrator's story of the hapless scrivener ultimately undermines Paul's claim that "Charity never faileth" (1 Cor. 13:8). This, perhaps, is the ultimate ironic biblical inversion illustrated by Melville's parabolic tale. When the narrator asserts at the end of the story, "Ah Bartleby! Ah humanity!" (45), he is inadvertently conveying a modern kerygma, or proclamation, of humanity's spiritual homelessness modeled on the life and death of his clerk as existential Everyman.

In the narrator's account of his dealings with Bartleby, then, Melville's story reveals why unconditional Christian loving kindness was increasingly difficult to achieve in the urbanizing and industrializing nation of the antebellum era. For as Walter E. Anderson notes, "The lawyer's Wall Street world does not so much give us a clue to the cause of his limitation as express the general—and natural—condition of which he is an exponent. Capitalism represents the dominant institutionalized form of self-interest. Melville's juxtaposition of Wall Street and Trinity Church (which actually stands at the head of that famous street) marvelously symbolizes the central paradox. The radical reappraisal to which Melville subjects 'the Word' questions the very idea of its being (or of its ever having been) perfectly practiced." In this economic world, the idea of Christian charity must yield to the newly established ethos of competitive individualism, in keeping with practical effects of the market revolution, as summarized by John Lauritz Larson: "Once comfortably embedded in relatively small communities governed by personal relations that were colored by kinship, friendship, and familiarity, Americans now moved restlessly in and out of pluralistic cities and towns, conducted business with strangers at home and abroad, and felt themselves increasingly powerless to shape the world in which they lived."[29]

The seeming negation of the Christian idea of charity toward humanity illustrated by "Bartleby" can be seen as a continuation of a central theme of Melville's *Pierre*, the novel he had published in the summer of 1852, a year before his turn to short story writing. Despite differences in their ages and the gender of their beneficiaries, *Pierre*'s nineteen-year-old Pierre Glendinning and the elderly lawyer in "Bartleby" offer comparable models of charitable behavior, both of which prove lethal in their effect. Pierre thus passionately but blindly precipitates a tragedy for himself and others by championing the cause of his oppressed half sister, while the lawyer's more modest efforts at assistance lead to the gratuitous death of his copyist. Unlike the example of the youthful Pierre, who quickly becomes the moral champion of his alleged half sister Isabel based on the idealistic teachings of the Sermon on the Mount, the narrator in "Bartleby," as a cautious older man and prudential lawyer, only becomes firmly committed to charitable assistance to Bartleby after a tepid conversion experience and a gradually developed sense of moral concern. In both narratives, Melville thus presents varied scenarios for exploring the viability of Christian commitment to those in need.

The core of this moral issue had been explicitly set forth by the narrator of *Pierre*, who noted the "solecism" found in the contradiction between the message of Christianity and the materialistic morality of the mid-nineteenth-century Anglo-American world: "That while, as the grand condition of acceptance to God, Christianity calls upon all men to renounce this world; yet by all odds the most Mammonish part of this world—Europe and America—are owned by none but professed Christian nations, who glory in the owning and seem to have some reason therefor." The grand contradiction between the moral demands of God and Mammon thus informs both *Pierre* and "Bartleby." In *Pierre*, the narrator goes on to note that, for such a young enthusiast as Pierre, "unless he can find the talismanic secret, to reconcile this world with his own soul, then there is no peace for him, no slightest truce for him in this life. Now without doubt this Talismanic Secret has never yet been found; and in the nature of human things it seems as though it never can be." Just as Pierre Glendinning fails to find a formula for reconciling the selfish mores of his upper-class world with his naïve attempt to save Isabel from a life of poverty and neglect, the narrator of "Bartleby" discovers that there is no available means to solve the problem that the scrivener presents to him, for although initially committed to the materialistic world of his Wall Street office, he nevertheless attempts to reconcile his "soul" to this world by assisting his helpless employee but eventually discovers that all such assistance is futile.[30]

The narrator of *Pierre*'s representation of the lack of a "talismanic secret" to reconcile the moral precepts of Christianity with the materialistic ethics of the modern world is contradicted by the pamphlet of the philosopher Plotinus Plinlimmon that Pierre reads during his journey from Saddle Meadows to New York City, for Plinlimmon's major point in the fragment that Pierre reads is that although these two ethical systems appear to be contradictory, they are paradoxically in harmony with each other. Plinlimmon accordingly teaches that "in things terrestrial (horological) a man must not be governed by ideas celestial (chronometrical); that certain minor self-renunciations in this life his own mere instinct for his own every-day general well-being will teach him to make, but he must by no means make a complete unconditional sacrifice of himself in behalf of any other being or any cause, or any conceit." The philosopher thus advocates a "virtuous expediency" as "the highest desirable or attainable earthly excellence for the mass of men, and is the only earthly excellence that their Creator intended for them." In *Pierre*, the youthful protagonist is depicted as someone who acts out a ruinous "chronometrical" act of charity and thereby destroys himself and others through sacrificing himself to save his half sister and atone for his father's sins; whereas in "Bartleby," the lawyer embodies Plinlimmon's ideal of a "virtuous expediency" in his treatment of Bartleby, even though the lawyer is increasingly drawn into sacrificing more and more of his own self-interest in taking care of his employee.[31]

In this reading of "Bartleby, the Scrivener," we have traced Melville's use of biblical language and symbolism in a story that uses the familiar motif of putting a Christ-like figure in a modern setting to show the clash in values between Christian ethical norms and the mores of an increasingly impersonal, individualistic, and materialistic modern society. It should be noted that Melville's suggestion in "Bartleby, the Scrivener" of the inadequacies of Christianity in the modern world is a repeated motif in Melville's post-*Pierre* fiction, reaching its ultimate literary expression in the final chapter of *The Confidence-Man* (1857), when the Cosmopolitan extinguishes the emblematic "solar lamp" of biblical revelation—the conclusion to the novel's elaborate satirical variations on the theme of Christian charity and its cultural manipulations and failings. "Bartleby" similarly anticipates the ironic critiques of institutional Christianity and the inadequacies of modern charity found in Melville's three so-called "diptychs"—"The Two Temples," "Poor Man's Pudding and Rich Man's Crumbs," and "The Paradise of Bachelors and the Tartarus of Maids"—all of which were written between the late summer of 1853 and the spring of 1854 in the first phase of Melville's career as a writer of short fiction.[32] Considered in the context of his writings in the early 1850s, Melville's "Bartleby, the Scrivener" thus continues his skeptical examination of the Christian teachings on charity and brotherly love that served as a basic moral touchstone for nineteenth-century Anglo-American society and culture. In Melville's next published short story, "Cock-a-Doodle-Doo!," he would subject the Christian dogma of the Resurrection and the idea of the immortality of the soul to comparable skeptical and seriocomic scrutiny.

CHAPTER 3

Conversion, Infatuation, Resurrection

Christian Salvation in "Cock-a-Doodle-Doo!"

As a story that suggestively hovers between parable, beast fable, and fairy tale, "Cock-a-Doodle-Doo! Or, The Crowing of the Noble Cock Beneventano" has remained something of an outlier in the canon of Melville's short stories. Published in the December 1853 *Harper's New Monthly Magazine*, the story, like its immediate predecessor, "Bartleby, the Scrivener," tells of the narrator's dealings with an enigmatic individual (and employee) who unexpectedly dies at the end of the story, along with his whole family; in this case, the individual is possessed of a mysteriously redemptive rooster whose symbolic significance has eluded critical consensus. Early criticism of the story proposed that it was intended to satirize the Transcendental idealism of Thoreau, but this theory has foundered on the problematic later dating of some of the Thoreauvian texts considered relevant to the story and the lack of a preponderance of convincing rather than suggestive evidence. If for many modern readers the idea of the magical "cock" sought by the narrator immediately suggests an off-color joke, a basic question remains concerning what the spirited cock, denominated "Trumpet" by his owner, ultimately represents, and whether the story was written to convey a subversive or affirmative spiritual message.[1]

Critical opinion on the story has thus offered a broad range of approaches to these questions. Richard Harter Fogle, for example, interprets the story within a Christian framework with clear biblical associations: "The crow of the cock is, first of all, a paean of Christian hope." William Bysshe Stein similarly argues that the story is a satire directed at the apostle Paul. William B. Dillingham, on the other hand, summarily asserts, "'Cock-a-Doodle-Doo!' is clearly not a religious story. The hell of this tale is the world which the narrator finds himself already living in, and divine intervention does not come as God's grace manifested in religious conversion." Marvin Fisher claims the story "is Melville's most prolonged look at the psychic imbalance to which the artist is particularly susceptible because the force of his commitment can so readily make the values of art superior to those of life, the charm of illusion preferable to mundane realities." Beryl Rowland, in contrast, explores the larger religious, philosophical, and folkloric significance of Melville's "cock" while claiming that Melville's story is an allegory on the delusion of faith: "There is no divine inspiration, Melville is saying, no plan of redemption, no life after death. There are only human beings who, in order to endure the daily misery of their lives, have a desperate need to believe in an illusion."[2]

More recently, Michael Colacurcio has examined the story in the context of Marx's well-known idea of religion as the opiate of the people, asserting that "Cock-a-Doodle-Doo!" is "a tale that intuits all on its own the Marxist relation between oppression and apocalypse. For clearly the sort of religion that Marx has in mind is precisely that which offers salvation in another world as the only fit recompense for so much suffering in this one." Claiming that Melville's story must be read as a symbolist, not an allegorical fiction, Matthew R. Bardowell argues that "a symbolist interpretation of the story asserts the immortal, otherworldly nature of the human spirit and its ability to triumph over materialistic constraints." Finally, Ib Johansen has analyzed Melville's story as an example of the fantastic mode in American literature in which the narrator's quest for the magical cock is framed by supernatural elements and fairy tale motifs in an imaginative critique of modernity: "The cock, with its defiant, jubilant outcry against whatever enslaves human beings in a class-divided, socially segregated world, triumphs over the enemies of the common people (the latter represented in the story by the poor wood-sawyer and his family)—the bird can die by its song, if not live by it."[3]

In keeping with Melville's obsessive exploration in much of his fiction in the 1850s of the apparent obsolescence of Christian doctrine and belief in mid-nineteenth-century America, my reading of "Cock-a-Doodle-Doo!" will argue that it is a modern parable satirically critiquing the allegedly redemptive powers of Christian faith in which the narrator's mock conversion is shown to be an act of supreme Pauline folly. Thus the spiritual "awakening" performed by the rooster—in keeping with the ongoing religious revivals of the era—brings about not spiritual renewal but only death for the owner of the rooster, his family, and finally the magnificent bird itself. Saint Paul made the truth of Christianity contingent on belief in the Resurrection of the body of Christ (1 Cor. 15:12–19), but the end result of the redemptive rooster's message in Melville's story is universal annihilation for all the members of the Merrymusk family, including the rooster. And if the narrator claims to have vanquished his depression at the end of the story, his redemptive conversion experience has reduced him to mindless crowing in keeping with a new identity as a "born-again" Pauline fool of Christ; it is thus appropriate that his final act is to inscribe the apostle's words regarding the resurrection of the body on the grave of the Merrymusk family. As a subversive commentary on the largely Protestant faith of antebellum America, the story ultimately implies that the Pauline fable of the resurrection of the spirit is equivalent to the fairy tale of a magical rooster's crowing forth a mysterious message of spiritual empowerment. Melville's well-known declaration to Hawthorne in 1856 that he had "pretty much made up his mind to be annihilated" is the underlying rationale for the astringent satirical allegory of "Cock-a-Doodle-Doo!"[4]

Before turning to Melville's tale, we must examine some of its relevant biblical and theological background. The most famous "cock" in the New Testament is, of course, the one that Christ predicted would provide confirmation of Peter's betrayal on the morning of his arrest (Matt 26:34; Mark 14:30; Luke 22:34); but the more relevant New Testament passages for Melville's tale relate to the general religious metaphor of spiritual awakening associated with the crowing of a rooster at daybreak. Thus, in the gospel of Mark, Christ tells his disciples to be vigilant and watch carefully for his Second Coming, which could come "at even, or at midnight, or at the cockcrowing, or in the morning" (Mark 13:35). In two of his most influential epistles, Saint Paul uses the metaphor of awakening to convey Christian truth to his readers: "And that, knowing the time, that now it is high time to awake out of sleep: for now is our salvation nearer than when we believed. The night is far spent, the day is at hand: let us therefore cast off the works of darkness and let us put on the armour of light" (Rom. 13:11–12). The spiritual awakening described here must be based on faith in the idea of spiritual resurrection, as Saint Paul teaches in his well-known disquisition in 1 Corinthians 15. Using the analogy of a seed that creates new life only when being buried in the ground, Paul notes of the dead body of the believing Christian, "It is sown in corruption; it is raised in incorruption: It is sown in dishonor; it is raised in glory; it is sown in weakness; it is raised in power: It is sown a natural body; it is raised a spiritual body" (1 Cor. 15:42–44). Later in the same passage, Paul reveals the ultimate "mystery" of the resurrection of the Christian soul after death: "For the trumpet shall sound, and the dead shall be raised incorruptible, and we shall be changed. For this corruptible must put on incorruption, and this mortal must put on immortality" (1 Cor. 15:52–53).[5]

In colonial Massachusetts, Jonathan Edwards further elaborated on the crowing cock as a symbol of evangelical Christianity and the need for Christian spiritual awakening, writing in *Images or Shadows of Divine Things*, "The awakening and crowing of the cock to wake men out of sleep and to introduce the day seems to signifie the introducing the glorious day of the church by ministers preaching the Gospel. Many shall be awakened and roused to preach the Gospel with extraordinary fervency, to cry aloud and lift up their voice like [a] trumpet. Peter's being awakened out of that deep sleep he had fallen into, and brought to repentance by the crowing of the cock at break of day, signifies the awakening of Christ's church that is built upon Peter." Edwards's description of the "fervency" of preachers of the gospel who will lift their voice like a "trumpet" is consonant with the name of Melville's rooster. As the leading theologian of the Great Awakening in the mid-eighteenth century, Edwards was frequently invoked as a guiding evangelical spirit for influential preachers like Lyman Beecher and Charles Grandison Finney during the Second Great Awakening.[6]

Melville's "Cock-a-Doodle-Doo!" dramatizes the seemingly miraculous but ultimately illusory spiritual benefits of listening to the crowing of a mysterious cock, which is repeatedly given an underlying Christian message of the triumph of spirit over matter, and life over death. It is thus no coincidence that the name of the cock in the story is "Trumpet," in keeping with Saint Paul's assertion of the general resurrection of the spiritual body "when the trumpet shall sound" (1 Cor. 15:52). Following his strategy to hide subversive meanings in his fiction, as described in his 1850 review of Hawthorne's *Mosses from an Old Manse*, in "Cock-a-Doodle-Doo!" Melville has created an entertaining beast fable and parable critiquing the Christian doctrines of spiritual salvation and resurrection. Through multiple allusions to Christian doctrines, institutions, and biblical teachings, Melville satirizes the psychology of religious conversion and the alleged salvific qualities of Christian belief in gaining a victory over death—a satire partly directed at the ubiquitous antebellum preoccupation with the joys of a posthumous heaven. Enhancing this underlying message is the fact that Melville's story takes place in the early spring, the season of Easter and the formal celebration of the Resurrection.[7]

Dominated by the dyspeptic mood of the unnamed narrator, the beginning of "Cock-a-Doodle-Doo!" depicts a depressing world of political injustice, deadly accidents, chronic disease, and insalubrious weather. We thus hear at the start of the story that political reaction is in the ascendant, as was historically the case in Europe in the early 1850s with the suppression of the 1848 democratic revolts on the Continent; so, too, lethal accidents from exploding steamboats and derailed or colliding trains have repeatedly taken place in the United States. Thinking over these manifold ills, the narrator is initially depicted as out walking in the morning on a hillside pasture in the early spring. Climbing up a hill with his body bent into the ascent, he comments on the analogy between his bowed physical stance and his oppressed attitude: "This toiling posture brought my head pretty well earthward, as if I were in the act of butting it against the world. I marked the fact, but only grinned at it with a ghastly grin."[8] It is mud season in New England, and the land is damp and unhealthy looking, with a "lagging, fever-and-aguish river, over which was a duplicate stream of dripping mist" (269), while chimney smoke from the village has created a "great flat canopy of haze, like a pall" (269). Looking over the landscape, the narrator thinks of the gruesome calamities that have killed people on both water and land. He thus alludes to a steamboat accident on the Ohio River "where my good friend and thirty other good fellows were sloped into eternity at the bidding of a thick-headed engineer, who knew not a valve from a flue" (269). The narrator goes on to complain about a train accident closer to home:

> And that crash on the railroad just over yon mountains there, where two infatuate trains ran pell-mell into each other, and

climbed and clawed each other's backs; and one locomotive was found fairly shelled, like a chick, inside of a passenger car in the antagonist train; and near a score of noble hearts, a bride and her groom, and an innocent little infant, were all disembarked into the grim hulk of Charon, who ferried them over, all baggageless, to some clinkered iron-foundry country or other. Yet what's the use of complaining? What justice of the peace will right this matter? Yea, what's the use of bothering the very heavens about it? Don't the heavens themselves ordain these things—else they could not happen? (269)

With righteous indignation, the narrator presents an ironic scene in which the ruined train cars and locomotive he mentions suggest a grotesque parody of copulation, while the innocent passengers, including those celebrating a wedding, have been horribly maimed and gone to a hellish afterlife resembling an industrial wasteland. The utter senselessness of the accident obsesses the narrator; despite realizing the futility of complaining, he is still upset by the cosmic injustice of this loss of life. The fact that such accidents are allegedly ordained by heaven implies that a divine power must condone them, casting doubt on the benevolence of God.

Like many of the contemporary public, the disgruntled narrator here is outraged at the ongoing occurrence of steamboat disasters and the beginnings of major railroad accidents in the United States at the time Melville was writing. For example, while engaged in a race with another steamboat down the Hudson River on July 28, 1852, the *Henry Clay* caught fire and sank off Riverdale, New York, with forty-seven bodies later recovered from the water, including those of Nathaniel Hawthorne's younger sister Louisa and the noted landscape architect Andrew Jackson Downing. Regarding the narrator's allusions to railroad accidents noted above, historian Christian Wolmar writes, "The year 1853 was a seminal one in terms of rail accidents and the public attitude toward them. . . . Two major disasters took place within a fortnight of each other in the spring of 1853, and their proximity exacerbated the sense that railroads were dangerous." The first, on April 25, was a collision of two trains at a crossing outside Chicago that caused the deaths of twenty-one German immigrants, while the second, on May 6, involved a train that plunged into the Norwalk River in Connecticut when a drawbridge was still open, with the loss of forty-six lives. A third shocking collision, to which Melville's narrator may obliquely be referring, occurred on August 12 when fourteen people were killed after two trains collided head-on at Valley Falls, Rhode Island, on the line between Providence and Worcester. The scores of grisly deaths, including that of the son of president-elect Franklin Pierce, resulting from railroad accidents in 1853 created an appalling new record of mortality that garnered considerable public indignation.[9]

Despite the depth of outrage at the catastrophic failure of modern technology expressed by the narrator in Melville's story, he displays an aggressively un-Christian attitude of sadistic revenge, for he goes on to remark that he would like to exercise retribution on "the thousand villains and asses who have the management of railroads and steamboats, and innumerable other vital things in the world. If they would make me Dictator in North America a while, I'd string them up! and hang, draw, and quarter; fry, roast, and boil, stew grill and devil them, like so many turkey-legs" (269–70). The frustrated narrator, with his violent fantasies of absolute power, is obviously far from exercising the Christian virtues of temperance and nonresistance to evil even as he shows pronounced signs of aggravated clinical depression in his obsession with death and destruction. The narrator's fit of righteous indignation continues as he rails against the "improvements" of the age, especially the new railroad system, which he demonizes as "that old dragon" and a "gigantic gad-fly of a Moloch" while comparing its lethal impact to "the Asiatic cholera cantering on a camel" (270). Refusing to see any benefits in the railroad, the narrator considers it a legally tolerated but monstrous agent of mortality: "Here he comes, the chartered murderer! the death monopolizer! judge, jury, and hangman all together, whose victims die always without benefit of clergy" (270). The injustice of premature mortality from the increasing number of railroad and steamboat accidents of the era thus weighs heavily on the narrator's mind. Yet a more immediately threatening source of his indignation is the unavoidable presence of "that smaller dunning fiend, my creditor, who frightens the life out of me more than any locomotive—a lantern-jawed rascal, who seems to run on a railroad track too, and duns me even on Sunday, all the way to church and back" (270)—an obvious violation of the proprieties of churchgoing and the cessation of business on the Sabbath.

The narrator's lack of money and his constant harassment by a dun are thus another prime source of his depression, while his desperate financial situation is aggravated by the widespread perception that money was "plentiful—a drug in the market; but blame me if I can get any of the drug, though there never was a sick man more in need of that particular sort of medicine" (270). His mention of sickness brings to mind the powder he was going to give to the sick baby of a nearby poor Irish laborer, a thought that in turn reminds him of the many childhood diseases rampant in the area. This obsessively negative trend in his thought also reminds the narrator that he himself suffers from rheumatism in the shoulder, which he ironically claims to have acquired when he gave up his berth "to a sick lady, and staid on deck till morning in drizzling weather. There's the thanks one gets for charity!" (270). The injustice of acquiring an illness through an act of charity is yet another example to the narrator of humanity's gratuitous suffering, to which he adds the example of the acute dyspepsia that also afflicts him. Clearly, the divine superintendence of the world is lacking in the narrator's mind as he seems to undergo a series of intense physical and mental sufferings.

Based on the reader's introduction to the narrator's long roster of grievances, we find ample confirmation of the fact that, as he himself confesses, he suffers from a case of "hypoes" (268), or depression, and therefore may be characterized as possessing the classic "sick soul" that often precedes the experience of religious conversion. Thus it comes as no surprise that when on his morning walk the narrator suddenly hears a mysterious rooster crowing in the distance, the sound is associated with religious exultation: "Hark again! How clear! how musical! how prolonged! What a triumphant thanksgiving of a cock-crow! *'Glory be to God in the highest!'* It says those very words as plain as ever cock did in this world" (271). Listening to the crowing of the cock, to which he imputes the joyful message of the angelic host at the Nativity in Luke 2:14, the narrator asserts that he already feels better—one might say reborn—after hearing the rooster's exultant crowing. For when he hears the crowing again, the narrator feels spiritually empowered by a sound that he now characterizes as "clear, shrill, full of pluck, full of fire, full of fun, full of glee. It plainly says—*'Never say die!'*" (271). The narrator thus finds a message of self-assertion and perseverance in the crowing of the cock, but the larger message of "Never say die!" also hints at the central Christian doctrine of the resurrection of the body and the immortality of the soul, and we will find this idea increasingly associated with the rooster as the story progresses.

In a sign of self-deprecation, the narrator makes a joke of the fact that he has unwittingly been talking about the rooster to the two-year-old calves he sees in his pasture, yet when doing so he is again suddenly overwhelmed by the sound of the unknown cock, which now inspires him to more extreme behavior when he jumps on a rotten log and flaps his elbows, imitating the crowing rooster in a foreshadowing of the end of the story. Thinking that such a cock can only crow in such a manner in the morning but will inevitably sound less inspiring as the day goes on, the narrator is surprised to hear the rooster as "he rings out again, ten times richer, fuller, longer, more obstreperously exulting than before. Why this is equal to hearing the great bell of St. Paul's rung at a coronation!" (272). The comparison of the cock to the bell of St. Paul's cathedral in London—likely referring to "Great Paul," at sixteen tons the largest bell ever cast in Britain—provides a clear hint of the religious significance associated with the rooster's crowing, as well as its association with the New Testament writings of Saint Paul himself setting forth the Christian doctrine of the resurrection. In keeping with his sudden spiritual transformation, the narrator seems to experience immediate psychological relief in a reversal of his previous angry mood. Thus he now feels positive about the existence of railroad travel while observing one train passing by, noting the cheerfulness of the locomotive's whistle and commenting on how the passengers are all going into the city to enjoy themselves: "Gay are the passengers. There waves a handkerchief—going down to the city to eat oysters, and see their friends, and drop in at the circus" (272). Even the sight of nature around him is no longer dismal and depressing, as he sees the sun shining through the mist and now compares the smoke over the village to "the azure tester over a bridal-bed" (272). Such a dramatic reversal in attitude is tangible proof that the rooster's crowing has already begun to transform the narrator's negative mind-set. For as he goes home at the end of his walk, he is in a much better mood, although in anticipation of having his creditor show up at his house he will go into the woods to obtain a club as a potential weapon. While acts of violence against the creditor would not seem to be a part of the joyful message of the cock, the narrator's new spiritual empowerment now seems to authorize such self-righteous violence, which continues his earlier desire to retaliate against the manifest evils of the world.

The ensuing meeting with the dun at the narrator's house takes place when he is reading a copy of Laurence Sterne's *Tristram Shandy*, injecting another note of comedy and sexual wordplay into the narrative as the narrator offers to read a scene from the novel concerning Uncle Toby's romantic admirer, the Widow Wadman, who aggressively pursues Uncle Toby despite his trepidation about women and his groin injury in battle; the courtship ultimately unravels when Toby finally agrees to show her where he was wounded, and while the widow waits for anatomical clarification about his masculine organs, he instead points to a map showing the 1695 siege of Namur in Belgium. While the dun in Melville's story obviously wants to get down to business with the narrator concerning the latter's debt, the narrator's desire to talk about *Tristram Shandy* hints at issues of personal impotence and potency that match his manic-depressive moods and his obsession with the invigorating crowing of the mysterious local "cock." When the dun thrusts his bill at the narrator, the latter contemptuously offers to twist it up to light his pipe and then asks if the dun has heard the extraordinary rooster before he precipitously forces the man out of his house, telling his boy helper to get a sack of potatoes to throw at the man to make him go away, adding insult to injury.

While we admire the verbal cleverness with which the narrator interacts with the dun, the violence of his ejection shows that the narrator's infatuation with the rooster's message of inspiration has not made him a newly reborn Christian who eschews violence and forgives injuries; indeed, the primary message that the narrator acquires from the cock is egotistical empowerment, not Christian charity and nonresistance to evil. For he says to himself after his creditor's eviction, when hearing the crowing of the cock again, "Bless my stars, what a crow! Shanghai sent up such a perfect paean and *laudamus*—such a trumpet-blast of triumph, that my soul fairly snorted in me. Duns!—I could have fought an army of them! Plainly, Shanghai was of the opinion that duns only came into the world to be kicked, hanged, bruised, battered, choked, walloped, hammered, drowned, clubbed" (273). The crowing of the cock here is again given a religious connotation in its comparison to a *laudamus*, the name for a hymn used by the early Christian Church and later incorporated into Catholic, Anglican, and Methodist services; the hymn thus begins with the words *Te Deum laudamus*, or "We praise thee God." The narrator's ensuing verbal threat of violence against his creditor again shows that the rooster has enhanced his sense of self-righteousness without fundamentally altering his previous moral grievances against the world.

When the narrator goes outside again at midday he again hears the rooster crowing and ascribes to it a new set of attributes. It is at this point that the sound of the cock's crowing moves toward a more obvious sexual significance, for the narrator now notes, "I had heard plenty of cock-crows before, and many fine ones;—but this one! so smooth and flute-like in its very clamor—so self-possessed in its very rapture of exultation—so vast, mounting, swelling, soaring, as if spurted out from a golden throat, thrown far back" (274). The description here of the "vast, mounting, swelling, soaring" of the cock's crow, climaxed by the "spurting" of the sound from its "golden throat," clearly adds a provocative orgasmic element to the rooster's appeal to the newly inspired narrator. The narrator goes on to characterize the sound as "the crow of a cock who had fought the world and got the better of it, and was now resolved to crow, though the earth should heave and the heavens should fall. It was a wise crow; an invincible crow; a philosophic crow; a crow of all crows" (274). When the narrator proceeds to think over the same potentially upsetting subjects that had depressed him at the beginning of the story, he now instead feels "a calm, good-natured rapture of defiance" (274). Indeed, he feels so superior to his troubles that he almost considers himself immortal: "I felt as though I could meet Death, and invite him to dinner, and toast the Catacombs with him, in pure overflow of self-reliance and a sense of universal security" (274). Anticipating the end of the story when he does indeed meet death in the rapid extinction of Merrymusk's family, the narrator has apparently gained a message from the rooster that corresponds to the Christian doctrine of the resurrection of the spirit after death. And before he goes to bed, the narrator goes outside and, after hearing the rooster crowing again, thinks of it as coming "like Xerxes from the East with his double-winged host. It was miraculous" (274-75). The crowing is thus compared to the famous Persian invader of Greece, whose miraculous "double-winged host" coming from the "East" suggests an angelic army of the lord ready to accomplish miracles.

The narrator's main task from this point to the end of the story will be finding the location of the rooster and then attempting to acquire it for himself in order to ensure himself its benefits. Based on the fact that the rooster is so impressive and persistent in his crowing, the narrator imagines that it must belong to a local wealthy individual. So the next morning he goes in quest of this unknown owner with the single clue that the crowing is apparently coming from somewhere to the east: "All that I could decide upon was this: the crow came from out of the East, and not from out of the West" (275). When he soon hears the crowing again, he reiterates the same idea: "There was no telling, further than it came from out the East" (275). The emphasis on the eastern direction of the sound of the rooster accords with the tradition that Christians were supposed to pray and worship while facing east toward Jerusalem and the Holy Land, the geographical epicenter of their faith; this was also the direction in which Western churches were supposed to be aligned in their architecture. The second advent of Christ was also traditionally supposed to come from the east: "For as the lightning cometh out of the east, and shineth even unto the west; so shall also the coming of the Son of man be" (Matt. 24:27).

The narrator's quest for the location of the cock at first involves him in a comically futile endeavor, for when he asks his first interlocutor, an old man fixing a rail fence, if he has heard "an extraordinary cock-crow of late," the man can only give him a "a long, bewildered, doleful, and unutterable stare" (277) of incomprehension. His second interlocutor is a "portly gentleman—nay a *pursy* one—of great wealth, who had recently purchased him some noble acres, and built him a noble mansion with a goodly fowl-house attached" (277); he would seem the likely candidate as owner of the inspirational cock, and he in fact owns ten "Shang-hai" roosters. But when the narrator sees these "carrot-colored monsters, without the smallest pretension to effulgence of plumage," he is convinced that none of them could be his "royal cock" (278). So the narrator must return home without success, and he spends several days haunted by the sound of the rooster, whose distant but regular crowing reinspires him, for his "soul, too, would turn chanticleer, and clap her wings, and throw back her throat, and breathe forth a cheerful challenge to all the world of woes" (278). Whatever temporary relief the narrator has obtained from throwing the dun out of his house, he now faces renewed financial difficulties and is forced to take out another mortgage on his estate to pay his debts. The persistent dun, meanwhile, has begun legal proceedings against him, and he is served a "civil-process" rolled up around the cigar that he went to retrieve after dining in his village tavern, and a constable rudely tells the narrator to "put that in your pipe and smoke it!" (278). The narrator is thus inadvertently reminded of his desperate financial situation, and after reading the process again meditates on his sense of being an unfortunate victim: "Nay, while many a stingy curmudgeon rolls in idle gold, I, heart of nobleness as I am, I have a civil-process served on me! I bowed my head, and felt forlorn—unjustly used—abused—unappreciated—in short, miserable" (279). But after hearing the rooster crow again, the narrator is inspired to make one last effort to remain solvent by consolidating all his debts into another mortgage on his estate so he can begin looking again for the "noble cock" that gives him inspiration and that he continues to hear every day, even briefly suspecting it to be the voice of "some wonderful ventriloquist" (279) haunting his vicinity.

The narrator's final discovery of the identity and location of the rooster comes unexpectedly when he is talking to the self-effacing workingman who has sawed and split his wood for the winter. The narrator's description of Merrymusk highlights the fact that even though he has a menial job, he does not complain about his situation and possesses an inherent dignity of manner to match a mysterious interior source of happiness that will soon be revealed: "He was tall and spare, with a long saddish face, yet somehow a latently joyous eye, which offered the strangest contrast. His air seemed staid, but undepressed" (280). Despite the narrator's previous attempt to make him tell something about himself while working outside, the woodcutter showed no desire to talk but merely kept up with his sawing. The narrator's initial estimate of his character envisages him as having lived a difficult life but still being reconciled to his lot through religious teaching or affiliation; thus he has concluded "that he was of a solemn disposition; that he was of the mind of Solomon; that he lived calmly, decorously, temperately; and though a very poor man, was, nevertheless, a highly respectable one. At times I imagined that he might even be an elder or deacon of some small country church" (280). In fact, the narrator is able to learn something about the woodcutter's life, which has involved an early stint as a sailor and then almost a decade in the region, where he has married a wife who is now an invalid, and has four sick children, one of them suffering from "white-swelling" (281), or tuberculous arthritis of the joints, and the three others having rickets, caused by a nutritional deficiency. Despite his depressing situation, Merrymusk uncomplainingly works and supports his infirm family, all of whom live in a shanty next to the railroad track, a model of the largely invisible pious poor.

When the narrator eventually comes around to ask Merrymusk if he knows of any "gentleman" in the area who might be the owner of the mysterious rooster, their verbal exchange offers a provocative play of sexual double-entendres:

> "My friend," said I, "do you know of any gentleman hereabouts who owns an extraordinary cock?"
>
> The twinkle glittered quite plain in the wood-sawyer's eye.
>
> "I know of no *gentleman*," he replied, "who has what might well be called an extraordinary cock."
>
> Oh, thought I, this Merrymusk is not the man to enlighten me. I am afraid I shall never discover this extraordinary cock. (281)

The narrator's verbal collocation of "gentleman" and "cock" here highlights their comic incongruity, while Merrymusk, as the coy but secret owner of the "extraordinary cock" playing along with the joke, has a twinkle in his eye because though a poor man, he can consider himself well-endowed in the possession of his prize rooster. The very name *Merrymusk* similarly hints at the wood sawyer's possession of a jolly temperament combined with sexual allure, musk being a male sexual secretion in animals.

Still in ignorance that the wood sawyer is the cock's owner, the narrator later arrives at his shanty to pay him the remainder of what he owes the sawyer for his work; the narrator is now surprised to discover the familiar sound of the cock and then sees the miraculous bird in front of the family shanty. The cock appears as extraordinary as it sounds, as it initially looks like a military hero: "A cock, more like a field marshal than a cock. A cock, more like Lord Nelson with all his glittering arms on, standing on the Vanguard's quarter-deck going into battle, than cock. A cock more like the Emperor Charlemagne in his robes at Aix la Chapelle, than a cock" (282). Appropriately impressive, the rooster has "a mighty and symmetrical crest, like unto Hector's helmet, as delineated on antique shields" and seems "like some Oriental king in some magnificent Italian Opera" (282). When the narrator shows his higher cultural and socioeconomic status by alluding to a character in a contemporary Italian opera in asking if the cock is named "Signor Beneventano," the sawyer understandably expresses puzzlement over this allusion, which was based on the name of a well-known opera singer who had performed in Italian operas in New York in the late 1840s and whose Italian name, appropriately enough, means "good wind."[10] But Merrymusk clearly has the advantage here, since the desired "cock" is his, and the narrator is manifestly envious of Merrymusk's possession of this homegrown creature, as seen in the narrator's comic astonishment on learning this startling fact: "Good heavens! do you own the cock? Is that cock yours?" (283).

Given what we have said about the evangelical significance of the cock's crowing, it is appropriate that its owner is a poor but virtuous man whose socioeconomic situation puts him in the class of impoverished individuals who were the intended beneficiaries of Christ's teachings. The covert irony of the narrator's discovery of the mysterious cock stems, however, from the fact that he immediately wants to buy it from the woodcutter, hoping to acquire its magical power and take advantage of Merrymusk's poverty. Indeed, the narrator's aggressive attempt to purchase the miraculous cock from Merrymusk makes him into a modern version of the notorious New Testament figure, Simon Magus, a sorcerer from Samaria who attempted to buy from the apostles the power of the Holy Ghost transmitted by the laying-on of hands, as described in the book of Acts, and whose name was later the basis for the sin of "simony" or the buying and selling of church offices. The narrator thus initially asks what Merrymusk would take for his rooster, beginning with an offer of fifty dollars and then upping it to a hundred, and then five hundred, all of which offers Merrymusk firmly refuses. In the biblical book of Acts, Simon Magus's comparably brazen attempt to buy spiritual gifts reveals his mercenary nature: "And when Simon saw that through laying on of the apostles' hands the Holy Ghost was given, he offered them money, Saying, Give me also this power, that I on whomsoever I lay hands, he may receive the Holy Ghost. But Peter said unto him, Thy money perish with thee, because thou hast thought that the gift of God may be purchased with money. Thou hast neither part nor lot in this matter: for thy heart is not right in the sight of God" (Acts 8:18–21).

By taking on the self-interested identity of a Simon Magus, the narrator shows his seeming unfitness to possess the miraculous powers of the cock, even though he thinks he is merely engaged in a simple commercial transaction by purchasing the charismatic rooster. Under the circumstances, however, Merrymusk does not act like an angry Peter condemning the sorcerer's greed, as in the New Testament story; and despite the narrator's brief anger at Merrymusk's refusal to sell his cock, the narrator is not as corrupt as his biblical model here since he accepts the poor man's invitation to come into his shanty, where the cock joins them, and where the narrator "stood awhile admiring the cock, and wondering at the man" (284). As might be expected, the shanty is a primitive space with bare rafters and a dirt floor, provisioned with beef jerky hanging from the ceiling, and potatoes and Indian cornmeal in bags in the corners. The narrator can hear, if not see, Merrymusk's ailing wife and children hidden behind a blanket hung in the middle of the shanty. Yet in contrast to this dismal scene, the noble-looking cock provides a complete contrast in appearance; indeed, the narrator describes it as possessing a light-filled supernatural glory suggestive of the *shekhinah* indicating divine presence, or "glory," in the Bible: "There was a strange supernatural look of contrast about him. He irradiated the shanty; he glorified its meanness. He glorified the battered chest, and tattered gray coat, and the bunged hat. He glorified the very voices which came in ailing tones from behind the screen" (284). The cock thus appears to have the ability to "glorify" its surroundings as though it were a divine agent in some fairy tale or medieval saint's life—a symbolism conveying both the blessedness of the honest poverty of the Merrymusk family according to traditional Christian belief, and the ironic incongruity between the magnificent-looking bird and the impoverished family home.

The cock's putative divine identity is additionally suggested by the request of one of Merrymusk's sickly children to hear Trumpet crow, which Merrymusk commands and the rooster duly renders with a crowing that literally jars the roof. When the narrator expresses astonishment that such noise doesn't disturb the ailing family members, Merrymusk replies, "Don't *you* like it? Don't it do *you* good? Ain't it inspiring? don't it impart pluck? give stuff against despair?" (285). Yet when the cock crows again, the narrator suddenly becomes frightened at its overwhelming power, suggesting in his mind the punitive actions of the Judeo-Christian god against divine enemies: "The cock frightened me, like some overpowering angel in the Apocalypse. He seemed crowing over the fall of wicked Babylon, or crowing over the triumph of righteous Joshua in the vale of Ajalon" (285). This is the first time that the narrator considers the crow of the cock almost a threat, implying that the magical rooster has both redemptive and potentially destructive apocalyptic capabilities in its seemingly divine nature.

The narrator's visit to Merrymusk continues with an introduction to his ailing wife behind the curtain, who looks "wasted" but with a "strangely cheerful human face"; and he sees the sickly children, too, who look on Trumpet "with a wild and spiritual delight. They seemed to sun themselves in the radiant plumage of the cock" (285). In their father's opinion, the rooster acts as a spiritual physician to the family: "'Better than a 'pothecary, eh?' said Merrymusk. 'This is Dr. Cock himself'" (285). Yet the magical rooster is clearly not able to physically cure the wife and children, whom Merrymusk expects to die of their illnesses; but in the meantime the presence of Trumpet keeps them all cheerful, according to the poor woodcutter, who imputes the redemptive message of Luke 2:14 to his cock: "He crows through all; crows at the darkest; 'Glory to God in the highest!' continually he crows it" (286). And in a confirmation of the Christian elevation of the heavenly over the earthly, Merrymusk claims that rather than his being a poor man as the narrator suggests, his possession of the rooster gives him unlimited spiritual riches: "Don't the cock *I* own glorify this otherwise inglorious, lean, lantern-jawed land? Didn't *my* cock encourage *you*? And I give you all this glorification away gratis. I am a great philanthropist. I am a rich man—a very rich man, and a very happy one. Crow, Trumpet" (286). Just as the poor embrace Christianity for its consolatory value and promise of heavenly reward, thereby laying up potential "treasures in heaven" in keeping with Christ's command (Matt. 6:19), the impoverished woodcutter is convinced of the manifold spiritual benefits provided by his magical cock.

The narrator does not see the woodcutter for several weeks after this, during which time he hears the cock crowing and is ultimately convinced that the lesson he has learned from the woodcutter concerning his redemptive rooster is valid. He is accordingly inspired to take out yet another mortgage on his farm and even not to mourn for some of his relatives who have died; indeed, he "wore no mourning, but for three days drank stout in preference to porter, stout being of the darker color" (286). Confirming the symbolic link between the crowing of Trumpet and human mortality is the fact that he hears the crowing just as he receives news of these family deaths. The narrator's reality-defying infatuation created by the woodcutter's rooster thus continues; but his final visit to Merrymusk now reveals the whole family to be mortally ill, with each one dropping dead as the magical rooster crows in a grotesquely incongruous tableau. Before Merrymusk himself dies, he confidently tells the narrator that his children are "all well," these two words being "shouted forth in a kind of wild ecstasy of triumph over ill" (287). With its owner's ecstatic death, the cock makes a glorious display of its plumage as the narrator compares it yet again to a visible feature of London's great cathedral: "The cock hung from the shanty roof as erewhile the trophied flags from the dome of St. Paul's" (287). After Merrymusk's wife asks if her husband is indeed dead, she too expires, and the cock again crows "in a rapture of benevolent delight," with this particular act of crowing so strong that it sounded "as if he meant the blast to waft the wood-sawyer's soul sheer up to the seventh heavens" (287). "Trumpet" is thus overtly performing the role of raising up the dead at the "last trump" in the scenario outlined by Saint Paul in 1 Corinthians 15.

As might be expected, the three children are also ready to expire and be transported to heaven by means of the cock's ecstatic crowing: "He seemed bent upon crowing the souls of the children out of their wasted bodies. He seemed bent upon rejoining instanter this whole family in the upper air. The children seemed to second his endeavors. Far, deep, intense longings for release transfigured them into spirits before my eyes. I saw angels where they lay" (288). The dying children are thus transfigured into angels, in keeping with a tenet of the sentimental Christian culture of the era. Yet in a surprising reversal of expectation, the magical cock itself makes one last "supernatural note, and dropped dead" (288) at the narrator's feet, having completed its task of crowing the Merrymusk family into a presumed spiritual immortality. The extinction of the whole family at the crowing of the cock, sustained by their belief in the redemptive powers of the rooster and supported by the narrator's vision of the children's dying transfiguration, is in keeping with the pervasive contemporary Christian idea of heaven as a place of blissful family reunion in the afterlife. In the brief sequel to the serial extinction of the Merrymusk family and its iconic rooster, the narrator mentions that he has buried the whole family along with their cock near the railroad tracks, and he has engraved a memorial stone containing Saint Paul's famous words on the immortality of the soul for the believing Christian: "Oh! death, where is thy sting? Oh! grave, where is thy victory?" (288). In a sign that the salvific message of the cock has taken over his own life, he ends his story with the claim that he is now never depressed but instead repeatedly imitates the sound of the rooster in a graphic demonstration of his embrace of the Pauline doctrine of holy foolishness (1 Cor. 1:18–25). The narrator's final act of crowing displays the dramatic reversal of his mood from the beginning of the story, as though he is permanently cured of his morbidly depressive spirits stemming from his contemplation of the "miserable world" (269) where death and injustice were seemingly pervasive. In reality, he has succumbed to a fantasy of salvation emanating from the magical cock, and his final gesture of crowing over the ills of the world suggests a deluded act of self-destructive folly, as he is still massively in debt to his creditors.

What are we to make of this absurdist modern fable of rural poverty, depression, serial mortality, and unexpected redemption in which a magical rooster proves to be a panacea for all the narrator's physical and spiritual ills? We can better understand the narrator's change of heart if we view it as equivalent to a case study in religious conversion, performed by the narrator's discovery of the sage-like Merrymusk and the strategic crowing of his charismatic rooster. In a recent study of the morphology of religious conversion based on a synthesis of psychological, sociological, anthropological, and historical models, Lewis R. Rambo has set forth seven general stages of religious conversion as relating to *context, crisis, quest, encounter, interaction, commitment*, and *consciousness*.[11] Examining Melville's story, we might use these seven stages to better comprehend the narrator's development from disgruntled debtor to ecstatic convert. Melville accordingly sets the larger *context* of the story in the initial depiction of the narrator's vocal discontent with the world while walking outdoors on a damp morning in early spring during New England mud season. The *crisis* he faces in his life is his pervasive sense of physical and psychological malaise, and the thought of the creditor who is constantly dunning him for an unpaid debt. The narrator's *quest* is initiated by the stirring sound of a distant cock crow, whose uplifting message to the narrator of *"Never say die!"* (271) provides both a spiritual tonic and a mystery over the cock's location and identity. Following his repeated experience of hearing the mysterious rooster crowing, and in a continuing quest to find its owner, the narrator finally has an *encounter* with the rooster's owner Merrymusk, an impoverished woodcutter who had earlier cut and split wood for the narrator. The narrator's subsequent *interaction* with Merrymusk leads to the discovery that this impecunious, modest, and self-effacing man is the owner of the prize rooster with the transcendent cock crow. Once he makes this surprising discovery, the narrator's ensuing *commitment* to acquiring the cock leads to his further acquaintance with Merrymusk and his family, who are all terminally ill but consoled for their sufferings by the crowing of their rooster. A final transformation of the narrator's *consciousness* occurs when Merrymusk, his wife, and his four children all die in the narrator's presence as the cock seems to crow their spirits to heaven and then itself finally expires after one last "supernatural note" (288)—an experience leading to the narrator's alleged cure of his depression and his perpetual exultant crowing like the rooster in the last sentence of the story.

If Melville's parable-like tale rehearses the formal stages of the narrator's religious conversion to a Christian hope for spiritual immortality based on Pauline doctrine, William James's classic discussion of conversion in *The Varieties of Religious Experience* is also relevant here. The narrator of Melville's story clearly belongs to James's category of the "sick soul" who is most susceptible to conversion, as illustrated by the narrator's morbid obsessions with disease, death, and cosmic injustice at the beginning of the story. These are the individuals James characterizes as those "for whom evil is no mere relation of the subject to particular outer things, but something more radical and general, a wrongness or vice in his essential nature, which no alteration of the environment, or any superficial rearrangement of the inner self, can cure, and which requires a supernatural remedy." Like one of James's representative subjects for conversion, the narrator attains a dramatic transformation by the end of the story, akin to those "born again" through an encounter with a climactic quasi-supernatural catalyst, whether human or divine: "What is attained is often an altogether new level of spiritual vitality, a relatively heroic level, in which impossible things have become possible, and new energies and endurances are shown. The personality is changed, the man *is* born anew, whether or not his psychological idiosyncrasies are what give the particular shape to his metamorphosis." In his manic energy of his "continual crow" (288), Melville's narrator thus illustrates a basic model of the born-again Christian conversion according to James's paradigm as well as the more recent multidisciplinary model of Rambo.[12]

If in "Cock-a-Doodle-Doo!" Melville reveals himself to be a skeptic concerning the Christian doctrine of the resurrection of the body and the immortality of the soul, in this he was of the same mind as a contemporaneous literary explorer of Christian mysteries, Emily Dickinson, whose poem #592, written about a decade after Melville's story, portrays the dead as perpetually locked in their underground vaults and eternally cut off from the things of the world:

> What care the Dead, for Chanticleer—
> What care the Dead for Day?
> 'Tis late your Sunrise vex their face—
> And Purple Ribaldry—of Morning
>
> Pour as blank on them
> As on the Tier of Wall
> The Mason builded, yesterday,
> And equally as cool—
>
> What care the Dead for Summer?
> The Solstice had no Sun
> Could waste the Snow before their Gate—
> And knew One Bird a Tune—
>
> Could thrill their Mortised Ear
> Of all the Birds that be—
> This One—believed of Mankind
> Henceforward cherished be—

What care the Dead for Winter?
Themselves as easy freeze—
June Noon—as January Night—
As soon the South—her Breeze

Of Sycamore—or Cinnamon—
Deposit in a Stone
And put a Stone to keep it Warm—
Give spices—unto Men—[13]

For Dickinson's dead, the crowing of the cock at dawn does not wake them from their eternal sleep or usher in a general resurrection; nor does the loud birdsong of the morning affect them, for they are as spiritually inert as a newly built stone wall. By the same token, the summer sun cannot revive the lifeless condition of the dead. If a bird knew one song that could reach the hearing of the dead, that bird would henceforth be cherished by humanity; but such a bird or song does not exist. Finally, the dead are as little affected by the cold of winter as by the warmth of summer, for it is as easy for the spice-scented breezes of the south to be kept in a stone container as for the dead to be affected by changes of season. In her poem, Dickinson is offering an ironic critique of a core Christian belief of the era—the ability of the dead to live again—just as Melville was doing in "Cock-a-Doodle-Doo!"

Melville's second published short story of December 1853 thus offers further evidence of an ongoing skeptical examination of Christian doctrine—in this case, the idea of the resurrection of the body as the basic Christian hope on which the church was founded, based on the Gospel accounts of the Crucifixion and Resurrection, and the related writings of Saint Paul. From its saturation with religious allusions and its depiction of a magnificent cock named Trumpet—whose name recalls the musical instrument that will summon the dead from their graves at the Last Judgment—one can hardly escape the notion that Melville was making an ironic statement about the delusive power of Christian myth in the lives of his contemporaries. Melville's employment of a flagrantly sexual pun on Merrymusk's magical "cock" underlines his perception of Christian notions of spiritual immortality as a Shandean "cock-and-bull" story. Reading the story in this manner transforms it from a charming fable of Christian redemption in the manner of a contemporary religious tract to an ironic and sexually provocative beast fable illustrating the underlying absurdity of the belief in the dead attaining spiritual immortality. In the next two chapters, we will see how Melville shifts his theological focus from fictive critiques of key New Testament doctrines to narratives largely rooted in Old Testament sources, portraying individuals facing the grievous challenges of human and divine injustice. Here Melville draws on the skeptical wisdom of the books of Job and Ecclesiastes in order to subvert the idea of a benevolent and providential Christian god overseeing humanity.

CHAPTER 4

The Genealogy of Melville's Female Job

Griselda, "Wakefield," Agatha, Hunilla

In a letter of August 13, 1852, Herman Melville wrote to his friend Nathaniel Hawthorne in West Newton, Massachusetts, about a long-suffering Cape Cod woman named Agatha Hatch Robertson, whose story he had heard from a New Bedford lawyer while on a tour of Nantucket and the Cape the previous month with his father-in-law, Lemuel Shaw. The letter was the first of the so-called "Agatha" letters offering Hawthorne the woman's story, as written up by the lawyer John Clifford, for possible literary use based on its perceived resemblance to Hawthorne's "Wakefield," which Melville had read the previous year in his friend's *Twice-Told Tales*. Melville's August letter to Hawthorne contained the lawyer's summary of Agatha's prolonged abandonment by her husband and her remarkable forbearance and magnanimity when confronted with his unexpected return after seventeen years following the death of a second bigamous wife in Alexandria, Virginia, and again after his removal to Missouri, where he eventually died, leaving a third wife there unaware of his marital irregularities. For an author whose most recent publications, *Moby-Dick* and *Pierre*, were devoted to chronicling the self-destructive moral and metaphysical revolt of outspoken male rebels, Melville's interest in the pathos-laden endurance of a long-suffering uncomplaining wife might seem peculiar—except that, as a modern enactment of the existential abandonment depicted in the biblical book of Job, it would prove to be the gateway to another phase of his career as a writer of short fiction, now focusing on themes of submission, patience, and reticence, as seen in such literary creations as Bartleby, Benito Cereno, and Hunilla.[1]

Melville's interest in the story of Agatha Hatch Robertson, whose last name he changed to "Robinson" in his letters to Hawthorne, is significant in other respects because it evokes a larger literary tradition of exemplary female suffering based on the model of the biblical Job. Developed in the Middle Ages in accordance with the traditional Christian interpretation of the figure of Job as exhibiting a disciplinary model of patience in distress, this tradition is perhaps best known in late medieval stories of the "patient Griselda," who acts as a model of uncomplaining submission to the cruel testing and pretended abandonment by her aristocratic husband. Such a female character is found in the last story of Boccaccio's *Decameron*, which was translated into Latin by Petrarch and then used by Chaucer in the Clerk's Tale in *The Canterbury Tales*. Interpreting the character of Agatha Robertson as a female Job figure and a spiritual descendant of the "patient Griselda" leads to a new understanding of the character of Hunilla in the eighth, and longest, sketch of "The Encantadas, or Enchanted Isles," a character also partly based on the historical model of Agatha Robertson. Melville's literary portrait of the long-suffering Hunilla in "Norfolk Island and the Chola Widow" followed Hawthorne's decision in early December 1852 not to write the proffered story of Agatha, and after Melville's apparent use of the story in his lost novella, *The Isle of the Cross*, which the Harper Brothers refused to publish in the spring of 1853 and was likely destroyed by the author.[2]

In this chapter, I will examine the genealogy of the female Job figure that descends from the heroine of Chaucer's Clerk's Tale to the testing of the silent wife of Hawthorne's "Wakefield," then to the story of feminine forbearance that Melville discovered in the marital history of Agatha Robertson, and finally to Melville's use of this female character type exhibiting extraordinary endurance of spirit in his story of Hunilla in "Norfolk Isle and the Chola Widow" in "The Encantadas," the series of sketches first appearing in *Putnam's Monthly Magazine* in 1854 and then forming part of *The Piazza Tales* (1856). In the tradition of the female Job I will be examining, the heroine will be seen to exemplify the submissive Job found at the end of the biblical story—the basis for the traditional Christianized Job—while it is the narrator or commentator who will lodge the moral protests at divine injustice that characterize the Old Testament patriarch before his climactic encounter with the deity in the biblical story.

Framed as a "test" of a wealthy patriarch's faith, as suggested to God by Satan, the divinely sanctioned "adversary" in the Old Testament God's heavenly court, the book of Job includes extended dialogues between Job and his three so-called comforters—later joined by a fourth—over the reason for the terrible calamities that have inexplicably struck him, with Job's voice raised in outspoken protest during many of these exchanges. When God eventually appears to answer Job directly as a Voice from the Whirlwind, Job is shown his ignorance, marginality, and impotence in the scale of creation, and he accordingly humbles himself to his creator ("Wherefore I abhor myself and repent in dust and ashes" [Job 42:6]), receiving as his reward a new family and estate. For most of the history of Christianity, readers of Job approached the text not as an outspoken challenge to divine justice, despite the formidable rhetoric that Job brings to his protests, but as an example of wise human submission to God's will, which was in keeping with the only reference to Job in the New Testament in the Letter of James: "Behold, we count them happy which endure. Ye have heard of the patience of Job, and have seen the end of the Lord: that the Lord is very pitiful, and of tender mercy" (James 5:11). The "patience of Job" thus became proverbial in Christian interpretive approaches to this Old Testament book.[3]

As the central biblical text dealing with the problem of evil and the related issue of theodicy, the book of Job has exerted a profound influence on the theology, literature, and culture of the West.[4] Pervading the Christian thought of the Middle Ages, Job continued to provide religious and literary inspiration to writers in the Renaissance and Reformation and was particularly important in the theology of John Calvin. In Puritan New England, the book of Job was well designed to reinforce the Calvinist message of divine authority and inscrutability; the *New England Primer* for the letter *J* thus read, "Job feels the rod / Yet blesses God." Job maintained its strong influence in Anglo-American culture well into the nineteenth century when it began to be read as much for its existential protests against divine injustice as for its quietist message of human submission; thus it became a key source for *Moby Dick* and remained an important text for Melville as he was composing his short fiction in the mid-1850s. In order to trace the thematic path that ultimately led to Melville's literary interest in Agatha Robertson and then to the Job-like character of Hunilla in the eighth sketch of "The

Encantadas," we must begin with Chaucer's *Canterbury Tales* and the creation of the literary prototype of the "patient Griselda" in the Clerk's Tale, which Melville read and marked in one of his two copies of Chaucer's poetry.[5]

Chaucer's Clerk's Tale was largely based on Petrarch's 1374 Latin version of Boccaccio's tale (with some additions from the anonymous French *Le livre Griseldis*) of a lower-class woman who uncomplainingly suffered the apparent murder of her children and divorce from her aristocratic husband in a prolonged secret "test" of her character and her fidelity to him as lord and master.[6] In the Clerk's Tale, Walter, the handsome young Marquis of Saluzzo, is encouraged by his subjects to find a wife and provide an heir. His choice soon falls on the virtuous and beautiful peasant girl Griselda, whom he has seen on his hunting expeditions. Only on his wedding day does Walter tells Griselda of his wish to marry her and makes sure she knows that she must ungrudgingly obey his every wish and command. The two are then married, and she goes on to be a virtuous wife much beloved of her husband's subjects, giving birth to a daughter after a year. When the baby is still young, Walter feels the need to test her constancy and tells her he must take her daughter away because his subjects allegedly resent his marriage to a lower-class woman, an announcement to which she uncomplainingly submits, even though when a servant comes to take the child away she thinks it will be killed: "And as a lambe she sitteth mekee and stille / And leet this cruel sergeant doon his wille" (ll. 538-39). Walter then directs the man to secretly carry his baby daughter to be raised by his sister, the Countess of Panaro, in Bologna. Four years later, Griselda gives birth to a son, and when it is two years old Walter now tells his wife that his disgruntled subjects don't want a future ruler having such a lowly descent on his mother's side, and he must take this child from her—a fate that Griselda again uncomplainingly accepts and so yields up a second child to presumed death, as Walter secretly conveys this child, like the previous one, to his sister in Bologna.

Looking for some sign of his wife's dissatisfaction, Walter sees that Griselda continues to show him perfect obedience; it is the marquis's own subjects, however, who now begin to murmur against the cruelty of their ruler who has seemingly killed his own children because of their mother's lowly origin. In a final test of her obedience, Walter tells his wife that he must have their marriage annulled to please his subjects, and he fabricates a papal bull to confirm this while telling his sister in Bologna to send his twelve-year-old daughter to come home, pretending that this is the young woman he will marry. Acceding to her husband's wishes to divorce her and marry another woman, Griselda agrees to return to her father's house, only asking to be able to wear the smock she is wearing so she won't return home naked. After she has gone home, Walter asks her to decorate the chambers of his palace for the new bride, to which she unhesitatingly agrees. Admiring the beauty of the young woman who is allegedly replacing her as Walter's spouse, Griselda is now finally told by Walter that this is in fact her own daughter, while the boy accompanying the girl was her son; everything he has done has thus been a test of her wifely obedience: "For no malice, ne for no crueltee, / But for t'assaye in thee thy wommanheede" (ll. 1074–75). Fainting with emotion, Griselda is overjoyed to be reunited with her two children and returns to the household of her husband, who treats her with love and respect, and the two subsequently enjoy an uninterrupted happy life together.

Modern readers may find the Clerk's Tale difficult to appreciate because of what appears to be the sustained sadism of Walter's actions and the masochistic submissiveness of Griselda, but the tale becomes less of a study in improbable pathological behavior when we factor in the story's religious dimensions. As in the source for the story in Petrarch, the testing of Griselda's marital faith in Chaucer's version provided a displaced example of the traditional Christian's submission to the vicissitudes of the deity. In an amplification of her moral significance, Chaucer cast Griselda as a supremely suffering Christ-like figure, whose humble birth suggested Christ's Nativity and whose relationship with her husband might be seen as that of an all-forgiving Christ to sinful man. Walter's Job-like "testing" of this wife could thus be seen as a "tempting" by her sinful husband, on the model of the devil's three temptations of Christ, and Griselda then becomes an ideal exemplar of Christian virtue rather than a fallible human being.[7]

Yet in a typological conflation of her identity, Chaucer's tale clearly makes Griselda a Job-like figure, using this biblical paragon of patient suffering in the Middle Ages.[8] Thus, when Griselda is getting ready to return to her father's house after Walter announces his divorce from her, she is resigned to give up all her possessions and return naked: "'Naked out of my fadres house,' quod she, / 'I cam, and naked moot I turne agayn'" (ll. 871–72). Griselda is mimicking Job here, for when first told of the loss of his children and property, the patriarch similarly announced his resignation when facing calamity: "Naked came I out of my mother's womb, and naked shall I return thither; the lord gave, and the Lord hath taken away; blessed be the name of the Lord" (Job 1:21). So, too, after she has returned to her father's humble dwelling, Griselda shows no indication of suffering or regret at her unenviable fate, with the narrator now explicitly comparing her to Job:

> Men speke of Job, and moost for his humblesse,
> As clerkes, when hem list, konne wel endite,
> Namely of men, but as in soothfastnesse,
> Though clerkes preise women but a lite [little],
> Ther kan no man in humblesse hym acquite
> As womman kan, ne kan been half so trewe
> As wommen been, but it be falle of newe [unless it has
>   happened recently].
>
> (ll. 932–38)

According to the narrator, although the virtue of Job-like humility is usually found in men, women can outdo men in this virtue, even though "clerks" (i.e., religious scholars like him) inevitably overlook it to focus on male examples. As in the book of Job, Walter first feels a perverse desire to test his wife's constancy by taking away her daughter, like the Satan who tests Job's faith by destroying his family; and as in Job, Griselda is rewarded with a miraculously restored family, just like a humbled Job is given new children following God's decision that he has passed his test of faith. Unlike Job after his second testing by Satan, however, Griselda never utters any objections, which are instead displaced onto other characters within the story, including the narrator, Walter's subjects, and, after Griselda is sent home, her father, who imitates Job by wishing he had never been born (see Clerk's Tale, ll. 901–3; Job 3:11–16). In the Clerk's Tale, then, the establishment of the literary type of the patient Griselda is heavily dependent on biblical models of behavior—especially that of the long-suffering Job—for dealing with the grievous injury perpetrated as a moral test by a perversely motivated husband.[9]

Hawthorne's "Wakefield" is in part a later thematic variation on Chaucer's tale of Griselda's marital testing and pretended abandonment. "Wakefield" was first published in May 1835 in the *New England Magazine* and then appeared again in 1837 in *Twice-Told Tales*; Melville read the story in early 1851, having received the newly published two-volume edition as a gift from the author. Drawing on his memory of an article in an older magazine or newspaper for his sketch, the narrator of "Wakefield" begins with an outline of a story in which the title character, living a comfortable domestic life in London, after some years of marriage commits the freakish "marital delinquency" of abandoning his wife for twenty years to live on an adjacent street. "During that period he beheld his home every day, and frequently the forlorn Mrs. Wakefield. And after so great a gap in his matrimonial felicity—when his death was reckoned certain, his estate settled, his name dismissed from memory, and his wife, long, long ago, resigned to her autumnal widowhood—he entered the door one evening, quietly, as from a day's absence, and became a loving spouse till death." After presenting the outline of his story, the narrator spends the rest of the narrative imagining how Wakefield would have decided to perform his perverse act, how he inadvertently prolonged his separation from his wife, and how he finally arbitrarily decided to resume his prior life with her. Throughout the story, then, the narrator speculates on the enigma of Wakefield's inexplicably cruel action, while noting his morbid curiosity about his wife and the gratuitous but largely hidden suffering inflicted on her—and himself.[10]

Pondering what he terms Wakefield's "folly," the narrator thus imagines Wakefield in the middle period of his married life, at which point his affection for his spouse has somewhat abated in what today might be called a midlife crisis: "With a cold, but not depraved nor wandering heart, and a mind never feverish with riotous thoughts, nor perplexed with originality, who could have anticipated, that our friend would entitle himself to a foremost place among the doers of eccentric deeds?" (131). Yet the narrator notes that Wakefield's wife could have identified the traits that might have led to her husband's actions, these being a "quiet selfishness," a "peculiar sort of vanity," "a disposition to craft," and a "little strangeness" in the man (132). Wakefield's abandonment of his wife begins with his telling her that he would be away on business for a few days while simultaneously thinking that he will extend this period to a week, and his wife remembers the enigmatic smile on his face while he goes out the door. The narrator then follows the progress of Wakefield's life as he engages lodgings only a block away from his own residence, where the narrator chastises him for abandoning his wife and warns him about how quickly the place he occupied in his wife's affections might be lost: "It is perilous to make a chasm in human affections; not that they gape so long and wide—but so quickly close again!" (133).

Without having a fully formed plan and thinking he might end his freakish abandonment, after one night alone Wakefield is curious to know how his wife looks without him and walks up to the door of his residence, where he suddenly stops himself from entering and goes to the end of the street. He then glimpses his wife in the window looking in his direction and quickly hastens back to his new lodgings, thereby beginning the process of Wakefield's prolonged separation. The narrator imagines Wakefield purchasing a red wig and new clothes to disguise his identity while deciding not to return to his wife because of the assumed inadequacy of her reaction to his loss, even though he now sees her on the street looking pale and anxious, and after three weeks there are signs that she is ill and being attended by a physician. Eventually recovering from her illness, Wakefield's wife has now presumably reconciled herself to her loss, and the separation between husband and wife goes on for ten years. At this time Wakefield is visibly more aged than his wife when they unexpectedly run into each other on the street as the wife is going to church; she fails to recognize him, and Wakefield feels a brief revival of affection together with a sense of the madness of his actions. The narrator notes the kind of death-in-life condition in which Wakefield exists: "He had contrived, or rather he had happened, to dissever himself from the world—to vanish—to give up his place and privileges with living men, without being admitted among the dead" (138).

After twenty years, Wakefield finally decides to return to his wife after he looks into the window of his former house and sees the shadow of his wife enjoying the warmth of a good fire while he is outside in the cold rain; the appeal of domestic comfort, not love of his wife, thus makes him commit the momentous act of reunion. "The door opens. As he passes in, we have a parting glimpse of his visage, and recognize the crafty smile, which was the precursor of the little joke, that he has ever since been playing off at his wife's expense. How unmercifully has he quizzed the poor woman! Well, good night's rest to Wakefield!" (139–40). The narrator thus notes the return of the delinquent husband to his wife without further comment but with careful attention to Wakefield's ambiguous smile and the designation of his monstrous behavior as a private "joke" on his wife. The narrator's statement that Wakefield has unmercifully "quizzed" his wife implies how heartlessly he has tested, mocked, and made a fool of her by his actions. The narrator's final "moral" focuses on the lesson that Wakefield's dangerously irresponsible behavior puts him at risk of losing his place in the world because "individuals are so nicely adjusted to a system, and systems to one another, that, by stepping aside for a moment, a man exposes himself to a fearful risk of losing his place forever" (140). But the narrator's cautionary remark about the risks of spiritual anomie is oddly opposed to how the story of Wakefield's marital delinquency actually ends, with his successful return to his original place beside his wife, even as it conforms to Hawthorne's recurrent theme of the magnetic chain binding humanity and the perils of human isolation that Wakefield enacts but ultimately chooses to escape.

The narrator's commentary on Wakefield's career lacks any explicit association between Wakefield's wife and the stories of Griselda or Job.[11] But like Griselda, Mrs. Wakefield submits to her husband's disappearance and accepts his return without any bitterness or complaint. And like the Job who is afflicted by God in order to implement Satan's theory that Job only worships God for personal gain, Mrs. Wakefield is abandoned by a "crafty" husband whose mysterious departure is marked by an ambiguous smile, in a scheme ostensibly designed to "test" his wife's patience. Wakefield thus lives in an adjacent street and periodically looks at her through the window of his house in a potential parody of God's all-seeing eye. The abandoned wife's Job-like suffering is on display when she becomes seriously ill following his disappearance, and her religious faith is evident when years later she is seen carrying her prayer book to church when Wakefield physically runs into her. Wakefield's spontaneous return to his wife after twenty years similarly corresponds to the return of Job's family and property after he has been shown his lowly place in the universe by God in the Voice from the Whirlwind, except that it is now a suffering Wakefield himself who has been playing God in his surveillance of his wife, who restores himself to his abandoned spouse and home. By focusing on Wakefield's enigmatic behavior, the narrator makes his wife voiceless while taking on the role of commentator on her husband's perverse actions in trying to fathom his motives, just as Job tried to fathom the reasons for God's abandonment of him. It is relevant to note that Hawthorne's use of the name "Wakefield" for his protagonist is appropriate in this context because of the name's previous literary use for the protagonist of Goldsmith's *Vicar of Wakefield* (1766), which, as critics have noted, is a modern retelling of the book of Job, with the beleaguered vicar, who suffers a series of unparalleled adversities, taking on the role of the Old Testament patriarch.[12]

Following its first identification by Austin Warren, Ruth Perry has traced the historical source of Hawthorne's sketch to a story that may have appeared in the early eighteenth century in the *Gentleman's Magazine* and was later recounted in the *Political and Literary Anecdotes of His Own Times* by the writer and scholar Dr. William King (1685–1763), originally completed in 1761 but only published in 1818.[13] The original of Wakefield was thus a Mr. Howe, a London merchant of comfortable means who in about 1706, after some seven or eight years of marriage, abandoned his wife for seventeen years while he inhabited a small lodging in another neighborhood. Hawthorne's sketch clearly borrows many of the essential details of the story from this source, for like Wakefield, Howe presents himself as an entirely unexceptional man whose act of abandonment defies any rational motive. And like Wakefield, Howe disguises himself with a wig and enjoys observing his solitary wife; in this case he has befriended a merchant who lives across from Mrs. Howe where she has moved from her original married habitation, and the two men frequently dine together as the merchant recommends the lady they are observing as a potential spouse to her disguised husband. Both Wakefield and Howe ultimately return to their wives not because of any compunctions of conscience but for practical reasons; for Wakefield it is the lost comfort of the domestic environment, while for Howe it is the fact that he has run out of money. By adapting this perverse tale of marital abandonment that also illustrates the growing impersonality of the city of London, Hawthorne transformed the main figure into the parable of a man driven by cold intellect and perverse curiosity to perform an unethical "test" on his wife, which she inadvertently passes. But in "Wakefield" the scenario also conforms to the archetypal models of Griselda and Job, with the test improbably resulting in a final restoration to domestic felicity.

As earlier noted, Melville's reading of Hawthorne's "Wakefield" was apparently a deciding factor that made him think the account of Agatha Hatch Robertson's life would be another pathos-laden story of marital delinquency that Hawthorne could bring to life in fiction. Melville accordingly wrote to Hawthorne on August 13, 1852, to tell him about how he obtained the story while accompanying his father-in-law Lemuel Shaw on court duty on Cape Cod and Nantucket Island in July. Traveling to Nantucket with Shaw and John Clifford, currently the attorney general for Massachusetts, Melville noted the latter's admiration for "the great patience, & endurance, & resignedness of the women of the island in submitting so uncomplainingly to the long, long absences of their sailor husbands" (232), and Clifford went on to tell the story of Agatha Robertson that he had first learned about in 1842 during a legal proceeding in Falmouth, Massachusetts. Agatha's history of marital abandonment thus suited the experience of the sailors' wives that Clifford mentioned, but in a manner more akin to that of Wakefield's deliberate delinquency rather than unavoidable absence at sea. After Melville asked for the details of Agatha's story because of possible literary interest, Clifford sent him a transcription of the case in a letter dated July 14, 1852, and it is this transcription that Melville sent to Hawthorne while offering the story for his use.[14]

The marital history of Agatha was first revealed to Clifford because the son of Robertson's third wife from a previous marriage, a Mr. Janney, came east from Saint Louis in 1842 to investigate the legitimacy of a claim on the recently deceased James Robertson's estate from Agatha Robertson and her married daughter, Rebecca H. Gifford, the sole child of the shipwrecked Robertson after he married Agatha when she was living in Pembroke, Massachusetts, near Duxbury on Cape Cod Bay. As the administrator of Robertson's substantial estate of $20,000, Janney not only learned that the claim was legitimate (Robertson had only told his third wife, the former Mrs. Irvin, that he had an illegitimate daughter), but the whole history of Robertson's irregular marital history then emerged. An English sailor who had been shipwrecked on the nearby coast, Robertson married Agatha in 1807 after she had nursed him back to health, and then after two years of marriage and two trips to sea he left his wife pregnant, telling her he had to leave to find work. He then disappeared and made his way to Alexandria, Virginia, where he married a second wife, and after seventeen years returned to Pembroke to see his wife and daughter, to whom he tried to make vague excuses for his disappearance; he also gave them money but wouldn't tell anything about where he was living or what he was doing. Promising to return again for good, Robertson left but came back again a year later to give his daughter a present on the eve of her marriage.

Following Robertson's subsequent return to Alexandria, his second wife died, and he wrote to his new son-in-law, Mr. Gifford, to come down for a short visit, subsequently giving him a gold watch and three shawls to bring back to his daughter and first wife, who, based on the evidence of the shawls, now had suspicions of Robertson's bigamous second marriage. Robertson then again returned north, now to Falmouth, Massachusetts, where his daughter and first wife were living, and invited them to move with him to Missouri, which they declined to do. Once established in Missouri, Robertson wrote letters, sent money, and even told his daughter and wife about his new marriage to a Mrs. Irvin, who had two children from a previous marriage and whom Agatha and her daughter did not inform about the illegality of her marriage to Robertson, thinking that it would only cause her needless shame and suffering. Clifford's account ends with the recognition that Agatha and her daughter had a legitimate claim to Robertson's estate, although Clifford was not involved in negotiating a final settlement.

Near the end of his account, Clifford noted Agatha's explanation for not telling Robertson's third wife the truth about her bigamous husband: "'I had no wish' said the wife [Agatha] 'to make either of them unhappy, notwithstanding all I had suffered on his account'—It was to me a most striking instance of long continued & uncomplaining submission to wrong and anguish on the part of a wife, wch made her in my eyes a heroine" (624). Such a recognition of Agatha's magnanimity and nobility of spirit in response to long-term emotional and material injury was doubtless what attracted both Clifford and Melville to the story, for she showed a forgiveness epitomizing the Christian virtue of nonresistance to evil (she was a Quaker by faith); but Melville doubtless would have also been interested in Agatha as a modern female Job figure. As a concrete reward for her forbearance, Agatha—whose name derives from the Greek word for "good"—is thus ultimately rewarded for her patience by becoming an inheritor of her delinquent husband's estate, just as Job saw his property and family restored after God's test of his faith.

It should be noted that during his trip to Nantucket Melville was likely reminded of the biblical patriarch by his encounter with George Pollard, who had been captain of the whaleship *Essex* when it was sunk in 1819 by a sperm whale, as recounted in Owen Chase's *Narrative* of the horrifying events undergone by the crew of survivors, including Pollard. Melville had in fact alluded to Pollard's experience in chapter 45 ("The Affidavit") of *Moby-Dick* while providing evidence of a sperm whale's ability to sink a whaleship. After Pollard suffered the wreck of another whaleship, he left the sea to work as a lowly Nantucket night watchman, humbled but not destroyed by his calamities, like the humbled Job at the end of the biblical book who has been shown by God his impotence in relation to the sea monster leviathan.[15]

In his August 1852 letter, Melville gave Hawthorne literary cues on how to set the initial scene of Robertson's arrival in Agatha's life by shipwreck along the Massachusetts coast, where Agatha lived with her father, a lighthouse keeper. He thus described a potential symbolic contrast between the image of an innocent lamb browsing on the top of a cliff overlooking the ocean, and the malignancy of the sea itself from which Robertson will emerge as the sole survivor of a shipwreck—a clear indication that the story would have covert allegorical resonances. By the same token, Melville suggested that the image of the wrecked prow of Robertson's sunken ship visible from the beach would be a reminder of her husband's prolonged absence, together with the rotting postbox that would never contain a letter from him. Likely reflecting his recent encounter with the chastened George Pollard on Nantucket, Melville also suggested that "the father of Agatha must be an old widower—a man of the sea, but early driven away from it by repeated disasters. Hence, he is subdued & quiet & wise in his life" (237). Apologizing for what might appear as "impertinent officiousness" in telling Hawthorne how to write the story, Melville justified his literary advice by noting that his descriptions "seem legitimately to belong to the story; for they were visably suggested to me by scenes I actually beheld while on the very coast where the story of Agatha occurred" (237).[16]

With her submission to her husband's cruel vagaries evoking the example of Chaucer's Griselda, Agatha Robertson also suggested aspects of the wife of Hawthorne's Wakefield, who spent twenty years away from his spouse and perversely enjoyed observing her in her assumed widowhood. When seeking to account for Robertson's motives, Melville in an October 1852 letter to Hawthorne offered reasons that sound like the narrator's speculations about the likely motivations of Wakefield, telling Hawthorne he didn't think that Robertson's desertion "was a premeditated thing. If it had been so, he would have changed his name, probably, after quitting her.—No: he was a weak man, & his temptations (tho' we known little of them) were strong. The whole sin stole upon him insensibly—so that it would perhaps have been hard for him to settle upon the exact day when he could say to himself, 'Now I have deserted my wife[']; unless, indeed upon the day he wedded the Alexandian lady" (234 35). In "Wakefield," Hawthorne's narrator similarly claimed that Wakefield had no larger scheme in mind when he left his wife on an allegedly short trip that he was planning to extend, and then thinks to return to his wife after a single night in a nearby lodging. Of course, Wakefield, unlike Robertson, doesn't marry another woman but spies on his wife and then returns to live with her after two decades, while Agatha was left alone for seventeen years before her husband briefly returned to her, keeping his former life a secret; she subsequently discovered that he had married a second wife, and after he left for Missouri, she learned that he had again entered into a bigamous marriage. It is only by associating the story of Agatha with a larger theme of prolonged, unjustified Job-like female suffering through arbitrary abandonment that we can understand Melville's interest in Agatha as a character, an interest that he carried over into the depiction of the Chola widow Hunilla in "The Encantadas."

The sketches in "The Encantadas, or Enchanted Isles" had been written in late 1853 or early 1854, at which time Melville had also proposed to his publisher and then abandoned a book on tortoise hunting in the Galápagos.[17] Melville had himself visited and cruised around the Galápagos Islands from October 30 through November 25, 1841, while he was a sailor on the *Acushnet* (and again when he briefly returned over a year later on the *Charles and Henry*), thereby providing a solid autobiographical basis for the series of ten sketches, several told in the first person, that he later composed about various aspects of the human and animal life on the strange, desolate, and seemingly enchanted group of equatorial islands that had earlier inspired Charles Darwin to begin conceptualizing his theory of evolution. In "The Encantadas," Melville thus created a group portrait of a desiccated, fallen realm inhabited by creatures seemingly under the spell of a malign enchantment. Melville's "Norfolk Isle and the Chola Widow" tells the story of Hunilla, a solitary "Chola, or half-breed Indian woman," discovered after the narrator had spent two days hunting tortoises on Norfolk Island with a crew from his whaling boat anchored nearby. Hunilla's tale of suffering and survival on the island following the deaths of her husband and brother, her betrayal by the French captain who was supposed to retrieve her, her perilous survival on the desiccated island, and her apparent gang rape by visiting sailors—all these add up to a portrait of extraordinary emotional and physical suffering, which magnifies her in the eyes of the narrator into an embodiment of moral endurance and spiritual nobility. In other words, Hunilla is a female Job, whose testing by an absent and perhaps indifferent god inspires faith in the dignity of a spiritually orphaned humanity. It is thus appropriate for her status as a female Job figure that the name Hunilla evokes the Spanish verb *humillar*, meaning to humiliate, humble, or abase.[18]

"Norfolk Isle and the Chola Widow" begins the narrator's account of how he and his fellow crewmen accidentally discover the presence of Hunilla on the island they are in the process of leaving when an inebriated sailor on the windlass they are turning happens to see a handkerchief fluttering from the top of a distant elevation. When the sailors return to the island, they pick up Hunilla on the shore, and, following their return to the ship, she tells her story in Spanish to the captain. Three years previous, Hunilla and her Spanish husband Felipe, her brother Truxill, and two young dogs had come to the island to collect the valuable oil of the tortoises, making an arrangement with the French whaling captain who delivered them there that he would return to pick them up in four months to take them back to the Peruvian mainland. Seven weeks into their stay, Felipe and Truxill are drowned while Hunilla watched from a distance, as the log raft they had made to go fishing broke up in the waves and the two were buffeted against a coastal reef—a scene suggesting Melville's symbolic juxtaposition of the innocence of the lamb on a cliff observing the malignity of the sea, as mentioned in his August 1852 letter to Hawthorne suggesting details for the story of Agatha. When her husband's body washes ashore, Hunilla buries him in a secluded clearing near the primitive shelter they had earlier built. The description of Hunilla's witnessing the death of her husband and brother, while drawing aside some branches for a view, places the tragedy within a demarcated frame and presents the scene as an initially picturesque but horrifyingly surreal *tableau vivant*: "They [the branches] formed an oval frame, through which the bluely boundless sea rolled like a painted one. And there, the invisible painter painted to her view the wave-tossed and disjointed raft, its once level logs slantingly upheaved, as raking masts, and the four struggling arms undistinguishable among them; and then all subsided into smooth-flowing creamy waters, slowly drifting the splintered wreck; while first and last, no sound of any sort was heard. Death in a silent picture; a dream of the eye; such vanishing shapes as the mirage shows."[19]

Reference to the seemingly "painted" sea here implicitly presents the divine creator as an "invisible painter" who is indifferent to the tragedy he is depicting. The narrator's description of how Felipe's body washes up on shore also suggests an invisible god who is removed from direct involvement in human affairs: "Lock-jawed in grim death, the lover-husband, softly clasped his bride, true to her even in death's dream. Ah, Heaven, when man thus keeps his faith, wilt thou be faithless who created the faithful one? But they cannot break faith who never plighted it" (154–55). In an implicit reprimand to the Judeo-Christian creator, the narrator insists that no contemporary covenant exists between humanity and its God, who inexplicably takes away human life regardless of human fidelity. The narrator's denial of the efficacy of faith here suggests Melville's covert subversion of the contemporary evangelical Christian belief in divine providence while ironically absolving the deity of direct responsibility for a senseless death within his human creation.

The narrator and his fellow crew are witness to the pathos of Hunilla's story, especially when, amid her narration, she momentarily breaks down while stating "in impassioned pain" (155) that she had to bury her husband herself. Driven to look for her brother's body by "the strong persuasion of her Romish faith," she is unable to find it, while her search for signs of the returning French captain is also unsuccessful: "With equal longing she now looked for the living and the dead; the brother and the captain; alike vanished, never to return" (155). Hunilla's task will now be trying to survive as a solitary human inhabitant with no indications of the passage of time on her island in the "selfsame sea" (155) as the island of Robinson Crusoe—the obvious literary comparison, except that the latter established a comfortable life on his solitary island and was eventually joined by a human companion, Friday. Hunilla's only hope to remain sane lies in her belief that the French whaler was already on its way to retrieve her; the narrator thus notes the incongruity of her building her hope on a lie—a fact that elicits his admiration for her admirable spiritual strength: "See here Hunilla, this lone shipwrecked soul, out of treachery invoking trust. Humanity, thou strong thing, I worship thee, not in the laurelled victor, but in this vanquished one" (157). It is Hunilla's power to endure and to sustain hope in the midst of disaster that inspires the narrator's "worship," not the missing god who has allowed her calamity to take place. Again, it is this solitary female Job, who has not only lost her family but, as we will shortly discover, whose very flesh has also been obscenely violated, who is the focus of the narrator's reverence, not the invisible Catholic god of Hunilla's conventional faith.

A length of hollow reed washed ashore provides Hunilla with the means to record the passage of days as well as other important information about the results of her foraging for food. As the narrator notes, "Hunilla leaned upon a reed, a real one; no metaphor" (157); but even this form of therapeutic support fails her like a weak reed when her ability to mark the shaft of the reed is visibly interrupted after six months. When the captain inquires why she didn't mark any more days, Hunilla tells him not to ask, and when he goes on to inquire if other ships passed by, she is again reluctant to reply, saying to the captain,

"'Nay, Senor;—but—" (157). To this pained breaking off of her speech, the captain replies with his own unfinished question: "Then the captain asked whether any whale-boats had—" (157). Following this double use of the figure of *aposiopesis*, or the interruption of speech because of unwillingness or inability to continue, the narrator himself turns to the figure of *apophasis*, which highlights a subject by deliberately not mentioning it. For the narrator now refuses to divulge any more information, noting that he can't tell anything more about her calamities: "But no, I will not file this thing complete for scoffing souls to quote, and call it firm proof upon their side. The half shall remain untold. Those two unnamed events which befell Hunilla on this isle, let them abide between her and her God. In nature, as in law, it may be libelous to speak some truths" (158). Based on the reluctant manner in which the "two unnamed events" are here evoked that provided (literally) unspeakable suffering for Hunilla, it is evident that these involved gang rapes by visiting sailors. While implying that some evils should not be directly exposed to his middle-class readership, the narrator's claim that "to speak some truths" may be "libelous" also suggests that their revelation might slander human nature, or sailors in particular, or even the alleged providential goodness of God.[20]

Having finished hearing out her story, the narrator and crew take Hunilla back to her cane shelter overlooking the sea, where the narrator inspects the primitive arrangements that have allowed her to collect water and where she keeps the tortoise oil initially collected by her husband and brother in kegs and calabashes. In a final act of fascination and curiosity, the narrator secretly follows Hunilla to the sandy mound that marks her husband's grave as she says a last goodbye to him: "Hunilla was partly prostrate upon the grave; her dark head bowed, and lost in her long, loosened Indian hair; her hands extended to the cross-foot, with a little brass crucifix clasped between; a crucifix worn featureless, like an ancient graven knocker long plied in vain" (161). The worn crucifix, with its comparison to a worn-down door knocker that has failed to gain a response, implies a uselessly repeated ritual of invoking aid from the divine comforter. The simile suggests an ironic inversion of the blessings offered by Christ in the Sermon on the Mount when he asserted, "Ask, and it shall be given you; seek, and ye shall find; knock, and it will be opened unto you" (Matt. 7:7). So, too, in the book of Revelation, Christ tells believers that he is standing at their door ready to help them: "Behold, I stand at the door, and knock; if any man hear my voice, and open the door, I will come in to him, and will sup with him, and he with me" (Rev. 3:20). Hunilla's plying of her crucifix like a potential door knocker underlines the suffering and sense of divine abandonment ensuing from her husband's senseless death.

The final pathos-laden coda to Hunilla's tragic ordeal on the island is that she must leave behind eight of the ten dogs that have kept her company, as the captain insists that she can only take the two she is carrying back on the ship because of scarcity of provisions; the abandoned dogs thus howl out their agony, but Hunilla is so inured to emotional pain at this point, she is resigned to this agony: "To Hunilla, pain seemed so necessary, that pain in other beings, though by love and sympathy made her own, was unrepiningly to be borne. A heart of yearning in a frame of steel. A heart of earthly yearning, frozen by the frost which falleth from the sky" (162). In the final image here of terrible events coming down like "frost" from above, the narrator hints at a heavenly source for Hunilla's sufferings, as implicitly confirmed by the divine Voice from the Whirlwind in Job when it tells the patriarch, "By the breath of God frost is given" (Job 37:10).[21]

After the ship has made port on the Peruvian coast and Hunilla departs from her rescuers, the narrator's final image of her conveys an impression of her exalted spiritual identity as she rides into Payta, like Christ into Jerusalem, on a "small grey ass; and before her on the ass's shoulders, she eyed the jointed workings of the beast's armorial cross" (162). Just as she has plied in vain her worn crucifix like a door knocker, as she rides on her ass Hunilla watches the "jointed workings" of the "armorial cross" on the animal's shoulders, both rider and beast of burden sharing in their submissiveness and suffering. The image of the cross here is likely borrowed from the description of the cross on the ass in Wordsworth's "Peter Bell" (l. 971 ff.), a narrative poem dramatizing the title character's discovery of the universality of human and animal suffering. But the "armorial cross" facing Hunilla also potentially suggests Saint Paul's well-known advice for faithful Christians to "take unto you the whole armour of God, that he may be able to withstand the evil day"; and to bear "the shield of faith, wherewith ye shall be able to quench all the fiery darts of the wicked" (Eph. 6:13, 16). No armorial shield of Christian faith, however, has been able to protect the Chola widow from her traumatic Job-like ordeal.[22]

Robert Sattelmeyer and James Barbour have pointed to a key historical source for "Norfolk Isle and the Chola Widow" in the news of the discovery, by an American sealer and sea-otter hunter living in Santa

Barbara, of a "Female Robinson Crusoe" who had lived alone for eighteen years on the island of San Nicolas sixty miles off the coast of California, an event reported in the *Albany Evening Journal* on November 3, 1853, and slightly expanded in the *Springfield Republican* of western Massachusetts on November 22. The article reported the past history of Indian tribes inhabiting the island, the alleged events by which this woman had been left alone on the island when the rest of her small tribe had been taken back to the mainland, her mode of survival on the island, and the fact that she had died in mid-October 1853, six weeks after her retrieval. Sattelmeyer and Barbour carefully review the apparent uses to which Melville put this article while incorporating elements of the Agatha story, claiming that Hunilla "combines the subtle mental agony and attenuation of spirit of Agatha Robertson with the childlike simplicity and the brutal physical isolation of the Indian castaway." More recently, Scott Norsworthy has presented his discovery of an earlier news item on the solitary "female Crusoe" on San Nicolas Island in the *Boston Atlas* for January 9, 1847, suggesting that Melville might have known the details of this female "isolato" several years before he wrote "The Encantadas." Melville's familiarity with this remarkable Native American woman when he was still an apprentice author living with his family in Lansingburgh, New York, in early 1847 would seem unlikely, and there is a clearer line of transmission to his writing of "Norfolk Isle and the Chola Widow" based on the November 1853 articles on a "female Robinson Crusoe" in two newspapers he is known to have read, just at the time when he was composing the sketches for "The Encantadas" in Pittsfield.[23]

Evidently combining his previous knowledge of the history of Agatha Robertson with his more recent discovery of the "female Robinson Crusoe" rescued from San Nicolas Island, Melville also gave his story of "Norfolk Island and the Chola Widow" a distinctly religious cast by presenting Hunilla as a type of a female Job figure while implicitly posing the question of theodicy concerning the seeming contradiction between the goodness of God and the existence of evil. We should first note that Hunilla's major traumatic experiences are divided between the loss of her husband and brother and the failure of the French captain to return, in one concentrated phase of spiritual testing, and then by the occurrence of gang rape in a second spiritual testing. Such a two-phase structure duplicates the example of Job, who is first tested by Satan with the loss of his property and children, and then when God approves a second test on Job's body ("But put forth thy hand now, and touch his bone and his flesh, and he will curse thee to thy face" [Job 2:5]). Job thus suffers a second phase of testing when Satan strikes him with a physical affliction (boils) all over his body, just as Hunilla's body is brutally violated by predatory whalemen. And like the Christianized Job, the narrator depicts Hunilla as submitting herself to punitive misfortunes while maintaining her Catholic faith throughout her ordeal. Finally, like Job who survives his ordeal and eventually sees God replace his lost wealth and children, Hunilla survives her long traumatic isolation and violation (her dogs being her only "comforters") and returns to her native community with the money from the sale of tortoise oil while "adding to the silver a contribution from all hands" (162), just as, at the end of the book of Job, "every man also gave him [Job] a piece of money, and every one an earring of gold" (Job 42:11).

Even though Hunilla does not question God's responsibility for her long suffering as Job does in much of his debate with his three comforters, it is the story's narrator who hints at the injustice of the deity, taking on the voice of Job's protests at his treatment, as implied by the narrator's repeated hints of divine abandonment accompanied by subversive allusions to biblical texts. We have previously remarked the narrator's depiction of the death of her husband and brother as framed in a silent picture devoid of any voice of protest, as well as his reference to the faithfulness of human beings versus the faithlessness of God in connection with this event, and his representation of Hunilla's plying of her worn crucifix like a repeatedly used door knocker over her husband's grave. Sattelmeyer and Barbour demonstrate how Melville seemingly inverted the statements of conventional piety in the November 1853 accounts describing the providential rescue of Hunilla. Such reversals contribute to the framing of the story of Hunilla's life as a modern representation of a female Job whose faith in God remains intact while the narrator of the story points out the flaws in the arguments supporting the creator's providential care for his creation.[24]

Based on the previous discussion of Griselda, "Wakefield," Agatha, and Hunilla, we can clearly see emerging a genealogy of the female Job figure in the stories we have examined. In Chaucer's Clerk's Tale, the lower-class Griselda uncomplainingly submits to all the emotional testing performed by her aristocratic husband, who in effect assumes the combined role of God and Satan in Job's ordeal. Moreover, the book of Job is explicitly cited in the story of Griselda's trials; thus the clerk mentions the fact that Job's ordeals are always invoked for the sufferings of men, but it is women who more perfectly embody the ideal of uncomplaining acceptance of whatever God or men send their way. In Hawthorne's "Wakefield," the narrative focus is primarily on the husband who abandons his wife for twenty years, but the details of the narrative suggest a similar testing of wifely virtue comparable to that found in the Clerk's Tale and, with a change of gender, the deity's test of Job. Thus after his abandonment of his wife, the husband becomes a God-like observer of her reaction to his disappearance. And like Walter in the Clerk's Tale and God in the book of Job, Wakefield feels no compunction about putting his wife through prolonged unmerited pain after his abandonment but capriciously offers her a final reward with his unexplained return.

In Melville's discovery of the life history of Agatha Robertson, he found a story comparable to Hawthorne's story of "the London husband" (as he called "Wakefield") that clearly interested him as an example of how, with patient forbearance, an abandoned wife rose above the spirit of bitterness and resentment when dealing with prolonged abandonment by her husband—a man whose life she had saved. Melville's suggestion to Hawthorne of using a sunken ship's prow as symbolic measure of the slow passage of time during which Agatha's husband has been gone was accordingly converted in the story of Hunilla to the washed-up reed on which she scores the passage of days she has lived alone on her island. In Agatha Robertson, Melville was also faced with a life history in which the moral burden of the story of Job was illustrated. Like Job, Agatha kept her faith despite her abandonment by her husband and provider; she showed exemplary forbearance by not exposing her husband's marital crimes, and like Job she was ultimately rewarded for her patience, in this case by a share of her husband's sizable estate. Unlike the wife in "Wakefield," Agatha did not have to suffer alone (she raised and married off a daughter), but the lengthy duration of her suffering was nevertheless comparable.

In Melville's mind, then, the story of Agatha demonstrated that the suffering of Job under divine testing was not just limited to men but could also be inflicted on women; thus there is a clear literary genealogy from Agatha Robertson, to the heroine of Melville's unpublished novel *The Isle of the Cross*, and finally to Hunilla in "The Encantadas." In Hunilla, like Chaucer's Griselda, we find a lower-class female Job figure who remained religiously devout like the wife of "Wakefield" and who was betrayed on multiple occasions like Agatha Robertson (Hunilla by multiple men, Agatha by one man at different times). Hunilla's ordeal lasts three years—not the twelve years of Chaucer's heroine, the two decades of the wife of "Wakefield," or over three decades for Agatha—but in many ways it is the most intense of the four women, based on the traumatic deaths of her husband and brother, her betrayal by the French captain, her prolonged solitude on the island, and her literally unspeakable rape by sailors. It is no accident that the last word of her story is "cross," for she survives a kind of prolonged crucifixion while typifying an occurrence of extended unmerited suffering that ultimately casts doubt on the justice and benevolence of the creator.

As the only story of a woman in the ten sketches of "The Encantadas," "Norfolk Isle and the Chola Widow" shows that the aura of malign enchantment characteristic of the Galápagos Islands extends beyond the male world of violence, exploitation, predation, and degeneration to the more vulnerable world of women, showing Hunilla as a victim of a malign fate, corrupt human nature, and—by implication—a morally delinquent deity. Thus Melville's 1851 reading of "Wakefield," his fortuitous discovery of the marital history of Agatha Robertson in July 1852, his unsuccessful attempt to present her story in the spring of 1853 in the novella *The Isle of the Cross*, and his November 1853 reading about the Native American "female Crusoe" retrieved from San Nicolas Island—all these came together, with possible influence from Chaucer, to make possible the creation of a nineteenth-century "patient Griselda" and Job-like Chola widow, Hunilla.[25]

CHAPTER 5

Revolutionary Skepticism in *Israel Potter*

The Role of Ecclesiastes

Writing to Nathaniel Hawthorne in early May 1851 while completing the composition of *Moby-Dick*, Melville commented to his Berkshire friend on the evanescence of literary celebrity: "I have come to regard this matter of Fame as the most transparent of all vanities. I read Solomon more and more, and every time see deeper and deeper and unspeakable meanings in him." As mentioned in chapter 1 of this study, by referring to "Solomon" and invoking the keyword of "vanity," Melville was demonstrating that he had been reading the book of Ecclesiastes, a compilation of skeptical wisdom that was traditionally associated with the legendarily rich, supremely wise second king of Israel—an authorship based on the biblical writer's claim of being "the son of David, king in Jerusalem" (Eccles. 1:1). In *Moby-Dick*, Ishmael conspicuously alluded to the skeptical teachings of Ecclesiastes in chapter 96 ("The Try-Works"), quoting the biblical writer's well-known claim that "All is vanity," and Melville continued to promote the same idea in Ishmael's description of the endless round of physical labor associated with harvesting and processing whale blubber, as evoked in chapter 98 ("Stowing Down and Cleaning Up").[1]

If Ecclesiastes intermittently informed Melville's philosophical vision in *Moby-Dick*, four years later he would devote a novella to confirming its pessimistic vision of human affairs. That literary work was *Israel Potter*, a historical narrative first serialized in *Putnam's* magazine from July 1854 to March 1855, at which time it was also published in book form. In *Israel Potter*, Melville would adapt the teachings of Ecclesiastes to a variety of purposes, ringing the changes on the theme of "vanity" to show that America's Revolutionary founding was not the mythically providential event that it was widely conceived to be, while also undercutting the Founders' ideal of the United States as a democratic society under the protection of a beneficent and just god.[2]

Melville's philosophical endorsement of the wisdom of Ecclesiastes was in keeping with his decisive turn toward religious skepticism during his career as a novelist. For the book of Ecclesiastes is a well-known anomaly in the Old Testament canon, posing a direct challenge to the idea of a personal and providential God of Israel and emphasizing the futility or "vanity" (Hebrew *hebel* = mist or vapor) that characterizes human endeavors—a keyword repeated thirty-eight times in a book of only twelve chapters. Scholars still debate the reasons for Ecclesiastes' inclusion in the Hebrew canon, and the Greek name also presents something of an anomaly, being an equivalent to the Hebrew "Qohelet," meaning the "leader" of an assembly, a word translated into English as "Preacher" in the King James Version (Eccles. 1:1-2, 12). The likely product of a fourth- or third-century BCE Israelite scribe living in late Persian or early Ptolemaic (Hellenistic) Jerusalem, Ecclesiastes articulates a vision of the world in which chance and contingency have replaced divinely mandated moral laws, with no assurance of ultimate justice for the good, or assured retribution for evildoers. Ecclesiastes also teaches that the modest pleasures of human life should be enjoyed because of the very ephemerality of the individual's life and the futility of human existence, which ends in universal death from which no resurrection or spiritual redemption can be expected, and which obliterates all memory of individual achievement.[3]

Writing to publisher George Putnam in early June 1854 to introduce his new Revolutionary War narrative for serial publication, Melville described it as containing "nothing of any sort to shock the fastidious. There will be little reflective writing in it; nothing weighty. It is adventure." Understandably cautious with his publisher because of the critical and financial disaster of *Pierre* two years earlier, as well as the recent rejection by *Putnam's Magazine* of his story "The Two Temples" for its ironic critique of Manhattan's Grace Church, Melville was emphasizing the broad popular appeal of his new work of fiction, which for much of its length did indeed contain some of his best writing in the category of dramatic "adventure." But the novella was still infused with a strain of moralistic "reflective" writing bearing a "weighty" burden of skepticism and pessimism—a strain that we may trace to the dominant influence of Ecclesiastes.[4]

Melville's serialized narrative was loosely based on the narrative of a Revolutionary War soldier, Israel Potter (1744–1826), whose pamphlet-length biography was—unknown to Melville—a blend of truth and fabrication, produced at a time when surviving Revolutionary veterans were writing their stories in the hope of belatedly obtaining a government pension. Allegedly following the outlines of the historical Potter's life, the protagonist of Melville's *Israel Potter* thus proves himself a dedicated soldier of the nation's cause, fighting in the battle of Bunker Hill, living as a fugitive in England after his capture at sea, acting as secret courier from English political sympathizers to Benjamin Franklin in Paris, and fighting alongside John Paul Jones during the latter's famous naval depredations on the coasts of Britain. Yet in a crushing irony illustrative of the "vanity" of human affairs, Potter's patriotic enthusiasm for his country's cause against Britain leads to his accidental boarding of a British warship and de facto captivity in England, followed by decades of poverty when he is forced to remain in London after the war with a wife and growing family to support. At the end of his first chapter, which evokes Israel Potter's birthplace in the rugged hills of western Massachusetts and the ironic contrast between his sturdy yeoman birth and his prolonged transatlantic captivity, Melville's narrator sets forth the allegorical and typological identity of his hero: "Such, at this day, is the country which gave birth to our hero: prophetically styled Israel by the good Puritans, his parents, since for more than forty years, poor Potter wandered in the wild wilderness of the world's extremest hardships and ills." Unlike the Israelites who eventually reached their Promised Land, Potter spends most of his life in renewed captivity in the Egypt of the oppressor he fought to obtain his country's freedom, and dies soon after his unheralded return to his native country as an octogenarian—ironic reversals consonant with the teachings of the "preacher" of Ecclesiastes.[5]

As we will see, the philosophical message of Ecclesiastes largely frames Melville's narrative of Israel Potter's career. It is particularly salient in the mordant dedication by the "Editor" of the narrative to the Bunker Hill Monument in Charlestown, Massachusetts, site of his hero's first military engagement and a historic site of Revolutionary providential history and hagiography—featured, most notably, in Daniel Webster's formal addresses at the monument at the beginning and end of construction in 1825 and 1843, respectively. The ironies evident in Melville's dedication begin with his addressing the 221-foot obelisk with the punning appellation of "His Highness"—a peculiar designation for a monument commemorating the birthplace of American democracy. Such an honorific term is in fact part of a sardonic tribute intended to recall a former era of royal patronage. Yet amid these ironies, the larger rhetorical message of the dedication is the futility of human accomplishment and the ubiquity of death, both prominent themes in Ecclesiastes. For beginning with a nod to the disinterestedness of the biographical enterprise when dedicated to the heroic dead, Melville quickly moves on to an ironic tribute to the subject of his fictional "biography," whose service to his country earned him a forgotten grave and an imaginary annual "pension" of greenery covering his gravesite, in an emblematic example of human vanity: "Israel Potter well merits the present tribute—a private of Bunker Hill, who for his faithful services was years ago promoted to a still deeper privacy under the ground, with a posthumous pension, in default of any during life, annually paid him by the spring in ever-new mosses and sward" (vii). Unlike the twenty-two thousand war veterans who were able to take advantage of the 1818 Revolutionary War Pension Act, amended for means testing two years later, Potter has been left unrewarded except for the universally available pastoral renewal of nature's verdure over his grave.[6]

Also reminiscent of the message of Ecclesiastes is Melville's insistence that Potter's "little narrative of his adventures, forlornly published on sleazy gray paper," was an obscure document by mid-century, and "like the crutch-marks of the cripple by the Beautiful Gate, this blurred record is now out of print" (vii). While the allusion here to the cripple at the gate of the Jerusalem temple miraculously healed by the apostle Peter (Acts 3:1–11) would seem to align Israel Potter's forgotten history with the pathos of Christian legend, Potter's fate of unrewarded service and oblivion is more consonant with the repeated argument in Ecclesiastes that the human past is always erased ("the dead know not anything, neither have they any more a reward; for the memory of them is forgotten" [Eccles. 9:5]), for even a prominent man is doomed to oblivion: "For he cometh in with vanity, and he departeth in darkness, and his name shall be covered with darkness" (Eccles. 6:4). Implicitly challenging Melville's assertions of his biographical subject's obscurity,

The Life and Adventures of Israel R. Potter was in fact published in three editions in the 1820s and was still known to at least one of *Israel Potter*'s early reviewers in the spring of 1855. While heightening the pathos of Potter's fate, Melville's deliberate, if somewhat overstated, emphasis on the obscurity of his hero's original story was likely intended to confirm the pessimism regarding human importance or achievement found in the book of Ecclesiastes.[7]

In the "Dedication" Melville again emphasizes the vanity of Israel Potter's patriotic efforts in view of his ironic fate of poverty and prolonged exile when Melville as "Editor" notes that Potter's full biography has not "appeared in the volumes of Sparks" (viii), thus drawing attention to the acclaimed work of historian Jared Sparks as author of a celebrated life of Washington, editor of the papers of Franklin and Washington, and editor and contributor to the twenty-five-volume Library of American Biography in the 1830s and '40s. For Melville's Editor, Potter's life has awaited publication until June 17, 1854—the seventy-ninth anniversary of the battle of Bunker Hill—allegedly in order to receive a more elevated (but insubstantial) benefit "under the present exalted patronage" of the monument; "seeing that your Highness, according to the definition above, may, in the loftiest sense, be deemed the Great Biographer: the national commemorator of such of the anonymous privates of June 17, 1775, who may never have received other requital than the solid reward of your granite" (viii). Adapting the term "Great Biographer" from its previous reference to James Boswell for his classic *Life of Johnson*, the Editor again plays on the bitter futility of the common soldiers' service to their country while hinting at an off-color Boswellian pun in reference to "anonymous privates" and showing mordant humor in calling the monument a "solid reward" in lieu of a pension.[8]

As in the rest of Melville's Dedication, the Editor's invocation of "solid reward" is also an implicit parody of the commemorative patriotic rhetoric of Daniel Webster, whose famous 1825 dedication speech at the laying of the cornerstone is likely parodied in the Editor's birthday wishes to the "prematurely gray" monument, while hoping that "each of its summer suns may shine as brightly on your brow as each winter snow shall lightly rest on the grave of Israel Potter" (viii). Webster had said of the unbuilt pillar in his dedication speech, "We wish that this column, rising towards heaven among the pointed spires of so many temples dedicated to God, may contribute also to produce, in all minds, a pious feeling of dependence and gratitude. We wish, finally, that the last object to the sight of him who leaves his native shore, and the first to gladden his who revisits it, may be something which shall remind him of the liberty and the glory of his country. Let it rise! let it rise, till it meet the sun in his coming; let the earliest light of the morning gild it, and parting day linger and play on its summit." Webster had died in October 1852, a much-maligned figure in New England because of his notorious speech of March 7, 1850, endorsing the national political Compromise of that year. Sardonically pointing out the vanity of Israel Potter's patriotic service, the Editor is apparently enlisting the shade of the great New England statesman and orator in an implied comment on the vanity of the liberties won by the American Revolution—a message that, for the discerning contemporary reader, would have evoked the growing sectional crisis over slavery illustrated by the massive civil disturbance in Boston in late May and early June 1854—just as *Israel Potter* was about to be serialized—over the rendition of the fugitive slave Anthony Burns.[9]

In adapting the personal history of Israel Potter, Melville found a protagonist whose name was well suited to the larger themes of his historical novella, with their underlying biblical associations. Throughout the narrative Potter is thus compared with a number of biblical types, including Jonah when he languishes in the fetid "black bowels" (15) of an English prison ship, a Daniel-like figure in "the very den of the British lion" (29) when he works in the King's Gardens at Kew and converses with King George III there, an Ishmael figure when "all hands" (138) are against him as he seeks to blend in with the crew of the British frigate onto which he accidentally leaped, and a Prodigal Son when he returns to the long-abandoned site of "his father's homestead" (168) in western Massachusetts in old age. But his larger biblical significance is embedded in both his Christian name and surname. The name Israel clearly made him an allegorized representative of the new American nation as a modern spiritual and political Israel, based on a typological model developed by the Puritans of New England and given a newly relevant meaning for the political leaders of the Revolutionary era, notably when they considered putting the scene of the Exodus on the Great Seal of the United States. As James P. Byrd remarks in a study of the role of the Bible in the American Revolution, "the fact that Adams, Jefferson, and Franklin all pondered the Exodus narrative in those decisive months of 1776 indicates that no biblical narrative surpassed the Exodus in identifying the major themes, plots, characters, and subplots of the Revolution. Revolutionaries could not get enough of the

Exodus story. They saw in the Exodus the providential hand of God, which would orchestrate the Revolution." The American colonies were thus widely viewed as the modern Israel escaping from the bondage of the English pharaoh—an archetypal narrative ironically reversed in the career of Melville's protagonist.[10]

Commentators have noted that the surname "Potter" evokes the idea of his hero's long impoverished existence in London, based on the name's association with the traditional "potter's field" where the destitute were buried—a term originating in the gospel of Matthew's account of Judas's supposed return of the thirty pieces of silver to the chief priests, who bought the potter's field outside Jerusalem for the burial of strangers (Matt. 27:3-8). But the symbolic resonances of "potter" go deeper when the larger biblical associations of the word are traced. In the Old Testament prophets, humanity is seen as clay in the hand of the divine potter (Isa. 64:8; Jer. 18:4-6), while in Saint Paul's Letter to the Romans, the apostle expounded the same theme of human dependence on the divine creator: "Hath not the potter power over the clay, of the same lump to make one vessel unto honour, and another unto dishonour?" (Rom. 9:21). By bearing the name "Israel Potter," then, Melville's Revolutionary antihero was given a Christian name connoting his exalted spiritual destiny, but his surname associated him with the whims of an inscrutable god who created human beings from clay and molded them into pottery vessels, some arbitrarily fated to reap reward and some to suffer misfortune—capricious behavior in keeping with the absent god of Ecclesiastes.

A major theme of Ecclesiastes is in fact its teaching of the arbitrary and unpredictable nature of life, which is not governed by a providential personal God but instead by chance and contingency. As the Preacher states, "For who knoweth what is good for man in this life, all the days of his vain life which he spendeth as a shadow? for who can tell a man what shall be after him under the sun?" (Eccles. 6:12). In what is perhaps the most famous articulation of this theme, the biblical author wrote, "The race is not to the swift, nor the battle to the strong, neither yet bread to the wise, nor yet riches to men of understanding, nor yet favour to men of skill; but time and chance happeneth to them all" (Eccles. 9:11). Not coincidentally, this same sense of life being governed by chance and contingency is pervasive in Melville's retelling of the life of Israel Potter. The trajectory of Israel Potter's career thus repeatedly goes back and forth between the United States, Britain, and France;

ships fighting for America and Britain; stints on sea and land; and the varied professions of surveyor, hunter, peddler, sailor, whaleman, and soldier in America, and laborer, gardener, courier, sailor, brick maker, porter, chair mender, match maker, and ragpicker in Britain. The picaresque structural pattern of Melville's narrative thus supports a thematic grounding in the author's use of Ecclesiastes as the narrative's religious and philosophical touchstone.[11]

Ecclesiastes can accordingly be related to a number of distinct narrative sequences throughout *Israel Potter*. For example, the Preacher's claim that the "race" is not won by the "swift" is particularly germane to the repeated depictions of Israel's running from his pursuers to escape capture. Thus, in chapter 3, Israel is first taken to England as a prisoner along with the other crew from the brig *Washington*, and after spending a month on a pestilential prison hulk in Spithead, he is given a place in the crew of the British commander's barge; and when the British crew all go to a local alehouse, Israel manages to escape by pleading the need to urinate before entering: "No sooner does Israel see his companions housed, than putting speed into his feet, and letting grow all his wings, he starts like a deer. He runs four miles (so he afterwards affirmed) without halting" (15). Caught again while seeking to escape after being challenged to identify himself in a public house, Israel is put under guard at the inn and only allowed to drink with his two guards. When the latter are thoroughly inebriated and half asleep, Israel obtains permission to relieve himself outdoors and is escorted down a dark passage to the door by the two drunken guards whom he eludes by butting them with his head; then leaping over the garden wall, a manacled Israel sprints away and "once more lets grow all his wings" (17), spending the remainder of the night on the run. Later, after he has escaped from his confinement in the secret compartment of Squire Woodcock's house following the squire's unexpected death, Israel manages to escape from the house and surrounding estate first by pretending to be the squire's ghost, and then, following his dressing up in the tattered clothes of a scarecrow, he engages in a comic charade with a pitchfork-wielding farmworker who runs after him and is soon joined by others in a chase sequence worthy of the silent movie era; but Israel again "proved to have better wind and bottom than any. Outstripping the whole pack, he finally shot out of their sight in an extensive park, heavily timbered in one quarter" (80).

But Israel's ability to flee from his English captors is ironically reversed in chapter 20 ("The Shuttle") as a result of a freak accident that causes Israel's unexpected return to England as a disguised member of the crew of an English frigate—the narrative's most poignant example of the dominant influence of chance in human affairs, as evoked in Ecclesiastes. While on a voyage back to the United States with John Paul Jones on the armed ship *Ariel*, Israel thus precipitously boards a British frigate that had allegedly surrendered to Jones's cannonading, only to find himself stranded alone on the enemy warship. Here the narrator notes how Israel eagerly responded to the call of duty when a spar of the enemy ship was thrust toward him on the *Ariel* and he "instinctively caught hold of it—just as he had grasped the jib-boom of the Serapis— and, at the same moment, hearing the call to take possession, in the valiant excitement of the occasion, he leaped upon the spar, and made a rush for the stranger's deck, thinking, of course, that he would be immediately followed by the regular boarders" (132). But the sails of the enemy ship suddenly fill, and it rapidly moves away from Jones's ship, with Israel now stranded amid the two hundred sailors of the British vessel, which had played a trick on Jones by pretending to be surrendering after falsely reporting half its men killed. Now facing the terror of indefinite imprisonment if his identity is discovered, Israel is forced to improvise an extended and ultimately successful masquerade of being a legitimate sailor on the British ship. If Israel's absurdist entrapment on an British ship after an act of naval deception strikingly illustrates the verse of Ecclesiastes claiming that the "race" is not won by the "swift" nor the "battle" by the "strong," the manner of his capture is also illustrated by the biblical text's ensuing lines: "For man also knoweth not his time: as the fishes that are taken in an evil net, and as the birds that are caught in the snare; so are the sons of men snared in an evil time, when it falleth suddenly upon them" (Eccles. 9:12). Israel is one such hapless "bird" unexpectedly caught in a deadly "snare."

Israel's capture by the British frigate also subjects him to a kind of social death in which his deliberate erasure of individual identity demonstrates the ephemeral identity of all humanity, as the Preacher taught in Ecclesiastes: "For he cometh in with vanity, and departeth in darkness, and his name shall be covered with darkness" (Eccles. 6:4). Thus, when Israel is being interrogated by the officer of the deck after his failed attempt to join various posts on the ship, the officer responds to the sailing master's claim that Israel is "out of his mind" by elaborating on the strange sailor's lack of any social or natural community, reducing him (literally) to a nonentity: "'He's out of all reason; out of all men's knowledge and memories! Why, no one knows him; no one has ever seen him before; no imagination, in the wildest flight of a morbid nightmare, has ever so much as dreamed of him. Who are you?' he again added, fierce with amazement. 'What's your name? Are you down in the ship's books, or at all in the records of nature?'" (137). Israel's strategic response to these remarks is to claim the identity of "Peter Perkins," a whimsical generic name that helps him to begin resolving his anomalous position on the ship, as he successfully fabricates a new improvised identity while again forced to join the naval forces of his country's enemy, following his earlier impressment.

Another significant indication of Melville's use of Ecclesiastes in *Israel Potter* is the story's subversion of the "great man" theory of biography popularized in the 1840s and '50s by Carlyle and Emerson, and reflected in the hagiographic writings on Revolutionary leaders during this era in the Library of American Biography edited by Jared Sparks, as mentioned in Melville's ironic dedication to his novel. At the start of the first chapter of *On Heroes, Hero-Worship, and the Heroic in History* (1841), Carlyle had boldly asserted: "For, as I take it, Universal History, the history of what man has accomplished in this world, is at bottom the History of the Great Men who have worked here. They were the leaders of men, these great ones; the modellers, patterns, and in a wide sense creators, of whatsoever the general mass of men contrived to do or attain"; indeed, "the soul of the world's history, it may justly be considered, were the history of these." In "Uses of Great Men," the first essay in *Representative Men* (1850), Emerson similarly claimed, "Mankind have, in all ages, attached themselves to a few persons, who, either by the quality of that idea they embodied, or by the largeness of their reception, were entitled to the position of leaders and law-givers. These teach us the qualities of primary nature,—admit us to the constitution of things."[12]

Daniel Reagan has insightfully argued that *Israel Potter* was written in dialogue with the dominant theories of biography of its era, notably those developed by Carlyle and Emerson, in which biographical subjects effectively act as living "epitomes" of their times.[13] But an enlarged perspective on this subject is gained when the exaltation of exemplary individuals in the writings of Carlyle and Emerson is juxtaposed to the skeptical teachings of Ecclesiastes that dominate *Israel Potter*. For if any text was designed to cast doubt on the glorifications of great men, it is this Old Testament book, which emphasizes the common mortal fate of all individuals, arguing for the futility of human accomplishment and placing man and animal on the same level of importance: "For that which befalleth the sons of men, befalleth beasts; even one thing befalleth them: as the one dieth, so dieth the other; yea, they have all one breath; so that a man hath no preeminence above a beast: for all is vanity. All go unto one place; all are of the dust, and all turn to dust again" (Eccles. 3:19–20). Unlike the positioning of Adam above the animals as the crown of creation in Genesis, in Ecclesiastes the skeptical Preacher demotes the human race to a level of shared mortality and oblivion with all living creatures.

In *Israel Potter*, the title character performs heroic service for the two Revolutionary giants depicted at length in the narrative, Benjamin Franklin and John Paul Jones, but he is not ultimately rewarded for his pains. Indeed, his heroic service to the Revolutionary cause in the persons of Franklin and Jones, which is supposed to earn him a return to America, instead leaves him stranded as a fugitive in England who must conceal his identity for the duration of the war and live in exile for over four decades afterward. In his narrative of Israel Potter's life, there is no doubt that Melville recognized the gifts and accomplishments of both Franklin and Jones, the first for his many-sided scientific, political, and literary genius, and the latter for his extraordinarily daring exploits while leading the naval war against Britain. But the ultimate irony of Israel's experience with these "great" men offers an implicit Ecclesiastes-related reproof to the universal popular exaltation of their accomplishments.

In the case of Franklin, the narrator provides an incisive portrait of this famous American polymath in a late phase of his long career as a celebrated natural philosopher, inventor, publisher, author, politician, and now his country's chief diplomat in Paris. Above all, Franklin is a worldly philosopher who attempts to educate a young Israel to be successful in all of his pursuits and to give him the moral direction he allegedly needs. The narrator's evocative description of Franklin repeatedly pays homage to Franklin as a "wise" man, or one possessed of unique "wisdom" or "sapience." Franklin is thus an appealing figure who has carefully studied the world and its ways: "It was a goodly sight to see this serene, cool and ripe old philosopher, who by sharp inquisition of man in the street, and then long meditating upon him, surrounded by all these queer old implements, charts and books, had grown at last so wondrous wise" (39). Seemingly possessed of an almost supernatural insight, Franklin also exhibits "far foresight, pleasant wit, and working wisdom" (39). At seventy-two years old, he thus displays many "years of sapience" (39). A figure of supreme worldly "wisdom" and a paragon of the American Enlightenment, Franklin is an embodiment of rational inquiry and problem solving. Tellingly, on a map of the New World covering a wall of his Paris apartment, "the word 'D E S E R T' diffusely printed" in the middle of a large empty space has been crossed out by a confident Franklin, "as if in summary repeal of it" (38).

Franklin advises Israel on the virtues of a wise frugality in both business and personal matters, treating him to a meal while not allowing him to drink any wine. When Potter goes into the adjoining chamber that Franklin has reserved for him, the young man is fascinated by the sight on the mantel of a sealed bottle of cognac marked "Otard," among other fragrant delights such as a bottle of cologne water, and he soon afterward encounters an attractive chambermaid who hints that she is available for more than housekeeping duties. But Franklin quickly puts a stop to Potter's potential to enjoy himself during his brief overnight stay in Paris by confiscating the cognac and cologne and warning him against the chambermaid. Left only with a copy of Franklin's *Way to Wealth*, Potter meditates over the "sly" wisdom of Franklin's persona, Poor Richard, as found in the well-known saying that "God helps them that help themselves" (54), a typical example of Franklin's prudential, worldly teachings.

Yet the worldly "wisdom" embodied by Franklin, when seen in relation to the ultimately unhappy fate of his secret courier Israel Potter, is comparable to the traditional utilitarian and pragmatic "wisdom" found in the book of Proverbs as compared to the skeptical higher wisdom of Ecclesiastes. For if Franklin preaches the prudential rules of conduct that will make one money and advance one in the world, he ignores the more pessimistic wisdom that sees the limitations of worldly morality and the uncertainty and injustice that prevail in most worldly affairs. Traditional wisdom, as found in the book of Proverbs, is thus based on a rationalized system of reciprocity and retribution, offering dichotomies of wisdom and foolishness, righteousness and wickedness, humility and hubris, and the clean and the unclean, among others. Such moral oppositions are meant to promote the notion that following the correct form of behavior will lead to worldly success, whereas Ecclesiastes asserts that there is no guaranteed reward for virtuous behavior.[14] The larger message of Ecclesiastes, to which Israel Potter's life will conform, is thus an implicit rejection of the rationalization of biblical wisdom found in the book of Proverbs, which served as an implicit literary model for *Poor Richard's Almanac*. Potter tellingly reveals his exasperation with Franklin: "Oh confound all this wisdom! It's a sort of insulting to talk wisdom to a man like me" (54). All he wants is a chance to eat, drink, and enjoy himself in Paris, as the book of Ecclesiastes explicitly enjoins men to do in their limited lives (Eccles. 2:24-26; 3:12-13; 5:18-19; 8:15; 9:7-9); but Franklin prudently keeps him from doing this.

In the career of Israel Potter, faithful service to Franklin will in fact lead to several life-threatening situations and the final misfortune of not being able to return to Paris to take advantage of Franklin's promise to send him home. For when Israel returns to the house of Squire Woodcock and delivers him the secret dispatches from Paris, circumstances require that Potter be hidden away in a secret cell above the chimney in what turns into a three-day entombment when the Squire unexpectedly dies, leaving Potter trapped in his cell. Potter's terrified experience in the constricted space, with its past history of medieval Templar tortures, constitutes a Poe-like premature burial and psychological ordeal that tests Potter's sanity while also parodying Christ's Resurrection—just as Ecclesiastes cast doubt on human spiritual immortality.[15] But once he has successfully escaped from the cell and exited the secret entry in the chimney, Potter's desperate flight turns to farce as he dresses himself in the deceased Woodcock's clothes so he can masquerade as the squire's ghost and escape the house. Despite his narrow escape from the mansion and the estate dressed first as a squire and then as a scarecrow—a reminder of Potter's fluid identity as a fugitive prisoner of war—he manages to make it all the way back to Dover, only to discover that all communication between England and France has been suspended. Potter's perilous services to Franklin and the interests of his country as a secret courier thus do not receive their deserved reward; instead, he is soon impressed into the British navy and only fortuitously finds himself involved in extended service at sea as the right-hand man to John Paul Jones.

First introduced to Potter in Franklin's Paris apartment, John Paul Jones is a strange hybrid of elegantly mannered gentleman and tattooed savage. "He was a rather small, elastic, swarthy man, with an aspect as of a disinherited Indian Chief in European clothes. An unvanquishable enthusiasm, intensified to perfect sobriety, couched in his savage, self-possessed eye" (56). Jones's greatest asset in the American war with England was his remarkable daring and aggression against the British ships and ports that he targeted. Unlike the portrait of the superlatively "wise" Franklin who embodies the rationalistic wisdom of Proverbs and not the pessimistic wisdom of Ecclesiastes, Jones's character and naval exploits offer potential confirmation for the important role of chance and contingency in human life, as Ecclesiastes teaches.

Potter's prolonged dramatic adventures with John Paul Jones begin with Potter's heroic action in subduing a British revenue cutter by killing some of its crew when Jones unexpectedly confronts the cutter during his wide-ranging depredations along the coasts of Britain. In the midst of his description of Jones's ensuing naval exploits, the narrator notes the captain's successes were the result of a kind of calculated recklessness based on the recognition that human affairs are always unsettled; or as Ecclesiastes notes, "time and chance happeneth to them all" (Eccles. 9:11): "The career of this stubborn adventurer signally illustrates the idea, that since all human affairs are subject to organic disorder; since they are created in, and sustained by, a sort of half-disciplined chaos; hence, he who in great things seeks success, must never wait for smooth water; which never was, and never will be; but with what straggling method he can, dash with all his derangements at his object, leaving the rest to Fortune" (114). Now operating with his ship the *Ranger* on which Potter serves as his quartermaster, Jones performs a daring predawn attack on the northwestern British coal port of White Haven in which the guns of its fort are spiked and at least one of its many moored colliers burnt; and it is Potter who daringly obtains the necessary fire by asking a local inhabitant for a light for his pipe. As a result of this and other bold actions such as the raid on the Earl of Selkirk's estate and the capture of the *Drake*, Jones receives all the credit even though Potter is instrumental in some of his captain's successes: "This cruise made loud fame for Paul, especially at the court of France, whose king sent Paul a sword and a medal. But poor Israel, who also had conquered a craft, and all unaided too—what had he?" (113). The question, with its assertion of Israel's "unaided" heroism on the British revenue cutter, is a foreshadowing of the ultimate "vanity" or futility behind Potter's heroic service to his celebrated captain.

The most noteworthy account of John Paul Jones's sea battles is, of course, his victory over the fifty-gun frigate *Serapis* off the coast of Yorkshire while commanding his next ship, the *Bonhomme Richard*—a battle that the narrator notes was precipitated by "luck" (119). To set up the scene for this famous naval engagement, the narrator introduces the eerie stage prop of "the Man-in-the-Moon" who watches the evening battle from just above the horizon of the sea: "this queer face wore a serious, apishly self-satisfied leer, as if the Man-in-the-Moon had somehow secretly put up the ships to their contest, and in the depths of his malignant old soul was not unpleased to see how well his charms worked. There stood the grinning Man-in-the-Moon, his head just dodging into view over the rim of the sea:—Mephistopheles prompter of the stage" (123). Conflated with the modern gentleman devil of Goethe's poetic drama *Faust*, the Man-in-the-Moon here is a stand-in for the recognizably amoral and capricious god of Ecclesiastes, all while acting as an embodiment of the fickleness of Fortune, which the moon traditionally represents.[16] Framed as a kind of stage performance during which the narrator employs a wealth of figurative language, the ensuing battle is savagely destructive, as each ship launches point-blank broadsides into the other while engaging in ghastly close-range combat separated only by a narrow stretch of water in which combatants are instantly obliterated from history. "Into that Lethean canal,—pond-like in its smoothness as compared with the sea without—fell many a poor soul that night;—fell, for ever forgotten" (125). It is only when Potter, following Jones's instructions, is able to throw a grenade down the *Serapis*'s main hatchway while hanging from a yardarm sixty feet above the deck that the lethal explosion "restored the chances of battle, before in favor of the Serapis" (127).

The actual surrender of the *Serapis* ironically occurs when both ships are on the verge of mutual destruction and the British captain hauls down his colors to end the carnage. "So equal was the conflict that, even after the surrender, it could be, and was, a question to one of the warriors engaged (who had not happened to see the English flag hauled down) whether the Serapis had struck to the Richard, or the Richard to the Serapis" (129). The arbitrary nature of the victory is in keeping with the arbitrary nature of human life depicted in Ecclesiastes. By the same token, even though it is Potter who turns the wavering tide of battle, it is Jones who gets all the credit. As we have previously noted, Potter soon experiences the catastrophe of leaping onto a passing British warship because of his very zeal to serve his captain. So, too, Potter's elaborate improvised charade of belonging to the enemy ship's crew inadvertently evokes his earlier masquerade when escaping from Squire Woodcock's, as though all Potter got for his heroic service to his two Revolutionary masters was a radical loss of identity, confirming the utter futility, or vanity, of his labors, again suggesting the message of Ecclesiastes: "For what hath man of all his labour, and of the vexation of his heart, whereby he hath laboured under the sun? For all his days are sorrows, and his travail griefs" (Eccles. 2:22–23).

Escaping from the British warship in Portsmouth, Potter sees the imprisoned Ethan Allen, a third Revolutionary giant whom the narrator evokes, but whose role in the narrative excites the narrator's unalloyed admiration as a figure of heroic defiance against the cruelty of his captors, whom he rhetorically intimidates into treating him humanely. Yet if the celebrated Allen provides a model of active defiance of his captivity and is eventually exchanged as a prisoner of war, Israel Potter, now a wandering fugitive, is forcibly resigned to patient endurance of his implicit "captivity" as he returns to London to find work and blend in with the population there, starting with his employment in the hellish brickyard outside the city.

Revealingly, the most explicit association of Melville's protagonist with the biblical resonances of his name occurs in a chapter that also features the most explicit association in the narrative with the message of the book of Ecclesiastes. Thus, in chapter 23 ("Israel in Egypt") Israel ponders the ironies of his situation working in the brickyard outside London, manufacturing building materials for the nation against which his own country was fighting for independence. While indirectly evoking Ecclesiastes' repeated emphasis on the endless unprofitable labor that characterizes human life (Eccles. 1:8–9; 2:22–23; 3:9–10), the narrator describes the brickmaking operation in which an impoverished Israel and his fellow laborers, implicitly imitating their divine creator, recklessly slap clay into molds and then smooth off the top, an operation in which the traditional biblical equation of humanity and clay is pessimistically asserted: "To these muddy philosophers, men and bricks were equally of clay. What signifies who we be—dukes or ditchers? thought the moulders; all is vanity and clay" (155). The conflation of "vanity" and "clay" here thus combines the moral burden of Ecclesiastes and the history of the creation in Genesis, both emphasizing the ephemerality of human existence and the inevitability of mortality. Laboring in "a sort of earthy dungeon, or grave-digger's hole" (155), Israel Potter works in this debilitating manufacture for thirteen weeks, giving the narrator (and Potter) a chance to play on the archetypal nature of his trade: "brick is no bad name for any son of Adam; Eden was but a brick-yard; what is a mortal but a few luckless shovelfuls of brick, moulded in a mould, laid out on a sheet to dry, and ere long quickened into his queer caprices by the sun? Are men not built into communities just like bricks into a wall?" (156). The overlap of Edenic and ancient Egyptian modes of creation and postlapsarian hard labor here conveys a memorably reductive view of the human condition—one in keeping with a pessimistic motif of universal "vanity."

By the same token, the equation of bricks and men is extended in the narrator's subsequent description of the action of the kiln in which the transition from the lower to higher layer of bricks suggests a symbolic range of humanity, from hardened and twisted proletariat scorched by adversity, to effete and overprotected scions of the upper class, with the most durable "bricks" in the middle section. Yet the chapter reaches a climax when the previously suggested themes all come to a head in a list of bitterly ironic reversals in Israel Potter's mind:

> Sometimes, lading out his dough, Israel could not but bethink him of what seemed enigmatic in his fate. He whom love of country made a hater of her foes—the foreigners among whom he now was thrown—he who, as soldier and sailor, had joined to kill, burn and destroy both them and theirs—here he was at last, serving that very people as a slave, better succeeding in making their bricks than firing their ships. To think that he should be thus helping, with all his strength, to extend the walls of the Thebes of the oppressor, made him half mad. Poor Israel! well-named— bondsman in the English Egypt. But he drowned the thought by still more recklessly spattering with his ladle: "What signifies who we be, or where we are, or what we do?" Slap-dash! "Kings as clowns are codgers—who ain't a nobody?" Splash! "All is vanity and clay." (157)

In this second iteration of keywords from Ecclesiastes and Genesis, Israel re-creates the "genial, desperado philosophy" of Ishmael's fatalistic initiation into whaling in chapter 49 of *Moby-Dick* while realizing that his (Israel's) fate exemplifies a typological reversal of the Exodus narrative identified by the American colonies as their chief model for their Revolution; for Israel will spend most of his life as a spiritual and economic "captive" in the "Egypt" of England and not in the transatlantic "Promised Land" of the new United States. Underlining this fact is the image of the brickworks being surrounded by the horizon like a noose or snare ("The blank horizon, like a rope, coiled round the whole" [156]), in keeping with Ecclesiastes' image of fate suddenly snaring human beings with a rope like trapped animals (Eccles. 9:12).

In Israel Potter's final return to London as an anonymous fugitive and exile, the teeming metropolis is characterized as "the City of Dis" in the chapter title, and a proliferation of Dantean imagery suggestive of a contemporary urban hell accentuates the black funereal atmosphere, based on the prevalence of coal smoke and coal dust covering every object. The description of London Bridge conveys an infernal scene: "Hung in long, sepulchral arches of stone, the black, besmoked bridge seemed a huge scarf of crape, festooning the river across. Similar funeral festoons spanned it to the west, while eastward, towards the sea, tiers and tiers of jetty colliers lay moored side by side, fleets of black swans" (159). On the sewerage-clogged river, "here and there, like awaiting hearses, the coal-scows drifted along, poled broadside, pell-mell to the current" (159). Like the various rivers of Hades in classical mythology (Styx, Acheron, Lethe, Phlegethon, Cocytus), or the two rivers over which Charon transported the dead (Styx and Acheron), the tidal currents of the Thames are comparable to the dark tides of humanity that pour over London Bridge "all bespattered with ebon mud" (159) like the dead entering the underworld in preparation for posthumous punishment: "It seemed as if some squadron of centaurs, on the thither side of Phlegethon, with charge on charge, was driving tormented humanity, with all its chattels, across" (159).

If chapter 24 of *Israel Potter* is filled with a series of evocative classical and Dantean images of hell, the portrayal of a dark, funereal-looking city is also consonant with the somber wisdom of Ecclesiastes, with its regular reminders of human oppression and mortality:

> So I returned, and considered all the oppressions that are done under the sun: and behold the tears of such as were oppressed, and they had no comforter; and on the side of their oppressors there was power; but they had no comforter.
>
> Wherefore I praised the dead which are already dead more than the living which are yet alive.
>
> * * *
>
> It is better to go to the house of mourning than the house of feasting: for that is the end of all men; and the living will lay it to his heart.
>
> * * *
>
> This is an evil among all things that are done under the sun, that there is one event unto all: yea, also the heart of the sons of men is full of evil, and madness is in their heart while they live, and after that they go to the dead. (Eccles. 4:1–2; 7:2; 9:3)

The last chapter of Ecclesiastes is in fact devoted to a portrait of old age and death as the Preacher warns his hearers against the coming of evil days in their advanced years by telling them to enjoy the days of their youth, "while the sun, or the light, or the moon, or the stars, be not darkened, nor clouds return after rain" (Eccles. 12:2). This implied future era of cosmic darkness will be characterized by a fear of death and a pervasive funereal atmosphere: "and desire shall fail: because man goeth to his long home, and the mourners go about the streets" (Eccles. 12:5). The images of death that haunt the book of Ecclesiastes and pervade its last chapter thus potentially provide a somber backdrop to the death-in-life existence of the exiled Israel Potter in London, where his wife and ten of his eleven children will die prematurely.

In view of the typological symbolism of Israel Potter's name and career, it is ironic that he re-creates in parody the allegedly providential history of his countrymen during the Revolutionary era. He thus first experiences a kind of onerous Egyptian captivity while working in the suburban brickyard, as described in chapter 23, and then relives the experience of the ancient Israelites' forty-year ordeal wandering in the Wilderness while struggling to survive as a chair mender in London, as described in chapter 25—except that here the divine pillar of cloud was the London fog; and there was "no pillar of fire by night, except the cold column of the monument; two hundred feet beneath the mocking gilt flames on whose top, at the stone base, the shiverer, of midnight, often laid down" (161). The narrator refers to the column adjacent to the Thames near London Bridge designed by Christopher Wren commemorating the catastrophic London fire of 1666. Unlike the Israelites in the Wilderness, who were fed with heavenly manna (Exod. 16:1–36; Num. 11:4–9) and drank of a miraculous spring obtained by Moses from a rock (Num. 20:7–13), Israel Potter is barely able to feed himself among the destitute of London and, following his marriage, must support his numerous children and wife on a tiny income largely derived from caning old chairs. In the end, however, after his wife and most of his children die, Israel and his only surviving son are finally able to return to the United States, the long-remembered "Canaan beyond the sea" (166) idealized by the elderly veteran, thereby fulfilling the typological pattern of final entry to the Promised Land. But contrary to the future "scenes of nestling happiness and plenty" (166) that he evokes for his son, his return to his native country will lead only to a climactic disappointment and death, and a final reassertion of the Ecclesiastes-based theme of vanity that dominates the last chapters of the narrative.[17]

Melville's historical novella concludes with an illustration of another well-known teaching of Ecclesiastes, namely, the inherent circularity of human and natural life as human generations appear and disappear, and the sun, winds, and rivers perform their cyclical movements; for "unto the place from whence the rivers come, thither they return again" (Eccles. 1:7). In keeping with this cyclical model of existence, Melville's life of Israel Potter ends where it began, at his original home in western Massachusetts. Israel is thus able to return to the United States after his son has listened to his father's evocative stories about his early life in America, and upon learning the Revolutionary veteran's story, the American consul in London is persuaded to help pay their way back to Boston. Arriving on July 4, 1826, on the fiftieth anniversary of Independence, Potter is able to view the commemorative exercises to honor the heroes of the Revolution and of the battle of Bunker Hill; but in a symbolic enactment of his historical fate, and the triumph of Revolutionary myth over individual witness, he "narrowly escaped being run over by a patriotic triumphal car in a procession" flying a banner that hailed the ancient veterans of Bunker Hill: "GLORY TO THE HEROES THAT FOUGHT!" (167). If the venerated Founding Fathers, Jefferson and Adams, both providentially expired on this day and thus began their careers of posthumous immortality, the unknown living veteran Israel Potter is almost killed during festivities allegedly devoted to celebrating his military service.

The fiftieth anniversary of the Declaration of Independence—the day of Israel's return to his native country—was historically denominated America's Jubilee, the term being derived from an ancient Hebrew festival (Lev. 25, 27) when slaves were freed and land returned to its original owners after fifty years. In keeping with this biblical prototype, the national celebrations on July 4, 1826—not represented in Melville's novella—constituted a key occasion within the nation's evolving civil religion dedicated to the Revolution. In Boston, Mayor Josiah Quincy gave the official oration at the Old South Meeting House, ending his remarks with a high-flown prophecy:

> And so this temple of liberty, the foundations of which were laid on the fourth of July, 1776, in blood and peril, by our fathers, shall, by the labours, councils, and virtues, of all the good and great, of present and future times, be enlarged and extended, in true proportions of moral architecture, till its pillars embrace the universe, and its dome vault upwards, with a more than human skill,—with glorious archings of celestial wisdom,—resplendent with purest faith,—radiant with immortal truth,—crowned with

revealed hope,—to the joy and rest of man, on the promise, and in the presence of the Eternal.

At the celebratory dinner at Faneuil Hall that day, Daniel Webster similarly proposed a toast to "the political miracle—that bright sun, which on the 4th of July 1776, had its rising in the WEST,—may it keep above the horizon, until it shall have shown [*sic*] on all nations."[18]

Contrary to these high-minded historical orations and celebrations devoted to the country's sacred history, the fictional Israel Potter's experience of the nation's jubilee in Boston is filled with pathos and alienation, for he will reap no recognition or reward from the occasion, thereby becoming a living martyr to his country's Revolutionary cause. Indeed, while Potter sits among the gravestones on Copp's Hill across the Charles River from the historic battlefield, the narrator notes of Potter that the original wound he had received on his chest at Bunker Hill was traversed by another cutlass wound obtained during the battle with the *Serapis*, so that he was "now the bescarred bearer of a cross" (167). Here assuming a Christ-like identity for his lifelong suffering and sacrifice, the inadvertently exiled veteran subsequently returns to his original home in western Massachusetts, where his homecoming is "less a return than a resurrection. At first, none knew him, nor could recall having heard of him" (168), for the last of Israel's family has migrated west more than thirty years previous. Returned home at last, Israel Potter is still a spiritual exile.

Confirming Ecclesiastes' larger message of human ephemerality, Israel Potter is thus unknown in his native region of the Berkshires, and when he goes to find his actual homestead, he sees a man plowing with oxen next to the ruin of an ancient fireplace; when the plow hits an old hearthstone in the ground, Israel discovers that this is the burnt-out ruin of the house where he grew up. Suddenly filled with emotion as he looks at the remains of the fireplace, Israel tells his son, " 'here,' raking with his staff, '*my* father would sit, and here, my mother, and here I, little infant, would totter between, even as now, once again, on the very same spot, but in the unroofed air, I do. The ends meet. Plough away, friend'" (169). The re-creation of Potter's childhood for his son many decades later suggests the closed circuit of history, in accordance with the message of Ecclesiastes: "The thing that hath been, it is that which shall be: and that which is done is that which shall be done, and there is no new thing under the sun" (Eccles. 1:9). In the same vein, the final paragraph of Melville's narrative underlines the pathos and supreme vanity of Israel Potter's life: "He was repulsed in efforts, after a pension, by certain caprices of law. His scars proved his only medals. He dictated a little book, the record of his fortunes. But long ago it faded out of print—himself out of being—his name out of memory. He died the same day that the oldest oak on his native hills was blown down" (169). Unrewarded for his heroic actions because of legal technicalities, Potter's name has disappeared into the void of past human endeavor. As the biblical Preacher remarked, "There is no remembrance of former things" (Eccles. 1:11).[19]

What additional insights does *Israel Potter* offer concerning the historiography of the American Revolution, and what relationship does it bear to the biography of its author? In keeping with a dominant theme of *Israel Potter*, the question of public recognition for common soldiers of the Revolutionary War was in fact a frequent subject for debate in the decades following the war. Sarah J. Purcell has thus detailed the gradual democratization of public memory for the sacrifices of common soldiers in the half-century following the battle of Bunker Hill, eventuating in the public tour of Lafayette in 1824–25 and construction of a Egyptian-style pillared monument beginning in 1825 intended to commemorate not just heroic martyrs like Dr. Joseph Warren, but all the common soldiers who had fought there or given their lives. This was a time when many aged veterans were writing down their experiences of the war for posterity, or for proof of their claims following passage of the 1818 Revolutionary War Pension Act—both being reasons for the historical Israel Potter to have his *Life and Remarkable Adventures* transcribed by the Providence, Rhode Island, writer, editor, and publisher Henry Trumbull in 1824. As Michael Kammen and others have shown, the larger meaning of the Revolution for the new nation was a complex, heavily loaded subject for the many veterans who participated in the fighting, and the citizens who were obligated to honor the fallen and pay tribute to living participants; the subject would continue to inform the nation's politics, culture, literature, and art throughout the nineteenth century. Within this larger tradition, Melville's *Israel Potter* registers a brilliant minority report, showing that the myth of the American Revolution as a providential event, with its chief biblical archetype in the Exodus, was an imaginative fiction; for the experience of a common soldier like Israel Potter more authentically reveals the ragged edges of history, for which only the skepticism and pessimism of the book of Ecclesiastes would provide a more reliable guide.[20]

The theme of unrewarded service to one's country as found in Melville's eighth extended work of fiction was also one that the author would likely have felt very keenly by the mid-1850s when he wrote *Israel Potter*. As the descendent of two Revolutionary heroes on his mother's and father's side—Colonel Peter Gansevoort, the defender of Fort Stanwix in Rome, New York, and Major Thomas Melvill, a participant in the Boston Tea Party and later a long-serving naval officer of the port of Boston—Melville could rightly claim a double Revolutionary descent that should have brought honor to his name. Instead, in the absence of an adequate income from his writing he was facing financial ruin by 1855, with defaults on an unpaid loan and overdue mortgage putting his Pittsfield property in jeopardy. Melville's transposition of the setting of Israel Potter's birth from Cranston, Rhode Island, to Berkshire County, Massachusetts, manifestly demonstrates a personal identification with his protagonist. Moreover, the fact that the historical Potter, as attested by the frontispiece and first sentence of his pamphlet biography, had the same birthday as Melville himself—August 1—would have created an additional bond of sympathy between his unrewarded Revolutionary-era hero and himself.[21]

A final illustration of the correspondence between the fictional Israel Potter and his literary creator, as citizens in a country that failed to remunerate or appreciate their service, is evident in a letter that Melville wrote to his mother on May 5, 1870, when he was working as a deputy inspector in the New York custom house and beginning the composition of *Clarel*. The letter describes his experience of asking a clerk in the lobby of the Gansevoort Hotel, at the corner of Twelfth and West Streets in Manhattan, whether the clerk knew where the name "Gansevoort" came from; whereupon a man sitting reading a newspaper said that it came from a wealthy old family that once lived in the area. As Melville indignantly reported to his mother, "The dense ignorance of this solemn gentleman,—his knowing nothing of the hero of Fort Stanwix, aroused such an indignation in my breast, that, disdaining to enlighten his benighted soul, I left the place without further colloquy. Repairing to the philosophical privacy of the District Office, I then moralized upon the instability of human glory and the evanescence of—many things."[22]

Melville's remark on the "evanescence" of the memory of heroic individuals like his grandfather—whose defense of Fort Stanwix contributed to the subsequent American victory at Saratoga in 1777—is, as we have seen, a major theme of both the book of Ecclesiastes and *Israel Potter*. The skeptical wisdom of Ecclesiastes may also help explain the author's deliberate retreat from the last vestiges of his literary fame in the final decades of his life in New York City, when occasional literary devotees and commentators noted his obscurity; and at his death in September 1891 a *New York Times* obituary notice mistakenly called him "Hiram" Melville. As the biblical Preacher had claimed, "vanity of vanities; all is vanity. What profit hath a man of all his labour which he taketh under the sun?" (Eccles. 1:2–3). Melville would have been repeatedly reminded of such wisdom while seeing his fiction largely forgotten and his last books of poetry self-published in tiny editions, with a novella remaining in manuscript at his death.

Given Melville's incorporation of the Ecclesiastes-inspired theme of vanity into his picaresque narrative on the experience of a common soldier during the American Revolution and its aftermath, it is a remarkable reversal that in a subsequent volume of Civil War poetry published a decade later, he assumed a voice of civic consecration and austere piety in order to chronicle the Union war effort and ensure lasting fame for the heroic dead. For if in *Israel Potter* Melville conveyed a message of Old Testament skepticism while critiquing the patriotic legacy of the American founding and lamenting the unrecognized sacrifices of common soldiers, in *Battle-Pieces* Melville assumed the openly patriotic voice of a noncombatant citizen-poet in order to chronicle the Northern war effort. And if, as we have seen in the first chapter of this study, Melville's private attitude to Christianity reached a nadir in the later 1850s, with the onset of war in the early 1860s and his decision to abandon fiction for poetry, Melville recognized the importance of imparting civic immortality to the dead through the use of both Christian and classical motifs in *Battle-Pieces*. It is to this volume of Civil War poetry that we now turn.[23]

CHAPTER 6

Memorializing the Dead in *Battle-Pieces*

Christian and Classical Motifs

Within the history of America's wars, the Civil War dwarfed all previous records of mortality. Compared with roughly 25,000 soldiers' deaths in the Revolutionary War, the 15,000 deaths in the War of 1812, and the 13,283 deaths in the Mexican War, the staggering sum of mortality in the Civil War, at approximately 655,000—with 214,938 deaths in combat and the rest from disease and noncombat events—constitutes a statistical enormity with massive repercussions. As a conflict occurring within a modern industrialized nation of over thirty-one million (almost four million of them slaves), with a total of three million doing military service, the Civil War launched armies that were rendered more lethal by dramatic advances in weaponry, while the logistical feats needed to send two massive armies into the field were made possible by new networks of transportation, communication, and procurement supported by newly organized government bureaucracies. The combatants began the struggle hoping for a brief and decisive war but were soon faced with a rapidly expanding scale and intensity of fighting. As a result, the sentimentalized view of death and the afterlife that characterized the evangelical culture of antebellum America was given a severe test by the ruthless slaughter of the Civil War battlefield. Indeed, as Mark M. Schantz argues, "Americans came to fight the Civil War in the midst of a wider cultural world that sent them messages about death that made it easier to kill and be killed."[1]

As a poetic historian of the Civil War, Herman Melville composed his *Battle-Pieces and Aspects of the War* (1866) to commemorate the Union struggle and ultimate victory while also highlighting the war's unfolding as a national tragedy involving an unprecedented degree of death and destruction; appropriately enough, the volume is "dedicated to the memory of the Three Hundred Thousand who, in the war for the maintenance of the Union, fell devotedly under the flag of their fathers." Once a long-neglected part of Melville's oeuvre, his Civil War poetry, with its varied forms, techniques, attitudes, and implications, has begun to be appreciated by an increasing number of critics.[2] In addition to his poetic evocations of important battles in a variety of theaters, events on the home front, and other "aspects" of the war, the poems in *Battle-Pieces* assume the task of memorializing the dead either in the person of important officers or of common soldiers. In keeping with the innovative and experimental approach he took to his new vocation of poet, the memorial poems in *Battle-Pieces* run a gamut of elegies, requiems, epitaphs, dirges, and other recognized poetic or liturgical forms of mourning and commemoration, the most commonly used being the pastoral elegy, in which nature offers consolatory compensation for the poet's grief. Among the poems of *Battle-Pieces*, Melville varied his techniques of memorialization while situating them within a blend of Christian and classical traditions.[3]

Melville had produced fictional works in the 1850s reflecting his persistent religious skepticism, but when he turned to writing his Civil War poetry he willingly embraced the role of public poet espousing a forensic Christianity, a stance the author shared with Abraham Lincoln, who as president similarly embraced and articulated the nation's dominant Christian faith despite his own previous religious doubts. Melville thus celebrated the spiritual immortality attained by some Northern heroes of the war in explicitly Christian terms, even if he was not personally committed to such doctrines. As in his previous writings, he also relied on biblical allusions to provide a larger context for his descriptions of events when commemorating the deaths of soldiers whose self-sacrifice was translated into divinely sanctified acts. Such religious references confirm that the moral and spiritual support provided by Christian institutions and beliefs was an essential part of the war effort in both the North and South.[4]

Along with his use of Christian motifs, Melville also evoked the pathos of the war dead in terms that recall the funerary poetry of classical Greek tradition in which only a nebulous afterlife was available, as opposed to the more important idea of the immortality of the hero's fame, or *kleos*, as exemplified by Homer's *Iliad*. A number of poems in Melville's *Battle-Pieces* thus grow out of the nation's classical heritage of Greece and Rome, which had been essential to its founding and had been widely inculcated in schools and colleges during the antebellum era, with a correspondingly broad impact on literature, politics, theater, art, architecture, and other cultural forms. Such standard classical authors as Homer, Plutarch, Caesar, Cicero, Virgil, Horace, and Ovid were a common literary possession for many better-educated soldiers going to war from both North and South. While drawing on the tradition of the classical pastoral elegy created by Theocritus and later adapted by Renaissance and Romantic-era English poets, Melville in his *Battle-Pieces* also showed his awareness of such notable poets as Simonides among the contributors to the sepulchral epitaphs of the collection of classical verse known as the *Greek Anthology*, as in the Greek poet's famous quatrain commemorating the Spartan dead at the battle of Plataea in 479 BCE: "These men having clothed their dear country in inextinguishable glory, donned the dark cloud of death; and having died, yet they are not dead, for their valour's renown brings them up from the house of Hades."[5]

This chapter's examination of poems from *Battle-Pieces* memorializing the dead will analyze the form, technique, and historical context of the poems while discussing Melville's use of both Christian and classical motifs drawn from the two major traditions that informed the nation's larger cultural identity. Melville claimed to have written—or perhaps completed—the poems in *Battle-Pieces* in the immediate aftermath of Lee's surrender; the collection is accordingly noteworthy for its lack of vengeful rhetoric toward the Confederacy, and the same is true for the poems specifically designed to memorialize the fallen, which in a few cases include Confederate as well as Union soldiers, thereby helping to defuse sectional antagonism. In addition, in his prose supplement Melville claimed that he wrote the poems as a series of spontaneous lyric meditations on the war, in keeping with the Romantic metaphor of the Aeolian harp that he mentions in his preface; but his poems also relied on historical cues from the multivolume journalistic compilation on the war contained in *The Rebellion Record*. In general,

Melville embraced a patriotic Northern sentiment toward his subject, largely viewed through the Protestant Christian lens with which the public interpreted the war, yet with borrowings from classical antiquity. Among the seventy-two poems in *Battle-Pieces*, Melville designated a set of nineteen poems at the end as "Verses Inscriptive and Memorial," sixteen of which merit the term "Inscriptive" for their brevity, while the last three—"The Scout toward Aldie," "Lee in the Capitol," and "A Meditation"—are of more substantial length and could be designated "Memorial" for their commemoration of representative events both during and after the war. The discussion below will include poems from *Battle-Pieces* devoted to the solemn task of memorializing the named, as well as the nameless, dead in a variety of forms in order to help bring healing to the nation at the conclusion to the war.

"The Portent"

As the elegiac introductory poem of *Battle-Pieces*, "The Portent" illustrates the common belief that the hanging of John Brown in Charles Town, Virginia (now West Virginia), on Friday, December 2, 1859, was a cosmic sign, or "meteor," of the impending arrival of the Civil War. The two-stanza, fourteen-line poem renders this popular idea both haunting and profound through its terse allusive descriptions and cosmological associations. The poem focuses on the momentous scene of Brown's execution at 11:15 a.m. on a scaffold in a field surrounded by fifteen hundred Virginia militia stationed to secure order and prevent any attempt to free the prisoner. Following his trial in late October and conviction on November 2, Brown spent a month in jail in Charles Town, where he received correspondence from a wide variety of admirers and detractors and wrote about his religious mission to end slavery in letters that often appeared in the Northern press; these communications helped assure his future fame as an abolitionist martyr, especially following his final written statement given to one of his guards on the morning of his execution, phrased in the manner of a last will and testament: "I John Brown am now quite *certain* that the crimes of this *guilty, land: will* never be purged away; but with Blood. I had *as* I now *think: vainly* flattered myself that without *verry much* bloodshed; it might be done." Brown's words were ultimately inspired by the assertion in the New Testament Letter to the Hebrews that "without shedding of blood is no remission" of sin (Heb. 9:22), a key biblical text in the abolitionist's violent prophetic vocation.[6]

The accuracy of Brown's prediction thus becomes part of his "weird" (i.e., uncanny) aura in Melville's poem:

> *Hanging from the beam,*
>   *Slowly swaying (such the law),*
> *Gaunt the shadow on your green,*
>   *Shenandoah!*
> *The cut is on the crown*
>   *(Lo, John Brown),*
> *And the stabs shall heal no more.*
>
> *Hidden in the cap*
>   *Is the anguish none can draw;*
> *So your future veils its face,*
>   *Shenandoah!*
> *But the streaming beard is shown*
>   *(Weird John Brown),*
> *The meteor of the war.*

In the first stanza, the speaker evokes the image of Brown's swaying body as it hangs from its support beam, casting both a literal and a figurative shadow on the tranquil and fertile "green" of the Shenandoah Valley, which will soon be turned into a contested and ravaged landscape throughout the war. The harsh alliteration of the first and last word in the third line ("*Gaunt the shadow on your green*") reinforces the destructive force of the dead man's "shadow," implying the impending realities of violence and war. In keeping with the imagery of green in Melville's poem, one journalist at the scene of execution noted, in spite of the late fall season, the striking beauty of "the Blue Ridge bathed in soft purple haze, and the green, undulating wheat fields on the opposite horizon."[7]

After setting the historical scene in "The Portent," the poet then refers to the wounds to the head that Brown had received on October 18 from First Lieutenant Israel Green of the Marines when soldiers stormed the Harpers Ferry engine house where Brown and his remaining men had taken their last stand: "*The cut is on the crown / (Lo, John Brown), / And the stabs shall heal no more*" (ll. 5–7). On a literal level, the "stabs" that Brown has received won't heal after his death, but the description of Brown hanging from the "beam" implicitly evokes an image of the Crucifixion, with the wounds to Brown's body recalling the Jesus who had been mocked with a "crown" of thorns and a reed scepter as Roman soldiers "spit upon him, and took the reed, and smote him on the head" (Matt. 27:30). While such hatred was duplicated in the many pro-slavery spectators at Brown's hanging (including John Wilkes Booth), his own overriding sense of martyrdom to the antislavery cause and execution on a Friday would facilitate comparison to the Crucifixion of Christ. In "The Portent," Melville's parenthetical citation of Brown's name—the first actual identification of the hanged man—is prefaced with the biblical "lo," meaning "look" or "see," as though the poet is citing Pontius Pilate's famous remark to the hostile Jerusalem crowd, "Behold the man" (John 19:5). The stanza's final assertion that "The stabs shall heal no more" postulates a metonymy implying that the injuries to Brown's body are injuries to the American body politic, and that the execution of Brown is an event beyond which the mutual antagonism of North and South would lead to an irrepressible conflict; indeed, the transformation of Brown's body into a Northern rallying cry would soon be evident in the marching song named after him, based on a Methodist hymn.[8]

In the second stanza of "The Portent," the poet points to the invisible suffering face of the executed man in his hood of execution—the actual physical suffering caused by the agonizing constriction of the windpipe and blood vessels to the head, and the larger generalized suffering of the coming war in the nation at large: "*Hidden in the cap / Is the anguish none can draw; / So the future veils its face, / Shenandoah!*" (ll. 8–11). The hanged man's expression of physical and psychological pain hidden by the hood here hints at the medieval legend of the "veil" of Veronica with which this Christian saint allegedly wiped the blood and sweat off Christ's face as he made his way down the Via Dolorosa, memorialized by Catholics as the Sixth Station of the Cross. The veil—a staple of medieval, Renaissance, and Baroque art—allegedly captured an image or impression of Christ's anguished features while going to the Crucifixion. Like the hidden face of Brown, which is ostensibly inaccessible to artistic representation, the impending war in America will create an unspeakable anguish comparable to Christ's.[9]

In the last three lines of the stanza and poem, the speaker compares the ample beard escaping from the hood as a prophetic cosmological sign of discord: "*But the streaming beard is shown / (Weird John Brown), / The meteor of the war*" (ll. 12–14). Like the word "comet," which was ultimately derived from a Greek word for "wearing long hair," the image of the "meteor" here ascribes prophetic cosmological significance to the streaming white beard of the aged-looking abolitionist. The use of the word "weird" to describe Brown—suggestive of the witches of *Macbeth* and implying the power to control fate, chance, or destiny—conveys the uncanny and fateful significance of the abolitionist's seemingly mad attempt to free the slaves, and the widespread political repercussions of his death, thereby coupling a non-Christian supernatural identity with the implied Christian association of Brown in the previous stanza. Moreover, as William Spengemann first noted, Melville's image of Brown's beard streaming out from under his hood likely draws on the description of the subject of Thomas Gray's influential poem "The Bard" (1757), which depicted the confrontation between the last surviving Welsh bard and Edward I (1239-1307), with his conquering armies; in the poem, the bard rehearses in prophetic accents the misfortunes of the Plantagenet line, to be followed by a more accomplished Welsh-descended line of Tudor rulers. Gray thus writes of the old poet previous to his death leap into the river below:

> On a rock, whose haughty brow
> Frowns o'er old Conway's foaming flood,
> Robed in the sable garb of woe,
> With haggard eyes the poet stood;
> (Loose his beard, and hoary hair
> Streamed, like a meteor, to the troubled air).
> And with a master's hand, and prophet's fire
> Struck the deep sorrows of his lyre.
>
> (ll. 15–22)

Like Melville's figure of John Brown, Gray's bard, with his streaming hair and beard, is a symbol of prophetic resistance to tyranny—in Brown's case, the institution of slavery and its seeming death-grip on the nation's political, social, and economic life.[10]

In its use of Christian imagery, Melville's depiction of the significance of Brown's death in "The Portent" is comparable to many other Northern writers' estimates of the controversial abolitionist's righteous cause and martyrdom. Among transcendentalists, Thoreau began the response with his address, "A Plea for Captain John Brown," delivered in Concord on October 30 during Brown's trial but before his conviction on November 2 and anticipating his capital punishment: "Some eighteen hundred years ago Christ was crucified; this morning, perchance, Captain Brown was hung. These are the two ends of a chain which is not without its links. He is not Old Brown any longer; he is an angel of light." So, too, in a November 8 lecture on "Courage," Emerson famously (or infamously) called Brown a "new saint, waiting yet his martyrdom; and who, if he shall suffer, will make the gallows glorious like the Cross." In a sermon to his New York church delivered on the day of Brown's execution, the black abolitionist Henry Highland Garnet addressed the old abolitionist in absentia: "Go up to meet the army of departed heroes that have gone before thee to the Kingdom of Heaven. Go, and with joy receive thy martyr's crown, which the Lord has prepared for thee." And in a January 1860 poem titled "With a Rose That Bloomed on the Day of John Brown's Martyrdom," Louisa May Alcott similarly claimed that "the gallows only proved to him / A stepping-stone to heaven."[11]

As we have seen in the second stanza of his poem, Melville invokes the martyrdom of Brown in connection with classical and Christian traditions of comets, meteors, and other unusual cosmological events as portents of historical change. The tradition was notably evident in Roman history with the uncanny disturbances of the earth and heavens reported in connection with the assassination of Caesar in 44 BCE, as mentioned in Virgil's *Georgics*. So, too, in the New Testament, the birth of Christ was heralded by the star of Bethlehem (Matt. 2:2, 9–10), while the Crucifixion caused the sun to go into eclipse and the earth to shake (Matt. 27:45, 51). Innumerable cosmological disturbances were subsequently reported throughout Western history as signs of God's judgment, in keeping with the cosmic imagery of the book of Revelation and other biblical texts—a tradition reflected in Shakespeare's plays, as in the violent cosmological events following the murder of King Duncan in *Macbeth*. Seventeenth- and eighteenth-century Puritan historians such as Increase and Cotton Mather recorded a number of irregularities of the stars, moon, meteors, and comets in connection with perceived civic crisis and moral decline or admonition. As Sarah J. Schechner has remarked of the development of modern cosmology, "widespread endorsement of the new, periodic theory of comets had not mitigated the perception of comets as agents of upheaval or renewal, nor indeed as tools God might use to punish the wicked or save the elect."[12]

Significantly, many Americans at the time of John Brown's raid, arrest, and execution were aware of an unusual number of meteor showers that autumn and connected these to Brown's actions. Thus, in a sermon of October 30 to his Brooklyn church, Henry Ward Beecher praised Brown's virtue and heroism while asserting, in an anticipation of the cosmological symbolism of Melville's poem, "A burning fragment struck the earth near Harper's Ferry. If the fragment of an exploding aerolite had fallen down out of the air, while the meteor swept on, it would not have been more sudden or less apparently either with a cause or an effect!" So, too, in a July 4, 1860, address titled "The Last Days of John Brown," written for delivery (by another speaker) at Brown's family home in North Elba, New York, Thoreau began, "John Brown's career for the last six weeks of his life was meteor-like, flashing through the darkness in which we live. I know of nothing so miraculous in our history." In his poem "Year of Meteors (1859–1860)" published in May 1865 in the collection *Drum-Taps*, Walt Whitman associated the ominous state of the nation following Brown's execution with the unusual cosmological disturbances of the year of the presidential election, noting "the strange huge meteor procession dazzling and clear shooting over our heads, / (A moment, a moment long it sail'd its balls of unearthly light over our heads, / Then departed, dropt in the night, and was gone)." The signs of unusual astronomical activity seen in the wake of John Brown's execution ranged from the impressive meteor showers of mid-December 1859 to the remarkable meteor procession of July 20, 1860, depicted in a painting by Frederic Church as *The Meteor of 1860*.[13]

As the first poem of Melville's *Battle-Pieces*, "The Portent" integrated two widely popular beliefs in regarding John Brown as a martyred Christ figure and seeing a cosmically portentous significance of his death. Compared with the hagiographic references to Brown by Emerson and Thoreau in their speeches, Melville's poetic representation of Brown's implicit religious identity was understated and indirect, as his Christological imagery focuses on the untold "anguish" of the abolitionist's hidden face, which serves as a figure for the country's anguish in the coming war. By the same token, Melville's identification of Brown as the "meteor" heralding Southern secession and war elevates his role to cosmological proportions while conveying the fateful impact of his historic execution.

"Lyon"

In "Lyon," Melville memorialized the fearless courage of General Nathaniel Lyon (1819–1861), the Northern commander killed at the battle of Wilson's Creek, near Springfield, Missouri, on August 10, 1861, in an initially successful engagement leading to a tactical defeat for the Union army. As the first Union general killed in the Civil War, Connecticut-born Nathaniel Lyon became one of the North's first recognized war heroes for his dedicated and resourceful efforts, with the backing of antislavery German American troops, to keep Missouri in the Union at the start of national hostilities. A West Point graduate, Seminole and Mexican War veteran, and officer in frontier service first in California and then "Bleeding Kansas," Lyon had become a staunch Unionist and Republican before taking command of a unit of United States infantry in Saint Louis in March 1861, followed by appointment to the federal arsenal there. Lyon thereupon successfully maneuvered to keep the weapons in the arsenal out of the hands of the secession-inclined governor Claiborne F. Jackson, who sought to ally the state militia with the Confederacy and fled Saint Louis in June with the secessionist elements of the state government, first to Boonesville and then farther southwest to join forces with Confederate general Benjamin McCulloch. A native Texan, McCulloch had been appointed a colonel in the Confederate army in the spring of 1861 and began assembling an Army of the West in Indian Territory in Arkansas, having made alliances with the Cherokee, Choctaw, and Creek nations. By July the newly appointed brigadier general Nathaniel Lyon had taken over command of all Union troops in the Department of the West before the position was superseded by John C. Frémont in late July 1861. In an attempt to thwart the secessionist Missouri State Guard under the command of former governor Sterling Price, Lyon moved his six thousand troops to Springfield to meet an enemy composed of poorly trained and badly equipped militia soldiers allied with a regionally mixed Confederate army from neighboring Arkansas. In the ensuing battle of Wilson's Creek, fought in the blistering summer heat, Lyon had his horse shot out from under him and was shot in the calf and then grazed in the head. Commandeering an orderly's horse, Lyon led a charge of the Second Kansas Infantry and was killed on "Bloody Hill" by a bullet through the heart by midmorning of the battle. Because of his inflexible commitment to the Union, firm sense of duty, and fanatical hatred of slavery, Lyon had preemptively forced an officially Unionist but militarily neutral Missouri into the national conflict using actions that ironically helped precipitate the ruthless guerrilla war that afflicted the state during the Civil War and after.[14]

In "Lyon," Melville presents an idealized account of Lyon's last hours at the battle of Wilson's Creek and in doing so stays true to the hagiographic image of Lyon as an early martyr for the North who sacrificed himself to keep Missouri in the Union. So Melville writes in "Lyon" that although outmatched by almost four to one, or twenty thousand Confederates to some five or six thousand Federals (the proportion of troops was actually closer to two to one), the Union general insists on engaging with a mixed foe of "Texans and Indians" (l. 46), in reality a blend of soldiers from the Missouri State Guard and Confederate regiments from Texas, Louisiana, and Arkansas, with a few Cherokee volunteers from nearby Indian Territory. Although the general foresees his certain death, he "willed the fight" (l. 62) and in his death joins prophets and angelic armies on Mount Zion. The general is thus depicted as a holy warrior, but his sanctified status stems not from victory in the Union cause but from his willingness to do battle despite the overwhelming odds against him, and to die as a martyr for his country. The rhymed trochee of the final couplet of each stanza accordingly creates a solemn incantatory effect in the sacred repetition of his name.

Commentators have generally criticized both the form and content of "Lyon," with Stanton Garner calling it "the least fortunate poem of *Battle-Pieces*" and Tony McGowan attempting to find an oppositional subtext in Melville's poem that would interpret Lyon's self-sacrifice as suicide and a symptom of an alleged devaluation of heroic officers in the collection as a whole.[15] Such critics have weakened their case by failing to account for the meaning of the poem in the context of early Civil War history and by misreading the punning emphasis on the dead general's name (Lyon/lion) by implying that he is being commemorated solely as an embodiment of courage. In his annotated edition of *Battle-Pieces*, Hennig Cohen suggests that Melville is highlighting Lyon's resolute "heart" by making him another Richard the Lion-Hearted. There is no doubt that Nathaniel Lyon was a brave Union officer whose name seemed perfectly suited to his combative character and whose actions in the spring and summer of 1861 appeared to save the Union by keeping Missouri from joining the Confederacy; for as a fellow officer noted in a magazine article twenty years after the Civil War,

> There was no middle ground with him in any matter that engaged his attention, and he conceived that it was his duty to enforce his doctrines or ideas upon all with whom he came in contact, even to the point of being offensive. At the same time, he was possessed of as tender a heart as ever beat in a man's breast. . . . He had in him an indomitable spirit that was always awake, a fixity of purpose that never faltered, and a courage that was never for an instant met by the slightest feeling of fear. He did not know what fear was.

Lyon was also subject to a full-length commemorative biography by another officer immediately after the end of the war, who noted, "He believed in the ultimate triumph of Good. . . . The government on whose side he was arrayed was the work of the good men of all the ages. It had grown out of the blood of martyrs and the fires of persecution, hastened by the mistakes of statesmen, and the might of peoples. He called this union 'the Ark of the Covenant.' "[16]

A key to interpreting Melville's "Lyon" is to realize that the recurrent stress on Lyon's name in the last line of each stanza implicitly identifies the Union general not just as a courageous officer, or military "lion," but also as a type of the "Lion of Judah," a symbolic savior figure appearing in the Bible. Thus, in the climactic blessing given to the twelve sons of the dying Jacob at the end of Genesis, the fourth son, Judah—head of the tribe to which both David and Christ will later belong—is called a "young Lion" when blessed (Gen. 49:9), and the title "lion of Judah" was thereafter associated with this dominant Hebrew tribe, which gave its name to the pre-exilic land of Israel formed around David's new capital of Jerusalem. The title was subsequently given to Christ in the book of Revelation when one of the elders says to John regarding the book in the right hand of God the Father, "Weep not: behold, the Lion of the tribe of Juda, the Root of David, hath prevailed to open the book, and to loose the seven seals thereof" (Rev. 5:5). Viewed from this typological perspective, the "Lyon" of Melville's poem becomes both a heroic warrior for the Judah-like North and a Christlike martyr who foresees his own death and still goes into battle, ascending in spirit to be received by the holy prophets and angelic armies of Zion, the sacred mountain of Jerusalem. It is retrospectively ironic that Lyon considered himself a religious skeptic, but this private opinion was overlooked in the patriotic commemorations of his death.[17]

The historical Nathaniel Lyon may have been an abrasive, emotionally unbalanced personality and fanatical disciplinarian whose occasionally ruthless actions as an officer often provoked controversy, as his modern biographer depicts him; but Melville's poetic presentation is based on the uniformly positive public perception of this early fallen hero of the Union. For as Alice Fahs remarks, "Within Northern popular literary culture, an elaborate martyrology grew up around the early wartime deaths of a small group of officers in the summer and fall of 1861. Newspaper poems, patriotic envelopes, engravings, illustrations in weekly newspapers, and elaborate memorial volumes all celebrated officers' wartime deaths as redemptive sacrifices in the nation's cause." Following Lyon's death, for example, the casket bearing his body was ceremonially honored during its trip from Saint Louis to Hartford,

Connecticut, and it lay in state for three days in City Hall in New York. In addition, a corps of the Twenty-Fourth Missouri Volunteer Infantry, dubbed the "Lyon Legion," was created bearing a regimental flag with a lion positioned below a constellation of six stars, and the deceased general was given an official resolution of thanks by Congress on December 24, 1861.[18]

As noted above, the image of Nathaniel Lyon in Melville's poem freely blends fact and fiction. In keeping with the hagiographic celebration of General Lyon's single-minded devotion to duty, he is introduced by the poem's speaker as one having a heart "of deeper sort, / Prophetic, sad, / Which yet for cause are trebly clad" (ll. 1–3). Following a widely reported legend of the era, the general, a lifelong bachelor, is depicted as making his country the beneficiary of his will: "By candlelight he wrote the will, / And left his all / To Her for whom 'twas not enough to fall" (ll. 16–18). Early Northern newspaper accounts of Lyon's death reported that the general had made the Union the beneficiary of his substantial estate of $30,000, when in fact he died intestate; the mistaken report nevertheless became a fixture in his legacy. Moreover, just as Lyon had told a fellow officer of his "presentiment" that he would die in the coming battle, Melville's poetic portrait of the general presents him as engaged in a deliberately sought act of self-sacrifice for the Union on the morning of the battle: "Day broke, but trooping clouds made gloom of it: / 'A field to die on,' / Presaged in his unfaltering heart, brave Lyon" (ll. 23–25). In "Lyon," Melville also invents a symbolic stellar name, "Orion," for the general's horse—perhaps suggested by the constellation of stars on the Lyon Legion regimental flag—and he creates a Corporal "Tryon" as the soldier calling out for an officer to lead a broken Iowa regiment back into battle.[19]

In Melville's elegy, the Union general's beloved black horse, "Star-browed Orion" (l.29), is shot out from under him, but he still bravely fights on despite the wounds to his head and leg:

"General, you're hurt—this sleet of balls!"
    He seemed half spent;
With moody and bloody brow, he lowly bent:
    "The field to die on,
But not—not yet; the day is long," breathed Lyon.

For a time becharmed there fell a lull
    In the heart of the fight;
The tree-tops nod, the slain sleep light;

Warm noon-winds sigh on,
And thoughts which he never spake had Lyon.

Texans and Indians trim for a charge:
    "Stand ready, men!
Let them come close, right up; and then
    After the lead, the iron;
Fire and charge back!" So strength returned to Lyon.

The Iowa men who held the van,
    Half drilled, were new
To battle: "Some one lead us, then we'll do,"
    Said Corporal Tryon:
"Men! *I* will lead," and a light glared in Lyon.

On they came: they yelped, and fired,
    His spirit sped;
We levelled right in, and the half-breeds fled,
    Nor stayed the iron,
Nor captured the crimson corse of Lyon.

This seer foresaw his solider-doom,
    Yet willed the fight.
He never turned; his only flight
    Was up to Zion,
Where prophets now and armies greet pale Lyon.

                                    (ll. 36–65)

At the battle of Wilson's Creek, Lyon's aides attempted to keep Lyon from exposing himself to rifle fire after he was wounded, but he replied, "I am but doing my duty"—a fixed determination reflected in the poetic portrait presented above. Of the regular breaks in fighting, as noted in one of the stanzas above, owing to the intense heat and exhaustion of the soldiers, Lyon's modern biographer observes: "Lulls settled periodically over the battlefield, marred only by desultory firing, as if both armies needed to catch their breath and take water before resuming the desperate struggle. Then the great crash of musketry and the thunder of cannon fire would resume almost spontaneously, to continue with wavelike intensity until another respite mysteriously occurred." Melville's use of personification in the images of the trees, the dead, and the winds adds to the eerie sense of quiescence in the midst of battle. Lyon's alleged remarks to the troops partly correspond to the general's documented last instructions to his newly trained troops before battle: "Don't shoot until you get orders. Fire low—don't aim higher than their knees; wait until they get close; don't get scared; it's no part of a soldier's duty to get scared." Lyon met his end when, as reported in the poem, soldiers in the broken ranks of the First Iowa called for someone to lead them back into battle, and Lyon decided to mount a borrowed horse and lead the assault; but he was mortally wounded as he attempted to rally his troops while shouting, "Come on, my brave boys, I will lead you! Forward!" Apart from ambiguously noting that "his spirit sped," the description of Lyon's death is omitted in the poem, as the reverential speaker—to be differentiated from Melville himself—instead denigrates the enemy as cowardly frontier "half-breeds" who are kept from seizing the general's dead body.[20]

Even though the Union ultimately lost the battle of Wilson's Creek, with heavy casualties on both sides, Lyon is nevertheless represented in Melville's poem as a Union "lion of Judah" who merits immortal ascent to "Zion," a prime dwelling place of God in the Old Testament, as repeatedly mentioned in the Psalms, Isaiah, Jeremiah, and the minor prophets. In Psalm 2, for example, God declares, "Yet have I set my king upon my holy hill of Zion" (l. 6), and in Psalm 48, the psalmist remarks, "Great is the Lord and greatly to be praised in the city of our God, in the mountain of his holiness. Beautiful for situation, the joy of the whole earth, is mount Zion" (ll. 1–2). In the book of Revelation, Zion is again the location of the host of the blessed: "And I looked, and lo, a Lamb stood on the mount Sion, and with him an hundred forty and four thousand, having his Father's name written on their foreheads" (Rev. 14:1). Situated between "The March into Virginia" and "Ball's Bluff," both of which depict the pathos of naïve young Union soldiers experiencing sudden death in stinging defeats, "Lyon" glorifies the bravery and self-sacrifice of an older commander whose name associates him with a biblical typology of courage and national redemption.

"Ball's Bluff"

In "Ball's Bluff: A Reverie," the poet creates an elegy mourning the loss of freshly recruited Federal soldiers in the self-inflicted disaster at Ball's Bluff outside Leesburg, Virginia, on October 21, 1861, thirty-five miles west of Washington, DC. As another reminder of the senseless slaughter that marred the early Union war effort, the Union forces at Ball's Bluff, under the command of Brigadier General Charles Pomeroy Stone, suffered an ignominious defeat in which the recently resigned senator Colonel Edward Dickinson Baker of Oregon, a close friend of Lincoln's, was killed, and the early Union war effort suffered another demoralizing setback. During this battle, Confederates broke the Union line and chased the Federals down the bluffs and into the Potomac River, where boats were swamped and soldiers drowned or were shot in the water, some of their bodies floating all the way downriver to the Union capital.[21]

In Melville's poem on the battle, the speaker, living in an unnamed Northern town, focuses on the experience of seeing a troop of young Federal soldiers on parade, and then hearing a few weeks later about the Union defeat in which many have been killed or wounded. Melville himself was still living on his Pittsfield farm in the fall of 1861 but would move into a rented house in the town in November 1862 before permanently moving to New York City a year later. The three-stanza poem offers a stark contrast in the image of the enthusiastic daytime send-off of the soldiers in the town, as compared with the poet's later melancholy musings when thinking about the terrible loss of young lives. The poet's depiction of the departure of the enthusiastic Federal troops in the flower of their youth, soon followed by their unexpected deaths in a botched military operation, has a likely biblical proof text in the book of Job: "Man that is born of a woman is of few days, and full of trouble, He cometh forth like a flower, and is cut down: he fleeth also as a shadow, and continueth not" (Job 14:1–2). The speaker's consciousness of such biblical wisdom underlies the basic structural contrast between the speaker's depiction of the town's celebratory send-off of youthful soldiers and their ultimately shadowy fate by the Potomac, echoed in the dying footfalls heard by the speaker at the end of the poem.[22]

The speaker begins by noting his observation out his window of a parade of Union troops being cheered by the citizens of the town:

> One noonday, at my window in the town,
>   I saw a sight—saddest that eyes can see—
>   Young soldiers marching lustily
>   Unto the wars
>
>   (ll. 1–4)

While the soldiers march with "fifes" playing and "flags in mottoed pageantry," all the "ladies" from within their traditional domestic realms of "porches, walks, and doors" are "cheering royally" (ll. 5, 7).

The speaker thus sets up a dramatic contrast between his own feeling of melancholy in watching the soldiers, in view of their coming ordeal and possible death, juxtaposed with the naively enthusiastic women sending them off. Continuing the description of the marching young soldiers, the speaker notes the youthful vigor and innocence of the soldiers who move "like Juny morning" and whose hearts are "fresh as clover in its prime" (ll. 8, 9); however, their youth is paradoxically an impediment to their anticipating the possible death that awaits them in the South: "Life throbbed so strong, / How should they dream that Death in a rosy clime / Would come to thin their shining throng?" (ll. 1–13). Suggesting an image of celestial beings in their "shining throng," the poet affirms a common theme in the psychology of adolescence: "Youth feels immortal, like the gods sublime" (l. 14).

In the third stanza, the speaker is now aware of the disastrous battle named in the title; for some weeks after the scene described in the first two stanzas, he goes to his window one night, unable to sleep, and muses "on those brave boys (Ah War! thy theft); / Some marching feet / Found pause at last by cliffs Potomac cleft" (ll. 17–19). Here the poet is aware that some of the earlier marchers were finally halted on the bluffs outside Leesburg, the "pause" in their marching acting as an understatement for death and disaster. We only hear now of the poet's wakefulness as he muses, "while in the street / Far footfalls died away till none were left" (ll. 20–21). The end of Melville's poem thus deliberately heightens the pathos of the youthful soldiers' deaths by noting the contrast between the earlier sounds of their marching on parade and the gradual silence of unidentified "footfalls" on the street below, thereby blending, in reverie, the sound of the soldiers and an anonymous pedestrian on the nighttime street. The tragic loss of young men depresses the poet, as the terrible contrast between their celebrated departure and wasteful death confirms what the poet of the book of Job had written of humanity's fleeting existence.

"Shiloh"

One of the best-known poems of *Battle-Pieces*, "Shiloh (A Requiem) (April, 1862)" commemorates the historic battle taking place on April 6 and 7, 1862, around a small Methodist church in southwestern Tennessee between the Army of the Tennessee of General Ulysses Grant and the Confederate Army of the Mississippi led by General Albert Sidney Johnston. Facing an unexpected Confederate attack in their position just west of the Tennessee River, the Union army retreated on the first day of battle, but reinforced by reserve divisions as well as those provided by a newly arrived General Don Carlos Buell, a strengthened Union force pushed the Confederates back beyond its former position in a decisive but costly Union victory. As the bloodiest battle of the war up to that point, with over thirteen thousand Union and ten thousand Confederate casualties, the conflict became notorious for the masses of the dead and the suffering of the wounded, which was increased by a fierce thunderstorm late in the evening of the first day. Historian James M. McPherson has noted of the battle, "Soldiers on both sides passed a miserable night. Rain began falling and soon came down in torrents on the 95,000 living and 2,000 dead men scattered over twelve square miles from Pittsburgh Landing back to Shiloh church. Ten thousand of the living were wounded, many of them lying in agony amid the downpour." The Union soldier Daniel McCook's description of the battlefield provides a graphic account of its horrors: "The disordered hair, dripping from the night's rain, the distorted and passion-marked faces, the stony, glaring eyes, the blue lips, the glistening teeth, the shriveled and contracted hands, the wild agony of pain and passion in the attitudes of the dead—all the horrid circumstances with which death surrounds the brave when torn from life in the whirlwind of battle, were seen as we marched over the field."[23]

Labeled as a "requiem," or musical service for the repose of the dead, Melville's "Shiloh" borrows elements of the pastoral elegy to commemorate both the Union and Confederate dead on a battlefield ironically centered on a church in the Tennessee backwoods. Indeed, the word "Shiloh," meaning "rest" in Hebrew, was used as an alternative term for the Messiah (Gen. 49:10) and later applied to Christ; Shiloh was also the geographical site of the Hebrew tabernacle (Josh. 18:1) where God revealed himself to Samuel to make the latter a prophet and priest. For the sixth-century BCE prophet Jeremiah, however, Shiloh had become a cursed place because of the wickedness of the Israelites (Jer. 7:12; 26:6). As the prophet spoke in the voice of an outraged Yahweh after the fall of Jerusalem to the Babylonians, "But go ye now unto my place which was in Shiloh, where I set my name at the first, and see what I did to it for the wickedness of my people Israel" (Jer. 7:12). Melville's poem "Shiloh" accordingly draws on this mixed Old Testament significance of Shiloh as both the site of a sacred temple and a later place of wickedness and desolation.

In the poet's initial description of the aftermath of battle in "Shiloh," the flight of the swallows over the battlefield conveys an image of pastoral peace:

> Skimming lightly, wheeling still,
>   The swallows fly low
> Over the field in clouded days,
>   The forest-field of Shiloh—"
>   (ll. 1–4)

The alliterative second and fourth lines, with their final rhyming trochee, also exhibit a chiasmic reversal. In the ensuing lines of the poem, we learn how the battle had created a myriad of desperately suffering wounded soldiers:

> Over the field where April rain
> Solaced the parched ones stretched in pain
> Through the pause of night
> That followed the Sunday fight
>   Around the church of Shiloh—
>   (ll. 5–9)

The fact that the battle of Shiloh began on a Sunday and took place around a church provides a key to the subsequent description of the wounded soldiers from both Union and Confederate armies moaning in pain and saying prayers as they die of their wounds:

> The church so lone, the log-built one,
> That echoed to many a parting groan
>   And natural prayer
> Of dying foemen mingled there—
> Foemen at morn, but friends at even—
>   Fame or country least their care:
>   (ll. 10–15)

If the irony of a church being at the center of a historically bloody battlefield hints at a critique of the ineffectuality of Christianity in the midst of the slaughter of war, the church nevertheless serves as a focus for the desperate prayers of the dying, who have found reconciliation with their foes in their shared suffering. With the brutal parenthetical exclamation "(What like a bullet can undeceive!)" (l. 16), the poet implies that the lethal wounds of the soldiers expose them to the ultimate truth of their shared mortality. The dead soldiers now "lie low" (l. 17) while the swallows skim over their bodies, "And all is hushed at Shiloh" (l. 18). The ostensible meaning of "lie low" is to avoid detection or conflict, but here it also means to be permanently cut down on the field of battle. The emphasis on the silence of the battlefield after the horrors of battle is in keeping with the pastoral imagery of the skimming swallows, whose presence commemorates only the peace of death.

As a haunting liturgical "requiem," Melville's "Shiloh" laments the masses of dead of both Union and Confederate armies and grieves for the suffering of the wounded. Although set in close proximity to a church, the poem hints at no formal spiritual redemption other than reconciliation of the dying with their former enemies, a Christian virtue (Matt. 5:20–25), while above them the swallows innocently fly, indifferent to the carnage on the battlefield, the rapidity of their flight contrasting with the unmoving dead. Nature's ultimate indifference to human suffering—despite the swallows' providing a kind of natural benediction—could also imply that the God of Christianity is remote from this scene, notwithstanding the rustic church at its center and its being named after a place where the Old Testament god established his tabernacle. As in the prophet Jeremiah, the battlefield at Shiloh is in any case now a place of physical and spiritual desolation. The poet's use of the musical term "requiem" in his title accordingly suggests that "Shiloh" is designed to assist the repose of the dead after their unspeakable suffering.[24]

"A Dirge for McPherson"

Among Melville's memorials for the dead, "A Dirge for McPherson: Killed in Front of Atlanta (July, 1864)" is noteworthy in its blending of Christian and classical motifs. Taking the form of a funeral dirge, or a slow and somber song of lament, Melville's "Dirge" commemorates the death of the celebrated Union officer who commanded the Army of the Tennessee under Sherman during the assault on Atlanta and was killed on July 22, 1864, the second-highest-ranking Union officer to die in the war. Having graduated first in his class in 1853 from West Point, where his classmates included Philip Sheridan and his Confederate opponent in Atlanta, John Bell Hood, James B. McPherson worked as a military engineer in the late 1850s before joining the Union army as a captain in the Corps of Engineers, working his way up the chain of command under Grant and Sherman in the western theater of war. Widely known as a model officer, McPherson was fatally shot a month before the fall of Atlanta when Confederates executed a flanking movement on part of the Union army and encountered McPherson riding back to rejoin his troops after conferring with Sherman, who thought the Confederates were retreating from Atlanta. McPherson's death was lamented by his commanding officer at Atlanta as well as by his former classmate and current opponent, John Bell Hood, who recognized McPherson's humane treatment of Southern civilians during the siege of Vicksburg.

In the "Dirge for McPherson," the poet begins by re-creating the funeral procession for the fallen officer, with all the formal trappings of the occasion:

> Arms reversed and banners craped—
>   Muffled drums;
> Snowy horses sable-draped—
>   McPherson comes.
>
> (ll. 1-4)

In the second stanza, the fallen general's sword is described as lying on the "pall" covering his casket, producing an alliterative "gleam in gloom" (ll. 7, 8); the image is used to confirm the paradoxical idea that "a bright name lighteth all / McPherson's doom" (ll. 9-10). The poet then assumes the imperative mood in the third stanza by ordering the procession to carry the body into a chapel where a "priest in stole" will "Pace before the warrior / Who led. Bell—toll!" (ll. 12, 13-14). In the ensuing stanza, the bearers are instructed to put down his casket in the nave of the church, and the funeral service's "Lesson" is read: "Man is noble, man is brave / But man's—a weed" (ll. 17-18). The final metaphor here evokes comparable metaphors of human ephemerality in the "Order for the Burial of the Dead" in *The Book of Common Prayer* used by the Episcopal Church, including the book of Job's claim that man "cometh forth like a flower, and is cut down" (Job 14:1), as well as Psalm 90: "In the morning it [the grass] flourisheth, and groweth up: in the evening it is cut down, and withereth" (l. 6). In stanza five, the poet again instructs the bearers to take up the casket and "wend / Graveward, nor weep: / There's a trumpet that shall rend / This Soldier's sleep" (ll. 19-22). Again in keeping with traditional Christian eschatological belief, the poet tells the dead general's bearers not to weep because, as a sanctified soul, he will participate in the resurrection of the body at the Last Judgment, when the sound of a trumpet will initiate the process of heavenly ascension from the grave (1 Cor. 15:52; 1 Thess.

4:16). The final stanza of the poem instructs the bearers to lower the casket into the grave, followed by ceremonial prayer and rifle salute to commemorate "McPherson's end" (l. 26).

"A Dirge for McPherson" represents a traditional Christian funerary ceremony and procession, except for the striking presence of two italicized couplets after the first and last stanzas. The first of these ("*But, tell us, shall we known him more, / Lost-Mountain and lone Kennesaw?*" [ll. 5–6]) interpolates the apparent voices of nature issuing from two mountain locations where McPherson fought before the Atlanta campaign, thereby invoking a feature of the traditional pastoral elegy showing the participation of nature in the poet's grief. Then at the end of the poem, another italicized assertion compares McPherson to a hero of the *Iliad*: "*True fame is his, for life is o'er— / Sarpedon of the mighty war*" (ll. 27–28). A leading warrior on the side of the ancient Trojans, Sarpedon was a king of Lycia and the son of Zeus and Laodamia, daughter of Bellerophon. After playing a key role in the defense of Troy, he was killed by Patroclus in book 16 of the *Iliad* after the latter entered the war bearing the armor of his close associate Achilles. By comparing the deceased Union general to the fallen Trojan hero Sarpedon, Melville is introducing a Homeric element to his ostensibly Christian funerary poem, creating a blend of ritualized Christian pomp with the assertion of Homeric fame for the poem's fallen general.

"On the Slain Collegians"

"On the Slain Collegians" is a pastoral elegy on the deaths of the myriad youth from both the North and South whose sacrifice is seen as rooted in the temper, ideals, and incentives that characterize this privileged group. In keeping with the subjects' status as college educated, the poem laments their loss with a series of classical allusions and an emphasis on the fate that drove them to their deaths on the battlefield. As in the poems of A. E. Housman lamenting the loss of the flower of young Englishmen in World War I, the pathos of the cultivated young men's deaths stirs the speaker's grief in Melville's poem. "On the Slain Collegians" thus serves as an illustration of the well-known classical proverb that those whom the gods love die young.

In the first stanza the poet describes the various elements motivating the young to fight in wars, including the incentives created by "woman," "duty," or the appeal of a fundamental "truth"; but in the end, the key motivation is found in the passionate temperament of the young: "Who can aloof remain / That shares youth's ardor, uncooled by the snow / Of wisdom or sordid gain?" (ll. 9–10). In the second stanza, the poet cites "the liberal arts and nurture sweet" (l. 11) as the key factors that "give his gentleness to man" (l. 12), providing honor and grace, and lending "sunniness to his face" (ll. 17–18). Thus, troops of "generous boys in happiness thus bred– / Saturnians through life's Tempe led, / Went from the North and came from the South" (ll. 20-22). The young men are thus imagined as living in a legendary golden age of the elderly Roman god Saturn—a time of peace and plenty—as they are led through the fabled valley of Tempe in northern Thessaly frequented by Apollo and the muses. Yet for all their "golden mottoes in the mouth" (l. 23) from their reading of classical authors like Plutarch, Caesar, and Cicero, the youths still meet on the battlefields and "lie down midway on a bloody bed" (l. 24), causing "woe" for the families of both North and South. The roughly alliterative metaphor of the youths' lying down to sleep on a "bloody bed" thus comes as a brutal shock following the previous aura of classical beauty and culture associated with their privileged status.

In the third stanza, the poet laments all the youth from North and South "who felt life's spring in prime" and were driven to war, or "swept by the wind of their place and time– / All lavish hearts, on whichever side, / Of birth urbane or courage high" (ll. 27-30). Such youth are temperamentally inclined to take on heroic tasks like that mythologically represented by the archer and sun god Apollo's slaying of the dragon-like Python in a primordial act of civilized good over anarchic evil: "Apollo-like in pride, / Each would slay his Python—caught / The maxims in his temple taught–" (ll. 33-35). In keeping with the classical motifs that pervade the poem, these youths have learned "maxims" in their "temples," referring to the collegial halls of academia where they studied. Each is "Aflame with sympathies whose blaze / Perforce enwrapped him" (ll. 36-37). In an echo of Lincoln's reference in his second inaugural address to the belief in their own righteousness shared by both the North and the South, the poet notes,

> Each went forth with blessings given
> By priests and mothers in the name of Heaven;
>   And honor in all was chief.
> Warred one for Right, and one for Wrong?
> So put it; but they both were young—
>
> (ll. 42–46)

Minimizing the contentious issues of slavery and states' rights, the poet asserts the shared motivation of these soldiers to fight based on the martial ardor of their adolescence and their engaged social communities. More important here than the antithetical ideology of the two sides is the shared pathos arising from their early deaths.

In the last stanza, the poet turns to the "anguish of maternal hearts" who must find some "balm divine" (ll. 49–50) in rationalizing the tragedy of the loss of their beloved young men. First is the assurance that the young men fought without disgracing themselves in their military roles, followed by the belief that fate had assigned them those roles: "well the striplings bore their fated parts / (The heavens all parts assign)—" (ll. 51–52). Moreover, in their premature deaths the soldiers were spared the ceaseless cares of adulthood. In keeping with the common belief of young people that they are immortal, the poet asserts that these soldiers had no knowledge of death before themselves expiring: "Nor dreamed what death was—thought it mere / Sliding into some vernal sphere" (ll. 55–56). Like a child on a slide, these youth imagined death as providing access to a perpetually green and spring-like postmortem paradise. Using an organic metaphor of human life as a plant that blossoms and then dies, as found in the biblical passages from Job and Psalms quoted above, the poet notes the consolatory idea that these dying youth avoided the "grief" of age and thus were "Like plants that flower ere comes the leaf— / Which storms lay low in kindly doom, / And kill them in their flush of bloom" (ll. 58–60). An oxymoronic "kindly doom" thus spares these youth possible future misfortune and suffering.

"On the Slain Collegians," then, evokes the deaths of youthful Union and Confederate soldiers using a classical frame of reference implicitly informed by the familiar adage that those whom the gods love die young. With no mention of Christian themes, the speaker instead provides a pathos-laden portrait of classically trained youth going to fight an idealized battle in which they are ineluctably driven to engage, and where they will sacrifice the flower of their youth. Imagining themselves going into battle like young Apollos, they will be killed by the destructive Python of war. The only redeeming feature of their deaths is that they will be spared the many inevitable griefs that come with a long life—a tenet of classical wisdom found throughout the ancient Greek playwrights.

"Inscription: For the Graves at Pea Ridge, Arkansas"

In the epitaphic "Inscription: For the Graves at Pea Ridge, Arkansas," Melville memorialized the Union dead from a battle occurring on March 7–8, 1862, in a small town in northwestern Arkansas. The battle's strategic importance came from the fact that it established Union control of most of the key border state of Missouri as well as northern Arkansas.[25] Melville's poem commemorating the Union dead in this battle relies on the conceit of the dead addressing the living, a poetic technique characteristic of many sepulchral epitaphs of the *Greek Anthology*. In the poem, the posthumous spirit of an imagined Union soldier tells the reader that no one should imagine these men "died amiss / When here we strove in furious fight" (ll. 1–2). Such a death was "Better than tranquil plight, / Tame surrender of the Cause / Hallowed by hearts and by the laws" (ll. 4–6). The men who died on this battlefield in fact "warred for Man and Right" (l. 7). With this repeated use of abstract nouns, the speaker emphasizes the superior righteousness of the Union war effort, which was backed by a higher "Cause" of "laws" (the Constitution), "Man" (human equality), and "Right" (superior moral justification). For these dead soldiers, the "choice of warring never laid with us" (l. 8) because their decision to fight directly resulted from "the traitor's choice" (l. 9) of secession. The ideas here suggest the influence of Simonides's famous epitaphic couplet to the fallen Spartan soldiers at the battle of Thermopylae in 480 BCE: "Stranger, bear this message to the Spartans, that we lie here obedient to their laws." These soldiers in Melville's poem were likewise precipitated into action without any verbal equivocations ("to trim and poise" [l. 10]) but instead "marched, and fell—victorious!" (l. 11). As in Saint Paul's famous assertion that for Christians "death is swallowed up in victory" (1 Cor. 15:54), the soldiers' violent deaths were paradoxically "victorious," not only on an individual spiritual level but also because of the ultimate Union victory and the fact that it was decisive in establishing Union control of a key border state so that Federal soldiers would not need to be transferred there from other theaters of war.[26]

"Inscription: For Marye's Heights, Fredericksburg"

In his "Inscription: For Marye's Heights, Fredericksburg" Melville dedicates another epitaphic poem to the graves of Union soldiers of the

Army of the Potomac who came under withering fire in the battle of Fredericksburg on December 13, 1862, after crossing the Rappahannock River from the north, trying to gain control of a hillside next to the Confederate-held town in a series of fourteen misdirected and futile charges. With massive deployments of both Union and Confederate soldiers totaling two hundred thousand in and around Fredericksburg, Union forces under the command of Joseph Hooker blundered into a trap as they repeatedly sought to advance up Marye's Heights but were cut down by rifle and artillery fire from impregnable elevated positions commanded by General James Longstreet, a disaster leading to some six to eight thousand Union casualties; it took two days to bury all the Union dead who fell in front of the stone wall on the Heights.[27]

In Melville's poem the deaths of these Union soldiers is sanctified by an aura of martyrdom that characterized their devotion to the civil religion of the Union cause:

> To them who crossed the flood
> And climbed the hill, with eyes
>   Upon the heavenly flag intent,
>   And through the deathful tumult went
> Even unto death: to them this Stone—
> Erect, where they were overthrown—
>   Of more than victory the monument.

For the Union soldiers here, their flag is "heavenly" in both a literal and a figurative sense, for they would be looking up the hill as their regimental flag bearers led their assault; yet they would also be "intent" upon following orders to climb the hill by virtue of their commitment to their nation's cause. To honor their sacrifice, the poet points to a single upright "Stone" that stands where the soldiers were "overthrown" and acts as a monument of their heroic sacrifice. The poet's claim that the stone represents "more than victory" in their actions again evokes Saint Paul's famous lines on death's lack of victory over the posthumous human soul; Melville's poem thus implies that these dead soldiers attain a spiritual victory through their selfless willingness to die for their country. The single erect stone, standing like the stele or cenotaph that commemorated the dead in the classical world, represents the immortal human spirit of selfless dedication associated with these dead soldiers.[28]

"An Uninscribed Monument: On One of the Battle-Fields of the Wilderness"

As another cenotaphic memorial, "An Uninscribed Monument" commemorates soldiers killed in the battle of the Wilderness taking place on May 5-7, 1864, that pitted Ulysses S. Grant against Robert E. Lee in a ferocious contest of forces fighting in the brush and forest around Spotsylvania, Virginia, resulting in 17,500 Union casualties at the beginning of Grant's war of attrition to vanquish the Confederacy.[29] Melville's poem memorializing the mass casualties on this battlefield represents the paradoxical image of a vocally animated gravestone or marker, a motif frequently found in the *Greek Anthology*. At the same time, "An Uninscribed Monument" functions as a literary cenotaph, or a verbal (and physical) monument standing in for an unspecified group of fallen soldiers. The speaker is imagined to be the "Uninscribed Monument" that informs the reader of the paradoxical "Silence" and "Solitude" that can only begin to suggest, by contrast, the "din which here befell" (ll. 1, 4). The proof of this previous roar of battle can be found in the "iron cones and spheres of death / Set round me in their rust" (ll. 6-7). Such rusty relics of spent shells and cannonballs will in fact also testify to the violence of the previous battle "with more than animated breath" (l. 9). By means of this personification of artillery shells, the speaker implies that the spent shells that created much of the thunderous noise of the battle, with their whistling trajectory and explosive impact, are eager to share their impressions of the noise of battle. The observer of the scene is then enjoined to contemplate the "import of the quiet here— / The after-quiet—the calm full fraught" (ll. 12-13). The meaning of this absolute stillness is in its strong contrast with the shocking roar of battle and its inevitable sequel of mass death. The observer (or reader) is thus invited to stand silently in front of the blank monument to appreciate the silence of the end of battle, which is "lonesome as the land" (l. 15) that has been devastated by mass carnage.

"An Uninscribed Monument" accordingly employs the paradoxical idea of an uncommunicative but still vocal monument that can't fully convey the message of silence that characterizes the desolate and abandoned battlefield with its visual evidence of death and debris. As such, the poem relies on the rhetorical figure of *adynaton*, or the so-called inexpressibility topos, in which an object or idea is claimed to be inexpressible in words, or compared to something that can't be fully articulated or measured. Melville's poem begins with such a rhetorical figure: "Silence and Solitude may hint /. . . / What I, though tabled, may never tell— / The din which here befell." The roaring destructive fury of the three-day battle can thus only be understood by its opposite of silence, although the evidence of rusting ordnance shells can partially communicate this fact through visual suggestion. The speaker's initial invocation of "Solitude" and his reference to the "lonesome" land in which the monument stands confirm the aura of desolation that characterizes this legendary battlefield, with its name suggestive of the deadly biblical Wilderness in which the Israelites wandered for forty years in the Exodus.[30]

"On the Grave of a Young Cavalry Officer Killed in the Valley of Virginia"

The elegiac epitaph "On the Grave of a Young Cavalry Officer Killed in the Valley of Virginia" mourns the gifted youthful life and noble death of an otherwise unidentified Union cavalry officer killed in the Shenandoah Valley. The unnamed officer was in fact Colonel Charles Russell Lowell (1835–1864), with whom Melville had spent several days in Northern Virginia in April 1864, beginning with a night at Lowell's camp in Vienna and then joining a three-day expedition to the west in search of the Confederate guerrilla fighter John Mosby, an experience Melville would dramatize in "The Scout toward Aldie," the longest poem in *Battle-Pieces*. Having an extended opportunity to become familiar with Lowell, Melville was doubtless impressed with this exemplary officer as a still youthful Harvard-educated kindred spirit who loved classical literature, especially Plato, and was familiar with Hawthorne and other Boston-area writers. Lowell had enlisted as a captain of cavalry in the Union army in June 1861 and served for two years on the staff of George McClellan during the Peninsular campaign and Antietam. Becoming a brigade commander of the Second Massachusetts Cavalry that he himself had organized in 1863, Lowell helped protect the outer defenses of Washington in the winter of 1863–64 before being ordered to lead the campaign against John Mosby in Northern Virginia, during which time he married Josephine (Effie) Shaw, sister of Robert Gould Shaw, the officer who died leading his black Union troops in an assault on Battery Wagner in Charleston, South Carolina, in July 1863.[31]

After defending the Union capital against a surprise Confederate attack by Jubal Early in July 1864, Lowell went to assist Philip Sheridan to secure the Shenandoah Valley against the Confederates. It was here that Lowell was mortally wounded on October 19, 1864, during the Union victory at Cedar Creek and died the next day in nearby Middletown, Virginia. Following Lowell's death, Sheridan called his slain officer "the perfection of a man and a soldier," while the Massachusetts state adjutant general, William Schouler, similarly noted, "Colonel Lowell was my *beau ideal* of an officer and a gentleman." Only twenty-nine at his death, Lowell was promoted to the rank of brigadier general the day of his mortal wounding, and the promotion was officially awarded posthumously. His funeral in Cambridge, Massachusetts, where Lowell had grown up as scion of a patrician family, was the occasion for an unprecedented turnout of leading families and literary figures to mourn one of their most distinguished sacrifices to the Union war effort. He was buried in Cambridge's Mount Auburn Cemetery.[32]

Melville's poem on Lowell's death is notable for its simplicity and compression, with the fallen officer transformed into an ancient Greek hero fallen in battle. The poet thus presents a salient paradox by claiming that the dead soldier's abundant gifts of beauty, youth, cultivation, friendship, wealth, and education were all inferior in value to the low earthen mound that now holds his dead body:

> Beauty and youth, with manners sweet, and friends—
>   Gold, yet a mind not unenriched had he
> Whom here low violets veil from eyes.
>   But all these gifts transcended be:
> His happier fortune in this mound you see.

As an epitaphic commemoration of the cavalry officer's death, the poem is strikingly devoid of any consolatory message of Christian redemption; indeed, it is noticeably classical in its insistence on the transcendent value of a noble death and in the simplicity and pathos of its message to the reader ("you"), who is assumed to be viewing the grave. The poet's insistence on the dead officer's "happier fortune" implicitly evokes the classical mythology of Fortune, which was deified in both Greek and Roman culture as *Tuche* and *Fortuna*, respectively. The invocation of "fortune" in connection with Lowell's life and death was particularly apt, as he had studied classics at Harvard, graduating in 1854 as valedictorian and showing himself to be an eager student of ancient and modern letters like his uncle, the poet and critic James Russell Lowell. Starting a career in business by managing an iron mill in Trenton, New Jersey, Lowell traveled in Europe from 1856 to 1858 to regain his health, which was threatened by a tubercular condition of the lungs. During his second visit to Italy in the winter of 1857–58, Lowell befriended Nathaniel and Sophia Hawthorne in Rome, where he visited art galleries and was particularly struck by a painting of *The Three Fates* in the Pitti Palace, considered at the time to be by Michelangelo (but now assumed to be the work of Francesco Salviati), and also found a favorite image of the goddess Fortuna, whom he called "the lady of the wheel." Lowell's modern biographer and descendant Carol Bundy describes the young man's embrace of classical culture:

> Lowell's letters home are full of classical allusions. Almost every one of his letters referred to his "luck" and "good fortune." He told his mother, "I shall trust as usual to the Gods." In a later letter he explained that "the Gods will hold me responsible and I am too superstitious to provide the avenging Goddess." His classical studies, his love of Plato, his fondness for epithets that alluded to that philosopher, and the prominence of Greek myth in his Commencement Day oration indicate an allegiance to the ancient world. But what might have simply been an affectation in a student became a more deeply held devotion during his months in Europe. He wrote of trusting to the gods, of how the gods "send you such chances," of "the gifts of Gods," of having "a great deal to thank the Gods for," of how "the wheel must turn sometime," of thanking "Fortune for playing me an ill turn now and then," of being "frightened when my spoke point too long at the zenith."[33]

Seen in the light of Lowell's fondness for the classical idea of fortune and the goddess Fortuna with her wheel, Melville's allusion to the "happy fortune" of the unnamed cavalry officer's death reflected the poet's apparent knowledge of the young officer's devotion to classical culture, as well as being a conscious strategy to emphasize the ancient Greek notion of a heroic death creating immortal fame (*kleos*) in the minds of the living. The modesty of the hero's grave site is reminiscent of numerous examples of poetic epitaphs in the *Greek Anthology*, in which the deceased are praised for the virtues that redeem them from the grave. While there is an obvious disparity between the simple mound of earth covering the fallen cavalry officer in Melville's poem and Lowell's elaborate funeral, burial, and grave site in Mount Auburn Cemetery, the poem deliberately fictionalizes the officer's humble last resting place in a manner consonant with the ancient Greek and Homeric cultural norms to which Lowell gave his allegiance.[34]

"A Requiem: For Soldiers Lost in Ocean Transports"

In "A Requiem: For Soldiers Lost in Ocean Transports," Melville again invokes the musical and liturgical tradition of the requiem while commemorating the deaths of the innumerable soldiers who drowned when their transport vessels were sunk by Confederate attack or bad weather off the North American coast. As a modified form of pastoral elegy, the poem uses the metaphor of a storm in relation to nature to illustrate the pathos of the men lost at sea, in contrast to the birds and fish that exult in the arrival of fair weather. The poem thus begins by describing how the various terrestrial and oceanic creatures emerge after a storm on land or sea, expressing their joy at being restored to their natural habitat without harm. So, the "robins blithe their orchard-sports renew; / And meadow-larks, no more withdrawn, / Caroling fly in the languid blue" (ll. 3–5). So, too, after a storm at sea, "Every finny hider wakes— / From vaults profound swims up with glittering scales; / Through the delightsome sea he sails" (ll. 11–13). The main subject of the poem only emerges two-thirds of the way through when the speaker mentions the example of the drowned sailors who will not be there to rejoice in a sunny morning following a storm; thus all creatures will rejoice,

> Save them forever from joyance torn,
>   Whose bark was lost where now the dolphins play;
> Save them that by the fabled shore,
>   Down the pale stream are washed away,
> Far to the reef of bones are borne;
>   And never revisits them the light,
> Nor sight of long-sought land and pilot more;
>   Nor heed they now the lone bird's flight
> Round the lone spar where mid-sea surges pour.
>   (ll. 18–26)

The repeated phrase "save them" is implicitly ironic in that these are not in fact saved but drowned men who cannot participate in the joyous celebration of life found in nonhuman nature. The idea of Christian salvation is raised in the imagery of the dolphin here, for dolphins were often depicted as a means of rescue, as in the myth of Arion, or acted as transporter of the dead in both classical and Christian cultures. Images of dolphins wrapped around anchors thus served as symbols of Christian redemption on the model of Christ and the cross. In Melville's poem, however, the dolphins do not seem to have any explicit salvific function but merely enjoy their own instinctive life. Instead, the drowned bodies of the lost soldiers are shown relentlessly sinking to the bottom of the sea, where lack of light prevents them from seeing the "long-sought land" or any "pilot more" (l. 24). The use of the word "pilot" here likely refers to both the navigator who guided the ship as well as the heavenly "pilot" (Christ) who is thus absent from their underwater burial ground. The last two lines of the poem highlight the pathos of these soldiers' deaths, for the description of the "lone bird's flight" (l. 25) circling the "lone spar where mid-sea surges pour" (l. 26) highlights the scene of shipwreck where they lost their lives. Melville's poem potentially ironizes the consolatory function of nature in traditional pastoral elegy for soldiers whose bones have no commemorative marker but rest at the bottom of the sea.[35]

A comparison with Milton's *Lycidas*, his pastoral elegy to his drowned Cambridge friend Edward King, immediately reveals the lack of any comparable redemptive message in Melville's poem except for the pathos communicated by nature's restoration following the storm. For as Milton wrote of King,

> Weep no more, woeful shepherds, weep no more,
> For Lycidas your sorrow is not dead,
> Sunk though he be beneath the wat'ry floor;
> So sinks the day-star in the ocean bed,
> And yet anon repairs his drooping head,
> And tricks his beams, and with new-spangled ore,
> Flames in the forehead of the morning sky:
> So Lycidas sunk low, but mounted high,
> Through the dear might of him that walked the waves,
> (ll. 165–73)

Milton's "day-star," a version of the biblical "light-bringer" (Isa. 14:12; 2 Pet. 1:9), is the planet Venus, but it is also a symbol of Christ, who rose from the dead like the drowned Lycidas, unlike the anonymous drowned soldiers in Melville's poem. Melville's "Requiem: For Soldiers Lost in Ocean Transports" thus figures the potential failure of pastoral elegy or formal requiem to redeem these soldiers from their lonely physical dissolution at sea.[36]

"The Martyr"

In "The Martyr: Indicative of the Passion of the People on the 15th of April, 1865," Melville took on the challenge of commemorating the shocking death of Abraham Lincoln early on the morning of April 15 after being shot by John Wilkes Booth at Ford's Theatre on Good Friday, April 14, 1865, only five days after the surrender of Robert E. Lee at Appomattox the previous Sunday. "The Martyr" largely conveys the immediate public reaction to Lincoln's death, combining grief at Lincoln's sudden demise shortly after Northern victory and rage at the insidious malice of the South, which was widely assumed to be responsible for the president's murder, employing the well-known actor John Wilkes Booth as assassin. As the historian Thomas Reed Turner writes, "The nation seemed to experience a feeling of betrayal. It was as if the prodigal son had been about to be welcomed home with celebration and the killing of the fatted calf, when suddenly it was discovered that the prodigal son not only was not penitent but had suddenly seized a dagger and plunged it into his father's back. Many people felt, with apparent justification, that the assassination might revive the dying Confederacy."[37]

The hagiographic figure of Lincoln in "The Martyr" thus subsumes the conspicuous parallels with the Passion and Crucifixion of Christ, and the beginnings of the national myth of Lincoln as the redeemer president whose words and actions form a central pillar of the nation's civil religion. The first stanza of the poem foregrounds the comparison with Christ while assuming an accusatory tone emphasizing the disparity between Lincoln's final stance of clemency toward the seceding states in early 1865, memorialized in his magnanimous claim of "malice toward none" and "charity for all" in his second inaugural address on March 4, and the malignity of those responsible for a murder that will only harden the will of the Northern victor:

> Good Friday was the day
>   Of the prodigy and crime,
> When they killed him in his pity,
>   When they killed him in his prime
> Of clemency and calm—
>   When with yearning he was filled
>   To redeem the evil-willed,
> And, though conqueror, be kind;
>   But they killed him in his kindness,

> In their madness and their blindness,
> And they killed him from behind.
>
> (ll. 1–11)

The stanza thus emphasizes the senseless cruelty and cowardice behind Lincoln's murder, here amplified by the hard "k" sound, or voiceless velar stop, evident in the repetition of the word "killed," balanced by the more benignant sounds of "clemency," "calm," and "though conqueror, be kind," all associated with the dead president. As Martha Hodes notes in a study of the popular reaction to the assassination, *"With malice toward none* and *with charity for all* were the words that mourners frequently chose to inscribe onto their signs and banners in the wake of Lincoln's death." By the same token, the word "prodigy" in the second line of "The Martyr" does not mean something exciting wonder but rather draws on older meanings of the word conveying the idea of monstrosity and prophetic significance. So, too, the poet's reference to a collective "they" as being responsible for the assassination, rather than John Wilkes Booth alone, matches the sentiments of the time. Thus according to Hodes, "A vitriol of stunning intensity runs through the record of personal responses to Lincoln's assassination. . . . Wartime is a powerful catalyst to acceptable anger, requiring as it does the demonization of the enemy. If surrender had softened those feelings among the victors, Lincoln's assassination recalled them, then multiplied the demonization a hundredfold." In like manner, in a study of the reaction of the Northern clergy to the killing of the president, David B. Chesebrough writes, "The great majority placed the blame upon the leaders of the South, the elite of the South, the slaveholders of the South, or the South as a whole as being the motivator and instigator of Lincoln's murder."[38]

While the speaker in Melville's poem draws on the general parallel of Lincoln's assassination with the martyrdom of Christ, his indignation at the president's murder plays up the evil-mindedness of his collective killers, just as the story of the Passion found in the four gospels plays up the malice of the Jewish crowds and Roman authorities who expressed their hatred for the crucified Messiah, in contrast to the sorrowing and forgiving Christ on the cross who remarked, according to Luke, "Father, forgive them; for they know not what they do" (Luke 23:34). The killers of Lincoln could only be overcome with "madness" and "blindness" to act against the larger interests of the South in the immediate aftermath of the war, and indeed John Wilkes Booth was often assumed to be touched with mental illness as well as a blind hatred of Lincoln as an alleged tyrant. The refrain to the first stanza turns from the senselessness of the death of the beneficent Lincoln to the collective grief of the Northern people ("There is a sobbing of the strong, / And a pall upon the land" [ll. 12–13]), whose mourning will inevitably lead to a more punitive attitude toward the defeated South: "Beware the people weeping / When they bare the iron hand" (ll. 16–17).

The second stanza begins and ends with allusions to Lincoln's blood, first emphasizing the pitiful scene of his death from a pistol wound to the back of the head, and then ultimately associating the president's blood with the ineffaceable guilt of his killer:

> He lieth in his blood—
> The father in his face;
> They have killed him, the Forgiver—
> The Avenger takes his place,
> The Avenger wisely stern,
> Who in righteousness shall do
> What the heavens call him to,
> And the parricides remand;
> For they killed him in his kindness,
> In their madness and their blindness,
> And his blood is on their hand.
>
> (ll. 18–28)

Although both Christ and Lincoln may have expressed forgiveness for their enemies, the poet echoes the feeling of the Northern peoples in their call for retribution, moving from the ethic of Christ the Forgiver (as in Luke 23:34) to Christ the apocalyptic Avenger, as Saint Paul had postulated: "That no man go beyond and defraud his brother in any matter: because that the Lord is the avenger of all such" (1 Thess. 4:6). Thus, despite the poem's apparent opposition to the nonviolent ethos of the Sermon on the Mount, in his call for retribution the poet draws on the idea of Christ as an "Avenger" of injury. Moreover, in his insistence that the conspirators had killed a father figure in Lincoln, who was popularly known, especially to the freed slaves, as "Father Abraham," the poet associates the crime of "parricide" with the murder of the president and implicitly endorses an Old Testament call for vengeance against the killers of the fallen patriarch. Finally, the "blood" on the "hand" of Lincoln's killers, and the South in general, suggests the end of the trial of Jesus, when Pilate washed his hands of the blood of "this just person," to which the crowd responded, "His blood be on us, and on our children" (Matt. 27:24–25).[39]

Historically speaking, the "Avenger" in Melville's poem would necessarily be an allusion to the figure of Andrew Johnson; but Johnson's notoriously cooperative behavior in his reintegration of the Southern secessionists in the year following Lincoln's death made him manifestly unfit for this role; but the specific dating of the poem as reflecting the mood of April 15, 1865, precludes any need to consider Johnson's impending performance in reestablishing the Union.[40] Indeed, Melville's historical note to his line anticipating an "Avenger" expresses evident relief that the South was not punished for Booth's assassination, for "the expectations built hereon (if, indeed, ever soberly entertained), happily for the country, have not been verified." By the same token, Melville is now glad that "the feeling which would have held the entire South chargeable with the crime of one exceptional assassin, this too has died away with the natural excitement of the hour." The depiction of the assassination of Lincoln in "The Martyr," with its accusation of collective guilt for Booth's act, was thus a representation of the universal Northern anguish and rage immediately following the murder of the president. The repetition of the refrain after the second stanza accordingly ends the poem with an ominous promise of retribution against the South as a whole—a policy that would in fact guide the Radical Republicans in the coming years based on the South's continuing injustice to its former slaves.

The accuracy of the depiction of the national mood following the assassination of Lincoln found in "The Martyr" is confirmed when comparing it with historical accounts of this period. Thomas Reed Turner's study of the aftermath of the assassination, *Beware the People Weeping*, in fact borrows a line from Melville's poem in its title. Moreover, in a study of over three hundred sermons by Protestant ministers delivered during the weeks following the assassination, David B. Chesebrough has extrapolated five common themes: first, intense grief for the death of the president; second, praise for the president's saintlike character of honesty, gentleness, homely wit, and profound wisdom; third, blame for the assassination on the South rather than on John Wilkes Booth; fourth, an angry call for retribution against the secessionists rather than forgiveness and reconciliation; and fifth, a larger view of Lincoln's death as a mysteriously providential event. Significantly, nearly all these same themes can be found in Melville's poem, from the near-universal comparison of Lincoln with Christ to the sense of anger and retribution toward the South. As Chesebrough notes, "To read the vast majority of sermons from Northern pulpits in those few weeks following the assassination of Abraham Lincoln is to become aware of how angry, bitter, and vengeful the passions were that gripped the North. Though the preachers were only reflecting the sentiments of the general populace, they legitimated and exasperated those sentiments by anointing them with divine approval."[41]

How were Melville's *Battle-Pieces*, including his memorializing verses to the dead, received by the newly reunited nation in 1866? In a largely negative review in the *Atlantic Monthly* for February 1867, William Dean Howells found reason to criticize Melville's volume of Civil War poetry chiefly for its seeming remoteness from recent events both on and off the battlefield, for it "not only reminds you of no poetry you have read, but of no life you have known." Seeing no tangible signs of the great national tragedy in Melville's verse, Howells asks, "Is it possible—you ask yourself, after running all over these celebrative, inscriptive, and memorial verses—that there has really been a great war, with battles fought by men and bewailed by women? Or is it only that Mr. Melville's inner consciousness has been perturbed, and filled with the phantasms of enlistments, marches, fights in the air, parenthetic bulletin-boards, and tortured humanity shedding, not words and blood, but words alone?" Howells's pointed remarks criticizing the apparent bloodlessness of Melville's war poetry reveal that the reviewer is unable to appreciate a style of war poetry that favored a more philosophical and meditative tone, and that avoided the patriotic sloganeering and sentimental pathos characterizing much of the popular Northern poetic output during the war. In his review, Howells similarly states of the author, "He treats events as realistically as one can to whom they seem to have presented themselves as dreams; but at last they remain vagaries, and are none the more substantial because they have a modern speech and motion." The poems in *Battle-Pieces* are thus insubstantial "vagaries," not solid, down-to-earth depictions of the war.[42]

The ironies of Howells's remarks on *Battle-Pieces* bear closer examination. First, it is particularly presumptuous for a man who spent the four years of the Civil War as the American consul in Venice—a reward for writing Lincoln's campaign biography—to be criticizing another author for the apparent detachment of his writing from the scenes of battle, especially an author who kept abreast of war news, interviewed officers, toured Union encampments, and even went on a scouting expedition against the Confederate guerrilla John Mosby during a visit to Northern Virginia in April 1864. Indeed, we may doubt whether Howells himself had the depth of personal experience of the war to do justice to Melville's poetry, which quickly disappeared from public attention thanks to negative reviews like his. Moreover, if Howells's remarks on Melville's Civil War poetry inadvertently reveal the literary and philosophical depth of Melville's *Battle-Pieces*, we can still question the accuracy of Howells's judgment of the poems' remoteness from the theater of war. For the most cursory perusal will reveal that the poems we have examined in *Battle-Pieces*, including those commemorating the deaths of civilian and military leaders as well as common soldiers, were carefully grounded in the historical unfolding of the war and accurately reflected a representative Northern attitude toward the conflict. Contrary to Howells's misguided evaluation, Melville well merits his current status as a leading poetic voice of the Civil War.

Whether offering harsh dismissals, mixed estimates, or faint praise, the roster of contemporary reviews of *Battle-Pieces* in fact illustrates the incapacity of American newspaper and magazine reviewers to appreciate Melville's poetic techniques. Among these perfunctory or extended appraisals, only the anonymous writer for the *Philadelphia Inquirer* saw the collection's full value, noting that Melville's poems "possess considerable merit, and deserve a permanent place in our war literature. They are characterized by a bold originality; the versification is at times uncouth, and the rhythm unmusical. Yet the graphic powers of the poet will cause the general reader to overlook and forget these deficiencies. The descriptions of battles and marches are remarkably life-like and accurate, and this is the chief merit of the 'Battle Pieces.'" Such a generous appraisal largely fell on deaf ears, and Melville's poetic attempt to honor the Union war effort and the heroic dead would wait a century for fuller understanding.[43]

CHAPTER 7

"Are Ye, Gods?"

Interrogating the Divine in Timoleon, Etc.

Although the posthumously appearing *Billy Budd* is often considered Melville's literary "last testament," the lesser-known work that actually terminated his career as a published writer was a collection of forty-two poems, *Timoleon, Etc.* (hereinafter *Timoleon*). Appearing a few months before his death in September 1891 in a self-published edition of only twenty-five copies, *Timoleon* officially ended the sequence of four volumes that Melville had published during his later career as a poet, although a substantial amount of poetry and prose, including a completed volume of poems dedicated to his wife, *Weeds and Wildings*, remained in manuscript at his death. Divided into two sections, the second of which was titled "Fruit of Travel Long Ago"—a reference to Melville's extended tour of Europe and the Levant in 1856–57—*Timoleon* distinguished itself from his previous volume of sea pieces and nautical reminiscences, *John Marr and Other Sailors* (1888), by its subject matter of religion, architecture, art, and the role of the artist in society. If we consider *Timoleon* a kind of last testament within Melville's total oeuvre, a significant part of this would be the religious skepticism that had shaped his imagination during the previous four decades. This chapter will examine the sequence of poems in *Timoleon* relating to religious belief and unbelief in order to understand the ultimate phase of the author's creative interrogation of the Judeo-Christian tradition, whose god had become increasingly conspicuous by his absence during the later nineteenth century.[1]

A few years after Melville published *Battle-Pieces*, he returned to his ponderings on Christianity in the modern world in the composition of his epic-length narrative *Clarel: A Poem and Pilgrimage in the Holy Land*, which appeared in 1876 during the nation's centennial celebrations. As the richly allusive, intricately braided narrative of a group of American and European pilgrims making an extended tour of notable biblical sites in Palestine, *Clarel* offers a broad panorama of possibilities and impossibilities for Christian faith in the post-Darwinian world. Significantly more challenging and sophisticated than the American reading public could absorb, Melville's narrative poem was only published through the generosity of his maternal uncle Peter Gansevoort, and it went virtually unnoticed by the reading public. Not for Melville would be the honors and acclaim that Tennyson would receive following publication of the book-length elegy on his lost friend Arthur Hallam, *In Memoriam* (1850); or the critical esteem given to Matthew Arnold's *Empedocles on Etna, and Other Poems* (1852), revealing the author's prolonged crisis of faith; or the unexpected popularity of Browning's four-volume "Roman murder story," *The Ring and the Book* (1868–69), told in interconnected dramatic monologues and touching on psychological, philosophical, and religious themes, with a setting in late seventeenth-century Rome.[2]

In the decade following the publication of *Clarel*, Melville continued his work as a New York customs inspector and pursued his literary and artistic interests with the same assiduity as he had throughout his life while he wrote more poetry and revised poetic materials that he had already produced beginning in the late 1850s. It should be noted that the Melville family rented a pew at All Souls Unitarian Church for Elizabeth Melville's use while they lived in New York City after the Civil War, and Melville himself became a member of the church in 1885; but the long unknown fact of Melville's church membership almost certainly did not constitute a late conversion to Christianity but was more likely an indication of continuing skeptical inquiry and possible nostalgia for religious belief in a man increasingly aware of his own mortality. In the wake of the 1888 publication of *John Marr and Other Sailors*, Melville was involved in the slow composition of his final work of fiction, *Billy Budd*, as well as polishing and assembling the poems for *Timoleon* as a final statement on the themes of art and faith that had preoccupied him from the start of his career. The volume was dedicated to the American artist Elihu Vedder (1836–1923), who resided in Italy and had provided illustrations to a deluxe edition of Edward Fitzgerald's *Rubáiyát of Omar Khayyám* (1886), a text much esteemed by Melville and popular with the late Victorian public. Never having met the artist, Melville had bought Vedder's illustrated volume of the *Rubáiyát* in 1886 to add to his two other copies of the poem; the artist's earth-toned illustrations created visual enhancements of the medieval Persian poet's pessimistic and Ecclesiastes-like themes of human vanity, ephemerality, and mortality.[3]

With their settings in a variety of eras from classical antiquity to the present, the poems in *Timoleon* would reveal that Melville was still exploring the varied possibilities and impossibilities of religious faith in the ancient, medieval, and modern world, following a path that had already been laid out by Tennyson and Arnold for the Victorian public. Many of the poems in *Timoleon* thus embodied the new religious situation of postbellum America in which a more extensive and open questioning of Christian faith was now possible. For as historian James Turner remarks, "Within twenty years after the Civil War, agnosticism emerged as a self-sustaining phenomenon. Disbelief in God was, for the first time, plausible enough to grow beyond a rare eccentricity and to stake out a sizable permanent niche in American culture." Despite the continued development of evangelical Protestant Christianity in postbellum America led by Dwight L. Moody, the embrace of unbelief was now no longer taboo: "An agnostic subculture had taken root—not a geographic community, but a community of ideas, assumptions, and values. The shared world view gave agnostics a coherent understanding of reality without benefit of God." Confirming Turner's claims here is the testimony of Octavius Brooks Frothingham (1822–1895), a freethinking Unitarian minister who broke with his denomination to preside over the Independent Liberal Church in the 1870s in New York after becoming the first president of the Free Religious Association in 1867, ultimately retiring from the ministry in 1879. In his "Attitudes of Unbelief" in the collection *The Rising and the Setting Faith and Other Discourses* (1878), Frothingham asserted,

> Ours is loosely called an age of unbelief; more so than any other age ever has been; and perhaps it is. Unbelief is more widely spread now than it ever was; it is more general; it comprehends more classes of people; it embraces more orders and varieties of minds.

It is more intelligent; it is more resolute; it is more earnest; it is more serenely content with itself; it is less passionately aggressive than it used to be, and it is far sweeter in its spirit. There are no statistics to describe the numerical or geographical extent of it. It is larger than can be expressed in figures, more diversified than can be described in words.

As the poems of *Timoleon* demonstrate, Melville was an honorary member of this community of skeptics, freethinkers, and unbelievers.[4]

The title poem in Melville's collection, "Timoleon" depicts a loss of moral confidence and guidance that was broadly representative of early fourth century Greece BCE—and, by implication, later nineteenth-century England and America.[5] Reconfiguring an episode in the history of ancient Corinth that Melville found in Plutarch's *Lives of the Noble Greeks and Romans* and Bayle's *Dictionary*, the poem narrates the moral history of the title character's crisis of conscience after conspiring to kill his older brother Timophanes for the latter's tyrannical seizure of power—an act partially enabled by the mother's early favoritism of the older sibling. As a variation of the conflict between public duty and private loyalty, "Timoleon" hints at Melville's early sibling rivalry with his prematurely deceased older brother Gansevoort, whose career as demagogic political orator on behalf of the expansionist James K. Polk in the presidential election of 1844 ended with his mysterious premature death in London in 1846 while filling a diplomatic post; the poem hints as well of Melville's long internal exile from the American public that had largely rejected him as a writer since the mid-1850s. Like Arnold's *Empedocles on Etna*, whose melancholy hero expounds a similar *Weltschmerz*, "Timoleon" raises contemporary religious and moral questions under the rubric of ancient Greek history. Set in the time of Plato, the later Sophists, and the decline of Athens as the leading Greek city state, "Timoleon" exemplifies the skeptical decoupling of morality and religion that also seemed to threaten the Victorian world with the decline of Christianity.

The poem begins with a relentless volley of questions about the ethics of dealing with an act of political usurpation that has been given the veneer of legitimacy—questions that will point to the seeming relativity of all moral action and the apparent inoperability of divine justice in the world. Thus, the speaker asks whether someone who does a public service by killing a political tyrant should be troubled with regret about his actions, lacking the overweening arrogance and opportunism that evildoers possess in their assurance that might makes right:

> Shall the good heart whose patriot fire
> Leaps to a deed of startling note,
> Do it, then flinch? Shall good in weak expire?
>   Needs goodness lack the evil grit
> That stares down censorship and ban,
> And dumfounds saintlier ones with this—
> God's will avouched in each successful man?
>
> (ll. 6–12)

Asking whether virtuous political action is ultimately less adapted to worldly success than tyranny, such a question is intimately related to some of Melville's most memorable fictions, as in Starbuck's inability to confront Ahab over the latter's usurpation of the *Pequod* to hunt Moby Dick, or Billy Budd's failure to understand Claggart's lethal prejudice against him. If good and evil are not equally balanced in the world, the former will always work at a disadvantage to a more ruthless and assertive evil—an idea dramatized in *Billy Budd*, which was written about the same time as "Timoleon" in the late 1880s.

Drawing on a theme that dominates Melville's *Pierre*, the speaker in "Timoleon" goes on to ask whether overly virtuous actions are self-defeating: "Seems virtue there a strain forbid— / Transcendence such as shares transgression's fate?" (ll. 15–16). The potentially fallible nature of moral idealism, with its basis in a divinely sanctioned knowledge of goodness and truth, is called into question here. Moreover, if the doer of a virtuous deed is at first blamed by the world but then restored to favor, is this change evidence of a providential divine plan or merely a chance event? As we will see by the end of the poem, all these questions are raised by Timoleon's history. The poet completes the first stanza by identifying his subject as having gained both glory and political martyrdom at the same time ("crowned with laurel twined with thorns"), while also identifying the Greek hero as a displaced Christ figure in his exemplary sufferings. Himself a kind of martyr to his career as literary prophet, Melville as speaker justifies his sympathetic interest in Timoleon's fate ("Not rash thy life's cross-ride I stem, / But reck the problem rolled in pang" [ll. 22–23]) in explicitly Christian terms; for the poet will "reach and dare to touch thy garment's hem" (l. 24), like those healed by Christ in the gospel of Matthew (9:20–21; 13:36).

Sections II, III, IV, and V of Melville's poem are taken up with narrating the earlier history of Timoleon and his brother, and the background events leading up to the decisive action of the poem, the killing of Timophanes to restore proper political authority in Corinth. Thus, section II relates how Timoleon heroically saved his brother in battle against Argos ("Covers him with his shield, and takes / The darts and furious odds and fights at bay" [ll. 35–36]), while section III tells of the mother's preference for the older brother Timophanes, whom the mother thinks will make her "An envied dame of power, a social queen." Timophanes's unscrupulously ambitious nature is thereupon revealed when he attains his rule in Corinth through a ruthless and lethal seizure of power: "Foresworn, with heart that did not wince / At slaying men who kept their vows, / Her darling strides to power, and reigns—a Prince" (ll. 74–76). Section IV reveals Timoleon's revulsion at Timophanes's actions and the beginning of his plan to kill his tyrannical brother, a plan foreshadowed in a dream in which he sees the executors of justice confronted by the demons of fratricide, a vision reminiscent of Orestes's career in Aeschylus's *Oresteia*: "He sees the lictors of the gods, / Giant ministers of righteousness, / Their *fasces* threatened by the Furies' rods" (ll. 90–92). Yet Timoleon decides to act on his divinely guided sense of moral righteousness and civic virtue: "He heeds the voice whose mandate calls, / Or seems to call, peremptory from the skies" (ll. 95–96). In section V we learn that Timoleon, with two confederates, sought to criticize the injustice of his brother's rule to his face; but Timophanes responds with laughter and contemptuous dismissal of his brother's accusation: "What to me is Right? / I am the Wrong, and lo, I reign, / And testily intolerant too in might" (ll. 106–8). In response to this flagrant display of hubris, Timoleon consents to his brother's death, and thus "Right in Corinth reassumes its place."

Sections VI and VII dramatize the moral center of Melville's poem. In section VI, the hitherto virtuous act of tyrannicide is interpreted by the "whispering-gallery of the world" as an immoral act of fratricide. The speaker goes on to provide the historical context for Timoleon's actions:

> The time was Plato's. Wandering lights
> Confirmed the atheist's standing star;
> As now, no sanction Virtue knew
> For deeds that on prescriptive morals jar.
>
> (ll. 121–24)

The "Wandering lights" here are the Sophists, who were notorious for spreading relativistic notions of morality throughout Greece at this time in their role as peripatetic instructors of rhetoric. Sophists like Antiphon and Thrasymachus taught that "nature" was paramount over artificially created human laws, and thus ultimately "might makes right"; a tyrant like Timophanes was a legitimate ruler by reason of his successful coup. For Timoleon, the unexpected result of his virtuous act of killing a tyrant is now seen as a guilty act of fratricide, which goes against "prescriptive morals" and has no special "sanction." The effect of this public rejection of his tyrannicidal action leads to a crisis of doubt in Timoleon's mind:

> Reaction took misgiving's tone,
> Infecting conscience, till betrayed
> To doubt the irrevocable doom
> Herself [i.e., conscience] had authorized when undismayed.
> Within perturbed Timoleon here
> Such deeps were bared as when the sea
> Convulsed, vacates its shoreward bed,
> And Nature's last reserves show nakedly.
>
> (ll. 125–32)

Timoleon suffers what amounts to a mental breakdown and suicidal depression, at first being tempted to end his life ("from Hades' glens / By night insidious tones implore— / Why suffer?" [ll. 133–35]), and then going into self-imposed exile that is described as a kind of spiritual decapitation: "In severance he is like a head / Pale after battle trunkless found apart" (ll. 143–44).

In section VII, Timoleon gives vent to his complaint against the gods for misleading him into a morally dubious action while dismissing the need to involve any merely human actors in his quandary:

> Like sightless orbs his thoughts are rolled
> Arraigning heaven as compromised in wrong:
> "To second causes why appeal?
> Vain parleying here with fellow clods.
> To you, Arch Principals, I rear
> My quarrel, for this quarrel is with gods.
> "Shall just men long to quit your world?
> It is aspersion of your reign;

> Your marbles in the temple stand—
> Yourselves as stony, and invoked in vain?"
>
> (ll. 147–56)

We can detect an echo here of Melville's greatest fictional rebels, Ahab and Pierre, as well as their ancient prototypes, Prometheus and Job, all of whom outspokenly questioned the workings of divine justice in keeping with the Christian issue of theodicy. In addition, Timoleon's reference to the statues of the gods as indifferent to human welfare may also remind us of the contemporary tragedies of Euripides, which mirrored the relativistic morality of the Sophists by highlighting the detachment and moral failings of the gods. The main difference between Melville's Timoleon and these literary and religious prototypes is that the former's aggrieved complaint modulates into a surprisingly deferential and apologetic appeal for divine magnanimity:

> Ah, bear with *one* quite overborne,
> Olympians, if he chide ye now;
> Magnanimous be even though he rail
> And hard against ye set the bleaching brow.—
>
> (ll. 157–60)

Like the Victorian intellectuals whose heads and hearts were at odds over the credibility of Christianity, Timoleon invokes the favor of the Olympian gods even as he arraigns them for their cruel absence and indifference. With his attack on their callousness, Timoleon's lament leads to his final agonized indictment of the moral neutrality of the gods, whose existence is simultaneously both affirmed and denied:

> "If conscience doubt, she'll next recant.
> What basis then? O, tell at last,
> Are earnest natures staggering here
> But fatherless shadows from no substance cast?
> "Yea, *are* ye, gods? Then ye, 'tis ye
> Should show what touch of tie ye may,
> Since ye too, if not wrung, are wronged
> By grievous misconceptions of your sway.
> "But deign, some little sign be given—
> Low thunder in your tranquil skies;
> Me reassure, not let me be
> Like a lone dog that for a master cries."
>
> (ll. 161–72)

If the gods exist, then they should sympathize with "earnest natures" like Timoleon, who is now desperate for some higher validation for his actions; for if the gods are not "wrung" by his plight, then humans have "grievous misconceptions" of their imaginary power. The moral agony of Timoleon stems from the painful disjunction of morality and religion in his thought, which is unresolved at the end of his remarks, when he is still pleading for a heavenly sign that he was not at fault for killing his corrupt and murderous brother.[6]

The fact that Timoleon's crisis of self-confidence was partly inspired by Melville's own religious doubts is demonstrated by two marginal notes he made to his reading in two key source texts that influenced his fiction and poetry. Thus, during a reading of *Don Quixote* in 1855, as mentioned in chapter 1, Melville remarked on the author's assertion of a knight's need for an idealized mistress by comparing it to Confucius's analogy of "a dog without a master" and then his own analogy of "a god-like mind without a God."[7] If the annotation reveals Melville's sense of bereavement over his loss of faith and felt need for a divine presence, a more outspoken rationalistic dismissal of divinity was evident in Melville's reading of Matthew Arnold's *Empedocles on Etna* in 1871. At this time he annotated the Greek philosopher's insistence that human beings have no god-given right to be happy ("Thou has no *right* to bliss, / No title from the Gods to welfare and repose" [I.ii.160-61]) by indignantly asserting, "A Western [i.e., American] critic here exclaims— What in thunder did the Gods create us for then? If not for bliss, for bale? If so, the devil take the Gods."[8] In this sharp critique of Old Testament creationist myth (Gen. 2; Job 10; Ps. 119:73-80; 139) and Protestant theology, if the "gods" have created humans only for misery—or Calvinist hell—then they should be summarily dismissed, for their only proper theological role is to assist their human dependents.

Although there is no answer to Timoleon's plea, he is eventually forgiven by his native city when he is sent to lead Corinthian troops at war in Sicily and is able to restore peace there:

> And Corinth clapt: Absolved, and more!
> Justice in long arrears is thine:
> Not slayer of thy brother, no,
> But saviour of the state, Jove's soldier, man divine.
>   (ll. 181–84)

In an unanticipated reversal of fortune, Timoleon is now a public benefactor, and his earlier "crime" forgiven. Yet despite this positive validation of his actions as a tyrannicide, and his previous experience of exile as a displaced form of death, Timoleon now "reposed" as a "loved guest" in Sicily and thenceforth never returned to his native Corinth. The Greek hero is now seemingly possessed of the spiritual equanimity that served as the implicit goal of classical skepticism. We thus return at the end of the poem back to the speaker's questions at the beginning, asking whether Timoleon's "emergence" after "eclipse" was "high Providence, or Chance?" In other words, were Timoleon's virtuous actions ultimately vindicated by supernatural authority, or were they accidentally rewarded by the workings of fate? Do the gods really exist? If so, what is their ultimate attitude toward human suffering? If not, on what authority do human beings base their morality? The questions at the start of the poem are unanswered at the end, conveying the persistently interrogative mood of Melville's religious skepticism.

If "Timoleon" represents the problematic nature of religious beliefs in the age of Plato and the late Victorian era, "After the Pleasure Party" depicts a modern educated American woman's struggle to overcome the confines of fleshly desire—including sexual jealousy—within a symbolic context of classical mythology, notably the dichotomy between the heavenly and earthly Aphrodite, and the mythological origins of sexual love, as set forth in Plato's *Symposium*. In heated accents recalling the dangers of sexual infatuation found in such classical heroines as Phaedra and Dido, the Urania of Melville's poem—who bears the name of the muse of astronomy and has a partial model in the pioneering American astronomer Maria Mitchell (1818–1889)—narrates the story of her involvement in a "pleasure party" of tourists visiting an Italian villa on the Mediterranean coast. In "After the Pleasure Party," we witness a display of spitefulness in the Greco-Roman god of love, Eros/Cupid/Amor, as well as an indictment of the unnamed creator god who was responsible for causing human unhappiness by dividing the human race into two interdependent sexes that only intermittently meet with a compatible partner.[9]

"After the Pleasure Party" has only gradually emerged to critical scrutiny as a poem shaped by a complex array of philosophical, biographical, and literary influences including works by Plato, Ovid, Milton, Schopenhauer, Hawthorne, Tennyson, and Arnold.[10] Important to an appreciation of Melville's use of the name Urania, for example, is Milton's invocation of her as astronomical muse at the start of book VII of *Paradise Lost*, where Urania is deemed the sister of divine Wisdom

(VII.9–10), a figure depicted in chapter 8 of the biblical book of Proverbs as coeval with the creation. Urania accordingly inspires the English
epic poet's heavenly flight: "Up led by thee / Into the Heav'n of Heav'ns
I have presum'd / An Earthly Guest, and drawn Empyreal Air" (VII.12–
14). On the other hand, in Matthew Arnold's poem "Urania," the heavenly Aphrodite represents a passionless ideal "muse" beyond the reach
of men because of their moral shortcomings:

> She smiles and smiles, and will not sigh,
> While we for hopeless passion die;
> Yet she could love, those eyes declare,
> Were but men nobler than they are.
> (ll. 5–8)

Beginning with the fifth stanza, the poem describes the potential transformation in Urania's demeanor if she could encounter better examples
of mankind:

> Yet oh, that Fate would let her see
> One of some better race than we;
> One for whose sake she once might prove
> How deeply she who scorns can love.
> (ll. 17–20)

But until that time, "Coldly she mocks the sons of men. / Till then her
lovely eyes maintain / Their gay, unwavering, deep disdain" (ll. 30–32).
Significantly, Melville marked the last stanza of the poem, double-
lining its final two lines. Unlike the mythological Urania figures of
Milton and Arnold, Melville's heroine is unable to transcend the fallen
world of human desire to attain celestial wisdom, for her celibate life
has unleashed the force of nemesis in the juvenile god of love.[11]

Following its epigraphic "Lines Traced Under an Image of Amor
Threatening" in which the spiteful son of Venus/Aphrodite warns of
the dire consequences of *"Taking pride from love exempt,"* Melville's "After
the Pleasure Party" is structured around the extended dramatic mono-
logue of a female astronomer whose confession of sexual passion and
jealousy during an Italian excursion leads to a final choric commentary
from the poet about the dangers arising from a vengeful Amor. The
poem takes place in two locations, first at an unnamed scenic villa on
the Mediterranean, and the second at the Villa Albani in Rome. The
poem is thus an account of a "fall" from heavenly wisdom into sexual
and emotional turmoil, fueled by an unrequited love for an unnamed

male companion who has shown more interest in an alluring younger woman. Like Hawthorne's Zenobia or James's Isabel Archer, Urania faces the devastating consequences of romantic infatuation and disillusionment after an attempt to lead a life dedicated solely to intellectual pursuits; in fact, Melville's depiction of Urania's angst over her unruly middle-aged passion was likely in part inspired by Zenobia's jealousy of her younger and more nubile half-sister Priscilla in competition for Hollingsworth's affections in *The Blithedale Romance*.[12]

After an initial evocation of the beauty of the sensual Italian scene where the "pleasure party" has taken place, Urania reveals the depth of her dismay as she attempts to control the eruption of passion that has occurred in her: "To flout pale years of cloistral life / And flush me in this sensuous strife. / 'Tis Vesta struck with Sappho's smart" (ll. 21–23). Upset at the incongruous nature of her feelings, she decries her shameful loss of control: "But baffled here—to take disdain, / To feel rule's instinct, yet not reign; / To dote, to come to this drear shame—" (ll. 33–35). Still feeling the passion that overwhelms her, which she depicts in a metaphor dating back to Sappho's lyrics ("Hence the winged blaze that sweeps my soul / Like prairie-fires that spurn control" [ll. 36–37]), Urania looks back on her previous life of solitary observation and study, at which time she lived as a votary to the stars in imagined self-coronation:

> "And kept I long heaven's watch for this,
> Contemning love, for this, even this?
> O terrace chill in Northern air,
> O reaching ranging tube I placed
> Against yon skies, and fable chased
> Till, fool, I hailed for sister there
> Starred Cassiopea in Golden Chair.
> In dream I throned me, nor I saw
> In cell the idiot crowned with straw.
>
> (ll. 39–47)

In the last two lines Urania reveals the vanity of her ambition, personified in the person of a self-crowned incarcerated lunatic. The life of the intellect has only led to her humiliation, as Urania expresses shock that she could fall so fast and far: "What gain I barrenly bereaved! / Than this can be yet lower decline— / Envy and spleen, can these be mine?" (ll. 51–53). Like Milton's Satan in his agony of jealousy over the sight of Eden (*Paradise Lost*, IV.9–120), Urania is dismayed by the eruption of envious emotions within herself. The source of her agony, of course, is her secret passion for an unnamed male in her party who seems to find more interest in a barefoot young woman carrying a blossoming, potentially phallic token of spring:

> "The pleasant girl demure that trod
> Beside our wheels that climbed the way,
> And bore along a blossoming rod
> That looked the scepter of May-Day—
> On her—to fire this petty hell,
> His softened glance how moistly fell!
> The cheat! on briars her buds were strung;
> And wiles peeped forth from mien how meek.
> The innocent bare-foot! young, so young!
> To girls, strong man's a novice weak.
> To tell such beads! And more remain,
> Sad rosary of belittling pain.
>
> (ll. 54–65)

Like a jealous Zenobia denigrating Priscilla during the May Day celebrations at Hawthorne's Blithedale, Urania is intensely jealous of her younger sexual competitor. The allusion above to rosary beads that she must still count in her penance foreshadows Urania's later unsuccessful attempt to find consolation in Christian retreat. Yet before that occurs, we first rehearse Urania's final despair at her attempt to divorce her intellect from her femininity. Like Timoleon, in the midst of her agony of frustration and rejection Urania expresses the desire to commit suicide, as Sappho was alleged to have done because of her unrequited love for the ferryman Phaon—a literary legend recorded in Ovid's *Heroides* and elsewhere. In Melville's poem, Urania laments:

> Could I remake me! or set free
> This sexless bound in sex, then plunge
> Deeper than Sappho, in a lunge
> Piercing Pan's paramount mystery!
>
> (ll. 80–83)

Urania's lunge will, she hopes, break through the "mystery" of nature and sexuality typified by the goat-god Pan. Urania's complaint continues in an indictment of the workings of sexual reproduction in nature; for if human selfhood is incomplete until each sex meets its intended other half, what happens if this never happens—how then can an individual attain spiritual wholeness? The condition of the human race thus resembles a kind of slavery to the flesh that, contrary to Christian teaching (Gal. 3:28), is impossible to transcend. The poem then recalls the myth of the androgyne set forth by Aristophanes in Plato's *Symposium*, in which human beings were originally created as self-sufficient sexual hybrids, but were punished for an attempt at revolt by being divided into male and female:

> For, Nature, in no shallow surge
> Against thee either sex may urge,
> Why hast thou made us but in halves—
> Co-relatives? This makes us slaves.
> If these co-relatives never meet
> Self-hood itself seems incomplete.
> And such the dicing of blind fate
> Few matching halves here meet and mate.
> What Cosmic jest or Anarch blunder
> The human integral clove asunder
> And shied the fractions through life's gate?
> (ll. 84–94)

The god of Nature in Urania's lament, who has torn apart the original human adrogyne, is thus either a cosmic jester or anarchic blunderer like the Gnostic creator god, who has divided human nature into male and female and then "shied"—or thrown with a swift movement—the "fractions" through "life's gate," a metaphor of the birthing process. As in the contemporary philosophy of Schopenhauer, human sexuality only adds to the oppressive forces of the will that characterize the universe. The "dicing of blind fate" in the assignment of a marriage partner—a potential reminder of several notoriously unhappy Victorian marriages including Melville's own—leads to Urania's bitter indictment of the cruel humor or stupidity of the gods.

The poem continues with the chorus-like intrusion of the poet declaring it unknown whether Urania "lived down the strain / Of turbulent heart and rebel brain" since Amor may have continued to express his "boyish spite"; but at some later date she visited Rome, where she was transfixed by the colossal statue of Athena ("form august of heathen Art") displayed at the Villa Albani (now Torlonia). Before this experience, however, she had visited a "convent shrine" where she was moved by an image of Mary to contemplate conversion to Catholicism and monastic retreat; but she now addresses a prayer to Athena as the "mightier one":

> "Languid in frame for me,
> To-day by Mary's convent-shrine,
> Touched by her picture's moving plea
> In that poor nerveless hour of mine,
> I mused—A wanderer still must grieve.
> Half I resolved to kneel and believe,
> Believe and submit, the veil take on.
> But thee, armed Virgin! less benign,
> Thee now I invoke, thou mightier one.
>   (ll. 125–33)

Like Hawthorne's Zenobia threatening to take the veil before her suicide, or Hilda seeking the confessional at St. Peter's in *The Marble Faun*, Urania has been tempted by the consolations of Catholicism to join a religious order; but she ultimately turns instead to the inspiration of Athena for strength to overcome her sexual malaise:

> Helmeted woman—if such term
> Befit thee, far from strife
> Of that which makes the sexual feud
> And clogs the aspirant life—
> O self-reliant, strong and free,
> Thou in whom power and peace unite,
> Transcender! raise me up to thee,
> Raise me and arm me!
>   (ll. 134–41)

Significantly, Urania prefers the armed wisdom of classical Athena to the passive self-denial of the Catholic Mary. Yet the ironic upshot of this choice is that the frame narrator of the poem denies Urania the peace of mind she craves, for "Nothing may help or heal / While Amor incensed remembers wrong." Just as the Roman poet Virgil famously asserted that *Omnia vincit amor* ("Love conquers all") in Eclogue X and depicted Amor/Cupid as secretly inspiring the widowed queen Dido with a fatal passion for Aeneas in *The Aeneid*, Urania in Melville's poem will apparently continue to be a victim of unfulfilled physical passion as an older single woman. At the end of the poem, the speaker in the role of chorus invokes aid for Urania from her virgin peers: "Then for

Urania, virgins everywhere / O pray! Example take too, and have care"
(ll. 150–51). In Melville's representation of Christian and classical gods
found in the poem, the latter are clearly more powerful; but they are
cruelly fickle (Eros/Amor) or unreliable (Athena), offering no hope of
moral support. Like "Timoleon," "After the Pleasure Party" represents
a universe out of joint, with an absence of gods to assist its beleaguered
human inhabitants.

In "After the Pleasure Party," Melville created a surprisingly modern
evocation of the conflict between intellect and desire, spirit and flesh,
love and vocation, in an educated American woman. While a seeming
anomaly in Melville's poetry, the poem evokes the work of his Victorian
contemporaries, for it exhibits a sexual candor comparable to the frustrated erotic fervor of Swinburne's *Poems and Ballads*, while the aura of
isolation, romantic disappointment, and religious questioning is evocative of Arnold's laments over lost love and faith such as "Switzerland,"
"Stanzas from the Grande Chartreuse," and *Empedocles on Etna*. By the
same token, Melville's indictment of the creator god who designed the
world so that sexuality is a torment to the individual evokes a familiar theme in Thomas Hardy's fiction; indeed, there are suggestive resemblances between the poem and Hardy's depiction of the conflict
between higher and lower natures and desires in *Tess of the D'Urbervilles*
and *Jude the Obscure*, both of which date from roughly the same period
as *Timoleon*.

Late nineteenth-century readers might have been led to associate the
female subject of "After the Pleasure Party" with the recently deceased
astronomer Maria Mitchell, whom Melville had met at her small ob-
servatory on Nantucket Island in July 1852, five years after she had
won international renown for discovering a new comet to which she
gave her name. A leading advocate for women's education, Mitchell was
the country's leading astronomer for much of the nineteenth century,
working as a "computer" of the planet Venus for the *Nautical Almanac*
for two decades and later serving as a well-regarded professor of astronomy at the new Vassar College from 1865 to 1888, training a generation
of young women in science. As a largely self-educated woman, Mitchell
was acquainted with a number of leading mid-nineteenth-century literary and scientific figures, and during her tour abroad traveled from
Paris to Rome in early 1858 with Nathaniel Hawthorne and his family
as her escort, spending time with the Hawthorne family during her
three months in Rome before she departed for Florence. Nathaniel
Philbrick has demonstrated that "After the Pleasure Party" was likely

shaped by Melville's reading of Hawthorne's *Passages from the French and Italian Notebooks* in 1872; Philbrick thus posits that a scene from Hawthorne's Italian notebook describing a visit by the Hawthornes and Mitchell to the Rospigliosi Palace in Rome—which Melville himself had visited a year earlier—provided him with a specific setting for the poem, transposed to the Mediterranean coast. There is no evidence that Maria Mitchell ever regretted her decision to remain single throughout her life, or felt remorse for her dedication to science and female education. Melville's poem thus rises above any specific biographical associations in its representation of the speaker's poignant dismay over the chaotic and wayward impulses of sexual desire and pair bonding, as embodied in the poem by the war between mythological personifications of erotic passion (Amor) and wisdom (Athena), whose enmity is part and parcel of a radically flawed creation.[13]

Following the first two long poems of *Timoleon, Etc.*, with their skeptical depictions of classical and Christian divinities, we encounter a series of poems depicting the perceived disappearance of God in contemporary Christianity, a phenomenon found among the educated elite within Anglo-American society. In an 1874 sermon titled *Why Go to Church?*, for example, Octavius Brooks Frothingham claimed that for many, the church had become "a simulacrum, a spectre, a ghost of things departed, a reminiscence of a tradition."[14] The first of Melville's poems from *Timoleon* overtly expressing the waning influence of Christianity, "The Night-March," describes the radical dissociation between an un-identified Roman army marching silently through the night and its absent "chief," whose existence is merely legendary. While the poem suggests the religious situation of the late empire between Constantine's formal recognition of Christianity in 325 CE and the fall of Rome in 476, the poem resists attempts at historicizing and has the impersonality of a dream. The first two stanzas describe the strangely noiseless appearance of the phantom army, with its battle standards furled and trumpets silent, its presence indicated only by flashing weaponry and armor:

> With banners furled, and clarions mute,
>   An army passes in the night;
> And beaming spears and helms salute
>   The dark with bright.
> In silence deep the legions stream,

With open ranks, in order true;
Over boundless plains they stream and gleam—
        No Chief in view!

(ll. 1–8)

It is only when we reach the third stanza that we discover that the poem expresses the insuperable divide between Christendom and Christ; for this is implied when the missing legendary "Chief" is associated with a "shining host," through whom he sends his unspecified "mandate":

Afar, in twinkling distance lost,
        (So legends tell) he lonely wends
And back through all that shining host
        His mandate sends.

(ll. 9–12)

A number of words and phrases here demonstrate a Christian context for this mysterious leader. The word "mandate" might be related to the biblical "commandments," which encompass the laws given to Moses by Yahweh on Sinai that were assimilated by Jesus into the Sermon on the Mount (Matt. 5–7). The original meaning of "host," on the other hand, is "army" or "great multitude"; thus the phrase "shining host" describing the marching army in Melville's poem also suggests the imagery of the heavenly "host" of angels (Psalm 103:20–21; 1 Kings 22:19) who accompanied Yahweh, the "god of hosts." In its one New Testament usage in Luke, Jesus's birth is announced to the shepherds by the appearance of a "heavenly host" (Luke 2:13). "Host," of course, also means the bread of the Eucharist; hence this "shining host" through which the unnamed leader sends his "mandate" is also potentially the "body" of Christ. The fact that the distant chief "lonely wends" his way suggests the image of Christ as rejected by the world he had come to save (John 1:10–11). Finally, the image of the "chief" lost in the "twinkling distance," as "legends tell," evokes the traditional association of Christ's birth with a star over Bethlehem (Matt. 2:2, 9–10) as well as the post-Resurrection Jesus who ascended into heaven.

In "The Night-March," the Christian soldiers are depicted with only spears and helmets, which "salute / The dark with bright." The "light" conveyed by the marching soldiers may be associated with the imagery of the redeemed in the New Testament, as in Saint Paul's claim "now ye are light in the Lord: walk as children of light" (Eph. 5:8). The metaphor of the Christian as a soldier is a familiar trope in the Letter to the Ephesians, which instructs the faithful to arm themselves with their faith: "Above all, taking the shield of faith, wherewith ye shall be able to quench all the fiery darts of the wicked. And take the helmet of salvation, and the sword of the Spirit, which is the word of God" (Eph. 6:16–17; see also 2 Tim. 2:3). Commenting on the phantom army in Melville's poem, William Bysshe Stein cites the contemporary Protestant hymn "Fling Out the Banner! Let It Float" as a possible influence; but the ideal of the Christian soldier would probably have been more familiar to late nineteenth-century Americans in the hymn "Onward Christian Soldiers," written by Sabine Baring-Gould in 1865 and set to music by Arthur Sullivan in 1871, the first verse of which reads,

> Onward Christian soldiers, marching as to war,
> With the cross of the Jesus, going on before.
> Christ the royal Master, leads against the foe;
> Forward into the battle, see his banners go!

In Melville's ironic dream vision, the army of Christian soldiers, their "banners furled," has no designated mission; nor does it have a visible leader. The *deus absconditus* of Christianity is only a distant memory in the darkness of the present.[15]

Like "The Night-March, "The Margrave's Birthnight" offers another oblique commentary on Christ as an enigmatic hidden god to his followers, demonstrating the essentially fictive nature of the Christian myth. In the latter poem, a mysterious German margrave—the hereditary title of certain princes in the Holy Roman Empire—fails to appear at his castle on his birth night, a scenario likely based on the two thousand year history of Christ's failure to return for his Second Advent. The fact that the leading proponents of the view of Christianity as a mythic creation were nineteenth-century German scholars like Strauss and Feuerbach makes the German setting of Melville's poem especially appropriate. The poem begins by depicting a scene of winter festivity in some unnamed German principality, an event with obvious resemblances to Christmas. With picturesque imagery worthy of Washington Irving's well-known portrayal of a traditional English Christmas in *The Sketch Book*, the poet details the gathering of rural peasantry to the unnamed margrave's castle in the middle of the winter:

> Up from many a sheeted valley,
> From white woods as well,
> Down too from each fleecy upland
> Jingles many a bell,

Jovial on the work-sad horses
Hitched to runners old
Of the toil-worn peasants sledging
Under sheepskins in the cold;

Till from every quarter gathered
Meet they on one ledge;
There from hoods they brush the snow off
Lighting from each sledge

Full before the Margrave's castle,
Summoned there to cheer
On his birth-night, in midwinter,
Kept year after year.

O the hall, and O the holly!
Tables line each wall;
Guests as holly-berries plenty,
But—no host withal!

(ll. 1–20)

The mentions of "cheer" and "holly" are appropriate for the poem's apparent context of Christmas celebration. The analogy between the missing "margrave" and Christ is also suggested by the pun embedded within the aristocratic title, for Christ was one who "marred" the "grave" with his Resurrection. In another pun, the feast depicted in the poem is analogous to a failed attempt at communion, for there is obviously no "host" present here. The speaker goes on to question whether the margrave's dependents can find satisfaction in their celebration without their noble "host," whose throne and table setting are both empty:

May his people feast contented
While at head of board
Empty throne and vacant cover
Speak the absent lord?

(ll. 21–24)

Another pun on "contented" implicitly raises the question of whether Christian communion, the ritual whereby Christ is remembered, can give "content," for despite the Catholic doctrine of the Real Presence, the margrave, like the "chief" in "The Night-March," is conspicuous by his absence. As William Bysshe Stein notes, "In the rhetorical question poised in the passage, Melville asks whether Christianity can endure without the New Testament vision of the living Christ."[16]

The poem continues by noting the radical disconnection between the festive activities and the absence of the individual for whom they are designed, as music is played, guests served, and old "observance" given; yet the noble host is not there to acknowledge the event:

> No, and never guest once marvels,
> None the good lord name,
> Scarce they mark void throne and cover—
> Dust upon the same.
>
> Mindless as to what importeth
> Absence in such a hall;
> Tacit as the plough-horse feeding
> In the palfrey's stall.
>
> (ll. 33–40)

In the first stanza above, the poet puns on the word "lord," a biblical honorific for Christ, while the "dust" on the throne and table setting conveys a hint of disuse and death. The guests are as "tacit" as the "plough-horse" stabled where the aristocratic "palfrey" was kept. The poem ends by asserting the functional nature of the birth-night holiday for the peasantry, who need the annual festivity as a change from their laborious routine: "Ah, enough for toil and travail, / If but for a night / Into wine is turned the water, / Black bread into white" (ll. 41–44). The mention of wine and bread here again implicitly alludes to the Christian sacrament of Communion as well as Christ's miracle of turning water into wine at the marriage in Cana (John 2:1–11), while the peasant's "travail" suggests a traditional Christian term for the labor, pain, and suffering that characterize the world according to Saint Paul (Rom. 8:22). In the poet's final statement, the ritual of attending the absent margrave's birthday celebration has a functional value in the welcome release it gives to the peasantry from the dreary routine of their mundane lives.

In a shift of time frame and philosophical vision, "The Garden of Metrodorus" evokes the materialist atomistic theories of the ancient Greek philosopher Epicurus, who advocated a life of spiritual withdrawal in keeping with the depiction of the secluded garden of the poem, named after one of the philosopher's chief followers. The poem thus continues the theme of the absent leader in *Timoleon*, but now he is the invisible inhabitant of a garden designed for intellectual contemplation, not metaphysical deception. As a pioneering proponent of the Democritan theory of matter, Epicurus undercut the sway of the gods by doubting their existence, or theorizing their ineffectual condition as diffuse configurations of matter. With no supernatural realm to fear, Epicurus advocated a life of quiet retirement fostering emotional equanimity, with friendship and intellectual inquiry at its center.[17]

In Melville's poem on the Epicurean ideal of seclusion, so contrary to the active public life of ancient Athens, each of the two stanzas of the poem provokes a question from the poet concerning the invisible occupant of the garden. In the first stanza, noting its "moss-grown gate" and "hedge untrimmed," the poet asks, "And who keeps here his quiet state? / And shares he sad or happy fate / Where never foot-path to the gate is seen?" (ll. 3–5). In the second stanza, noting the absence of signs of life and the silence of those frequenting the garden, the poet asks again, "Content from loneness who may win? / And is this stillness peace or sin / Which noteless thus apart can keep its dell?" (ll. 8–10). The implied answer here is that the Epicurean inhabitant of the garden has reached a state of equanimity that was an intended goal of classical skepticism. Echoing a series of conventional beliefs about human solitude, the poet asks how the occupant of the garden can avoid loneliness, and whether such withdrawal signifies a well-adjusted nature or one hiding from the world in shame. The fact that Melville himself was deliberately living in a comparable condition of spiritual withdrawal and solitude in the last years of his life in New York City makes such questions both poignant and ironic.

Another form of spiritual withdrawal can be found in two short poems, "The Weaver" and "Buddha," which depict the impulse toward transcendence of the physical world in two non-Western religions, Hinduism and Buddhism, respectively. In "The Weaver," the ascetic figure of the title, alone in his "mud-built room" over a period of "years," weaves a shawl for "Arva's shrine." The reference to "shrine" here implies that the site is a place of worship devoted to either a saint or god. The weaver exists devoid of human comforts or society, his only sign of life being his "busy shadow on the wall." Like a monk, the solitary figure has mortified his body and mind: "The face is pinched, the form is bent, / No pastime knows he nor the wine, / Recluse he lives and abstinent" (ll. 5–7). Given the weaver's shrunken body and solitary existence, the "shawl" that occupies his labors is a symbol of his living death, a virtual shroud; moreover, the impersonality of the scene described in "The Weaver" implies that the poem is a potential illustration of the ascetic impulse within many forms of religious worship, not just Hinduism. As the editors of the Northwestern-Newberry edition of Melville's *Published Poems* note, Melville first intended to give the poem an Islamic context by writing "Mecca's" in line 2 and "Allah's" in line 8, but he eventually settled on "Arva," an obscure figure from Hindu mythology, thereby demonstrating the ecumenical range of reference latent within the poem.[18]

An even greater impulse toward self-annihilation is manifested in "Buddha," a brief tribute to another major world religion. William B. Dillingham has demonstrated the wide interest in Buddhism in later nineteenth-century America, as found, for example, in William Rounseville Alger's *The Solitudes of Nature and Man* (1869), which Melville read some time in the early 1870s.[19] Melville's poem carries an epigraph from the New Testament Letter of James ("For what is your life? It is even a vapor that appeareth for a little time and then vanisheth away" [James 4:14]) that seems to echo the repeated claim in Ecclesiastes that all was "vanity"—the English translation of the Hebrew word for "vapor"—while also unorthodoxly hinting at the idea of spiritual annihilation characteristic of Buddhism. In only six lines, Melville's "Buddha" exemplifies the central doctrine of this pervasive Eastern faith, namely the desire to escape the cycles of pain and suffering in the world and attain nirvana, or nothingness: "Sobs of the worlds, and dole of kinds / That dumb endurers be— / Nirvana! absorb us in your skies, / Annul us into Thee" (ll. 3–6). Unlike the subject of "The Weaver," the religious aspirant here is part of a group of devotees ("us"), and there is a more explicitly pronounced impulse to transcend the sufferings of the physical world in quest of self-annihilation.

If many of the first section of poems in *Timoleon* constitute a rationalist critique of religious faith, "The New Zealot to the Sun" presents an implied criticism of the positivist, demythologizing impulse of modern science—a criticism earlier embodied in the character of the geologist Margoth in *Clarel*. The "zealot" of the poem's title is accordingly devoted to science as a type of surrogate religion. Addressing the sun (which in the new discipline of comparative religion was often considered the ultimate source for the idea of god), the speaker evokes the movement of the sun from east to west as a journey through both time and space, from a degrading and abject idolatry in ancient times to a modern enlightened rationalism, bent on "searching every secret out."

The movement of the poem thus suggests a version of the traditional idea of a progressive *translatio imperii* from east to west, as famously articulated in Bishop Berkeley's poem evoking the westward course of empire, "Verses on the Prospect of Planting Arts and Learning in America."

Initially addressing the sun as a "Persian"—an allusion to the Zoroastrian worship of the sun as chief deity—the speaker in the first stanza evokes the sun's rise in a realm of absolute human subjection, where "adulators sue" and "prostrate man" has followed traditional religious rites from time immemorial. In stanza two, the sun is described as an "Arch type of sway" shining over "Asia's plain" from which issue "many a wild incursive horde / Led by some shepherd Cain" (ll. 11-12), a likely allusion to the figure of Tamerlane (1336-1405) memorialized by Marlowe's two-part drama. In stanza three, like the ruthless military conquerors just mentioned, the gods ("brood of Brahma"), too, issue from the East, conquering peoples "like to the scythed car, / Westward they rolled their empire far, / Of night their purple wove" (ll. 16-18). While the allusion to the westward movement of empire here recalls the gist of Berkeley's poem, the ensuing line describes the union of power ("purple") and ignorance ("night") that characterizes these new faiths. Stanza four describes the theological tyrannies that ensue from these new gods, for the sun is now described as a "chemist" breeding each "sorcerous weed / That energizes dream," resulting in a series of oppressive and delusive "myths and creeds" that have reached their natural end in "Calvin's last extreme" of a tyrannical deity and theology.

In the penultimate stanza the poet questions whether the sun—whose primeval rays "In time's first dawn compelled the flight / Of Chaos' startled clan" (ll. 26-27)—will ever be capable of dispersing "worse Anarchs, frauds and fears, / Sprung from these weeds to man?" (ll. 34-36). However, in the final stanza the speaker suggests that "Science" can create a stronger "power" than sunlight that will "quell the shades you fail to rout, / Yea, searching every secret out / Elucidate your ray." According to the speaker's blindly rationalistic faith, science will explain everything in the cosmos, even the composition of sunlight itself. With an overweening ambition comparable to Ahab's, the new zealot inadvertently demonstrates that the Enlightenment-inspired rationalism of modern science can become a misguided enterprise reproducing the faith it allegedly scorns; for the very skepticism that questions the existence of gods has ironically failed to question the ultimate truth claims of science, with their denial of humanity's emotional and spiritual needs.

The symbolism of "light" in *Timoleon*, however, is more complex than reductive rationalism, for the dedication to "light" as a moral or creative ideal, as portrayed in "The Enthusiast," offers a nobler, if also more challenging, vocation than that of the scientist in "The New Zealot to the Sun." Bearing an epigraph from Job 13:15 relating to the need for keeping faith in one's self, "The Enthusiast" questions the dedication to ideals typical of "youth's magnanimous years," as opposed to the prudential wisdom of age, when he who began as an idealist might "Recant, and trudge where worldings go / Conform and own them right" (ll. 7–8). Continuing in the same vein, the speaker asks whether "Time" can make the idealist ultimately compromise with "palterers of the mart," so that they might eventually "shrink from Truth so still, so lone / Mid loud gregarious lies" (ll. 15–16). The last stanza offers encouragement to the idealist to "put the torch to ties though dear, / If ties but tempters be" (ll. 19–20), suggesting the teachings of Christ on transcending family ties (Mark 3:31–35; Luke 2:44–49); while the poem's final injunction not to complain if blindness or despair ensues evokes the example of Milton: "Nor cringe if come the night: / Walk through the cloud to meet the pall, / Though light forsake thee, never fall / From fealty to light" (ll. 21–24). We recall that the root meaning of the word "enthusiasm" means "filled with god or spirit" (*theos*). Hence Melville's poem offers praise of a moral or creative idealism that is willing to brave all odds to achieve its ends; the poem no doubt reflects the personal challenges that faced Melville as a virtually unknown writer in later nineteenth-century America. Unlike the reference to light in "The New Zealot to the Sun," the light in "The Enthusiast" is an interior, not an exterior phenomenon—the light of creativity and personal faith that are still crucial to the artist amid the decline of traditional religious faith.

The world's "darkness," however, is often not easily overcome, as the ensuing poem demonstrates. In "Fragments of a Lost Gnostic Poem of the 12th Century," Melville creates a two-part poetic fragment setting forth the basic tenets of medieval Gnosticism, a heretical branch of Christianity premised on the idea that the creation was an act of evil, not good, as Christianity taught based on the first chapter of Genesis. The implicit historical context for the poem was the rise of Gnostic beliefs among the medieval Cathars (or so-called Pure Ones) of Southern

France, who were exterminated by the armies of the pope in the early thirteenth century during the Albigensian Crusade. Essentially dualist in theology, Catharism, like its earlier ancestor Gnosticism, held as its most fundamental tenet the corrupt nature of the physical universe, which was seen as the creation of a radically flawed divinity called the *Rex Mundi*, or king of the world. Adepts who possessed this secret wisdom (or gnosis) would nurture their divine "spark" by transcending the corruptions of the flesh and worshipping a second god of pure spirit and love whose messenger was Jesus Christ. Proponents of Catharism were divided into the *Perfecti* (the perfect ones) and the *Credentes* (believers); the former acted as unofficial clergy and led lives of celibacy, simplicity, nonviolence, vegetarianism, and charitable acts, while the latter were allowed to lead regular lives in the world except that they avoided marriage and procreation, leading to charges of sexual perversion from Rome.[20]

In Melville's poem, the first quatrain presents an ironic juxtaposition of worldly achievement and its fatalistic result, a predictable product of the evil permeating the creation, asserted as a legal claim against the individual:

> Found a family, build a state,
> The pledged event is still the same:
> Matter in end will never abate
> His ancient brutal claim.
>   (ll. 1–4)

The negative view of sexual procreation and the state as an institution of power, as found in the Gnostic theology of Catharism, are echoed in the first line above. The succeeding and final stanza, following an implied gap in the text indicated by asterisks, presents the paradoxical relationship of action in the world and true redemption, according to Gnosticism's dualist beliefs:

> Indolence is heaven's ally here,
> And energy the child of hell:
> The Good Man pouring from his pitcher clear,
> But brims the poisoned well.
>   (ll. 5–8)

The quatrain summarizes the unworldly theology of the dualistic Cathars, who believed that the physical world was a hellish prison from which the believer should seek escape by the practice of asceticism but not suicide. The third line above subsumes a historical reference, for the Cathars, whose name was imposed on them by their enemies, originally called themselves the *Bonnes Hommes et Femmes* (Good Men and Women). If such Good Men indulge in pouring out their spirit by means of engagement with the world—especially in the form of procreative sexuality—they will only be contributing to the tainted "well" of the corrupt physical universe.

The final two poems of the first section of *Timoleon* examine the moral and spiritual deficiencies of the later nineteenth-century United States, with the nation's crass materialism coexistent with a decadent Christianity. In "The Age of the Antonines," Melville offered a comparison between the world of the second-century Roman Empire, as portrayed by Gibbon, with its string of "good" emperors culminating in the Stoic "philosopher king" Marcus Aurelius Antoninus (ruled 161–80 CE), and the world of Gilded Age America, with its political and commercial corruption led by the so-called robber barons. Stanton Garner has examined Melville's poem as a product of his many years as an inspector for the New York Custom House, with its vast network of bribery and political cronyism, as well as his concern with the collapse of republican virtues in an era dominated by venal politicians.[21] The poem begins by noting the disparity between the traditional millennial visions of the Protestant churches and the reality of war between major European powers (as in the Franco-Prussian War of 1870), and goes on to evoke pagan, second-century Rome as the zenith of Western civilization:

> While faith forecasts millennial years
> Spite Europe's embattled lines,
> Back to the past one glance be cast—
>   The Age of the Antonines!
> O summit of fate, O zenith of time
> When a pagan gentleman reigned,
> And the olive was nailed to the inn of the world
> Nor the peace of the just was feigned.
>   A halcyon Age, afar it shines,
> Solstice of Man and the Antonines.
>
> (ll. 1–10)

Proposing to look backward in history for an age of peace comparable to the Christian millennium, the poet, with Gibbon's Enlightenment historiography for guide, looks to a fabled era of the *Pax*

Romana under the rule of a pagan emperor before the transformation of Christianity into the official religion of the empire. In the ensuing stanza, the contrast between the unabashedly pluralistic polytheism of Rome and the salient vices of a declining Protestant Christianity are outlined:

> Hymns to the nations' friendly gods
> Went up from the fellowly shrines,
> No demagogue beat the pulpit-drum
>   In the Age of the Antonines!
> The sting was not dreamed to be taken from death,
> No Paradise pledged or sought,
> But they reasoned of fate at the flowing feast,
> Nor stifled the fluent thought.
>   We sham, we shuffle while faith declines—
> They were frank in the Age of the Antonines.
>
>   (ll. 11–20)

Instead of harboring the delusive hope for spiritual resurrection as posited by Saint Paul (1 Cor. 15), or the apocalyptic redemption from history set forth by the book of Revelation, the second-century Romans freely debated the operations of fate without the hypocritical "sham" of a providential universe that modern Christians must maintain, even while the dogmatic supports for the faith disintegrate.

In the third and final stanza, the poet notes the rule of law and political order that characterized the world of Marcus Aurelius, in contrast to the pervasive social climbing and political corruption of Gilded Age America, with its string of mediocre or ethically compromised presidents beginning with Grant:

> Orders and ranks they kept degree,
> Few felt how the parvenu pines,
> No lawmaker took the lawless one's fee
>   In the Age of the Antonines!
> Under law made will the world reposed
> And the ruler's right confessed,
> For the heavens elected the Emperor then,
> The Foremost of men the best.
>   Ah, might we read in America's signs
> The Age restored of the Antonines.
>
>   (ll. 21–30)

While Melville seems to echo the authoritarian political philosophy of Carlyle—the election of the emperor by the "heavens" suggests the anti-democratic stance of the Victorian chronicler of heroes—the emphasis on order presented here is the necessary precondition for the attainment of global peace in the poem. The final muted wish that America's "signs" (an ironic allusion to the "signs of the times" of Matthew 16:3) might indicate return to the world of the *Pax Romana*, although unrealistic, is an attempt to conclude the poem with a small consolatory hope for change.

The last poem in the first section of *Timoleon*, "Herba Santa" ("Holy Weed"; modern Spanish uses the spelling *hierba*, meaning "grass," "herb," or "weed"), proposes the sociable pleasures of smoking as a modern substitute for the god of Christianity who has failed to bring peace to the human race. While the modern reader must temporarily ignore contemporary knowledge about the health risks of smoking to fully appreciate this poem, the poem's representation of the ceremonial peace pipe, or Indian calumet, as a more likely instrument for bringing about a form of millennial peace than traditional Christian ritual is a deliberately provocative formulation that we can still appreciate. Moreover, the poem's praise of the peace pipe is additionally relevant in the context of the continuing decimation of Native American tribes in the later nineteenth century. As the poem implies, Christianity cannot fulfill its ostensible mission because Christ's loving sacrifice, commemorated in the Eucharist, has only led to two millennia of schism and war between sects of worshippers:

> Shall code or creed a lure afford
> To win all selves to Love's accord?
> When Love ordained a supper divine
>   For the wide world of man,
> What bickerings o'er his gracious wine!
>   Then strange new feuds began.
>   (ll. 8–13)

Instead of conflict, the lowly peace pipe as a form of smoky communion will ironically outdo Christ and Christianity at their own "pacific" mission of uniting the human race in one nonsectarian community:

> Effectual more, in lowlier way,
>   Pacific Herb, thy sensuous plea
> The bristling clans of Adam sway

At least to fellowship in thee!
Before thine altar tribal flags are furled,
Fain woulds't thou make one hearthstone of the world.
(ll. 14–19)

Through its access to the "soul" from the "nerve," the sacred herb can effectuate a relief from regret, or even sin, in a manner like that of conventional Christianity; "so canst win / Some from repinings, some from sin, / The Church's aim thou dost subserve" (ll. 30–32). While the working class can find relief and reconciliation with their lot in the act of smoking ("Him soothest thou and smoothest down / Till some content return again" [ll. 35–36]), even the worst classes of men can find a redemptive influence in the sacred herb, which offers a nonsectarian gospel:

Even ruffians feel thy influence breed
    Saint Martin's summer in the mind,
They feel this last evangel plead,
As did the first, apart from creed,
    Be peaceful, man—be kind!
(ll. 37–41)

Feeling the mellowness of Indian summer ("Saint Martin's summer") in their minds, the most recalcitrant human subjects will feel peace and charity toward their fellow man and woman. In the penultimate stanza, the speaker asks whether the sacred herb, a mere "weed," can act as a modern substitute for Christ's Second Coming, since the universal love promised by Christ's first advent has not been fulfilled:

Rejected once on higher plain,
O Love supreme, to come again
    Can this be thine?
Again to come, and win us too
    In likeness of a weed
That as a god didst vainly woo,
    As man more vainly bleed?
(ll. 42–48)

In the end, however, such hopes of a modern form of secular redemption may seem misguided; for the poet concludes by reminding himself to remain content with merely dreaming of such possibilities while enjoying the sensual delights of tobacco alone:

Forbear my soul! and in thine Eastern chamber
    Rehearse the dream that brings the long release:

Through jasmine sweet and talismanic amber
   Inhaling Herba Santa in the passive Pipe of Peace.
                    (ll. 49–52)

"Herba Santa," then, offers a modern naturalistic substitute for the repeatedly failed millennial dreams of Christianity, creating peace where
the latter only fomented division and conflict. Just as the act of smoking consecrated the friendship of Ishmael and Queequeg in the early
chapters of *Moby-Dick*, the same is proffered here as a remedy for the
ills of the later nineteenth-century world. If the spirit of Christ is conspicuous by its absence, then the poet will suggest a secular religion of
communal smoking. The poem thus augments Melville's argument in
the poems of *Timoleon* that Christianity has run its historical course,
and its savior god has no chance of return to redeem humanity from a
fallen world.

The second section of *Timoleon*, titled "Fruits of Travel Long Ago," consists of eighteen poems that are distinguishable from the first section
of the collection by their evocation of picturesque sights from Italy,
Greece, and Egypt, including historical cities and landscapes ("Venice," "Pausilippo," "The Attic Landscape," "Off Cape Colonna," "Syra,"
"In the Desert"), as well as architecture ("Pisa's Leaning Tower," "Milan Cathedral," "The Parthenon," "Greek Architecture," "The Great
Pyramid"). The overall impression left by many of these poems is the
spiritual beauty inherent in Mediterranean landscapes and cultures adhering to classical canons of aesthetics, which thereby demonstrate a
"reverence for the Archetype" ("Greek Architecture," l. 4). In these poems, the varied portrayal of the disappearance of God found in the first
section is replaced by the representation of classical forms of beauty as
objects of quasi-religious devotion—a transformation in keeping with
the various manifestations of Aestheticism in later nineteenth-century
culture and art.

    While most of the poems in "Fruits of Travel Long Ago" pertain to
art and classical aesthetics, however, the final two poems, both set in
Egypt, complete the whole collection's skeptical depiction of religious
themes by associating the monotheistic god of the West with the arid
landscape of ancient Egypt. Thus "In the Desert" describes in a series
of four quatrains the poet's overwhelming experience of the noonday
desert sun, whose power is depicted as comparable to the Hebrew god's.
Beginning with a striking paradoxical image, the poet in the first stanza
compares the intensity of the light of the desert sun to the "plague" of

total darkness that Yahweh brought the Egyptians as punishment for pharaoh's intransigence (Exod. 10:21–23): "Never Pharaoh's Night, / Whereof the Hebrew wizards croon, / Did so the Theban flamens try / As me this veritable Noon" (ll. 1–4). In the second stanza, the intense light is compared to the experience of a calm at sea, when "Undulates the ethereal frame; / In one flowing oriflamme / God flings his fiery standard out." Originally the red banner of Saint Denis, an "oriflamme" (i.e., gold flame) describes any flag that rallies troops for battle. God's act of flinging his "fiery standard out" (ll. 6–9)—a likely reminder of Yahweh as a military Lord of Hosts (Josh. 5:14) and Divine Warrior (Ps. 77:16–20; Isa. 13:13; Joel 2:11)—implies the omnipotent power of the sunlight on the open ocean, when the atmosphere of the sky "undulates" with radiant energy even as the ocean is hypnotically still. In the third stanza, the desert sunlight is described as so powerful that it vanquished Napoleon's soldiers during his Egyptian campaign; for "bayonetted by the sun / His gunners drop beneath the gun," another likely allusion to the Hebrew god of battles.

In the final stanza, we witness a shift in mood as the poet salutes the desert sunlight as the mystical manifestation of the Hebrew divinity: "Holy, holy, holy Light! / Immaterial incandescence, / Of God the effluence of the essence, / Shekinah, intolerably bright!" (ll. 14–17). At the start of book III of *Paradise Lost*, Milton had paid tribute to "holy Light," celebrating it as a visual form of the divine nature: "Bright effluence of bright essence increate" (III.6). In Melville's adaptation of the blind poet's salute, the divine light, or "shekinah," overwhelms human perception, just as the light of the burning bush had overcome Moses, so that the prophet "hid his face, for he was afraid to look upon God" (Exod. 3:6). As the "dwelling" or presence of God in post-biblical and rabbinical Judaism, the *shekhinah* was conceived as being present in the pillar of cloud and tent of meeting that accompanied the Israelites in the Sinai desert; hence Melville's use of the term is symbolically appropriate here. "In the Desert," then, confirms the mystical presence of a godlike force in the sunlight of the Egyptian desert; yet it is a force that is potentially inimical to human well-being. The poem thus hints at the ambiguous nature of the divine presence, as previously experienced by the prophet Moses and the Hebrew people generally, whose god was an inscrutable combination of redemptive and destructive characteristics.

If "In the Desert" salutes the blindingly godlike power of light, the poem's Egyptian counterpart, "The Great Pyramid," offers an antithetical image of the divine embodied in an ancient architectural wonder symbolizing the monotheistic god of Judeo-Christian tradition. Melville associates the creation of the monumental Great Pyramid of Giza with the creation of a monotheistic god synonymous with Yahweh of the Old Testament. Built in 2560 BCE as the tomb for King Cheops in the Fourth Dynasty, the limestone Great Pyramid at 455 feet high was the tallest manmade structure in the world until the completion of Lincoln Cathedral circa 1300. Basing his poem on the account he wrote in his travel journal of ascending the same stupendous architectural wonder on December 31, 1856, during his trip to Europe and the Levant, Melville created a portrait of an archetypal deity who is massive in size and power—a supreme embodiment of sublime wonder and terror.

As Melville recorded in his journal at the time, "I shudder at idea of ancient Egyptians. It was in these pyramids that was conceived the idea of Jehovah. Terrible mixture of the cunning and awful. Moses learned in all the lore of the Egyptians [Acts 7:22]. The idea of Jehovah born here." Moses's dependence on Egyptian religion for the development of Israelite monotheism had been debated throughout the Enlightenment, and Melville was no doubt aware of some of these debates, as shown by his remarks here. He then comments in his journal on the massive structures' oppressive presence: "Pyramids still loom before me—something vast, indefinite, incomprehensible, and awful." The very form of his poem on the pyramid, with two pairs of octosyllabic couplets followed by a shortened four-syllable line, accentuates the immoveable solidity of the massive stone structure. Sharing characteristics of the evil Gnostic creator god, the deistic notion of Yahweh as a product of Jewish priestcraft, and the cruelly predestinating god of Calvinism, Melville's enigmatic pyramid is ambiguously poised between human and supernatural influences, nature and culture; it is thus a fitting final manifestation of Melville's religious skepticism.[22]

In the poem's seven stanzas—the number being symbolic of divine perfection or completion—Melville creates an image of the overwhelming physical presence of the pyramid. Thus in the first stanza, the poet notes the enormous scale of the masonry of the monument, asking whether it is a product of a human or divine creator, culture or nature; for the huge rows of stone blocks, or "courses," in the pyramid—the pyramid's steplike structure after its polished outer limestone casing had worn away—create a question in the viewer's mind about the mysterious origins of such a structure:

> Your masonry—and is it man's?
> More like some Cosmic artizan's.

Your courses as in strata rise,
Beget you do a blind surmise
        Like Grampians.
            (ll. 1–5)

The Grampian Mountains of the Scottish Highlands, which exhibited rugged pyramid-like slopes comparable to those described in Melville's poem, contained the highest mountain peak in the British Isles, Ben Nevis (4,409 feet).

Continuing the image of the pyramid as mountain, the second stanza focuses on the tiny forms of those climbing the pyramid, who ascend it like those scaling an Alpine peak:

Far slanting up your sweeping flank
Arabs with Alpine goats may rank,
And there they find a choice of passes
Even like to dwarfs that climb the masses
        Of glaciers blank.
            (ll. 6–10)

The geological and architectural imagery become interfused here, as local Arabs ascending with their mountain-climbing "Alpine" goats face the same challenges as those climbing the empty white expanse ("blank") of gigantic European glaciers. In the third and fourth stanzas, the pyramid reveals itself as impervious to nature and the elements, a "sterile" arid structure that dominates the blue skies of the desert and weathers its sandstorms:

Shall lichen in your crevice fit?
Nay, sterile all and granite-knit:
Weather nor weather-strain ye rue,
But aridly you cleave the blue
        As lording it.
Morn's vapor floats beneath your peak,
Kites skim your side with pinion weak;
To sand-storms battering, blow on blow,
Raging to work your overthrow,
        You—turn the cheek.
            (ll. 11–20)

The truncated fifth line of each stanza here confirms the association between the pyramid and the Judeo-Christian god; for the

pyramid is "lording it" over its environment like the "Lord" of the
Old Testament, while the ironic image of the pyramid turning its
"cheek" to the sandstorm makes subversive use of Jesus's well-
known championship of nonresistance to violence in the Sermon
on the Mount (Matt. 5:39). Exemplifying impassivity instead of
pacifism, the pyramid is inhumanly indifferent to the vicissitudes
of time and weather. Then, in the fifth stanza, to the idea of the
pyramid's indifference to the elements is added the seemingly eternal nature of the structure's age:

> All elements unmoved you stem,
> Foursquare you stand and suffer them:
> Time's future infinite you dare,
> While, for the past, 'tis you that wear
>   Eld's diadem.
>   (ll. 20-25)

Since the pyramid does not show any sign of physical decline, its existence extends infinitely into the future, while its demonstrable antiquity has earned it a crown of divine sovereignty.

In the sixth stanza, those who seek to enter the pyramid's labyrin-
thine passages are driven mad and die, as legend relates:

> Slant from your inmost lead the caves
> And labyrinths rumored. These who braves
> And penetrates (old palmers said)
> Comes out afar on deserts dead
>   And, dying, raves.
>   (ll. 26-30)

"Palmers" are those who have made a pilgrimage to the Holy Land; the
heart of the enigmatic pyramid is thus depicted by legend as forbidden
to mortals, just as it was forbidden to enter into the inner sanctuary of
the Hebrew Temple in Jerusalem. The last stanza of the poem continues
the association of the pyramid with the Hebrew god:

> Craftsmen, in dateless quarries dim,
> Stones formless into form did trim,
> Usurped on Nature's self with Art,
> And bade this dumb I AM to start,
>   Imposing him.
>   (ll. 31-35)

The implicit paradox is that this godlike architectural structure was created by human "craftsmen," whose architectural creation "usurped" on nature with a form of "art." The word "art" here implies the notion of "artifice," for the pyramid is not an object of creative and imaginative beauty, as are the Greek temples described in other poems in this section of *Timoleon*; it is instead comparable to the elusive but strategically calculating Yahweh of the Old Testament, who enigmatically named himself "I AM THAT I AM" to Moses at the burning bush (Exod. 3:14). Like the Old Testament divinity, whose unlimited power was seemingly imposed by priestly "craftsmen," the pyramid was brought into existence by human builders working in "dateless quarries dim" but has then assumed a seemingly independent life of its own. The last stanza of Melville's poem thus evokes the traditional Enlightenment attack on Judeo-Christian religion as the product of designing priestcraft. In the end, Melville's evocation of the Great Pyramid implies the creation of the god of monotheism by the Hebrews as a blend of both human ingenuity and supernatural mystery—a mystery that the shape of the pyramid (named by the Greeks after its resemblance to the form of a flame, or *pyr*) has traditionally conveyed.

In August 1861, John Ruskin wrote to his American friend Charles Eliot Norton, "It is to me so fearful a discovery to find how God has allowed all who have variously sought Him in the most earnest way to be blinded—how Puritan—monk—Brahmin—Churchman—Turk— are all merely names for different madnesses and ignorances." Like Ruskin, Melville was a lifelong religious seeker whose fiction and poetry portrayed the various forms of "madness" and "ignorance" that possessed those who thought they had discovered the reality of the divine. Melville's last self-published volume of poetry reveals a similar concern with the deliberate or inadvertent betrayal that faith in God has perpetrated on various individuals and societies; yet here and elsewhere he demonstrates the recurrent human need—or instinct—for faith. Basem L. Ra'ad has noted this basic duality in Melville's attitude toward religion: "on the one hand, his recognition of the unconscious human need for mythic protection; on the other hand, his distrust of the self-deceptive obsessions that the religious mind creates." We may conclude that Melville's recurrent interest in the irresolvable problems of faith and belief reveals a mind devoted to the continued intellectual inquiry and suspended judgment—the skeptical outlook—that were integral to his creativity as a writer of both fiction and poetry. In the next, and last, chapter, we will explore how, despite his manifest disbelief in traditional Christian doctrine, Melville still embraced the symbolic truth of the Judeo-Christian myth of the Fall and adapted it as a major theme in his last, unpublished work of fiction.[23]

CHAPTER 8

Legends of the Fall

Genesis, Paradise Lost, *Schopenhauer,* Billy Budd

At about the same time as he was self-publishing *Timoleon, Etc.*, with its skeptical examination of a variety of gods and religious traditions from both West and East, but chiefly focused on his own Judeo-Christian heritage, Melville was engaged in finishing what turned out to be his final work of narrative fiction, which he left in semi-final form as a mass of manuscript sheets at his death—a sibylline text that would first see print in 1924, but only receive likely definitive textual form in the 2017 Northwestern-Newberry edition of Melville's works. *Billy Budd* would thus provide Melville with a final opportunity to probe the moral framework of the biblical myth of the Fall and the origin of evil within Judeo-Christian tradition, which saw its mythically redemptive counterpart in the atoning Crucifixion and Resurrection of Christ; and he drew on this archetypal drama not with any inclination to authenticate the literal truth claims of the Bible but to validate its continued relevance to human experience. *Billy Budd* would be neither Melville's final testament of faith nor of doubt, but a skeptical recognition of the power of biblical myth to represent the universal problem of evil in human nature, institutions, societies, and the cosmos. As a final statement of his skeptical engagement with Christianity for most of his adult life, *Billy Budd* would pay tribute to the ultimate source of many of his narrative themes and motifs in the Bible.

How exactly do we account for Melville's return to the form of prose fiction in order to write *Billy Budd, Sailor* in the late 1880s, more than three decades after publication of *The Confidence-Man*, the novel that ended his career as a professional writer of fiction? On a practical level, if the novella emerged from his effort to provide a headnote to "Billy in the Darbies," a poem originally intended to be included in his collection *John Marr and Other Sailors* (1888), the larger motivation to compose *Billy Budd* as a belated capstone to his literary career has also been plausibly traced to a variety of sources. These include Melville's extensive reading of Balzac's fiction in the 1880s, as evidenced by his purchase of numerous volumes from a new edition of the great French realist; the contemporary debate over the morality of capital punishment, especially two opposing journalistic accounts of the 1842 *Somers* naval mutiny case in which three sailors were hanged on evidence provided by Melville's cousin Guert Gansevoort; the influence of current labor unrest, notably the violent confrontation in 1886 of workers and police in Haymarket Square in Chicago, raising issues of state power versus workers' rights; and finally the haunting death of Melville's eighteen-year-old son Malcolm in September 1867 by a self-inflicted gunshot wound to the head.[1]

While some or all of these factors may have played a part in motivating Melville to return to prose fiction, the writing of *Billy Budd* was undoubtedly also based on Melville's lifelong preoccupation with the problem of evil. For writing *Billy Budd* provided Melville with a final opportunity to explore a core myth of Christianity—the Fall of Adam and Eve from paradise—and to meditate on his virtual obsession with what Saint Paul described as the "mystery of iniquity" (2 Thess. 2:7) and evil's paradoxical existence in relation to an allegedly good god. Following the lead of critics who have focused on Melville's use of Christian myth, symbolism, allegory, and typology in *Billy Budd*, in this chapter I will explore Melville's use of the theme of the Fall in *Billy Budd* in relation to his chief sources in the Bible and Milton's *Paradise Lost*. I will also suggest that Melville's immersion in the writings of Arthur Schopenhauer in the last year of his life, when he had largely completed his novella, provided him with timely confirmation of the philosophical and moral truth behind his depiction of biblical myth in *Billy Budd*.[2]

By dramatizing a modern version of the Fall in *Billy Budd*, Melville was demonstrating the tenacity with which he held to the symbolic truth of this traditional Christian doctrine, which had shaped the history of Christianity but was becoming a theological relic within the liberalizing churches of the late nineteenth century, including the All Souls Unitarian Church to which he and his wife belonged. We recall that Melville had written in his epochal 1850 review of Hawthorne's *Mosses from an Old Manse* that like Shakespeare, Hawthorne's greatest strength as a writer came from the depiction in his writing of the "power of blackness," which according to Melville "derives its force from its appeals to that Calvinistic sense of Innate Depravity and Original Sin, from whose visitations, in some shape or other, no deeply thinking mind is always and wholly free. For, in certain moods, no man can weigh this world, without throwing in something, somehow like Original Sin, to strike the uneven balance." Melville's elliptical phrasing here shows that he is suggesting a metaphysical, not a doctrinal, truth embedded within Christian theology; indeed, the ultimate responsibility for this "original sin" is left potentially ambiguous. In addition to his evocation in the *Mosses* review of the moral depth of Shakespeare's and Hawthorne's literary creations, an implicit purpose of Melville's claim here was to validate the thematic basis of his own novel-in-progress in 1850, with its revenge-obsessed whaling captain on a mission to fathom the metaphysical origins of evil. Four decades after he wrote his *Mosses* review, Melville would again show in *Billy Budd* that he held to the same idea that the onset of evil figured by a mythical Fall typified the ineluctable presence of evil and human suffering in the world—an idea shared by the "deeply thinking mind" of Arthur Schopenhauer, whose influence as a philosopher was pervasive in later nineteenth-century European cultures.[3]

The Judeo-Christian doctrine of the Fall had its origins in the third chapter of the Old Testament book of Genesis in which Adam and Eve are evicted from their paradisiacal state for disobeying the divine order not to eat the fruit of the tree of knowledge. Along with the ultimate punishments of sin and death, Adam and Eve were each given onerous gender-based physical labors—pain and sorrow in childbirth for the woman and sorrowful physical labor for the man—while the originally reptilian serpent was condemned to become a dust-eating snake at perpetual war with humanity, God telling it that there will be "enmity between thy seed and her seed; it shall bruise thy head, and thou shalt bruise his heel" (Gen. 3:15). In the New Testament only the Crucifixion and Resurrection of Christ will potentially end this divinely ordained war, when the redemptive "last Adam" (1 Cor. 15:45) will atone for humanity's original sin in Eden and restore humanity's lost condition of immortality, all according to a theological system developed by Saint Paul and the early Church Fathers.[4]

The influence of the archetype of the Fall in *Billy Budd* is evident throughout the narrative, with the major roles of Adam and Eve, Serpent, and God filled by Billy Budd, John Claggart, and Edward Fairfax Vere, respectively. At the start of *Billy Budd*, we are accordingly introduced by the narrator to the tradition of the "Handsome Sailor," an exemplar of physical strength and beauty, whose charismatic presence makes him a cynosure to his shipmates and an object of aesthetic contemplation with multiple archetypal associations beginning with the Judeo-Christian primordial man. Billy's example of Adam-like grace and appeal is also found, for example, in the black common sailor bearing "the blood of Ham," observed by the narrator half a century earlier on the docks of Liverpool surrounded by a diverse assemblage of sailors of all races, who are described as comparable to a group of Assyrian priests worshipping "their grand sculptured Bull when the faithful prostrated themselves." In a stormy sea, such a type of strong and fearless sailor might be seen reefing the topsail in the pose of "young Alexander curbing the fiery Bucephalus." With this initial representation of the moral and physical ideal that Billy Budd will exemplify—an adaptation suggesting the eighteenth-century cultural convention of the Noble Savage—the young sailor is formally introduced as the orphaned, blond-haired, and blue-eyed foretopman on the HMS *Bellipotent* who has been impressed into naval service in 1797 owing to the exigencies of the war with France, when a shortage of manpower and unrest against institutional abuses that had previously led to mutiny created the emergency conditions depicted in the narrative.[5]

As the narrator notes in the prelude to the story proper, Billy Budd began his sailing career in the British merchant marine, where his status as an iconic "Handsome Sailor" was first established. As Captain Graveling tells Lieutenant Ratcliffe during Billy's impressment from the *Rights-of-Man*—the ship being named after Thomas Paine's outspoken revolutionary rebuttal to Edmund Burke's *Reflections on the Revolution in France* (1790)—Billy was an effective peacemaker on his ship by his mere presence, as if "a virtue went out of him" (6). Like Christ, who blessed peacemakers and cured demoniacs (Matt. 5:9; 8:28–34), Billy has exerted a charismatically calming presence on his shipmates, but he will now be transferred to a ship whose sole mission is devoted to the business of killing, and whose institutional structure will reflect the strict regimentation necessary for its military mission. The initial association of Billy's Adam-like identity with a ship named the *Rights-of-Man* is appropriate in that Paine's argument in his Revolutionary-era treatise was partly based on the idea of innate human rights being traceable to primordial man: "It may be worth observing that the genealogy of Christ is traced to Adam. Why then not trace the rights of man to the creation of man?" Indeed, "every child born into the world must be considered as deriving its existence from God. The world is as new to him as it was to the first man that existed, and his natural right in it is of the same kind."[6] When Billy Budd thus good-naturedly bids farewell to his ship by saying "goodbye to you, old *Rights-of-Man*" (7), he is marking his forced exit from a realm of Adam-like natural rights into the fallen world of "Cain's city" (10), in which his archetypal innocence and personal beauty will stand out as a provocation to the corrupt and serpentine master-at-arms, John Claggart.

While Billy's status as a "foundling" associates him with the traditional biography of a mythical hero, the narrator's extended portrait of Billy also reveals the full extent of his identity as an androgynous Adam figure who implicitly incorporates the identity of Adam's God-given consort Eve. The latter association is evident in the description of Billy's introduction to the crew of the *Bellipotent* as "analogous to that of a rustic beauty transplanted from the provinces and brought into competition with the high born dames of the court" (9)—an anticipation of the envious desire that will motivate Claggart—as well as in the ensuing description of Billy's strikingly beautiful physical form "suggestive of a mother eminently favored by Love and the Graces; all this strangely indicated a lineage in direct contradiction to his lot" (9). After identifying himself as a foundling to the officer mustering him into the naval service, Billy also reveals his illiteracy, which inspires the narrator to make an explicit association between Billy and his prelapsarian mythical model: "He possessed that kind and degree of intelligence going along with the unconventional rectitude of a sound human creature, one to whom not yet has been proffered the questionable apple of knowledge" (10). Billy, in sum, "was little more than a sort of upright barbarian, much such as Adam presumably might have been ere the urbane serpent wriggled himself into his company" (10). Yet in a crucial caveat to Billy's seemingly unfallen Adamic identity, the narrator notes one slight defect in his physical makeup in his tendency to stutter under stress: "In this particular Billy was a striking instance that the arch interferer, the envious marplot of Eden, still has more or less to do with every human consignment to this planet of Earth" (11). While the characterization of an envious Satan or serpent here hints at Milton's representation of the Fall in *Paradise Lost*, the narrator's insistence on

Billy's inheritance of a small token of humanity's original sin is conso- nant with Saint Paul's influential assertion in the Letter to the Romans that a "law of sin" afflicts all human "members" (Rom. 7:23), in this case, Billy Budd's flawed vocal organs. While the young sailor's defect of a stutter is initially presented here as a physical disability illustrating the potential satanic interference on the body and soul of every human born on earth, it will become an inadvertent tragic flaw under the ex- traordinary circumstances presented later in the story.

Following the narrator's evocation of the historical background of the story in the time of the notorious mutiny against naval abuses by sailors in ships at the Nore anchorage in the Thames estuary, and the introduction of the philosophical character of Captain Vere, we are given a portrait of the satanic serpent figure in the master-at-arms, John Claggart, whose antagonism to Billy Budd will inspire the major events of the story. As the chief disciplinary officer on the *Bellipotent*, Claggart plays a role suggestive of the Old Testament origins of "the satan" as a moral "accuser" acting under the auspices of the deity (as in the book of Job), just as Claggart acts under Vere's authority—a role that also accords with the Germanic root of the first syllable of Claggart's name (klag = "complainer," "accuser").[7] In other respects, too, Claggart sug- gests the symbolic Old Testament lineage of the Christian devil in that the pale-complexioned, shady-looking Claggart is described as having initially entered the British navy from a higher social station: "His gen- eral aspect and manner were so suggestive of an education and career incongruous with his naval function that when not actively engaged in it he looked like a man of high quality, social and moral, who for rea- sons of his own was keeping incog [incognito]" (20). Claggart's fallen social status is comparable to that of the fallen Lucifer of the Old Tes- tament found in Isaiah 14, an important Old Testament prototype of the Christian devil providing many later literary and cultural variants. The characterization also evokes the image of Milton's Satan as a fallen archangel still bearing traces of his original nobility:

> Darkened so, yet shone
> Above them all th' Archangel: but his face
> Deep scars of thunder had intrenched, and care
> Sat on his faded cheek, but under brows
> Of dauntless courage, and considerate pride
> Waiting revenge.
>   (I, 599–604)

Claggart's distinguished, upper-class appearance similarly conforms to the model of the gentlemanly Mephistopheles often found in Romantic-era representations of the Christian devil, as influentially depicted in Goethe's *Faust*. With his prognathous jaw making him look like the perjury-convicted fabricator of the Popish Plot, Titus Oates, and a likely background as a criminal *chevalier* from Revolutionary France, Claggart has risen from the ranks and established himself aboard the *Bellipotent* as an efficient disciplinary officer with a genius for ferreting out presumed guilt with the help of a network of spies and informers.[8]

It doesn't take long for Billy to discover that no matter how conscientious he is about stowing his bag and keeping his hammock neat, he is still reprimanded for infractions of the rules by Claggart's agents, causing him anxiety about the risks of the flogging he has witnessed as a newcomer to the warship. His anxiety drives him to ask an experienced shipmate, the oracular "old Dansker," about his case, to which the veteran sailor replies that Claggart apparently had developed a grudge against him: "'Baby Budd, *Jemmy Legs*' (meaning the master-at-arms) 'is down on you'" (25). Mystified by this news, Billy is soon made aware of Claggart's presence in a direct encounter, but he mistakenly interprets the master-at-arms's behavior as favorable to him when he accidentally spills soup directly in front of the passing disciplinary officer. Claggart, however, perversely takes the soup as a personal affront, tapping Billy with his rattan and sarcastically remarking, "Handsomely done, my lad! And handsome is as handsome did it, too!" followed by "an involuntary smile, or rather grimace" (26). Claggart's suspicion that Billy Budd has deliberately insulted him confirms the perverse pathological hatred he has developed toward the newly impressed foretopman because of the latter's exemplary physical beauty and simple, ingenuous nature.

In three key chapters, the narrator examines the seemingly inexplicable basis for Claggart's instinctive hatred of Billy Budd, which leads to a desire to destroy the foretopman. Today we might say that Claggart's predatory personality accords with modern psychological research on the small class of conscienceless individuals afflicted with an antisocial personality disorder—one who blends in with social groups and excels at manipulative behavior and deception for his own selfish ends. In *The Science of Evil: On Empathy and the Origins of Cruelty*, psychologist Simon Baron-Cohen identifies acts that we denominate as "evil" as stemming from a complete absence, or "zero-degrees," of empathy, which Baron-Cohen identifies in individuals diagnosed with borderline, psychopathic, and/or narcissistic personality disorders; those afflicted with psychopathy in particular are often subject to "attributional bias," or ascribing a hostile intent to individuals who manifest no such motivation. In the case of Melville's fictional master-of-arms, we can place him within this diagnostic purview, as he demonstrates an absence of empathy for Billy following the young sailor's impressment into naval service. Indeed, Claggart wishes to destroy the innocent foretopman whom he accuses of plotting mutiny and whose attitude and actions he maliciously misinterprets in clear examples of pathological attributional bias. Billy's physical grace and uncorrupted character manifestly cause indelible injury to Claggart's narcissistic sense of self.[9]

Within the historical frame of the narrative, Claggart's perverse but enigmatic character causes the narrator to search through a roster of literary, social, philosophical, and biblical explanations of the master-at-arms' irrational motivations to hate Billy merely for his attractive appearance and good nature. If Plato's idea of "natural depravity" applies only to discrete individuals as products of nature, and Calvin's emphasis on humanity's corruption by original sin suggests a generalized perversity of disposition, only Saint Paul's well-known phrase "mystery of iniquity" (2 Thess. 2:7), describing the secretive subversive actions of demonic evil at the end-times, adequately suggests the type of Claggart's latently evil nature in its paradoxical combination of insanely destructive ends and calculated means: "Towards the accomplishment of an aim which in wantonness of atrocity would seem to partake of the insane, he will direct a cool judgment sagacious and sound" (26). Claggart's secret malice toward a benevolent Billy is, as the narrator notes, ultimately grounded in a combination of hatred and envy: "If askance he eyed the good looks, cheery health, and frank enjoyment of young life in Billy Budd, it was because these went along with a nature that, as Claggart magnetically felt, had in its simplicity never willed malice or experienced the reactionary bite of the serpent" (30). Claggart instinctively senses that Billy, in his radical innocence, leads an exemplary life because he has never committed evil acts nor been their victim.

With the mention of Claggart's motives of spontaneous envy, we are made aware of Melville's use here of Milton's influential characterization of Satan in *Paradise Lost* as motivated by comparable emotions in his destruction of Adam and Eve in their privileged paradise and special relationship with the divine parent.[10] Milton's Satan had been a model for several of Melville's most memorable characters, notably Captain Ahab, and here Melville makes superlative use of the fallen angel's depiction as an envious agent for the destruction of Adam and Eve. After Milton's Satan deliberates in book IV on his self-inflicted fall from heaven and his planned revenge on God's newly created human couple, the poet notes of the arch-fiend,

> Thus while he spake, each passion dimmed his face,
> Thrice changd with pale, ire, envy, and despair,
> Which marred his borrowed visage, and betrayed
> Him counterfeit, if any eye beheld.
> For Heav'nly minds from such distempers foul
> Are ever clear. Whereof he soon aware,
> Each perturbation smoothed with outward calm,
> Artificer of fraud; and was the first
> That practised falsehood under saintly show,
> Deep malice to conceal, couched with revenge:
>   (IV, 114–23)

Milton's depiction of Satan accordingly assumes a key role in the characterization of Claggart, with the archfiend's acute despair over his fallen condition, his corrosive envy of the innocent and beautiful Adam and Eve, and his practiced hypocrisy all being translated into Claggart's comparable attitude toward the androgynous and Adam-like foretopman Billy. Thus Claggart saw the "charm" of Billy's innocence, "and fain would have shared it, but he despaired of it" (30). In short, "With no power to annul the elemental evil in him, though readily enough he could hide it; apprehending the good, but powerless to be it; a nature like Claggart's, surcharged with energy as such natures almost invariably are, what recourse is left to it but to recoil upon itself and, like the scorpion for which the Creator alone is responsible, act out to the end the part allotted it" (30). Claggart is thus ironically condemned to exert his formidable powers of destruction (including self-destruction) because of his despairing powerlessness to change his God-given evil nature; ironically, his destructive impulse toward Billy Budd will indeed result in his own violent death as his intended victim unexpectedly becomes a deadly nemesis figure. It is important to note that Claggart's envy of Billy is largely hidden from his own consciousness; moreover, the foretopman has no idea of the master-at-arms's irrational antipathy to him because of his exemplary physical appearance and moral innocence.[11]

Imagining the foretopman as genuinely motivated by the disdain for him that he wrongly imputes to Billy because of his own pathological "attributional bias," Claggart makes an aggressive effort to entrap Billy in a manufactured plot of mutiny by deputizing one of his agents to approach Billy one night and tempt him with two guineas ("two small objects faintly twinkling in the night-light" [33]) to join an imaginary conspiracy of sailors who have been impressed like Billy—a visually appealing temptation like the fruit that the serpent offered Eve (Gen. 3:6) but that a virtuous Billy, unlike his archetypal Edenic models, indignantly rejects as appealing to his disloyalty. Yet Billy is mystified why he should be targeted for this particular test of loyalty to the ship and its officers, and the old Dansker is unwilling to tell him anything more than he has already said about Jemmy Legs being "down on" Billy. The test is continued when Billy notices that two minor officers, the armorer and the captain of the hold, who are both messmates with Claggart, begin to eye him suspiciously, but Billy's radical innocence again makes him unable to explain this further questioning of his integrity.

After watching Billy survive these trials to his innocence, Claggart now exhibits a paradoxical combination of frustrated love and malign hatred that infuses his feelings for the foretopman: "Then would Claggart look like the man of sorrows. Yes, and sometimes the melancholy expression would have in it a touch of soft yearning, as if Claggart could even have loved Billy but for fate and ban" (38). Claggart's attitude here manifestly matches Satan's ambivalent emotions when first viewing Adam and Eve enjoying themselves in their playful paradise in Milton's epic:

> O Hell! What do mine eyes with grief behold,
> Into our room of bliss thus high advanced
> Creatures of another mould, earth-born perhaps,
> Not Spirits, yet to Heav'nly Spirits bright
> Little inferior; whom my thoughts pursue
> With Wonder, and could love, so lively shines
> In them Divine resemblance, and such grace
> The hand that formed them on their shape hath poured.
>   (IV, 358–65)

Yet even if Claggart can at times conjure up a visage of suffering like the archetypal Old Testament image of the "man of sorrows" (see Isaiah 53), traditionally identified as a typological model for Christ, a more authentic Satan-like identity is evident in him when he unexpectedly runs into Billy on the ship on various other occasions: "But upon any abrupt unforeseen encounter a red light would flash forth from his eye like a spark from an anvil in a dusk smithy. That quick, fierce light was a strange one, darted from orbs which in repose were of a color nearest approaching a deeper violet, the softest of shades" (38). If the red light of the blacksmith's shop here suggests the devil's fiery pit, the deep violet in Claggart's eyes evokes a traditional color of royalty and power, as suited to a monstrous egotist who is bereft of sympathy for his innocent victim.

The events leading to the climax of the narrative begin with Claggart's desperate gamble of going directly to Captain Vere to accuse Budd of plotting mutiny, seeing that all his efforts to entrap him have failed to provoke any actionable response. As we now learn, Vere had from the first been impressed with Billy Budd's physical beauty and nautical prowess, congratulating his lieutenant after the impressment for "lighting on such a fine specimen of the genus homo, who in the nude might have posed for a statue of young Adam before the Fall" (43), an estimation in dramatic contrast to Claggart's jarring claim that the impressed sailor was really a satanic "mantrap under daisies" (43). Suspicious of the veracity of Claggart's accusations and conscious of the sensitivity of the charges at a time of recent mutinous discontent within the British fleet but on high alert for enemy engagement, Vere decides to have Budd respond to Claggart's accusation in person in his cabin, a situation that inadvertently dooms the foretopman when his speech impediment prevents him from responding to Claggart's accusation except by delivering a fatal blow to the master-at-arms's forehead. As we know from Claggart's intuitive awareness that Billy has never felt the "reactionary bite of the serpent," his first experience of apparently motiveless malignity in the master-at-arms's false accusation is an assault on his moral integrity and results in an instinctive act of retaliation.

The moment before the fatal blow, as Claggart repeats the outrageous charge of mutiny, we witness Budd's traumatic discovery of the master-at-arms's hidden malice, which is evident in the regressive transformation of Claggart's eyes into those of an Edenic snake and then a primordial creature of the oceanic deep—changing from a hypnotic predatory stare to a threatened discharge of electricity: "Meanwhile the accuser's eyes, removing not as yet from the blue dilated ones, underwent a phenomenal change, their wonted rich violet color blurring into a muddy purple. Those lights of human intelligence, losing human expression, were gelidly protruding like the alien eyes of certain uncatalogued creatures of the deep. The first mesmeristic glance was one of serpent fascination; the last was as the paralyzing lurch of the torpedo-fish" (46). As mirrors of the soul, Claggart's eyes are regressively transformed from having a human to a nonhuman appearance, initially resembling those of the archetypal biblical symbol of evil in the serpent, and changing into the ocular apparatus of predatory monsters of the sea. Following Billy's lethal blow to Claggart's forehead, his body continues to bear a serpentine character, for lifting the inert corpse off the floor "was like handling a dead snake" (47).

Throughout the scene in the captain's cabin, the biblical archetype of the Fall provides a necessary point of reference. Billy's act of striking and killing Claggart is an implicit fulfillment of one consequence of the biblical story in that a "seed" of Eve has lethally "bruised" the "head" of the serpent (Gen. 3:15) in the form of the corrupt master-at-arms. So, too, Captain Vere's designation of the foretopman as a "fated boy" (46) and his provocative remark to the ship's surgeon that Claggart has been "struck dead by an angel of God! Yet the angel must hang!" (47) is comparable to the Old Testament God's immediate sentence of Adam and Eve to exile and death for their violation of his ban on eating the fruit of the tree of knowledge—even though Billy's crime has ironically emerged from an earlier *refusal* to be tempted by Claggart. Vere's paradoxical awareness of Billy's angel-like innocence and the need for him to be immediately punished for his crime demonstrates the captain's consciousness of the inadequacies of earthly justice. Having immediately remarked the capital nature of the foretopman's crime, Vere assumes he must act quickly because of the perilous situation he faces with a crew partly composed of sailors earlier involved in mutinous protests and with a potentially imminent threat from enemy ships; and for that purpose he convenes a drumhead court of officers, a proceeding in which he will obtain the opinion of his peers while reserving to himself the responsibility to pass final judgment on the case: "Feeling that unless quick action was taken on it, the deed of the foretopman, so soon as it should be known to the gun decks, would tend to awaken any slumbering embers of the Nore among the crew, a sense of the urgency of the case overruled in Captain Vere every other consideration" (50). Billy is accordingly asked to give testimony, and as Vere suspected, the young sailor exonerates himself of any deliberate malice in killing the master-at-arms: "I did not mean to kill him. Could I have used my tongue I would not have struck him. But he foully lied to my face and in presence of my captain, and I had to say something, and I could only say it with a blow, God help me!" (51). Billy's homicide was thus not a deliberate act but the inadvertent result of the primordial "law of sin" in his "members" (Rom. 7:23), which have acted without his conscious control. And just as the devil is traditionally known as the father of lies, Billy identifies Claggart as a brazen liar while failing to provide a reason for the master-at-arms's malice—a phenomenon that Vere will suggestively call a "mystery of iniquity" (53) in Claggart's character during the proceedings, again hinting at the master-at-arms's symbolic antecedents in biblical myth.

During the drumhead court, Vere attempts to lay out the nature of the charges against the foretopman while emphasizing that extenuating circumstances should not detract from the basic fact of Budd's crime of striking and killing an officer of the ship, even if everyone in the court knows that he was innocent of any deliberate act of murder. And although the court feels compassion for the accused as having contemplated neither "mutiny nor homicide" (55), Vere reminds them of the stern nature of the law and the demands of duty, all while admitting that Budd is ultimately innocent in the eyes of God: "At the Last Assizes [Last Judgment] it shall acquit. But how here? We proceed under the law of the Mutiny Act. In feature no child can resemble his father more than that Act resembles in spirit the thing from which it derives— War" (55–56). Rationalizing his sense that historical necessity requires Budd's immediate execution, Vere ultimately justifies his decision to convict under the stringent requirements of military law enhanced by the current emergency conditions of wartime.

Critics have long debated whether Vere was legally justified in executing Billy, usually arguing against it—a controversy that has also been judged irresolvable, given the unfinished or deliberately ambiguous state of the surviving text. Closely related to this debate is the narrative's representation of the legal aspects of the story, which demonstrates Melville's likely awareness of controversial mid-century court cases of his father-in-law, Lemuel Shaw, and knowledge of later nineteenth-century legal formalism. Also relevant is the issue of whether Melville knew that according to the British naval law of the era, no shipboard court proceeding and execution should have been officially authorized by Vere, and that the captain repeatedly violated legal protocol. Yet in order to fully understand Melville's representation of Vere's moral predicament, it must be approached from other biographical, historical, and theological perspectives.[12]

In the narrator's brief allusion to the 1842 case of the *Somers* during the proceedings of the drumhead court on the *Bellipotent*, Melville was deliberately revisiting the dramatic circumstances confronting Captain Alexander Slidell Mackenzie when faced with the urgency of judging the three suspected mutineers—a midshipman, a mate, and a common sailor—on the naval training brig *Somers* in late 1842, when the officers' shared sense of impending peril to their lives (one of whom was Melville's cousin Guert Gansevoort) led to the execution of the demonstrably guilty—and likely dangerous—offenders before the ship reached port, acting under Articles XIII and XIV of the US Articles of War.[13] Upon the ship's return to its home port in New York, Mackenzie's actions, aided by his immediate subordinate Lieutenant Gansevoort, aroused a storm of controversy, especially since one of the hanged, midshipman Philip Spencer, was the son of the secretary of war—a dissolute, emotionally disturbed adolescent whose plan of mutiny envisaged the transformation of the training brig into a pirate ship based in the Caribbean, a scheme likely inspired by a reading of Cooper's *Red Rover*. As the narrator notes, "True, the circumstances on board the *Somers* were different from those on board the *Bellipotent*. But the urgency felt, well-warranted or otherwise, was much the same" (57). The narrator's point is that in both the *Somers* threatened mutiny case and the situation on the *Bellipotent*, the safety of the ship was of paramount importance in the captain's mind, overriding the need for legal due process. On the *Somers*, the danger arose from the threat of possible attack on its officers by its large juvenile crew led by Spencer and his coconspirators, while on the *Bellipotent* the threat stemmed from both the potentially defiant mood of the crew, provoked by the murder of the master-at-arms, and the threat of imminent hostilities with the French fleet.

Yet over and above its historical associations, the theological model providing a rationale for Billy's conviction and execution is God the Father's sacrifice of his guiltless son—an antitype of the prelapsarian Adam—in order to atone for the sins of a fallen humanity. And it is here that Billy's role as a modern avatar of the first Adam transmutes into his typological identity at the end of the story as the last Adam, or Christ, whose act of atonement redeems fallen humanity according to Saint Paul (1 Cor. 15:47). In the case of Billy Budd, Vere must make the decision to sacrifice the hapless young sailor in order to prevent possible revolt among the sailors that might ensue from extending Billy a clemency that would be interpreted as "pusillanimous" (56) by the crew. The narrator acknowledges Vere's deeper ambivalence about this case when comparing the captain's imagined last meeting with Billy to that of Abraham sacrificing his son Isaac to God (Gen. 22): "The austere devotee of military duty, letting himself melt back into what remains primeval in our formalized humanity, may in the end have caught Billy to his heart, even as Abraham may have caught young Isaac on the brink of resolutely offering him up in obedience to the exacting behest" (58). The significance of the simile here is augmented by the fact that in Christian typology Abraham and Isaac are considered to be representatives of God and Christ, respectively.

As an originally Adam-like and now increasingly Christlike sacrificial victim, Billy spends the final night before his execution guarded in irons on the gun deck, having recovered from the trauma of his encounter with a satanic Claggart and gone through a moral agony like Christ in the garden of Gethsemane (Matt. 26:36–46): "But now lying between the two guns, as nipped in the vice of fate, Billy's agony, mainly proceeding from a generous young heart's virgin experience of the diabolical incarnate and effective in some men—the tension of that agony was over now" (61). It is in this chapel-like setting that the ship's chaplain visits him twice in the attempt to reconcile the young foretopman to his death, the first time departing without speaking so as not to disturb Billy's tranquillity of mood, the second time attempting to interest him, without success, in Christian ideas of "salvation and a Savior" (62), leaving him with a kiss of inadvertent betrayal that matches the Judas-like role he plays as "the minister of the Prince of Peace serving in the host of the God of War—Mars" (63). As an uneducated and irreducibly innocent primordial man, Billy is thus immune to the persuasions of formal religion, being compared to a South Sea Islander of the late eighteenth or earlier nineteenth century who has been given a "primer of Christianity" (63) by missionaries but fails to embrace its doctrines. A mere youth at heart, in accordance with the organic symbolism of his last name, Billy is a modern pagan or barbarian whose moral nature compares favorably with that of the ineffective, civilized chaplain. For despite his recent Fall into a tragic encounter with evil, Billy remains at heart an archetypally innocent young man in the corrupt postlapsarian world of the *Bellipotent*.

During the scene of execution, Billy clearly acts in the role of Christ as a type of Pauline "last Adam," inadvertently expiating the sins of his fellow sailors and officers. The dawn of the morning of his execution thus offers salient Christological imagery in a sky in which the night withdraws like "the prophet [Elijah] in the chariot disappearing in heaven and dropping his mantle to Elisha [2 Kings 2:11–13]" (63), while the horizon in the East "stretched a diaphanous fleece of white furrowed vapor" (64), evoking the imagery of Christ as Lamb of God (John 1:29, 36). Before dying, Billy blesses Captain Vere, just as Christ forgave those who condemned him to the cross and commended his spirit into the hands of the Father (Luke 23:34, 46); while Billy's voice sounds like the "clear melody of a singing bird on the point of launching from the twig" (64), just as the figure of the dove was often placed above the scene of the Crucifixion in Western art. Hints of a symbolic resurrection are also evident when, concurrently with Billy's execution, "it chanced that the vapory fleece hanging low in the East was shot through with a soft glory as of the fleece of the Lamb of God seen in mystical vision" (65), a description again evoking the mystical image of Christ as Lamb of God in the Gospel of John, while drawing on the repeated references to his divine "glory" (John 1:14, 2:11, 17:5, 24). Unlike other hanged men's, Billy's body fails to move upon suspension from the rope, showing a passivity in mortal suffering that matches Christ's necessarily stationary position on the cross.

The scene of Billy's death thus extensively hints at the biblical depiction of Christ's Crucifixion and Resurrection. For immediately after his hanging, when the ship rolls back from leeward, the atmosphere conveys a mystic sign of blessing based on additional symbolism from the Gospel of John: "At the same moment it chanced that the vapory fleece of the Lamb of God seen in mystical vision and simultaneously therewith, watched by the wedged mass of upturned faces, Billy ascended; and ascending, took the full rose of the dawn" (65). During the subsequent ceremony to consign the foretopman's dead body to the sea, the narrator notes, "The fleece of low-hanging vapor had vanished, licked up by the sun that late had so glorified it. And the circumambient air in the clearness of its serenity was like smooth white marble in the polished block not yet removed from the marble-dealer's yard" (68)—language hinting at the angel's removal of the stone at Christ's tomb at the scene of the Resurrection (Matt. 28:2). The subsequent newspaper account of Billy's murder of Claggart and ensuing execution, which postulates the "enormity of the crime and the extreme depravity of the criminal" (70), is a grotesque misreading of the case comparable to the "scandal" or "stumbling block" of Christ's execution as a common criminal (Rom. 9.33; 1 Cor. 123; 1 Pet. 2.8). Finally, the sailors who have witnessed the execution venerate the spar from which

Billy was hung, treating it like a medieval relic ("To them a chip of it was as a piece of the Cross" [71]), and when Vere himself dies after an engagement with the French ship *Athée*, he is invoking Billy's name as though the executed sailor were a talismanic figure whose name alone conveys Christlike spiritual redemption.

So far we have explored the pervasive influence of the biblical and Miltonic representations of the Fall on *Billy Budd*, but a final significant circumstance in the composition of the narrative relating to the theme of the Fall remains to be mentioned. In the eight months before his death in September 1891, Melville was immersing himself in the writings of the German pessimistic philosopher Arthur Schopenhauer (1788–1860), who was frequently cited in American articles and books on the pervasive phenomenon of philosophical Pessimism in the 1870s and '80s when Melville likely first became acquainted with his thought. In early February 1891, Melville borrowed Schopenhauer's *Counsels and Maxims* (1890) from the New York Society Library and apparently thought so highly of it that he immediately bought a copy of the volume, going on to purchase and mark or annotate the German philosopher's *Religion: A Dialogue, and Other Essays* (1891), *Studies in Pessimism* (1891), and *The Wisdom of Life* (1891), as well as the three volumes of Schopenhauer's chief philosophical work, *The World as Will and Idea* (1888). One can imagine that Melville experienced something of a shock of recognition, like that he experienced reading Hawthorne, when immersing himself in Schopenhauer, whose major preoccupation concerned the pervasiveness of evil and human suffering in a phenomenal world determined by the noumenal forces of the will. In response to such forces, the German philosopher posited an atheistic metaphysic that advocated escape through asceticism and selflessness, as promoted by Buddhism and other Eastern religions, as well as through immersion in the higher artistic productions, especially music.[14]

Critics have argued that Melville might have drawn on specific passages in Schopenhauer's writings to create several key aspects of *Billy Budd*. For example, he might have turned to Schopenhauer's *The World as Will and Idea* for the characterizations of Billy Budd and John Claggart as prototypically "good" and "evil" men, while portraying Billy's ready acceptance of death as an example of Schopenhauer's ideas of the need for the cessation of the will; or he might have used the discussion of envy in Schopenhauer's essay on "Human Nature" in *The Wisdom of*

Life to help shape the character of Claggart.[15] Yet if Melville came to Schopenhauer's writings relatively late for them to have a significant impact on *Billy Budd*, they would still have provided uncanny philosophical confirmation for Melville's fictional depiction of the Fall in *Billy Budd*. In his essay on "The Sufferings of the World" in *Studies in Pessimism*, Schopenhauer thus declared that "the sole thing that reconciles me to the Old Testament is the story of the Fall. In my eyes, it is the only metaphysical truth in that book, even though it appears in the form of an allegory. There seems to me no better explanation of our existence than that it is the result of some false step, some sin of which we are paying the penalty." The final statement here may remind us of Melville's previously quoted remark in his 1850 review of Hawthorne's *Mosses from an Old Manse* that "in certain moods, no man can weigh this world, without throwing in something, somehow like Original Sin, to strike the uneven balance."[16]

Among Schopenhauer's writings, "Religion: A Dialogue" likely had an especially powerful appeal to Melville in that it debates the pros and cons of Christianity in an incisive manner while reviewing the history of religion in Europe through the mid-nineteenth century. Of the two classically named interlocutors (in likely imitation of Hume's *Dialogues*), Philolethes and Demopheles, the former is an outspoken opponent of Christianity as the enemy to the pursuit of truth through philosophy, while the latter is Christianity's apologist, seeing it as embodying important allegorical ideas of truth and morality for the masses. Philolethes accordingly praises the achievements of the classical age and blames Christianity for the stifling of human intellectual growth and the atrocities resulting from its self-righteous fanaticism, whereas Demopheles sees Christianity as providing a higher model of morality than the utilitarianism evident in classical ethics and furnishing the masses with a system of metaphysics under the veil of myth and allegory that helps guide them in their life while giving meaning to their death. "Such an allegorical representation of truth is always and everywhere, for humanity at large, a serviceable substitute for a truth to which it can never attain, for a philosophy which it can never grasp." In "Religion: A Dialogue" Melville would have discovered a deep ambivalence about the truth and value of Christianity that likely matched his own. So, too, he would have recognized that his use of the Christian myth of the Fall in *Billy Budd* was in keeping with Schopenhauer's assertion that religion used such myths and allegories to convey essential metaphysical truths to humanity.[17]

Even if it is more a matter of confluence than influence, comparing *Billy Budd* to the pessimistic themes of Schopenhauer suggests the broader literary and cultural transatlantic contexts in which *Billy Budd* was composed in the later 1880s. In the *Bible and Novel: Narrative Authority and the Death of God* (2013), William Vance has analyzed the works of four later Victorian authors—George Eliot, Thomas Hardy, Mary Ward (Mrs. Humphry Ward), and Rider Haggard—in relation to their extensive use of the Bible, which they continued to value despite the decline of biblical authority during the nineteenth century. Vance notes that from the perspective of the present "it has become easier to read ostensibly secular or post-Christian narratives as in fact post-secular, or religious by other means. Eliot, Hardy, Ward, and Haggard can now be seen not as secular novelists so much as pioneers of the post-secular. It is tempting to enroll them in a special 'school' of novelists devoted to reimagining the scriptures in the secular world, continuing the age-old process of rereading the Bible." Exhibiting varying degrees of belief and unbelief in their personal lives, these authors nevertheless drew on the Christian Bible as a key repository of themes and motifs in their works of fiction, which Vance denominates "secular scriptures." While there is no evidence that Melville was aware of the work of any of these four authors, he nevertheless belongs by extension in the same informal late Victorian "school" and shares their tendency toward crafting fiction strategically informed by vestiges of Christian myth and allegory.[18]

As a contemporaneous counterpart to the composition of *Billy Budd*, Hardy's *Tess of the D'Urbervilles* (1891), for example, dramatizes the story of an innocent young woman who impulsively commits murder against a cynically corrupt and persecuting male oppressor, Alec D'Urberville, and is then judicially condemned to death by hanging despite the ample moral justification for her crime. Like Melville's Billy, Tess serves as a Christlike sacrificial victim to a repressive society while offering a redemptive spiritual message to at least one survivor of her tragedy, Angel Clare. And like *Billy Budd*, *Tess of the D'Urbervilles* is filled with symbolism of the Fall, with the role of Satan filled by Tess's putative "cousin" Alec, and Tess herself playing the role of both pre- and postlapsarian Eve. In both narratives, too, the representatives of institutional Christianity—the navy chaplain in *Billy Budd*, Parson Tringham and Angel Clare's two brothers in *Tess*—are either inadequate to their spiritual task, or manifestly unfaithful to the teachings of Christ. Like Melville, Hardy was obsessed with the problem of evil and the apparent indifference to human suffering of the divine figure he called the "President of the

Immortals" at the conclusion to *Tess*. And like Hardy's *Tess*, with its protest of his heroine's moral purity in its subtitle (*A Pure Woman Faithfully Presented*) despite the sins she commits, Melville's *Billy Budd* uses the myth of the Fall to remind the reader of the atavistic presence of evil in the world, its embodiment in corrupt individuals and repressive social institutions, and its power to destroy archetypal innocents like Melville's foretopman.

Notes

Preface

1. For useful overviews of current debates on the concept of "secularization" see Rob Warner, *Secularization and Its Discontents* (New York: Continuum, 2010); William Vance, *Bible and Novel: Narrative Authority and the Death of God* (New York: Oxford University Press, 2013), chap. 1; and Michael Rectenwald, *Nineteenth-Century British Secularism: Science, Religion, and Literature* (New York: Palgrave Macmillan, 2016). On George Jacob Holyoake and the mid-Victorian Secularist movement see Edward Royle, *Victorian Infidels: The Origins of the British Secularist Movement, 1791–1866* (Totowa, NJ: Rowman & Littlefield, 1974); Rectenwald, *Nineteenth-Century British Secularism*, chap. 3. On the extended history of the relationship between Christianity and science see David C. Lindberg and Ronald L. Numbers, eds., *God and Nature: Historical Essays on the Encounter between Christianity and Science* (Berkeley: University of California Press, 1986).

2. On George Eliot's fiction as secular scripture see Vance, *Bible and Novel*, chap. 4. On Thomas Henry Huxley's reverence for the Bible see Timothy Larsen, *A People of One Book: The Bible and the Victorians* (New York: Oxford University Press, 2011), chap. 8.

3. See Christopher Grasso, *Skepticism and American Faith: From the Revolution to the Civil War* (New York: Oxford University Press, 2018); Eric Leigh Schmidt, *The Church of Saint Thomas Paine: A Religious History of American Secularism* (Princeton, NJ: Princeton University Press, 2021).

4. Hawthorne quoted in Steven Olsen-Smith, *Melville in His Own Time* (Iowa City: University of Iowa Press, 2015), 82; Melville, *Moby-Dick; or, the Whale*, ed. Harrison Hayford, Hershel Parker, and G. Thomas Tanselle (Evanston, IL: Northwestern University Press and the Newberry Library, 1988), 374.

5. See Damien B. Schlarb, *Melville's Wisdom: Religion, Skepticism, and Literature in Nineteenth-Century America* (New York: Oxford University Press, 2021). The present study was largely completed before I became aware of Schlarb's book. On Melville and the post-secular see also Brian Yothers, "Melville after Secularism," in *The New Melville Studies*, ed. Cody Marrs (New York: Cambridge University Press, 2019), 53–65. On the turn toward post-secular approaches to American literature see, for example, Jenny Franchot, "Invisible Domain: Religion and American Literary Studies," *American Literature* 67, no. 4 (December 1995): 833–42; Tracy Fessenden, *Culture and Redemption: Religion, the Secular, and American Literature* (Princeton, NJ: Princeton University Press, 2006); Steven John Bembridge, "'I Could Almost Believe in God': The Evolution of American Theology in American Literary Naturalism" (diss., University of East Anglia,

2017), https://core.ac.uk/reader/83923730; and Harold K. Bush and Brian Yothers, eds., *Above the American Renaissance: David S. Reynolds and the Spiritual Imagination in American Literary Studies* (Amherst: University of Massachusetts Press, 2018).

1. The Making of a Skeptic

1. On the development of Melville's ambivalent attitude toward Christianity see William Braswell, *Melville's Religious Thought: An Essay in Interpretation* (Durham, NC: Duke University Press, 1943); William H. Shurr, "Melville and Christianity," *Essays in Arts and Sciences* 5, no. 2 (July 1976): 129–48; Roland A. Sherrill, "Melville and Religion," in *A Companion to Melville Studies*, ed. John Bryant (New York: Greenwood, 1986), 481–513; Walter Donald Kring, *Herman Melville's Religious Journey* (Raleigh, NC: Pentland, 1997); Judy Logan, "The Catnip and the Amaranth: Melville's Struggle with the 'Ever-Encroaching Appetite for God,'" *Christianity and Literature* 51, no. 3 (Spring 2002): 387–406; Emory Elliott, "'Wandering To-and-Fro': Melville and Religion," in *A Historical Guide to Herman Melville*, ed. Giles Gunn (New York: Oxford University Press, 2005), 167–204; John Wenke, "The Many Masks of Melville's God," in *Critical Insights: Herman Melville*, ed. Eric Carl Link (Ipswich, MA: Salem Press, 2013), 142–62; Brian Yothers, *Sacred Uncertainty: Religious Difference and the Shape of Melville's Career* (Evanston, IL: Northwestern University Press, 2015); Jonathan A. Cook and Brian Yothers, introduction to *Visionary of the Word: Melville and Religion* (Evanston, IL: Northwestern University Press, 2016), 3–18; and Brian Yothers, "Melville after Secularism," in *The New Melville Studies*, ed. Cody Marrs (New York: Cambridge University Press, 2019), 53–65.

2. A. N. Wilson, *God's Funeral: The Decline of Faith in Western Civilization* (New York: Norton, 1999), 11. On loss of faith in the Victorian era see Howard R. Murphy, "The Ethical Revolt against Christian Orthodoxy in Early Victorian England," *American Historical Review* 60, no. 4 (July 1955): 800–817; Basil Willey, *Nineteenth Century Studies: Coleridge to Arnold* (New York: Harper & Row, 1966); Basil Willey, *More Nineteenth-Century Studies: A Group of Honest Doubters* (New York: Harper & Row, 1966); Richard Helmstadter and Bernard Lightman, eds., *Victorian Faith in Crisis: Essays on Continuity and Change in Nineteenth-Century Religious Belief* (Stanford, CA: Stanford University Press, 1991); Christopher Lane, *The Age of Doubt: Tracing the Roots of Our Religious Uncertainty* (New Haven, CT: Yale University Press, 2011); Michael Rectenwald, *Nineteenth-Century British Secularism: Science, Religion, and Literature* (New York: Palgrave Macmillan 2016); and Norman Vance, *Bible and Novel: Narrative Authority and the Death of God* (New York: Oxford University Press, 2013). On David F. Strauss and his revolutionary *Life of Jesus* see Frederick C. Beiser, *David Friedrich Strauss, Father of Unbelief: An Intellectual Biography* (New York: Oxford University Press, 2020).

3. Thomas Paine, *The Age of Reason*, in *Collected Writings*, ed. Eric Foner (New York: Library of America, 1995), 677, 825.

4. Saul K. Padover, ed., *The Washington Papers: Basic Selections from Public and Private Writings of George Washington* (New York: Harpers, 1955), 318–19. On the

mixed faith of Washington and most of the other Founders see David L. Holmes, *The Faiths of the Founding Fathers* (New York: Oxford University Press, 2006), quotation at 86. For studies of the leading American deists see Kerry Walters, *Revolutionary Deists: Early America's Rational Infidels* (Amherst, NY: Prometheus Books, 2010); Christopher Grasso, *Skepticism and American Faith from the Revolution to the Civil War* (New York: Oxford University Press, 2018), chaps. 1, 3, 4.

5. On controversies over freethought in the early republic see Martin E. Marty, *The Infidel: Freethought and American Religion* (Cleveland: World Publishing, 1961), chaps. 1–4; Susan Jacoby, *Freethinkers: A History of American Secularism* (New York: Metropolitan Books / Henry Holt, 2005), chaps. 1–3; Eric R. Schlereth, *An Age of Infidelity: The Politics of Religious Controversy in the Early United States* (Philadelphia: University of Pennsylvania, 2013); and Amanda Porterfield, *Conceived in Doubt: Religion and Politics in the New Nation* (Chicago: University of Chicago Press, 2015). On the development of freethought in the antebellum era see Albert Post, *Popular Freethought in America, 1825–1850* (New York: Columbia University Press, 1943); Marty, *Infidel*, chaps. 5–8; James Turner, *Without God, without Creed: The Origins of Unbelief in America* (Baltimore: Johns Hopkins University Press, 1985), chaps. 3–4; Jacoby, *Freethinkers*, chap. 4; Grasso, *Skepticism and American Faith*, chaps. 5–13; David Faflik, *Transcendental Heresies: Harvard and the Modern American Practice of Unbelief* (Amherst: University of Massachusetts Press, 2020); and Leigh Eric Schmidt, *The Church of Saint Thomas Paine: A Religious History of American Secularism* (Princeton, NJ: Princeton University Press, 2021), chap. 1.

6. On Robert Owen see J. F. C. Harrison, *Quest for the New Moral World: Robert Owen and the Owenites in Britain and America* (New York: Scribners, 1969). On Robert Dale Owen see Richard William Leopold, *Robert Dale Owen: A Biography* (Cambridge, MA: Harvard University Press, 1940). On Fanny Wright see Celia Morris Eckhardt, *Fanny Wright: Rebel in America* (Urbana: University of Illinois Press, 1984); Lori D. Ginzberg, "'The Hearts of Your Readers Will Shudder': Fanny Wright, Infidelity, and American Freethought," *American Quarterly* 46, no. 2 (June 1994): 195–226.

7. On Abner Kneeland see Henry Steele Commager, "The Blasphemy of Abner Kneeland," *New England Quarterly* 8, no. 1 (March 1935): 29–41; Roderick S. French, "Liberation from Man and God: Abner Kneeland's Free-Thought Campaign, 1830–1839," *American Quarterly* 32, no. 1 (Summer 1980): 202–21; Samuel Gridley Howe, "Atheism in New England," *New England Magazine*, vol. 7 (December 1834), 500–509, and vol. 8 (January 1835), 53–62.

8. Lyman Beecher, *Lectures on Scepticism* (Cincinnati, 1835), 87–88. For more on Lyman Beecher and the threat of freethought see Marty, *Infidel*, chap. 7.

9. On Melville's early life in New York City, Albany, and Lansingburgh, New York, see William H. Gilman, *Melville's Early Life and "Redburn"* (New York: New York University Press, 1951), chaps. 1–3; Hershel Parker, *Herman Melville: A Biography, Volume 1, 1819–1851* (Baltimore: Johns Hopkins University Press, 1996), chaps. 1–8; John Bryant, *Herman Melville: A Half Known Life*, 2 vols. (New York: Wiley Blackwell, 2021), vol. 1, chaps. 1–36.

10. David G. Hackett, *The Rude Hand of Innovation: Religion and the Social Order in Albany, New York 1652–1836* (New York: Oxford University Press, 1991), 150. On the Philo Logos Society controversy see Gilman, *Melville's Early Life*, 90–95; Parker, *Herman Melville*, vol. 1, chap. 6; Bryant, *Herman Melville*, vol. 1, chap. 31. For the exchange of letters in the *Albany Microscope* reflecting the tenor of the debates in the Philo Logos Society see Steven Olsen-Smith, ed., *Melville in His Own Time* (Iowa City: University of Iowa Press, 2015), 6–27 (Van Loon quoted at 12, Melville at 16). On Joel Munsell of the *Albany Microscope* see David S. Edenstein, *Joel Munsell: Printer and Antiquarian* (New York: Columbia University Press, 1950); on the impact of Munsell's reading of Thomas Paine see 56–61.

11. On Melville's life during this era of maturation and transition see Parker, *Herman Melville*, vol. 1, chaps. 8–31; Bryant, *Herman Melville*, vol. 1, chaps. 37–53, and vol. 2.

12. Sextus Empiricus, *An Outline of Pyrrhonism*, trans. R. G. Bury (Amherst, NY: Prometheus Books, 1990), 188. For an overview of classical skepticism see R. J. Hankinson, *The Sceptics* (New York: Routledge, 1998); on the ten modes of skepticism see chap. 9. On Sextus Empiricus in the context of classical atheism see Tim Whitmarsh, *Battling the Gods: Atheism in the Ancient World* (New York: Vintage Books, 2015), chap. 11. For a comprehensive history of religious doubt in the West see Jennifer Hecht, *Doubt: A History: The Great Doubters and Their Legacy of Innovation from Socrates and Jesus to Thomas Jefferson and Emily Dickinson* (San Francisco: HarperOne, 2004).

13. On Montaigne and skepticism see Richard Popkin, *The History of Skepticism, Savonarola to Bayle*, rev. ed. (New York: Oxford University Press, 2003), chap. 3.

14. On Bayle and skepticism see Popkin, *History of Skepticism*, chap. 18. On the impact of Melville's reading of Bayle on *Moby-Dick* see Millicent Bell, "Pierre Bayle and *Moby-Dick*," *PMLA* 66, no. 5 (September 1951): 626–48.

15. Popkin, *History of Skepticism*, 290, 300.

16. On Melville's assimilation of Emerson see Merton M. Sealts Jr., "Melville and Emerson's Rainbow," in *Pursuing Melville, 1940–1980* (Madison: University of Wisconsin Press, 1982), 250–77. For a complete record of Melville's reading see Steven Olsen-Smith and Peter Norberg, eds., *Melville's Marginalia Online* at www.melvillesmarginalia.org; see also Sealts, "The Records of Melville's Reading," in *Pursuing Melville*, 31–57. For Melville's comments on Shakespeare in his *Mosses* review see *The Piazza Tales and Other Prose Pieces, 1839–1860*, ed. Harrison Hayford, Alma A. MacDougall, G. Thomas Tanselle, et al. (Evanston, IL: Northwestern University Press and the Newberry Library, 1987), 244–46, 252. In chapter 58 of *Redburn*, written in the late spring of 1849, Melville noted that the unbeliever David Hume died in a composed state of mind (as famously recorded by Boswell), and late in life Melville also heavily annotated a passage in Schopenhauer's *The World as Will and Idea* praising the English philosopher. See Braswell, *Melville's Religious Thought*, 14, 51. Familiarity with the writings of Paine is demonstrated by the name of Billy Budd's first ship, the *Rights-of-Man*, and in the accompanying conflict between the political theories of Paine and Burke that provided an ideological backdrop to Melville's unfinished novella.

17. *Moby-Dick, or the Whale*, ed. Harrison Hayford, Hershel Parker, and G. Thomas Tanselle (Evanston, IL: Northwestern University Press and the Newberry Library, 1988), 107. On Bulkington's literary model as Hercules, and the paradigm of sea and shore as based on the philosophical model of the Choice of Hercules, see Jonathan A. Cook, "*Moby-Dick*, Myth, and Classical Moralism: Bulkington as Hercules," *Leviathan: A Journal of Melville Studies* 5, no. 1 (March 2003): 15–28. On the novel's engagement with the skeptical Old Testament wisdom of Job and Ecclesiastes see Cook, *Inscrutable Malice: Theodicy, Eschatology, and the Biblical Sources of "Moby-Dick"* (DeKalb: Northern Illinois University Press, 2012). For a study of philosophical skepticism in *Moby-Dick* see also Maurice S. Lee, *Uncertain Chances: Science, Skepticism, and Belief in Nineteenth-Century American Literature* (New York: Cambridge University Press, 2012), chaps. 2–3. On Ishmael as a skeptical narrator see Brian Yothers, "Ishmael's Doubts and Intuitions: Religion in *Moby-Dick*," in *Critical Insights: "Moby-Dick*," ed. Robert C. Evans (Ipswich, MA: Salem Press, 2014), 174–90.

18. *Moby-Dick*, 374. On "intuition" as a means of divine knowledge in the context of current belief see Turner, *Without God*, 104–9.

19. *Moby-Dick*, 374. On Melville's literary sources for his discussion of the whale's spout see Howard P. Vincent, *The Trying-Out of "Moby-Dick"* (1949; Kent, OH: Kent State University Press, 1980), 286–94. In the quoted passage from "The Fountain," Melville was possibly responding to a passage he had read in Hawthorne's "Sunday at Home" in *Twice-Told Tales*, a copy of which he had received as a gift of the author in January 1851: "Doubts may flit around me, or seem to close their evil wings, and settle down; but, so long as I imagine that the earth is hallowed, and the light of heaven retains its sanctity, on the Sabbath—while that blessed sunshine lives within me—never can my soul have lost the instinct of its faith. If it have gone astray, it will return again" (Hawthorne, *Tales and Sketches*, ed. Roy Harvey Pierce [New York: Library of America, 1982], 415).

20. *Moby-Dick*, 491, 492. The editors of the Northwestern-Newberry edition ("Discussions of Adopted Readings" in *Moby-Dick*, 901) ascribe the statements here on religious faith to Ahab by putting them in quotation marks, even though the original text of the English and American editions did not have such quotation marks. The assignment of the speech to Ahab is mistaken. The content of the remarks is clearly more suitable for Ishmael as narrator, echoing the cadence and tenor of his narrative voice, the skeptical content of his many previous remarks on religious belief, and his tendency to echo aspects of the book of Ecclesiastes. (On the well-known representation of cyclical flux in Ecclesiastes, see Eccles. 1:4–10; 3:1–8; on Ishmael and Ecclesiastes generally, see Cook, *Inscrutable Malice*, passim.) Ahab simply does not have the emotional or philosophical detachment to make such a speech at this point in the narrative, nor does its subject matter suggest anything found in his previous characterization.

21. Melville, *Correspondence*, ed. Lynn Horth (Evanston, IL: Northwestern University Press and the Newberry Library, 1993), 119.

22. *Correspondence*, 122.

23. Melville, *Journals*, ed. Howard C. Horsford with Lynn Horth (Evanston, IL: Northwestern University Press and the Newberry Library, 1989), 4–5.

Melville's erratic punctuation and spelling are preserved as written. For more on Melville's friendship with Adler see Sanford E. Marovitz, "More Chartless Voyaging: Melville and Adler at Sea," in *Studies in the American Renaissance*, ed. Joel Myerson (Charlottesville: University Press of Virginia, 1986), 373–84; Sanford E. Marovitz, "Correspondences: Paranoic Lexicographers and Melvillean Heroes," in *"Ungraspable Phantom": Essays on "Moby-Dick,"* ed. John Bryant, Mary K. Bercaw Edwards, and Timothy Marr (Kent, OH: Kent State University Press, 2006), 100–113.

24. Melville, *Journals*, 8.

25. Melville, *Correspondence*, 186. On Melville's friendship with Hawthorne in the Berkshires see Parker, *Herman Melville*, vol. 1, chaps. 36–40. On the recurrent religious and biblical allusions in Melville's letters to Hawthorne see Jonathan A. Cook, "An Endless Sermon: Religious Motifs in Melville's Letters to Hawthorne," *Religion and Literature* 51, no. 2 (Summer 2020): 1–22.

26. Melville, *Correspondence*, 186. For a review of Melville's possible sources for the idea of "Being" here in relation to comparable ideas in the writings of Plato, Plotinus, Milton, Bayle, Coleridge, and Shelling see Sanford Marovitz, "Melville's Problematic Being," *ESQ: A Journal of the American Renaissance* 28, no. 1 (First Quarter, 1982): 11–23.

27. *The Complete Works of Michael de Montaigne*, ed. William Hazlitt (London: John Templeman, 1842), 281. For more on Melville's edition of Montaigne see Olsen-Smith and Norberg, *Melville's Marginalia Online*, at www.melvillesmarginalia.org.

28. Melville, *Correspondence*, 186. For discussions of Melville's projection of his own rebellious doubts onto Hawthorne see James E. Miller Jr., "Hawthorne and Melville: No! in Thunder" and "Hawthorne and Melville: The Unpardonable Sin," in *Quests Surd and Absurd: Essays in American Literature* (Chicago: University of Chicago Press, 1967), chaps. 12 and 13; Jerome M. Loving, "Melville's Pardonable Sin," *New England Quarterly* 47, no. 2 (June 1974): 262–78.

29. Melville, *Correspondence*, 191–92, 193.

30. Olsen-Smith, *Melville in His Own Time*, 76.

31. Olsen-Smith, 77; Melville, *Correspondence*, 193.

32. Olsen-Smith, 81.

33. Brian Higgins and Hershel Parker, eds., *Herman Melville: The Contemporary Reviews* (New York: Cambridge University Press, 1995), 385, 380.

34. Higgins and Parker, 430, 436, 445. On Melville's struggles to maintain his literary career following the publication of *Moby-Dick* and *Pierre* see Hershel Parker, *Herman Melville: A Biography, Volume 2, 1851–1891* (Baltimore: Johns Hopkins University Press, 2002), chaps. 1–12.

35. Herman Melville, *Pierre; or the Ambiguities*, ed. Harrison Hayford, Hershel Parker, and G. Thomas Tanselle (Evanston, IL: Northwestern University Press and the Newberry Library, 1971), 204; Paine, *Age of Reason*, 820.

36. Melville, *Pierre*, 213; Paine, *Age of Reason*, 823.

37. In a letter of May 29, 1854, Helen wrote her brother declining his recommendation to read the essay of Plutarch: "'Plutarch on the Cessation of the Oracles' must be a work of deep interest, but, I'll take your word for it, having

no ambition to peruse the same" (Merton M. Sealts Jr., *Melville's Reading*, rev. and enlarged ed. [Columbia: University of South Carolina Press, 1988]), 205.

38. On Melville's annotation to Cervantes see Jay Leyda, *The Melville Log: A Documentary Life of Herman Melville, 1819–1891*, 2 vols. (New York: Gordian, 1951), 2:508, Duyckinck quoted at 2:523. On the philosophical skepticism of *The Confidence-Man* see Maurice S. Lee, "Skepticism in *The Confidence-Man*," in *The New Cambridge Companion to Herman Melville*, ed. Robert S. Levine (Cambridge: Cambridge University Press, 2014), 113–26. On the novel's religious skepticism see Jonathan A. Cook, *Satirical Apocalypse: An Anatomy of "The Confidence-Man"* (Westport, CT: Greenwood, 1996).

39. Olsen-Smith, *Melville in His Own Time*, 82. Commentators persistently misread this passage by failing to grasp the contemporary meaning of "annihilation" in a religious context, namely, the extinction of the soul at death. For a reliable discussion of Melville's reference to "annihilation" here see Parker, *Herman Melville*, 2:300–301. For a comparable example of Hawthorne's use of the term in the same sense see *Nathaniel Hawthorne: The American Notebooks*, ed. Claude Simpson (Columbus: Ohio State University Press, 1972), 429.

40. Richard D. Altick, *Victorian People and Ideas* (New York: Norton, 1973), 233.

41. For a complete account of Melville's travels in Europe and the Levant in 1856–57 see Parker, *Herman Melville*, vol. 2, chaps. 13–15. For a discussion of the significance of Melville's journal of this trip within his personal and creative development see Robert Milder, *Exiled Royalties: Melville and the Life We Imagine* (New York: Oxford University Press, 2006), chap. 7; see also Basem L. Ra'ad, "Melville's Art: Overtures from the Journal of 1856–1857," in *Savage Eye: Melville and the Visual Arts*, ed. Christopher Sten (Kent, OH: Kent State University Press, 1991), 200–217.

42. Melville, *Journals*, 75, 83, 88, 91, 94.

43. *Journals*, 97.

44. Weber's phrase was first used in his lecture "Science as a Vocation" (1917). Melville may have learned about the writings of Niebuhr and Strauss during his extended conversations with German scholar George Adler during his trip to England and the Continent in the fall of 1849. On Strauss's impact on biblical studies in the United States see Jerry Wayne Browne, *The Rise of Biblical Criticism in America, 1800–1870: The New England Scholars* (Middletown, CT: Wesleyan University Press, 1969), chap. 9 (Bulfinch quoted at 141); Elisabeth Hurth, "'The Last Impiety of Criticism': D. F. Strauss's *Leben Jesus* in New England," *ESQ: A Journal of the American Renaissance* 40, no. 4 (Fourth Quarter, 1994): 319–52.

45. Turner, *Without God*, 253; Melville, *Journals*, 99, 101, 102, 108, 111, 112.

46. Melville, *Journals*, 114, 115, 119, 121.

47. Olsen-Smith, *Melville in His Own Time*, 114. On Melville's life as a lecturer and a disgruntled resident of Pittsfield in the late 1850s see Parker, *Herman Melville*, vol. 2, chaps. 16–18.

48. For histories of freethought, atheism, and agnosticism in the postbellum United States see Sidney Warren, *American Freethought, 1860–1914*

(New York: Columbia University Press, 1943); Turner, *Without God*, chaps. 5-9; Jacoby, *Freethinkers*, chaps. 4-7; and Eric Leigh Schmidt, *Village Atheists: How Unbelievers Made Their Way in a Godly Nation* (Princeton, NJ: Princeton University Press, 2016).

49. Shurr, "Melville and Christianity," 142. For a survey of the influence of the Bible in Melville's writings see Nathalia Wright, *Melville's Use of the Bible* (Durham, NC: Duke University Press, 1949).

50. Melville, *Piazza Tales*, 244.

2. Biblical Inversion and the Ends of Christianity

1. See Bruce H. Franklin, *The Wake of the Gods: Melville's Mythology* (Stanford, CA: Stanford University Press, 1963), 126-36. For useful older reviews of the extensive criticism of the story see Lea Bertani Vozar Newman, *A Reader's Guide to the Short Stories of Herman Melville* (Boston: G. K. Hall, 1986), 19-78; Dan McCall, *The Silence of Bartleby* (Ithaca, NY: Cornell University Press, 1989). For informative essay collections see also Howard P. Vincent, ed., *The Melville Annual 1965, a Symposium: "Bartleby, the Scrivener"* (Kent, OH: Kent State University Press, 1966); M. Thomas Inge, ed., *Bartleby the Inscrutable: A Collection of Commentary on Herman Melville's Tale "Bartleby the Scrivener"* (Hamden, CT: Archon Books, 1979).

2. William Bysshe Stein, "Bartleby, the Christian Conscience," in Vincent, *Symposium*, 104-12 (quotation at 106); Donald M. Fiene, "Bartleby the Christ," *American Transcendental Quarterly* 7 (Summer 1970): 18-23 (quotation at 22); Stanley Brodwin, "To the Frontiers of Eternity: Melville's Crossing in 'Bartleby the Scrivener,'" in Inge, *Bartleby the Inscrutable*, 174-96 (quotation at 185); Graham Nicol Forst, "Up Wall Street towards Broadway: The Narrator's Pilgrimage in Melville's 'Bartleby, the Scrivener,'" *Studies in Short Fiction* 24 (Summer 1987): 263-70; Richard Kopley, "The Circle and Its Center in 'Bartleby, the Scrivener,'" *ATQ* 2, no. 3 (new series) (September 1988): 191-206; Steven Doloff, "The Prudent Samaritan: Melville's 'Bartleby, the Scrivener' as Parody of Christ's Parable of the Lawyer," *Studies in Short Fiction* 34 (Summer 1997): 357-61 (quotation at 360); Thomas Dilworth, "The Narrator of Bartleby: The Christian Humanist Acquaintance of John Jacob Astor," *Papers on Language and Literature* 38, no. 1 (Winter 2002): 49-75; Damien Schlarb, *Melville's Wisdom: Religion, Skepticism, and Literature in Nineteenth-Century America* (New York: Oxford University Press, 2021), 48-59 (quotation at 59). Hans Bergmann resists making too close a parallel between Bartleby and Christ, claiming that "Bartleby is perhaps the story of a god, but it is not Christ or Christ figure. Bartleby is on the one hand not *full* enough to be Christ and on the other not *empty* enough to be a Christ figure" (*God in the Street: New York Writing from the Penny Press to Melville* [Philadelphia: Temple University Press, 1995], 169). For other interpretations of Melville's story recognizing a religious perspective see Richard Harter Fogle, *Melville's Shorter Tales* (Norman: University of Oklahoma Press, 1960), chap. 2; John Gardner, "'Bartleby': Art and Social Commitment," *Philological Quarterly* 43 (January 1964): 104-12; Thomas Mitchell, "Dead Letters

and Dead Men: Narrative Purpose in 'Bartleby, the Scrivener,'" *Studies in Short Fiction* 27 (Summer 1990): 329–38; Walter E. Anderson, "Form and Meaning in 'Bartleby, the Scrivener,'" *Studies in Short Fiction* 18 (Fall 1981): 383–94; Harold Schechter, "Bartleby the Chronometer," *Studies in Short Fiction* 19, no. 4 (Fall 1982): 359–66; William H. Hildebrand, "Bartleby and the Black Conceit," *Studies in Romanticism* 27, no. 2 (Summer 1988): 289–313; and Justin Saxby, "Toadstools, Bartleby, and Badiou: Herman Melville's Response to the Quest for the Historical Jesus," *Religion and the Arts* 19 (2015): 51–73.

3. John F. Kasson, *Rudeness and Civility: Manners in Nineteenth-Century Urban America* (New York: Hill & Wang, 1990), 93. For an overview of the market revolution in the United States between the Revolution and the Civil War see John Lauritz Larson, *The Market Revolution in America: Liberty, Ambition, and the Eclipse of the Common Good* (New York: Cambridge University Press, 2009). For a discussion of biblical teachings on the morality of wealth and poverty see Conrad Boerma, *The Rich, the Poor—and the Bible* (Philadelphia: Westminster, 1979).

4. James Turner, *Without God, without Creed: The Origins of Unbelief in America* (Baltimore: Johns Hopkins University Press, 1985), 119. On contemporary signs of uneasiness about the moral perils of excessive wealth see Stewart Davenport, *Friends of the Unrighteous Mammon: Northern Christians and Market Capitalism, 1815–1860* (Chicago: University of Chicago Press, 2008); Lorman A. Ratner, Paula T. Kaufman, and Dwight L. Teeter Jr., *Paradoxes of Prosperity: Wealth-Seeking versus Christian Values in Pre–Civil War America* (Urbana: University of Illinois Press, 2009).

5. On New York City in the antebellum era see Edward K. Spann, *The New Metropolis: New York City, 1840–1857* (New York: Columbia University Press, 1981); on wealth and poverty in the 1840s see chaps. 4, 5, 9, and 10. On "Bartleby" and the changing urban landscape of New York City see Nick Yablon, *Untimely Ruins: An Archaeology of American Urban Modernity, 1819–1919* (Chicago: University of Chicago Press, 2009), chap. 3.

6. Spann, *New Metropolis*, 19. Herman Melville, *The Piazza Tales and Other Prose Pieces, 1839–1860*, ed. Harrison Hayford, Alma A. MacDougall, G. Thomas Tanselle, et al. (Evanston, IL: Northwestern University Press and the Newberry Library, 1987), 32. Further references to this edition of the story will appear parenthetically in the text. On "Bartleby" in the context of journalism and fiction devoted to the unparalleled urban growth of New York in the antebellum era see Bergmann, *God in the Street*. For a study of the urban milieu of clerks and copyists like Bartleby see Thomas Augst, *The Clerk's Tale: Young Men and Moral Life in Nineteenth-Century America* (Chicago: University of Chicago Press, 2003); on "Bartleby" see chap. 4. Barbara Foley attempts to recontextualize "Bartleby, the Scrivener" in New York history by arguing for the covert influence of the Astor Place Riot of May 1849 on the narrator's consciousness; see "From Wall Street to Astor Place: Historicizing Melville's 'Bartleby,'" *American Literature* 72, no. 1 (March 2000): 87–116.

7. George G. Foster, *New York in Slices: By an Experienced Carver* (New York: W. F. Burgess, 1848), 16, 18; Steve Fraser, *Every Man a Speculator: A History of*

Wall Street in American Life (New York: HarperCollins, 2005), 49. All quotations from the Bible are from the Authorized (King James) Version.

8. For Marxist-oriented and sociological criticisms of "Bartleby" depicting the scrivener as alienated worker see Louise K. Barnett, "Bartleby as Alienated Worker," *Studies in Short Fiction* 11 (Fall 1974): 379-85; James C. Wilson, " 'Bartleby': The Walls of Wall Street," *Arizona Quarterly* 37 (Winter 1981): 335-46; Michael T. Gilmore, *American Literature and the Marketplace* (Chicago: University of Chicago Press, 1985), 132-45; David Kuebrich, "Melville's Doctrine of Assumptions: The Hidden Ideology of Capitalist Production in 'Bartleby,' " *New England Quarterly* 69, no. 3 (September 1996): 381-405; and Naomi C. Reed, "The Specter of Wall Street: 'Bartleby, the Scrivener' and the Language of Commodities," *American Literature* 76, no. 2 (June 2004): 247-73.

9. On the circumstances surrounding the composition of "Bartleby, the Scrivener" see *Herman Melville: A Biography, Vol. 2, 1851–1891* (Baltimore: Johns Hopkins University Press, 2002), chap. 8. On Gansevoort and Allan Melville's successive appointments as examiner in chancery see Hershel Parker, *Herman Melville: A Biography, Vol. 1, 1819–1850* (Baltimore: Johns Hopkins University Press, 1996), 313, 321-22; Melville, *Correspondence*, ed. Lynn Horth (Evanston, IL: Northwestern University Press and the Newberry Library, 1993), 567. On Melville's likely inspiration for "Bartleby" in novelist James A. Maitland's *The Lawyer's Story* see Johannes Dietrich Bergmann, " 'Bartleby' and *The Lawyer's Story*," *American Literature* 47, no. 3 (November 1975): 432-36. On legal contexts for Melville's story see Nicholas Ayo, "Bartleby's Lawyer on Trial," *Arizona Quarterly* 28, no. 1 (Spring 1972): 27-38; Tal Kastner, " 'Bartleby': A Story of Boilerplate," *Law and Literature* 23, no. 3 (Fall 2011): 365-404. On the theme of "prudence" in the story and its basis in changes in mid-nineteenth-century legal practice associated with Melville's father-in-law Lemuel Shaw see John Matteson, " 'A New Race Has Sprung Up': Prudence, Social Consensus, and Law in 'Bartleby, the Scrivener,' " *Leviathan* 10, no. 1 (March 2008): 25-49.

10. On the role of the master of chancery in relation to the story see Herbert F. Smith, "Melville's Master in Chancery and His Recalcitrant Clerk," *American Quarterly* 17, no. 4 (Winter 1965): 734-41; Irving Adler, "Equity, Law and Bartleby," *Science and Society* 51, no. 4 (Winter 1987-88): 468-74.

11. James Parton, *Life of John Jacob Astor* (New York: American News, 1865), 52, 75. For a survey of Astor's life see Axel Madsen, *John Jacob Astor: America's First Millionaire* (New York: Wiley, 2001). For more on the narrator and John Jacob Astor see Mario D'Avanza, "Melville's 'Bartleby' and John Jacob Astor," *New England Quarterly* 41, no. 2 (June 1968): 259-64. Dilworth ("The Narrator of Bartleby") makes the contemporary controversy over Astor's real estate holdings a central factor in the meaning of the story while arguing that the narrator, like many other individuals, simply lacks the emotional ability to live up to Christian ideals of charity. For a critique of the lawyer's character with respect to contemporary notions of charity see Nancy D. Goldfarb, "Charity as Purchase: Buying Self-Approval in Melville's 'Bartleby, the Scrivener,' " *Nineteenth-Century Literature* 69, no. 2 (September 2014): 233-61.

12. The very name "Bartleby" recalls a roster of Dickens's similarly named characters such as the title characters in *Barnaby Rudge* and *Nicholas Nickleby*,

Josiah Bounderby in *Hard Times*, and the Jellyby family in *Bleak House*; Susan Nippers is Florence Dombey's nurse in *Dombey and Sons*. On the Dickensian aspects to Melville's story see David Jaffee, *"Bartleby, the Scrivener" and "Bleak House": Melville's Debt to Dickens* (Arlington, VA: Mardi, 1981); Robert F. Fleissner, "'Ah Humanity!' Dickens and Bartleby Revisited," *Research Studies* 50 (1982): 106–9; Brian Foley, "Dickens Revisited: 'Bartleby' and *Bleak House*," *Essays in Literature* 12, no. 2 (Fall 1985): 241–50; and Robert Weisbuch, *Atlantic Double Cross: American Literature and British Influence in the Age of Emerson* (Chicago: University of Chicago Press, 1986), chap. 2. Richard Harter Fogle notes that "Turkey and Nippers together . . . form an allegory of the English and American national characters, their virtues and their faults" (*Melville's Shorter Tales*, 129). On the lawyer's clerks as partly modeled on figures in the writings of Charles Lamb see Joel O. Conarroe, "Melville's Bartleby and Charles Lamb," *Studies in Short Fiction* 5 (Winter 1968): 113–18.

13. Joel O. Conarroe argues for Bartleby's origins in the writings of Charles Lamb, from whose essay "Oxford in the Vacation" Melville likely derived the word "scrivener" for legal copyist while also reading of "dead-letter days" and the flayed Christian martyr "Bartlemy" (Saint Bartholomew); see "Melville's Bartleby," 115–17. Christopher W. Sten argues that Bartleby's inanimate behavior reflects the unworldly attitude of the contemporary young transcendentalist as represented in Emerson's essay "The Transcendentalist"; see "Bartleby, the Transcendentalist: Melville's Dead Letter to Emerson," *Modern Language Quarterly* 35, no. 1 (March 1974): 30–44. John F. Kasson explores Bartleby's inert behavior as a tragicomedy of incivility in the mid-nineteenth-century world of manners; see *Rudeness and Civility*, 86–92. Ronald Wesley Hoag reads the scrivener as a *memento mori*, or reminder of death, who deepens the narrator's knowledge of the human condition; see "The Corpse in the Office: Mortality, Mutability, and Salvation in 'Bartleby, the Scrivener,'" *ESQ: A Journal of the American Renaissance* 38 (Second Quarter, 1992): 119–42. Richard J. Zlogar associates Bartleby with the treatment of lepers in the Bible; see "Body Politics in 'Bartleby': Leprosy, Healing, and Christ-ness in Melville's 'Story of Wall Street,'" *Nineteenth-Century Literature* 53, no. 4 (March 1999): 505–29. Wendy Anne Lee explores the philosophical implications of Bartleby's affectless personality in "The Scandal of Insensibility; or, the Bartleby Problem," *PMLA* 150, no. 5 (October 2015): 1405–19. In a biographical reading, John Cullen Gruesser argues that the characterization of Bartleby incorporates images of Poe as an impoverished New York author in the mid-1840s; see *Edgar Allan Poe and His Nineteenth-Century Counterparts* (New York: Bloomsbury, 2019), chap. 3. For another biographical reading linking the characters of "Bartleby" with Melville's sometime literary friend Evert Duyckinck and his literary associates see Daniel A. Wells, "'Bartleby, the Scrivener,' Poe, and the Duyckinck Circle," *ESQ: A Journal of the American Renaissance* 21, no. 1 (First Quarter 1975): 35–39.

14. On "Bartleby" and melancholy see Nathalia Wright, "Melville and 'Old Burton' with 'Bartleby' as *An Anatomy of Melancholy*," *Tennessee Studies in Literature* 15 (1970): 1–13. On schizophrenia see Morris Beja, "Bartleby and Schizophrenia," *Massachusetts Review* 19, no. 3 (Autumn 1978): 555–68. On autism see William P. Sullivan, "Bartleby and Infantile Autism: A Naturalistic

Explanation," *Bulletin of the West Virginia Association of College English Teachers* 3, no. 2 (Fall 1976): 43-60; Amit Pinchevski, "Bartleby's Autism: Wandering along Incommunicability," *Cultural Critique* 78, no. 1 (March 2011): 27-59.

15. *New York Tribune*, December 25, 1845, p. 2; partly quoted in Spann, *New Metropolis*, 73.

16. On the close relationship between the "Occupy Wall Street" protest of 2011-12 and Melville's uncooperative Wall Street scrivener see Russ Castronovo, "Occupy Bartleby," *J19: The Journal of Nineteenth-Century Americanists* 2, no. 2 (Fall 2014): 253-72.

17. For more on the John Colt-Samuel Adams murder as it relates to "Bartleby" see T. H. Giddings, "Melville, the Colt-Adams Murder, and 'Bartleby,'" *Studies in American Fiction* 2 (Autumn 1974): 123-32. For a full account of this sensational crime see Harold Schechter, *Killer Colt: Murder, Disgrace, and the Making of an American Legend* (New York: Ballantine Books, 2010). Graham Nicol Forst argues that the last names of the murderer (Colt) and victim (Adams) evoke the archetypal biblical murder by Cain of his brother Abel, both being literal sons of Adam; see "Up Wall Street," 267.

18. Davenport, *Friends of the Unrighteous Mammon*, 81; see also 93, 117-18, 160, 169.

19. For discussions of the narrator's reading of Edwards and Priestley see Walton Patrick, "Melville's 'Bartleby' and the Doctrine of Necessity," *American Literature* 41, no. 1 (March 1969): 39-54; Allan Moore Emery, "The Alternatives of Melville's 'Bartleby,'" *Nineteenth-Century Fiction* 31, no. 2 (September 1976): 170-87; and Hiroki Yoshikuni, "Kant with Bartleby: A Fate of Freedom," *Nineteenth-Century Literature* 71, no. 1 (June 2016): 37-63.

20. See Franklin, *Wake of the Gods*, 132.

21. Marvin Fisher, *Going Under: Melville's Short Fiction and the American 1850s* (Baton Rouge: Louisiana State University Press, 1977), 195.

22. George G. Foster, *New York in Slices*, 19-20. For more on the Tombs prison see Timothy J. Gilfoyle, "America's Greatest Criminal Barracks: The Tombs and the Experience of Criminal Justice in New York City, 1838-1897," *Journal of Urban History* 29, no. 5 (July 2003): 525-54. Graham Nicol Forst notes Bartleby's likely allusion to John 5:42 while arguing that the narrator, like the figure of Nicodemus, ultimately learns a lesson of compassion from his scrivener; see "Up Wall Street," 268-70. Donald M. Fiene remarks that "one might construe Bartleby's final refusal to eat the grub-man's food as a deliberate excision by Melville of the last supper and the sacrament of communion (and the promise of redemption) from his version of the Christian myth" ("Bartleby the Christ," 22).

23. For discussion of the relevance of the parable of the Good Samaritan in the story see Doloff, "Prudent Samaritan."

24. Turner, *Without God*, 119.

25. For discussions of the historical role of the "dead letter" office in the national postal system in relation to Melville's story see Lewis H. Miller Jr., "'Bartleby' and the Dead Letter," *Studies in American Fiction* 8, no. 1 (Spring 1980): 1-12; Thomas R. Mitchell, "Dead Letter and Dead Men: Narrative Purpose in 'Bartleby, the Scrivener,'" *Studies in Short Fiction* 27 (Summer 1990):

329–38; Richard R. Johns, "The Lost World of Bartleby, the Ex-Officeholder: Variations on a Venerable Literary Form," *New England Quarterly* 70, no. 4 (December 1997): 631–41; and Yoshiaki Furui, *Modernizing Solitude: The Networked Individual in Nineteenth-Century American Literature* (Tuscaloosa: University of Alabama Press, 2019), chap. 3. For background on dead letters see David M. Henkin, *The Postal Age: The Emergence of Modern Communications in Nineteenth-Century America* (Chicago: University of Chicago Press, 2006), 158–71.

26. Henkin, *Postal Age*, 161. On Melville's May 29, 1846, letter to Gansevoort see Melville, *Correspondence*, 39–41. On the contemporary popularity of "dead letter" stories see Hershel Parker, "The Sequel in 'Bartleby,'" in Inge, *Bartleby the Inscrutable*, 159–65. On resemblances between the sequel to "Bartleby, the Scrivener" and a passage from Charles Dickens's *The Pickwick Papers* see Allan H. MacLaine, "Melville's 'Sequel' to 'Bartleby the Scrivener' and Dickens' 'Story of the Bagman's Uncle' in *Pickwick Papers*," *American Transcendental Quarterly* 60 (July 1986): 37–39.

27. As William Bysshe Stein notes, "Symbolically, the failure of letters to reach the addresses parallels the failure of the New Testament Epistles (the organizing inspiration of the church, historically) to define the meaning and purpose of human existence" ("Bartleby, the Christian Conscience," 111).

28. Damien B. Schlarb notes the relevance of the book of Job to the scrivener's alleged employment in the Dead Letter Office: "In his epilogue, Melville conceives of a Joban plot without that text's [i.e., the book of Job's] uplifting resolution. The tragedy consists not of the individual undeliverable letter but of the ultimate impossibility of redressing human suffering" (*Melville's Wisdom*, 59).

29. Anderson, "Form and Meaning," 386; Larson, *Market Revolution*, 140.

30. Herman Melville, *Pierre; or The Ambiguities* (Evanston, IL: Northwestern University Press and the Newberry Library, 1971), 207, 208.

31. *Pierre*, 214. On Bartleby as a representative of heavenly chronometrical morality and the narrator as a practitioner of worldly horological "virtuous expediency" see Schechter, "Bartleby the Chronometer."

32. See Jonathan A. Cook, *Satirical Apocalypse: An Anatomy of "The Confidence-Man"* (Westport, CT: Greenwood, 1996); Cook, "Christian Typology and Social Critique in Melville's 'The Two Temples,'" *Christianity and Literature* 56, no. 1 (Fall 2006): 5–33; Cook, "Poverty, Class, and Christian Charity in 'Poor Man's Pudding and Rich Man's Crumbs,'" *Symbiosis: A Journal of Transatlantic Literary and Cultural Relations* 21, no. 2 (October 2017): 147–67; and Cook, "Moral Education in 'The Paradise of Bachelors and the Tartarus of Maids,'" *Leviathan: A Journal of Melville Studies* 19, no. 3 (October 2017): 79–99.

3. Conversion, Infatuation, Resurrection

1. For a detailed review of criticism of the story through the mid-1980s see Lea Bertani Vozar Newman, *A Reader's Guide to the Short Stories of Herman Melville* (Boston: G. K. Hall, 1986), 155–74. For previous critics arguing for a religious reading of Melville's story see Richard Harter Fogle, *Melville's Shorter Tales* (Norman: University of Oklahoma Press, 1960), chap. 3; William Bysshe

Stein, "Melville's Cock and the Bell of St. Paul," *Emerson Society Quarterly* 27 (Second Quarter 1962): 5–10; Beryl Rowland, "Melville and the Cock That Crew," *American Literature* 52, no. 4 (January 1981): 593–606; Michael Colacurcio, "Charity and Its Discontents: Pity and Politics in Melville's Fiction," in *There before Us: Religion, Literature, and Culture from Emerson to Wendell Berry*, ed. Roger Lundin (Grand Rapids, MI: Eerdmans, 2007), 49–79; and Matthew R. Bardowell, "Signor Beneventano and Man Inspirited: A Symbolist Reading of Melville's 'Cock-a-Doodle-Doo!,'" *Renascence* 61, no. 4 (June 2009): 221–34. On "Cock-a-Doodle-Doo!" as a satire on Thoreau and Transcendentalism see Egbert S. Oliver, "'Cock-a-Doodle-Doo!' and Transcendental Hocus-Pocus," *New England Quarterly* 21, no. 2 (January 1948): 104–16; William Bysshe Stein, "Melville Roasts Thoreau's Cock," *Modern Language Notes* 74 (March 1959): 218–19; Hershel Parker, "Melville's Satire of Emerson and Thoreau: An Examination of the Evidence," *American Transcendental Quarterly* 7 (Summer 1970): 61–76, and 9 (Winter 1971): 70; Allan Moore Emery, "The Cocks of Melville's 'Cock-a-Doodle-Doo!,'" *ESQ: A Journal of the American Renaissance* 28, no. 2 (Second Quarter 1982): 89–111; and Joseph Rosenblum, "A Cock Fight between Melville and Thoreau," *Studies in Short Fiction* 23 (Spring 1986): 159–67. Placing "Cock-a-Doodle-Doo!" high in the canon of Melville short fiction, Sidney P. Moss debunks the idea that the story satirizes Thoreau or Transcendentalism generally but thinks it should be interpreted without irony as the narrator's triumph over despair and death; see "'Cock-a-Doodle-Doo!' and Some Legends in Melville Scholarship," *American Literature* 40, no. 2 (May 1968): 192–210. William B. Dillingham denies a Christian meaning for the story but sees the narrator as experiencing a crisis of masculinity ending in a perverse self-glorification; see *Melville's Short Fiction: 1853–1857* (Athens: University of Georgia Press, 1977), chap. 3. On "Cock-a-Doodle-Doo!" as a critique of Wordsworth's failure to understand rural poverty, as found in the parody of "Resolution and Independence" included in Melville's story, see Arnd Bohm, "Wordsworth in Melville's Cock-a-Doodle-Doo!," *Leviathan* 9, no. 1 (March 2007): 25–42. On the story as a dramatization of the narrator's unstable mental health see Corey Evan Thompson, "Melville's 'Cock-a-Doodle-Doo!': A Case Study in Bipolar Disorder," *ATQ* 17, no. 1 (new series) (March 2003): 43–53. Marvin Fisher argues that Melville's story is a parable of the literary artist illustrating the danger of dedicating oneself to creating illusions; see *Going Under: Melville's Short Fiction and the American 1850s* (Baton Rouge: Louisiana State University Press, 1977), 161–78. On the story as an example of fantastic literature see Ib Johansen, *Walking Shadows: Reflections on the American Fantastic and the American Grotesque from Washington Irving to the Postmodern Era* (Leiden: Brill Rodopi, 2015), chap. 4.

2. Fogle, *Melville's Shorter Tales*, 33; Stein, "Melville's Cock"; Dillingham, *Melville's Short Fiction*, 68; Fisher, *Going Under*, 170; Rowland, "Melville and the Cock That Crew," 606.

3. Colacurcio, "Charity and Its Discontents," 76; Bardowell, "Signor Beneventano," 221; Johansen, *Walking Shadows*, 145.

4. On Melville's phallic punning in relation to the rooster Trumpet and his owner Merrymusk see Phillip Young, *The Private Melville* (University Park: Pennsylvania State University Press, 1993), 95–98.

5. All quotations from the Bible are from the Authorized (King James) Version. On Melville's recurrent allusions throughout his fiction and poetry to Saint Paul's doctrine of Christian resurrection see Gordon V. Boudreau, "Herman Melville, Immortality, St. Paul, and Resurrection: From *Rose-Bud* to *Billy Budd*," *Christianity and Literature* 52, no. 3 (Spring 2003): 343–64.

6. Jonathan Edwards, *Images or Shadows of Divine Things*, ed. Perry Miller (1948; Westport, CT: Greenwood, 1977), 92. On the continued influence of Jonathan Edwards on nineteenth-century Protestant Christianity see Joseph A. Conforti, *Jonathan Edwards, Religious Tradition, and American Culture* (Chapel Hill: University of North Carolina Press, 1995). Emery ("Cocks," 91–93) notes that Melville's interest in roosters may have been stimulated by a reading of the Episcopal minister Frederick W. Shelton's series "Letters from Up the River" appearing in the *Knickerbocker Magazine* in 1852 and 1853 in which the author discussed, among other things, his experience with Shanghai roosters and a variety of other chickens. An inhabitant of Dutchess County, New York, Shelton published his letters on the charms and challenges of rural life in book form as *Up the River* (New York: Scribners) in October 1853.

7. On the pervasive antebellum preoccupation with heaven see Mark M. Schantz, *Awaiting the Heavenly Country: The Civil War and America's Culture of Death* (Ithaca, NY: Cornell University Press, 2008).

8. Herman Melville, *The Piazza Tales and Other Prose Pieces, 1839–1860*, ed. Harrison Hayford, Alma A. MacDougall, G. Thomas Tanselle, et al. (Evanston, IL: Northwestern University Press and the Newberry Library, 1987), 268. All references to this edition will be cited parenthetically in the text.

9. On the sinking of the *Henry Clay* see the *New York Times*, July 30, 1852, at https://timesmachine.nytimes.com/timesmachine/1852/07/30/87838967.pdf. On antebellum railroad accidents see Christian Wolmar, *The Great Railroad Revolution: A History of Trains in America* (New York: Public Affairs, 2012), chap. 7 (quotation at 193, 194).

10. Melville and his wife had heard Ferdinando Beneventano singing in Donizetti's *Lucia di Lammermoor* in New York at the Astor Place Opera House on December 24, 1847. See Hershel Parker, *Herman Melville: A Biography, Volume 1, 1819–1850* (Baltimore: Johns Hopkins University Press, 1996), 570.

11. Lewis R. Rambo, *Understanding Religious Conversion* (New Haven, CT: Yale University Press, 1993).

12. William James, *The Varieties of Religious Experience: A Study in Human Nature*, in *Writings, 1902–1910*, ed. Bruce Kuklick (New York: Library of America, 1987), 127, 222.

13. *The Complete Poems of Emily Dickinson*, ed. Thomas H. Johnson (Boston: Little, Brown, 1955), 290.

4. The Genealogy of Melville's Female Job

1. See Melville, *Correspondence*, ed. Lynn Horth (Evanston, IL: Northwestern University Press and the Newberry Library, 1993), 231–37, 621–25. Subsequent references to this edition of Melville's letters will be cited parenthetically in the text. Damien B. Schlarb has recently examined the relevance of the book

of Job to "The Encantadas," noting that the series of sketches "adopts as its default subject position the moment when Job, having lost all possessions and even his health, sits in a ditch, scrubbing himself with potsherds while awaiting some explanation for his suffering" (*Melville's Wisdom: Religion, Skepticism, and Literature in Nineteenth-Century America* [New York: Oxford University Press, 2021], 60).

2. For more on Melville's attempted literary collaboration with Hawthorne on this project see Wynn Kelley, "Hawthorne and Melville in the Shoals: 'Agatha,' the Trials of Authorship, and the Dream of Collaboration," in *Hawthorne and Melville: Writing a Relationship*, ed. Jana Argersinger and Leland S. Person (Athens: University of Georgia Press, 2008), 173–95. On the biographical background to Melville's Agatha letters, his failed attempt to use this material for his own unpublished novel *The Isle of the Cross*, and his composition of "The Encantadas," see Hershel Parker, *Herman Melville: A Biography, Volume 2, 1851–1891* (Baltimore: Johns Hopkins University Press, 2002), chaps. 6–8. On the direct link between the story of Agatha and "Norfolk Isle and the Chola Widow" see Charles N. Watson Jr., "Melville's Agatha and Hunilla: A Literary Reincarnation," *English Language Notes* 6 (December 1968): 114–18. On the overall impact of the Agatha story on Melville's short fiction see Patricia Lacy, "The Agatha Theme in Melville's Stories," *University of Texas Studies in English* 35 (1956): 96–104.

3. All quotations from the Bible are from the King James (Authorized) Version.

4. On the broad historical impact of the book of Job see Mark Larrimore, *The Book of Job: A Biography* (Princeton, NJ: Princeton University Press, 2012); Franklin T. Harkins and Aaron Canty, eds., *A Companion to Job in the Middle Ages* (Leiden: Brill, 2016). On the influence of Job in *Moby-Dick* see Jonathan A. Cook, *Inscrutable Malice: Theodicy, Eschatology, and the Biblical Sources of "Moby-Dick"* (DeKalb: Northern Illinois University Press, 2012).

5. Melville owned two copies of Chaucer's writings, first a two-volume modernized edition *The Riches of Chaucer, in Which His Impurities Have Been Expunged . . .* (London, 1835), and an eight-volume *Poetical Works*, edited with a memoir by Robert Bell (London, 1854–56). See the listings at Steven Olsen-Smith and Peter Norberg, eds., *Melville's Marginalia Online* at http://melvilles marginalia.org.

6. See the Clerk's Tale in *The Works of Geoffrey Chaucer*, ed. F. N. Robinson (Boston: Houghton Mifflin, 1961), 101–14. Quotations from this edition of the tale will be followed by line number.

7. See Edward I. Condren, "The 'Clerk's Tale' of Man Tempting God," *Criticism* 26, no. 2 (Spring 1984): 99–114.

8. On Job and the Clerk's Tale see Lawrence Besserman, "Biblical Exegesis, Typology, and the Imagination of Chaucer," in *Typology and Medieval Literature*, ed. Hugh T. Kennan (New York: AMS, 1992), 183–205; Jane Beal, "Patience on Pilgrimage: Job in Chaucer's *Canterbury Tales*," in Harkins and Canty, *Companion to Job*, chap. 13; and Larrimore, *Book of Job*, 145–53.

9. See Larrimore, *Book of Job*, 149–50, and Besserman, "Biblical Exegesis." As Besserman notes, "By attributing the patient words of Job to Griselda and assigning Job's impatient curse to her father, Chaucer in effect

splits the biblical figure, and Griselda becomes a new, more perfect Job" ("Biblical Exegesis," 193).

10. Nathaniel Hawthorne, "Wakefield," in *Twice-Told Tales*, ed. William Charvat, Roy Harvey Pierce, and Claude M. Simpson (Columbus: Ohio State University Press, 1974), 130. Subsequent references to this edition will be cited parenthetically in the text. For a useful summary of mid-twentieth-century criticism of "Wakefield" see Lea Bertain Vozar Newman, *A Reader's Guide to the Short Stories of Nathaniel Hawthorne* (Boston: G. K. Hall, 1979), 311–17. Arnold Weinstein views the story as an anticipation of the modern fragmentation of the self; see *Nobody's Home: Speech, Self, and Place in American Fiction from Hawthorne to DeLillo* (New York: Oxford University Press, 1993), chap. 1. Milette Shamir similarly reads the story as marked by radical inconsistencies; see *Inexpressible Privacy: The Interior Life of Antebellum American Literature* (Philadelphia: University of Pennsylvania Press, 2008), 70–81.

11. Laura Laffrado argues that Wakefield's wife gains power and dignity as she is transformed from dependent wife to independent widow, but her argument downplays the evidence of the wife's suffering in the story and ignores the perversely God-like test of her husband. See Laffrado, "'Far and Momentary Glimpses': Hawthorne's Treatment of Mrs. Wakefield," in *New Interpretations of American Literature*, ed. Richard Fleming and Michael Payne (Bucknell, PA: Bucknell University Press, 1988): 34–44.

12. See Martin C. Battestin, *The Providence of Wit: Aspects of Form in Augustan Literature and the Arts* (Charlottesville: University Press of Virginia, 1989), chap. 7; James H. Lehmann, "The Vicar of Wakefield: Goldsmith's Sublime, Oriental Job," *ELH* 46, no. 1 (Spring 1979): 97–121.

13. See Austin Warren, ed., *Nathaniel Hawthorne: Representative Selections* (New York: American Book, 1934), 364–65; Ruth Perry, "The Solitude of Hawthorne's 'Wakefield,'" *American Literature* 49, no. 4 (January 1978): 613–19.

14. Melville's offer to Hawthorne of the history of Agatha Hatch Robertson for literary use, which the latter author declined, is oddly reminiscent of a similar true-life story that Henry Wadsworth Longfellow obtained from Hawthorne, his friend and Bowdoin classmate, and turned into *Evangeline* (1847)—a story, like that of Melville's abandoned spouse, of a woman's long-suffering separation from her husband following the forced deportation of the French Acadian peoples of Nova Scotia by the British in 1755. Hawthorne had himself learned of this story in October 1838 from his Salem minister friend Horace Conolly and allegedly brooded on it before writing an account of the Acadians' exile in his children's history, *Famous Old People* (1841). Hawthorne and Conolly had dined with Longfellow sometime in 1840, and Conolly recounted the history of the Arcadian woman and her lost husband, whom Longfellow later named Evangeline and Gabriel, respectively. After Hawthorne had relinquished use of the story for his fiction, Longfellow turned the saga into his commercially successful long poem. See Manning Hawthorne and H. W. Longfellow Dana, "The Origins of Longfellow's *Evangeline*," *Papers of the Bibliographical Society of America* 41, no. 3 (1947): 165–203.

15. On Melville's notes bound into his copy of Owen Chase's *Narrative* describing the sinking of the *Essex* see "Melville's Memoranda in Chase's *Narrative*

of the Essex," in Melville, *Moby-Dick; or The Whale,* ed. Harrison Hayford, Hershel Parker, and G. Thomas Tanselle (Evanston, IL: Northwestern University Press and the Newberry Library, 1988), 971–95. For more on Melville and Pollard see Henry F. Pommer, "Herman Melville and the Wake of the *Essex,*" *American Literature* 20, no. 3 (November 1948): 290–304; Cook, *Inscrutable Malice,* 252–53.

16. In view of Melville's mention of shipwreck and the malignancy of the sea in his August 13 letter to Hawthorne, it is both tragic and ironic that Hawthorne's younger sister Louisa had drowned in a steamboat accident on the Hudson River in late July 1852. See James R. Mellow, *Nathaniel Hawthorne in His Times* (Boston: Houghton Mifflin, 1980), 410–12. There is no mention of this family tragedy in Melville's extant letters to Hawthorne.

17. For useful studies of "Norfolk Isle and the Chola Widow" and "The Encantadas" see Richard Harter Fogle, *Melville's Shorter Tales* (Norman: University of Oklahoma Press, 1960), 92–115; Howard D. Pearce, "The Narrator of 'Norfolk Isle and the Chola Widow,'" *Studies in Short Fiction* 3 (Fall 1965): 56–62; I. Newberry, "'The Encantadas': Melville's Inferno," *American Literature* 38, no. 1 (March 1966): 49–68; Margaret Yarina, "The Dualistic Vision of Herman Melville's 'The Encantadas,'" *Journal of Narrative Technique* 3, no. 2 (May 1973): 141–48; Bruce Bickley, *The Method of Melville's Short Fiction* (Durham, NC: Duke University Press, 1975), chap. 7; Marvin Fisher, *Going Under: Melville's Short Fiction and the American 1850s* (Baton Rouge: Louisiana State University Press, 1977), 28–49; William B. Dillingham, Melville's *Shorter Fiction, 1853–1856* (Athens: University of Georgia Press, 1977), chap. 3; Maria Felisa López Liquete, "When Silence Speaks: The Chola Widow," in *Melville and Women,* ed. Elizabeth A. Schultz and Haskell S. Springer (Kent, OH: Kent State University Press, 2006), 213–28; Graham Thompson, *Herman Melville: Among the Magazines* (Amherst: University of Massachusetts Press, 2018), 72–85; Gary Shapiro, "Beasts, Sovereigns, Pirates: Melville's 'Enchanted Isles' beyond the Picturesque," in *Melville among the Philosophers,* ed. Corey McCall and Tom Nurmi (Lanham, MD: Lexington Books, 2017), 83–104; and Christopher Sten, *Melville's Other Lives: Bodies in "The Piazza Tales"* (Charlottesville: University of Virginia Press, 2022), chap. 5.

18. Fogle notes the depiction of a cruel but absent god in the story: "With the story of the Chola widow one is forced to face the issue, who or what is the god of the Encantadas? Who blasted them, who made Hunilla suffer? Melville will not allow us to escape from this question of questions, nor, conscientious in the method of knowledge, will he answer it" (*Melville's Shorter Tales,* 108). For a different interpretation of Hunilla as a potential female Job figure see Schlarb, *Melville's Wisdom,* 63–65.

19. Melville, *The Piazza Tales and Other Prose Pieces, 1839–1860,* ed. Harrison Hayford, Alma A. MacDougall, G. Thomas Tanselle, et al. (Evanston, IL: Northwestern University Press and the Newberry Library, 1987), 154. Subsequent references to this edition will be cited parenthetically in the text. Gary Shapiro ("Beasts, Sovereigns, Pirates," 91) notes Melville's inversion of picturesque convention in the depiction of the accidental deaths of Hunilla's husband and brother.

20. In a comparison of Frederick Douglass's and Melville's implied references to rape, Hester Blum notes the ambiguities and complexities of Melville's use of the long three-em dash as well as other semantic obliquities when referring to Hunilla's violation; see "Douglass's and Melville's 'Alphabets of the Blind,'" in *Frederick Douglass and Herman Melville: Essays in Relation*, ed. Robert S. Levine and Samuel Otter (Chapel Hill: University of North Carolina Press, 2008), 257–78. Maria Felisa López Liquete gives a political meaning to the narrator's reticence and Hunilla's silence concerning her traumatic experience: "The narrator's decision not to name rape as the violation Hunilla probably experienced exposes his complicity in silence and silencing. . . . He leaves the tale without closure, thereby avoiding the risks of presenting himself as an authoritative representative of the subaltern" ("When Silence Speaks," 225–26).

21. See also Psalms 147:16–17: "He giveth snow like wool: he scattereth the hoarfrost like ashes. He casteth forth his ice like morsels: who can stand before his cold?"

22. On the image of Hunilla's ass in relation to Wordsworth's "Peter Bell" see James Baird, *Ishmael* (Baltimore: Johns Hopkins University Press, 1956), 313–14. Caroline Alice Hofmann argues that the depiction of animal suffering of tortoises and dogs in the sketch, allegedly influenced by Rousseau's *Discourse on the Origins of Inequality* (1755), subverts the priority of the human suffering of Hunilla; see "Staging Sympathy: Hunilla, Suffering, Rousseauvian Beasts," *Leviathan: A Journal of Melville Studies* 23, no. 2 (June 2021): 53–72.

23. See Robert Sattelmeyer and James Barbour, "The Sources and Genesis of Melville's 'Norfolk Isle and the Chola Widow,'" *American Literature* 50, no. 3 (November 1978): 398–417 (quotation at 403); Scott Norsworthy, "Early Sources for Melville's 'Chola Widow' Sketch," Melvilliana, Saturday, February 16, 2013; and "Call Her Hunilla," *Melvilliana*, Sunday, October 21, 2018, both at http://melvilliana.blogspot.com.

24. As Sattelmeyer and Barbour note, "In Melville's tale the frame of providential care is retained, but it is grimly reversed in an attack on the platitudes about God's inscrutable ways which abound in the newspaper article" ("Sources and Genesis," 415).

25. As initiated in English literature by Chaucer, the tradition of the "patient Griselda" as a female Job figure continued in Elizabethan drama in Henry Chettle, Thomas Dekker, and William Haughton's *Patient Grissil* (1599), and it also informed the English novel in Samuel Richardson's *Clarissa* (1748). See Harry Kayishian, "Griselda on the Elizabethan Stage: *The Patient Grissil* of Chettle, Dekker, and Haughton," *Studies in English Literature, 1500–1900* 16, no. 2 (Spring 1976): 253–61; Veronica Bassil, "The Faces of Griselda: Chaucer, Prior, Richardson," *Texas Studies in Literature and Language* 26, no. 2 (Summer 1984): 157–82. Continuing the tradition are Maria Edgeworth's *The Modern Griselda* (1804) and Anthony Trollope's *Miss Mackenzie* (1865), the latter initially titled *The Modern Griselda*. The saintly, unjustly persecuted wife is a familiar figure in Victorian fiction; see John R. Reed, *Victorian Conventions* (Athens: Ohio University Press, 1975), 40–44.

5. Revolutionary Skepticism in *Israel Potter*

1. Melville, *Correspondence*, ed. Lynn Horth (Evanston, IL: Northwestern University Press and the Newberry Library, 1993), 193. The likely dating of this letter has been corrected from June 1 in *Correspondence* to early May by Hershel Parker; see *Herman Melville: A Biography: Volume 1, 1819–1851* (Baltimore: Johns Hopkins University Press, 1996), 841. On the use of Ecclesiastes in chapters 96 and 98 of *Moby-Dick* see Jonathan A. Cook, *Inscrutable Malice: Theodicy, Eschatology, and the Biblical Sources of "Moby-Dick"* (DeKalb: Northern Illinois University Press, 2012), 155–58. All references to the Bible are from the King James (Authorized) Version. Nathalia Wright notes of the biblical wisdom literature to which Ecclesiastes belongs, "No other group of Scriptural books is so extensively represented in his [Melville's] pages, or so profusely marked in his Bible" (*Melville's Use of the Bible* [Durham, NC: Duke University Press, 1949], 94). In his recent study, Damien B. Schlarb has analyzed the importance of Ecclesiastes in Melville's oeuvre while tracking its presence in *Redburn, Moby-Dick, Pierre*, and *Battle-Pieces*, but not in *Israel Potter*; see *Melville's Wisdom: Religion, Skepticism, and Literature in Nineteenth-Century America* (New York: Oxford University Press, 2021), chap. 3.

2. For studies that discuss or highlight some of the allegorical, typological, mythic, and religious dimensions to *Israel Potter* see John T. Frederick, "Symbol and Theme in Melville's *Israel Potter*," *Modern Fiction Studies* 8, no. 3 (Autumn 1962): 265–75; Arnold Rampersad, *Melville's "Israel Potter": A Pilgrimage and Progress* (Bowling Green, OH: Bowling Green University Popular Press, 1969); John R. Samson, *White Lies: Melville's Narratives of Fact* (Ithaca, NY: Cornell University Press, 1989), chap. 6; Alide Cagidemetrio, *Fictions of the Past: Hawthorne and Melville* (Amherst: Institute for Advanced Study of the Humanities / University of Massachusetts Press, 1992), 109–93; and Bill Christopherson, "Israel Potter: Melville's 'Citizen of the World,'" *Studies in American Fiction* 21, no. 1 (Spring 1993): 21–35. On historical themes in the narrative see Alexander Keyssar, *Melville's "Israel Potter": Reflections on the American Dream* (Cambridge, MA: Harvard University Press, 1969); Robert Zaller, "Melville and the Myth of Revolution," *Studies in Romanticism* 15, no. 4 (Fall 1976): 607–22; Michael T. Gilmore, *The Middle Way: Puritanism and Ideology in American Romantic Fiction* (New Brunswick, NJ: Rutgers University Press, 1977), 151–64; William B. Dillingham, *Melville's Later Novels* (Athens: University of Georgia Press, 1986), chap. 8; Chris Lackey, "The Two Handles of *Israel Potter*," *College Literature* 21, no. 1 (February 1994): 32–45; Russell Reising, *Loose Ends: Closure and Crisis in the American Social Text* (Durham, NC: Duke University Press, 1997), chap. 3; Christopher Sten, *The Weaver God He Weaves: Melville and the Poetics of the Novel* (Kent, OH: Kent State University Press, 1996), chap. 8; Edgar Dryden, *Monumental Melville: Transformation of a Literary Career* (Stanford, CA: Stanford University Press, 2004), 33–53; John Hay, "Broken Hearths: Melville's *Israel Potter* and the Bunker Hill Monument," *New England Quarterly* 89, no. 2 (June 2016): 192–221; Luke Bresky, "Pro-Americans, Proto-Americans, and Un-Americans in Melville's *Israel Potter*," in *A Passion for Getting It Right: Essays of Appreciation in Honor of Michael J. Colacurcio's 50 Years of Teaching*, ed. Carol M. Bensick (New York:

Peter Lang, 2016), 39–68; David Faflik, "Melville's Little Historical Method," *J19: The Journal of Nineteenth-Century Americanists* 5, no. 1 (Spring 2017): 51–77; Robert S. Levine, *Race, Transnationalism, and Nineteenth-Century Literary Studies* (New York: Cambridge University Press, 2018), chap. 7; and Jeffrey Insko, *History, Abolition, and the Ever-Present Now in Antebellum Writing* (New York: Oxford University Press, 2019), chap. 5.

3. Mark R. Sneed notes that Ecclesiastes is "a polemic against traditional wisdom that advises the futility of human striving, effort, and toil, and particularly the effort of traditional wisdom to master the world. Rather, the world is largely irrational and incomprehensible" (*The Politics of Pessimism in Ecclesiastes: A Social-Science Perspective* [Atlanta: Society of Biblical Literature, 2012], 174). See also Leo G. Purdue, *The Sword and the Stylus: An Introduction to Wisdom in the Age of Empires* (Grand Rapids, MI: Eerdmans, 2008), chap. 5.

4. Melville, *Correspondence*, 265. On the biographical circumstances of Melville's composition of *Israel Potter* see Hershel Parker, *Herman Melville: A Biography, Volume 2, 1851–1891* (Baltimore: Johns Hopkins University Press, 2002), chap. 10.

5. Melville, *Israel Potter: His Fifty Years of Exile*, ed. Harrison Hayford, Hershel Parker, and G. Thomas Tanselle (Evanston, IL: Northwestern University Press and the Newberry Library, 1982), 6. Subsequent references to this edition will be cited parenthetically in the text. On Melville's source for his narrative in the *Life and Adventures of Israel R. Potter* see "Melville's Basic Source," in *Israel Potter*, 277–394. For more on the historical Potter, whose fictionalized biography was accepted as legitimate history until well into the twentieth century, see David Chacko and Alexander Kulcsa, "Israel Potter: Genesis of a Legend," *William and Mary Quarterly* 41, no. 3 (July 1984): 365–89. For a discussion of the relation of Melville's *Israel Potter* and the historical Potter, including the shift to third-person from first-person narration, see Peter J. Bellis, "*Israel Potter*: Autobiography as History as Fiction," *American Literary History* 2, no. 4 (Winter 1990): 607–26. On the metafictional aspects to the narrative see Manuel Brancano, "Strategies of Textual Subversion in Herman Melville's *Israel Potter*," *Amerikastudien / American Studies* 53, no. 4 (2008): 491–505.

6. On the Revolutionary War Pension Act of 1818 see David Resch, *Suffering Soldiers: Revolutionary War Veterans, Moral Sentiment, and Political Culture in the Early Republic* (Boston: Northeastern University Press, 1999). For more on the ironies of Melville's dedication and its relation to Webster's Bunker Hill addresses and career see Dillingham, *Melville's Later Novels*, 253–58; Dryden, *Monumental Melville*, 334–39; Hay, "Broken Hearths," 202–8.

7. After quoting the third paragraph of Melville's dedication to *Israel Potter*, an editorial commentator in the May 1856 issue of *Putnam's* wryly noted, "The original, however, is not so rare as Mr. Melville seems to think. At any rate, we have a copy before us, as we write" (quoted in "Historical Note," in *Israel Potter*, 218).

8. As Scott E. Casper remarks, Melville "used fiction to tell his story and note the ideological and methodological limits of Sparksian biography" (*Constructing American Lives: Biography and Culture in Nineteenth-Century America*

[Chapel Hill: University of North Carolina Press, 1999], 153). On Jared Sparks as creator and editor of the Library of American Biography beginning in 1832 see Casper, *Constructing American Lives*, 135–58.

9. "The Bunker Hill Monument," in *The Works of Daniel Webster*, vol. 1 (Boston: Little, Brown, 1851), 62. For a full account of the crisis in Boston during the Anthony Burns rendition see Albert J. von Frank, *The Trials of Anthony Burns: Freedom and Slavery in Emerson's Boston* (Cambridge, MA: Harvard University Press, 1998).

10. James P. Byrd, *Sacred Scripture, Sacred War: The Bible and the Revolution* (New York: Oxford University Press, 2013), 47.

11. As John Samson argues, "In *Israel Potter*, the individual is guided not by Providence or will but by chance, nature, and other forces beyond his comprehension and control. Chance, more than divine purpose, directs Israel's course to an almost absurd degree. He is a sort of shuttlecock, blown and directed from unlikely event to unlikelier event" (*White Lies*, 205). Manuel Broncano similarly notes, "Israel may be said to be the first literary hero in the United States to meet with failure because of a mere whim of fate, thanks to the malignant power of a universe which is not governed by any criterion (or any divine rule) at all" ("Strategies," 499).

12. Carlyle, *On Heroes, Hero Worship, and the Heroic in History*, ed. David R. Sorenson and Brent E. Kinser (New Haven, CT: Yale University Press, 2013), 21; Ralph Waldo Emerson, *Representative Men*, in *Essays and Lectures*, ed. Joel Porte (New York: Library of America, 1983), 624.

13. See Daniel Reagan, "Melville's Israel Potter and the Nature of Biography," *ATQ* 3, no. 3 (new series) (September 1989): 257–76. David Faflik argues that Melville's novella anticipated the methods of the late twentieth-century New Historicism in its focus on minor, previously overlooked historical figures and trends; see "Melville's Little Historical Method." For discussions of Melville's portraits of Benjamin Franklin and John Paul Jones see Gilmore, *Middle Way*, 154–60; Dillingham, *Melville's Later Novels*, 258–82; Sten, *Weaver God*, 167–76. The most negative assessment of Melville's portrait of Franklin is in Reising, *Loose Ends*, 132–53. On *Israel Potter* in relation to nineteenth-century historical fiction see Brian Rosenberg, "*Israel Potter*: Melville's Anti-History," *Studies in American Fiction* 15, no. 2 (Autumn 1987): 175–86. On Melville's novella as the story of an unsuccessful search for Revolutionary Fathers see Charles N. Watson Jr., "Melville's *Israel Potter*: Fathers and Sons," *Studies in the Novel* 7, no. 4 (Winter 1975): 563–68.

14. See Sneed, *Politics of Pessimism*, chap. 7.

15. See Charles N. Watson Jr., "Premature Burial in *Arthur Gordon Pym* and *Israel Potter*," *American Literature* 47, no. 1 (March 1975): 105–7. As Watson notes, "the comic overtones of his resurrection in the clothes of the dead squire tend to obscure the seriousness of the implied analogy with that other Son, who submits to the will of his Father only to cry from the cross that his Father has forsaken him. But though Christ's Father ultimately keeps his promise . . . no father, heavenly or earthly, waits to redeem Israel from his lonely quest" ("Melville's *Israel Potter*," 566).

16. As Sneed writes, "Because Qohelet essentially views God as capricious and often rather malevolent (instead of omnibenevolent), even if Qohelet believes this is God's sovereign right, it affects Qohelet's view of God and the human capacity to have any meaningful relationship with him. Qohelet appears to have no real personal relationship with God. Qohelet's God, by definition, cannot. He is essentially impersonal, detached, and distant, which is the expected character of an amoral, capricious heavenly despot" (*Politics of Pessimism*, 188–89). Samson (*White Lies*, 206–7) notes that Melville likely borrowed the image of the Man-in-the-Moon from Hawthorne's story of revolutionary violence "My Kinsman Major Molineux" from *The Snow-Image, and Other Twice-Told Tales* (1852).

17. Samson claims that "Melville's typology shows the Revolution illustrative not of a genetics of salvation but of a genetics of oblivion, like Israel's Puritan parents' ruined homestead" (*White Lies*, 203). Christopherson ("Israel Potter") argues that Melville's protagonist develops from being a figure of nationalist typology to a universal allegorical Everyman by the end of the narrative.

18. Josiah Quincy, *An Oration Delivered on Tuesday, the Fourth of July, 1826* . . . (Boston: True and Greene, 1826), 29–30. On the significance of 1826 as the year of the nation's jubilee see Andrew Burstein, *America's Jubilee: A Generation Remembers the Revolution Fifty Years after Independence* (New York: Vintage, 2002); for descriptions of the July Fourth celebrations that year see chap. 10 (Webster quoted at 252).

19. Dryden (*Monumental Melville*, 47) compares Israel's discovery of his ruined home in the Berkshires to the Wanderer's story of the ruined cottage in book 1 of Wordsworth's *Excursion*. Hay ("Broken Hearths," 216–20) notes connections to Washington Irving's "Rip Van Winkle" and Melville's own late poem "Rip Van Winkle's Lilac."

20. See Sarah J. Purcell, *Sealed with Blood: War, Sacrifice, and Memory in Revolutionary America* (Philadelphia: University of Pennsylvania Press, 2010). For other useful studies of the legacy of the Revolution in relation to American memory and culture see Michael Kammen, *A Season of Youth: The American Revolution and the Historical Imagination* (New York: Oxford University Press, 1978); Alfred F. Young, *The Shoemaker and the Tea Party: Memory and the American Revolution* (Boston: Beacon, 1999); and Michael A. McDonnell, Clare Corbould, Frances M. Clarke, and W. Fitzhugh Brundage, eds., *Remembering the Revolution: Memory, History, and Nation Making from Independence to the Civil War* (Amherst: University of Massachusetts Press, 2013). As Dryden notes, "*Israel Potter* is a *Don Quixote* of national biography, written against the volumes in the Sparks Library of American Biography and undermining the story of America told in those representative lives" (*Monumental Melville*, 39). On the small class of nineteenth- or twentieth-century narratives that, like *Israel Potter*, seriously critiqued the American Revolution see Kammen, *Season of Youth*, 222–33.

21. On Melville's financial difficulties in the early 1850s see Hershel Parker, "Damned by Dollars: *Moby-Dick* and the Price of Genius," in *Melville Biography: An Inside Narrative* (Evanston, IL: Northwestern University Press, 2014),

481–597. For a more extended discussion of the autobiographical aspects of *Israel Potter* see Reising, *Loose Ends*, 178–85.

22. Melville, *Correspondence*, 412. Melville's lament over the public's forgetfulness of his heroic grandfather recalls a comparable example in Ecclesiastes of a wise man who once saved a city from siege warfare: "And he by his wisdom delivered the city; yet no man remembered that same poor man" (Eccles. 9:15).

23. On obituary notices at Melville's death see Parker, *Herman Melville*, 2:920–22.

6. Memorializing the Dead in *Battle-Pieces*

1. Mark M. Schantz, *Awaiting the Heavenly Country: The Civil War and America's Culture of Death* (Ithaca, NY: Cornell University Press, 2008), 2. On casualty and mortality statistics for American wars see www.en.wikipedia.com/wiki/United_States_military_casualities_of_war. Social historians have investigated the immediate and long-term consequences resulting from the massive scale of death in the Civil War. See John R. Neff, *Honoring the Civil War Dead: Commemoration and the Problem of Reconciliation* (Lawrence: University Press of Kansas, 2005); Drew Gilpin Faust, *This Republic of Suffering: Death and the American Civil War* (New York: Vintage, 2009); Ian Finseth, *The Civil War Dead and American Modernity* (New York: Oxford University Press, 2018). On the Civil War dead in broader cultural context see also Gary Laderman, *The Sacred Remains: American Attitudes towards Death, 1799–1883* (New Haven, CT: Yale University Press, 1996).

2. All quotations from *Battle-Pieces* will be from Melville, *Published Poems: Battle-Pieces, John Marr, Timoleon*, ed. Robert C. Ryan, Harrison Hayford, Alma MacDougall Reising, and G. Thomas Tanselle (Evanston, IL: Northwestern University Press and the Newberry Library, 2009). The most extensively annotated edition is Hennig Cohen, ed., *The Battle-Pieces of Herman Melville* (New York: Thomas Yoseloff, 1963). For criticism see William H. Shurr, *The Mystery of Iniquity: Melville as Poet, 1857–1891* (Lexington: University of Kentucky Press, 1971), chap. 1; Stanton Garner, *The Civil War World of Herman Melville* (Lawrence: University Press of Kansas, 1993); Michael Warner, "What Like a Bullet Can Undeceive?," *Public Culture* 15, no. 2 (Winter 2003): 41–54; Edgar A. Dryden, *Monumental Melville: The Formation of a Literary Career* (Stanford, CA: Stanford University Press, 2004), chap. 2; Martin Griffin, *Ashes of the Mind: War and Memory in Northern Literature, 1865–1900* (Amherst: University of Massachusetts Press, 2009), chap. 2; Andrew West, "Emersonian Pragmatism and Melville's *Battle-Pieces and Aspects of the War*," *Forum for Modern Language Studies* 46 (2010): 267–96; Randall Fuller, *From Battlefields Rising: How the Civil War Transformed American Literature* (New York: Oxford University Press, 2011), chap. 9; Faith Barrett, *To Fight Aloud Is Very Brave: American Poetry and the Civil War* (Amherst: University of Massachusetts Press, 2012), chap. 6; Jillian Spivey Caddell, "Melville's Epitaphs: On Time, Place, and War," *New England Quarterly* 87, no. 2 (June 2014): 292–318; Elizabeth Renker, "Melville and the Worlds of Civil War Poetry," *Leviathan* 16, no. 1 (March 2014): 135–62; Timothy Sweet, "Melville's *Battle-Pieces* and Vernacular Poetics," *Leviathan* 17, no. 3 (October 2015): 25–42;

and Juana Celia Djelal, *Melville's Antithetical Muse: Reading the Shorter Poems* (Valencia, Spain: University of Valencia Press, 2017), chap. 3.

3. On the development of the pastoral elegy in English literature see Peter M. Sacks, *The English Elegy: Studies in the Genre from Spenser to Yeats* (Baltimore: Johns Hopkins University Press, 1985). On the elegy in American literature see Max Cavitch, *American Elegy: The Poetry of Mourning from the Puritans to Whitman* (Minneapolis: University of Minnesota Press, 2007).

4. On Lincoln's relationship to Christianity during the Civil War see David S. Reynolds, *Abe: Abraham Lincoln in His Times* (New York: Penguin, 2020), chap. 19. On the importance of religion in the Civil War generally see George C. Rable, *God's Almost Chosen People: A Religious History of the American Civil War* (Chapel Hill: University of North Carolina Press, 2010); Sean A. Scott, *A Visitation of God: Northern Civilians Interpret the Civil War* (New York: Oxford University Press, 2010).

5. *The Greek Anthology*, trans. W. R. Paton, 5 vols. (New York: Putnam's, 1919), 2:141. On the pervasive influence of classical culture in antebellum America see Carl J. Richard, *The Golden Age of the Classics in America: Greece, Rome, and the Antebellum United States* (Cambridge, MA: Harvard University Press, 2009). On the concept of *kleos* and the ancient Greek hero see Gregory Nagy, *The Ancient Greek Hero in Twenty-Four Hours* (Cambridge, MA: Harvard University Press, 2013).

6. Brown quoted in Louis DeCaro Jr., *Freedom's Dawn: The Last Days of John Brown in Virginia* (Lanham, MD: Rowman & Littlefield, 2018), 302. For a comprehensive record of contemporary responses to John Brown's raid see John A. Stauffer and Zoe Trodd, eds., *The Tribunal: Responses to John Brown and the Harpers Ferry Raid* (Cambridge, MA: Harvard University Press, 2012).

7. Quoted in DeCaro, *Freedom's Dawn*, 323.

8. Shurr (*Mystery of Iniquity*, 16–17) sees "The Portent" as the beginning of the "Cycle of Law" in the poem; the "cut" to the "crown" (as legal realm) is the violation of civil law that Brown's raid will initiate. On the joint political and religious significance of Brown in Melville's poem see Dryden, *Monumental Melville*, 70–76. Tom Nurmi focuses on the poet's allusions to the Shenandoah Valley as a shadowed realm of death, and the rhetorical functions of apostrophe and prosopopoeia in "The Portent"; see "Shadows in the Shenandoah: Melville, Slavery, and the Elegiac Landscape," *Leviathan* 17, no. 3 (October 2015): 7–24.

9. On the tradition of Christ's face depicted in Veronica's "veil," napkin, or handkerchief in Western art see Neil MacGregor, with Erika Langmuir, *Seeing Salvation: Images of Christ in Art* (New Haven, CT: Yale University Press, 2000), chap. 6. The Virginia illustrator and journalist David Hunter Strother, who provided unsympathetic accounts of Brown's raid and its sequel for *Harper's Weekly*, made unpublished drawings of Brown on the scaffold in his white hood and then hanging from the rope, and he also drew Brown's grotesquely contorted face shortly after his death when the hood was lifted. See DeCaro, *Freedom's Dawn*, 318–22, for the drawings' first appearance in print.

10. William Spengemann, "Melville the Poet," *American Literary History* 11, no. 4 (December 1999): 569–609; see also Dryden, *Monumental Melville*, 75.

Thomas Gray, "The Bard," Thomas Gray Archive at https://www.thomasgray.org/cgi-bin/display.cgi?text=bapo.

11. Stauffer and Trodd, *Tribunal*, 109 (Thoreau), 114 (Emerson), 155 (Garnet), 199 (Alcott).

12. Sara J. Schechner, *Comets, Popular Culture, and the Birth of Modern Cosmology* (Princeton, NJ: Princeton University Press, 1997), 3–4.

13. Stauffer and Trodd, *Tribunal*, 102 (Beecher), 109 (Thoreau); Walt Whitman, *The Complete Poetry and Collected Prose*, ed. Justin Kaplan (New York: Library of America, 1982), 381.

14. For a modern biography of General Nathaniel Lyon see Christopher Phillips, *Damned Yankee: The Life of General Nathaniel Lyon* (Columbia: University of Missouri Press, 1990); on the battle of Wilson's Creek see chap. 10. See also James M. McPherson, *Battle Cry of Freedom: The Civil War Era* (New York: Oxford University Press, 1988), 351–52.

15. Garner, *Civil War World*, 109; McGowan, "Melville's Low-Relief Officer Corps," *Leviathan* 17, no. 3 (October 2015): 43–62.

16. Cohen, *Battle-Pieces*, 214; William A. Hammond, "Brigadier General Nathaniel Lyon, U.S.A.—Personal Recollections," *Magazine of American History* 12, no. 3 (March 1885), quoted in Adam Goodheart, *1861: The Civil War Awakening* (New York: Vintage, 2012), 254; James Peckham, *Gen. Nathaniel Lyon, and Missouri in 1861* (New York, 1866), 332. Goodheart, *Civil War Awakening*, 251–66, shows why Lyon was revered by the Northern public as a martyr to the Union cause for his strategic actions in seizing the Saint Louis arsenal and creating a Home Guard of German immigrants in Saint Louis as a Unionist force within the state.

17. On Lyon's religious views see Phillips, *Damned Yankee*, 16–17, 29–30, 34, 46–49, 61, 70–71, 82, 85–86, 99, 123, 251.

18. Alice Fahs, *The Imagined Civil War: Popular Literature of the North and South, 1861–1865* (Chapel Hill: University of North Carolina Press, 2001), 83. Lyon's place in early Union hagiography is evident in Jeremiah Burns, *The Patriot's Offering; or, The Life, Services, and Military Career of the Noble Trio, [Elmer] Ellsworth, [Nathaniel] Lyon, and [Edward] Baker* (New York: Baker & Godwin, 1862). Burns noted of Lyon's death, "The falling of the body was but the dropping of the shell: the releasing of a life which was to go forth to breathe strength in the arms of others—to make a nation braver and better, to defend and enjoy the priceless blessings of liberty" (*Patriot's Offering*, 43).

19. In the nineteenth century the verb phrase "try on" meant to "try out" in modern English. On the circumstances surrounding Lyon's death and his remarks before and during the battle see Phillips, *Damned Yankee*, 252–56; on the mistaken journalistic account of his bequest of his estate to the Union war effort see 260–61.

20. Phillips, *Damned Yankee*, 253; Lyon quoted at 251, 255.

21. On the Union disaster at Ball's Bluff see McPherson, *Battle Cry of Freedom*, 362–63.

22. In her reading of the poem, Renker interprets the geographical word "bluff" in the title as hinting at the deception underlying the contrast between

the soldiers' patriotic enthusiasm and impending senseless death; see "Melville and the Worlds," 142–45.

23. On the battle of Shiloh see McPherson, *Battle Cry of Freedom*, 405–15 (quotation at 412). Daniel McCook quoted in Neff, *Honoring the Civil War Dead*, 26.

24. For Shurr, "Shiloh" dramatizes the ironic epigram "What like a bullet can undeceive!" (*Mystery of Iniquity*, 32–33). Griffin writes, "In its rich amalgamation of religious, Romantic, and pantheistic sensibilities, 'Shiloh: A Requiem' is a hymn sung in memoriam by Nature to wounded humankind" (*Ashes of the Mind*, 70). Claiming that the swallows in the poem hint at Christian redemption for the dead soldiers, Fuller argues that by focusing on the sky instead of the grisly battlefield, "the poem ensures that the war remains an abstraction, an idea. This strategy of abstraction emerges from Melville's understanding about the difficulty—the near impossibility—of presenting modern combat through the conventional medium of mid-nineteenth-century poetry" (*From Battlefields Rising*, 69).

25. On the battle of Pea Ridge see McPherson, *Battle Cry of Freedom*, 404–5.

26. On Simonides's epitaph see *Greek Anthology*, 2:139. Caddell notes of the poem that a "tension remains between the 'we' who are referenced by the single 'Inscription' and the material plurality of 'Graves' on which it is presumed to appear"; another tension arises from the epitaph's "fundamental task to praise the deceased and attach meaning to his life and the futility the poem expresses" ("Melville's Epitaphs," 308).

27. On the battle of Fredericksburg see McPherson, *Battle Cry of Freedom*, 570–74.

28. Caddell claims that the poem challenges the conventions of its genre: "Again, Melville seems to obstruct the epitaphic impulse, truncating the process of inscription and divorcing it from its creation and reception" ("Melville's Epitaphs," 315).

29. On the battle of the Wilderness see McPherson, *Battle Cry of Freedom*, 724–26.

30. For other discussions of "An Uninscribed Monument" see Griffin, *Ashes of the Mind*, 71–72; Caddell, "Melville's Epitaphs," 309–10.

31. See Carol Bundy, *The Nature of Sacrifice: A Biography of Charles Russell Lowell* (New York: Farrar, Straus and Giroux, 2005). On Melville's visit to Lowell's camp and his subsequent scout with Lowell see Fuller, *From Battlefields Rising*, 185–95; see also Bundy, *Nature of Sacrifice*, 378–81; Garner, *Civil War World*, 304–21.

32. On Sheridan and Schouler's responses to Lowell's death see Bundy, *Nature of Sacrifice*, 478.

33. Bundy, 129.

34. Without identifying the subject of the poem as Lowell and ignoring its classical associations, Caldwell claims that the poem expresses the idea of the deceased soldier's Christian resurrection. She also improbably asserts that the title implies the poem is literally inscribed on the fallen officer's grave, allegedly making it the only technical "epitaph" in the collection; but the preposition

"on" in the title is more likely figurative, meaning "devoted to." See Caldwell, "Melville's Epitaphs," 304–5. For an analysis of "The Scout toward Aldie" and the Lowell-like portrait of its commanding officer see Jonathan A. Cook, "History, Legend, and Poetic Tradition in Melville's 'The Scout toward Aldie,'" *ATQ* (new series) 17 (June 2003): 61–80.

35. As Griffin notes, "The poetic speaker is haunted by the impossibility of a monument, in any real sense connected to the place of loss, that could commemorate the soldiers who drowned as their troop-carrying ships went down" (*Ashes of the Mind*, 75).

36. John Milton, *The Complete Poems*, ed. John Leonard (New York: Penguin, 1998), 45–46.

37. Thomas Reed Turner, *Beware the People Weeping: Public Opinion and the Assassination of Abraham Lincoln* (Baton Rouge: LSU Press, 1991), 22. For an extensive account of the national reaction to the assassination see Martha Hodes, *Mourning Lincoln* (New Haven, CT: Yale University Press, 2015). On the assassination itself see Reynolds, *Abe*, chap. 22. Max Cavitch accurately notes, "As an occasional poem, 'The Martyr' . . . depends for its intelligibility upon its embeddedness in the historical present" (*American Elegy*, 278).

38. Hodes, *Mourning Lincoln*, 136, 119–20; David B. Chesebrough, *No Sorrow Like Our Sorrow: Northern Protestant Ministers and the Death of Lincoln* (Kent, OH: Kent State University Press, 1994), 52.

39. Lincoln's appellation of "Father Abraham" had first been popularized by the poem "We Are Coming, Father Abraham" by Quaker poet James Sloan Gibbons, published in William Cullen Bryant's *New York Evening Post* and then set to music by Stephen Foster and others, following Lincoln's call on July 1, 1862, for three hundred thousand more volunteers.

40. In their sermons in the aftermath of Lincoln's death, many Northern preachers looked to the figure of Andrew Johnson as offering potentially sterner justice toward the defeated Confederacy than Lincoln might have enacted; see Turner, *Beware the People*, chap. 10; Chesebrough, *No Sorrow*, 70–73. In a scathing indictment of the South for Lincoln's death, New Bedford Congregational minister Alonzo H. Quint opined, anticipating Melville's language in "The Martyr," "We will rally around this man [Andrew Johnson]. He, when generals said Nashville could not be held, sent the citizens into the trenches, and held it, and kept the flag flying. He will defend the flag as well now, and will man the ramparts with faithful men. The kindly heart is gone; the avenger has come" (*No Sorrow*, 73, 125).

41. Chesebrough, *No Sorrow*, 64–65; for a full discussion see chap. 4. See also Tuner, *Beware the People*, chap. 6; Hodes, *Mourning Lincoln*, chap. 5.

42. Brian Higgins and Hershel Parker, eds., *Herman Melville: The Contemporary Reviews* (New York: Cambridge University Press, 1995), 527; on the general critical response to *Battle-Pieces* see 507–28.

43. Higgins and Parker, 514.

7. "Are Ye, Gods?"

1. Citations of *Timoleon, Etc.* in the present essay will be from Melville, *Published Poems: Battle-Pieces, John Marr, Timoleon*, ed. Robert C. Ryan, Harrison

Hayford, Alma MacDougall Reising, and G. Thomas Tanselle (Evanston, IL: Northwestern University Press and the Newberry Library, 2009); on the printing and publishing history of *Timoleon, Etc.* see 565–78. The deliberately offhand inclusion of "Etc." in the collection's title was probably Melville's ironically dismissive acknowledgment of his marginal status as a contemporary poet. For critical discussions of *Timoleon* see Darrel Abel, "'Laurel Twined with Thorn': The Theme of Melville's *Timoleon*," *Personalist* 41 (1960): 330–40; William Bysshe Stein, *The Poetry of Melville's Late Years: Time, History, Myth, and Religion* (Albany: State University of New York Press, 1970), chaps. 5–6; William Shurr, *The Mystery of Iniquity: Melville as Poet, 1857–1891* (Lexington: University of Kentucky Press, 1972), chap. 5; Clark Davis, *After the Whale: Melville in the Wake of "Moby-Dick"* (Tuscaloosa: University of Alabama Press, 1995), 159–74; William B. Dillingham, *Melville and His Circle: The Last Years* (Athens: University of Georgia Press, 1996), 167–75; Douglas Robillard, introduction to *The Poems of Herman Melville* (Kent, OH: Kent State University Press, 2000), 34–47; Edgar Dryden, *Monumental Melville: The Formation of a Literary Career* (Stanford, CA: Stanford University Press, 2004), chap. 5; Sanford E. Marowitz, "Connecting by Contrast: The 'Art' of *Timoleon, Etc.*," in *Melville as Poet*, ed. Sanford E. Marowitz (Kent, OH: Kent State University Press, 2013), chap. 7; and Juana Celia Djelal, *Melville's Antithetical Muse: Reading the Shorter Poems* (Valencia, Spain: University of Valencia, 2013), chap. 5. Abel claims that *Timoleon, Etc.* was "unified by its varied reiteration of the theme that preoccupied his thoughts at the close of his career—that bold and original thinking alienates artists and intellectuals from their fellow-men" ("Laurel Twined," 330). Davis argues that the volume shows "the attempt once again to synthesize the dialectic between mind and body" (*After the Whale*, 159). Dillingham asserts that Melville's "primary subject is devotion to art" (*Melville and His Circle*, 171). Robillard (introduction to *Poems of Herman Melville*) suggests that the idea of pilgrimage and the quest for knowledge unifies the collection, as hinted by its concluding "L'Envoi." In Dryden's view, "Broadly speaking, the first group of poems examines the relation of poetry and history, and in the process obliquely suggests Melville's understanding of his own situation as a writer in America in 1881 [*sic*]. The second group focuses on the poet's own past" (*Monumental Melville*, 167). My own examination of the poems in *Timoleon, Etc.* comes closest to William B. Stein's analysis of the poems' varied religious symbolism. On Melville's reading of Matthew Arnold's poetry and the latter's influence on his characteristic themes and techniques as poet see Walter E. Bezanson, "Melville's Reading of Arnold's Poetry," *PMLA* 69, no. 3 (January 1954): 365–91.

2. On the larger religious context of *Clarel* see Jonathan A. Cook, "*Clarel* and the Victorian Crisis of Faith," in *Visionary of the Word: Melville and Religion*, ed. Jonathan A. Cook and Brian Yothers (Evanston, IL: Northwestern University Press, 2016), 21–70.

3. On Melville's affiliation with the Unitarian Church while living in New York City see Walter Donald Kring, *Herman Melville's Religious Journey* (Raleigh, NC: Pentland, 1997), chaps. 8–9. On the impact of Elihu Vedder's illustrations to Edward Fitzgerald's *Rubáiyát of Omar Khayyám* on the poetry of *Timoleon* see Elisa Tamarkin, "A Final Appearance with Elihu Vedder: Melville's Visions," *Leviathan* 18, no. 3 (October 2016): 68–107.

4. James Turner, *Without God, without Creed: The Origins of Unbelief in America* (Baltimore: Johns Hopkins University Press, 1985), 171; Octavius Brooks Frothingham, *The Rising and the Setting Faith and Other Discourses* (New York: G. P. Putnam's Sons, 1878), 185–86. On the evangelical career of Dwight L. Moody see Bruce J. Evensen, *God's Man for the Gilded Age: D. L. Moody and the Rise of Modern Mass Evangelicalism* (New York: Oxford University Press, 2003). For a survey of religious trends in the postbellum United States see Francis P. Weisenburger, *Ordeal of Faith: The Crisis of Church-Going America, 1865–1900* (New York: Philosophical Library, 1959).

5. For an insightful comparison of themes in "Timoleon" and *Billy Budd* see Robert Shulman, "Melville's 'Timoleon': From Plutarch to the Early Stages of *Billy Budd*," *Comparative Literature* 19, no. 4 (Autumn 1967): 351–61. For other discussions of "Timoleon" see Stein, *Poetry of Melville's Late Years*, 74–77; Shurr, *Mystery of Iniquity*, 153–57; Vernon Shetley, "Melville's 'Timoleon,'" *ESQ* 33, no. 2 (1987): 83–93; Dryden, *Monumental Melville*, 171–77; and Djelal, *Melville's Antithetical Muse*, 136–43. The editors of the Northwestern-Newberry edition of Melville's *Published Poems* (751–53) suggest that Melville relied on the translation of Plutarch's *Lives* by John and William Langhorne (New York: Harper & Brothers, 1875).

6. As Djelal has noted, "The tragic howl that concludes the stanza pleads for proof of godly connection. That cry echoes from myth through tragedy, in the tales of gods and their mortal sons who beg for signs of affiliation" (*Melville's Antithetical Muse*, 142).

7. Quoted in Shulman, "Melville's 'Timoleon,'" 359–60.

8. Quoted in Bezanson, "Melville's Reading," 381.

9. On the life of Maria Mitchell see Renée Bergland, *Maria Mitchell and the Sexing of Science: An Astronomer among the American Romantics* (Boston: Beacon, 2008). Melville first met Mitchell on a visit to Nantucket with his father-in-law in July 1852, but the details for the setting of "After the Pleasure Party" came from Melville's visit to Italy in early 1857 and the revelation this gave him of the art of classical antiquity and the Renaissance. See Melville, *Journals*, ed. Lynn Horth (Evanston, IL: Northwestern University Press and the Newberry Library, 1993), 100–124. The visual stimulus for the poem's depiction of a spiteful Amor was probably provided by his visit to the Villa Borghese, where he saw a bas relief or sculpture of "Venus & Cupid" and noted the "mischievous look of C. [Cupid]" (*Journals*, 107; see also 468–69). Dennis Berthold suggests that Melville may have used an 1863 guidebook to the Vatican museum containing 136 woodcuts of statues as a visual aid to represent the figures of Urania and Athena in his poem; see "Robert McPherson's *Vatican Sculptures*: An Iconographic Source for Herman Melville's 'After the Pleasure Party,'" *South Central Review* 35, no. 3 (Fall 2018): 40–54.

10. Walter Sutton, "Melville's 'After the Pleasure Party' and the Art of Concealment," *Philological Quarterly* 30 (July 1951): 316–27, has examined the poem's use of the images of heavenly and earthly love, as found in Plato's *Symposium*, as well as its echoes of Sappho's despairing self-representation in Ovid's *Heroides* XV. Shurr, *Mystery of Iniquity*, 155–60, has demonstrated that the poem

NOTES TO PAGES 179-194

echoes the pessimistic philosophy of Schopenhauer's *The World as Will and Idea*, which Melville likely read in the late 1880s; more particularly, the poem dramatizes ideas found in chapter 44, "The Metaphysics of the Love of the Sexes," including the philosopher's negative portrait of the figure of Cupid/Eros, which is reflected in the characterization of Amor in Melville's poem. On Melville's reading of Schopenhauer see also Dillingham, *Melville and His Circle*, 58–70. Hershel Parker, *Melville: The Making of the Poet* (Evanston, IL: Northwestern University Press, 2007), 139–40, has briefly noted linguistic echoes in the poem from Tennyson's *The Princess*, an extended examination of the contemporary debate on female education. For discussions of the astronomical muse Urania of Milton and Arnold in relation to Melville's poem see Dryden, *Monumental Melville*, 178–79, and Dillingham, *Melville and His Circle*, 93, respectively. Vernon Shetley, in "Melville's 'After the Pleasure Party': Venus and Virgin," *Papers on Literature and Language* 25 (Fall 1989): 425–42, has related Melville's poem to the writings of Henry Adams and Harriet Beecher Stowe on the contrast of Venus and Virgin in later nineteenth-century American culture.

11. John Milton, *Paradise Lost*, ed. Merritt Y. Hughes (Indianapolis: Odyssey, 1962), 164; Matthew Arnold, *Poems* (New York: Dutton, 1948), 79; Bezanson, "Melville's Reading," 372.

12. See Allan F. Stein, "Hawthorne's Zenobia and Melville's Urania," *American Transcendental Quarterly* 26 (Spring 1975): 11–14.

13. See Nathaniel Philbrick, "Hawthorne, Maria Mitchell, and Melville's 'After the Pleasure Party,'" *ESQ: A Journal of the American Renaissance* 37, no. 4 (1991): 291–308. On Melville's visit to the Rospigliosi Palace see *Journals*, 109–10. For another discussion of Mitchell in relation to Melville's poem focusing on the idea of sexual inversion see Bergland, *Maria Mitchell*, 243–47.

14. *Why Go to Church?*, in *Sermons, Volume 2* (New York: Francis, 1974), 5; quoted in Eric Leigh Schmidt, *The Church of Saint Thomas Paine: A Religious History of American Secularism* (Princeton, NJ: Princeton University Press, 2021), 122.

15. Stein, *Poetry of Melville's Late Years*, 78.

16. Stein, 79.

17. For a useful guide to Epicurean ideas see Catherine Wilson, *How to Be an Epicurean: The Ancient Art of Living Well* (New York: Basic Books, 2019).

18. See Melville, *Published Poems*, 787.

19. Dillingham, *Melville and His Circle*, 32–42.

20. Believing in reincarnation, the Cathars rejected the doctrine of the Trinity and the sacrament of the Eucharist, as well as the existence of hell and purgatory. Although defeated in their polemical battle with early Christianity, adherents to Gnosticism and Manichean dualism survived in parts of the eastern Roman Empire such as in Armenia among the Paulicians and in the Balkans among the Bogomils ("Friends of God") and later spread throughout parts of France, Germany, and Italy during the High Middle Ages. Gnosticism suffered its final defeat by the armies of the pope, whose extermination of the populace of Languedoc was meant to eliminate any future threat to Catholicism, while the newly established Inquisition dealt with any remaining heretics.

For another analysis of the Gnostic context of the poem see Shurr, *Mystery of Iniquity*, 164–66.

21. Garner, "Aging with the Antonines," in *Melville "Among the Nations,"* ed. Sanford E. Marovitz and A. C. Christodoulou (Kent, OH: Kent State University Press, 2001), 277–86.

22. Melville, *Journals*, 75, 76. On the historical debates on Moses's indebtedness to the Egyptians see Jan Assmann, *Moses the Egyptian: The Memory of Egypt in Western Monotheism* (Cambridge, MA: Harvard University Press, 1997), chaps. 3–4. Recent biblical research demonstrates the Yhwh was likely adopted as the god of the Hebrews in about 1200 BCE from an Edomite storm god and only became the exclusive god of Israel in about 500–400 BCE after a complex process of evolution. See Thomas Römer, *The Invention of God*, trans. Raymond Geuss (Cambridge, MA: Harvard University Press, 2015).

23. Ruskin quoted in A. N. Wilson, *God's Funeral: A Biography of Faith and Doubt in Western Civilization* (New York: Norton, 1999), 272; Basem L. Ra'ad, "Ancient Lands," in *A Companion to Herman Melville*, ed. Wyn Kelley (New York: Blackwell, 2006), 138.

8. Legends of the Fall

1. On the likely influence of Melville's late reading of Balzac on the novel see William B. Dillingham, *Melville and His Circle: The Last Years* (Athens: University of Georgia Press, 1996), chap. 3; Kevin J. Hayes, "Melville and Balzac," *Resources for American Literary Study* 26, no. 2 (2000): 159–83. On the influence of the *Somers* naval mutiny see Charles Robert Anderson, "The Genesis of *Billy Budd*," *American Literature* 12, no. 3 (November 1940): 329–46; H. Bruce Franklin, "*Billy Budd* and Capital Punishment: A Tale of Three Centuries," *American Literature* 69, no. 2 (June 1998): 337–59; Wyn Kelley, "'Tender Kinswoman': Gail Hamilton and Gendered Justice in *Billy Budd*," in *Melville and Woman*, ed. Haskell Springer and Elizabeth Schultz (Kent, OH: Kent State University Press, 2006), 98–117; and John Cyril Barton, *Literary Executions: Capital Punishment and American Culture, 1820–1925* (Baltimore: Johns Hopkins University Press, 2014), 193–224. On the novella's relation to contemporary labor unrest see Robert K. Wallace, "*Billy Buddy* and the Haymarket Hangings," *American Literature* 47, no. 1 (March 1975): 108–13; Larry J. Reynolds, *Righteous Violence: Revolution, Slavery, and the American Renaissance* (Athens: University of Georgia Press, 2011), chap. 7; see also Sanford E. Marovitz, "Melville among the Realists: W. D. Howells and the Writing of *Billy Budd*," *American Literary Realism* 34, no. 1 (Fall 2001): 29–46. On the covert biographical basis for the novella in the death of Malcolm Melville see Peter L. Hays and Richard Dilworth Rust, "'Something Healing': Fathers and Sons in *Billy Budd*," *Nineteenth-Century Fiction* 34, no. 3 (December 1979): 326–36.

2. On the use of Christian myth and symbol in the novella see John H. Timmerman, "Typology and Biblical Consistency in *Billy Budd*," *Notre Dame English Journal* 15, no. 1 (Winter 1983): 23–38; Eugene Goodheart, "*Billy Budd* and the World's Imperfection," *Sewanee Review* 114, no. 1 (Winter 2006): 81–92. All quotations from the Bible will be from the King James (Authorized) Version.

3. Herman Melville, *The Piazza Tales and Other Prose Pieces, 1839–1860*, ed. Harrison Hayford, Alma A. MacDougal, G. Thomas Tanselle, et al. (Evanston, IL: Northwestern University Press and the Newberry Library, 1987), 243. Significantly, while evoking a basic doctrine shaping Protestant Christianity in this passage, Melville employs two biblical metaphors, with "visitation" describing a revelation from God (Job 10:12; Jer. 8:12, 10:15, 46:23, 50:27; 1 Pet. 2:12), and the scales of justice used as a means to "weigh" guilt (Job 31:6; Isa. 26:7; Daniel 5:27).

4. For a discussion of the theological and cultural resonances of the Fall see Gary A. Anderson, *The Genesis of Perfection: Adam and Eve in Jewish and Christian Imagination* (Louisville, KY: Westminster John Knox, 2001).

5. *Billy Budd, Sailor*, in *"Billy Budd, Sailor" and Other Uncompleted Writings*, ed. Harrison Hayford, Alma A. MacDougall, Robert A. Sandberg, and G. Thomas Tanselle (Evanston, IL: Northwestern University Press and the Newberry Library, 2017), 3, 4. Subsequent references from this edition will be cited parenthetically in the text.

6. Thomas Paine, *The Rights of Man*, in *Collected Writings*, ed. Eric Foner (New York: Library of America, 1995), 462, 463.

7. See Robert Narveson, "The Name Claggart in *Billy Budd*," *American Speech* 43, no. 3 (October 1968): 229–32.

8. John Milton, *Paradise Lost*, in *The Complete Poems*, ed. John Leonard (New York: Penguin, 1998). Citations from this edition will be cited by book and line number in the text. On the civilized gentlemanly devil of nineteenth-century literature see Jeffrey Burton Russell, *Mephistopheles: The Devil in the Modern World* (Ithaca, NY: Cornell University Press, 1986). In a discussion of the alleged homoerotic subtext of *Billy Budd*, Caleb Crain notes that the comparison of Claggart's appearance to that of Titus Oates, the perjured instigator of the fabricated Popish Plot against Charles II in 1678, subsumes an allusion to Oates's notorious homosexuality implying Claggart's sharing this sexual orientation; see *American Sympathy: Men, Friendship, and Literature in the New Nation* (New Haven, CT: Yale University Press, 2001), chap. 6.

9. Simon Baron-Cohen, *The Science of Evil: On Empathy and the Origins of Cruelty* (New York: Basic Books, 2012), chap. 3.

10. See Henry F. Pommer, *Milton and Melville* (Pittsburgh: University of Pittsburgh Press, 1950), 84–90; and Norman Holmes Pearson, "Billy Budd: 'The King's Yarn,'" *American Quarterly* 3, no. 2 (Summer 1951): 99–114.

11. On the nature of Claggart's envy and Vere's punitive manner of handling Billy's crime see Lester H. Hunt, "Billy Budd: Melville's Dilemma," *Philosophy and Literature* 26, no. 2 (October 2002): 273–95.

12. On the incompletion of the novel in relation to the task of criticism see the essays in Robert Milder, ed., *Critical Essays on Melville's "Billy Budd"* (Boston: G. K. Hall, 1989); John Wenke, "Melville's Indirection: *Billy Budd*, the Genetic Text, and 'the Deadly Space Between,'" in Yanella, *New Essays*, 114–44; and Russell Weaver, *The Moral World of "Billy Budd"* (New York: Peter Lang, 2014). On legal formalism and Chief Justice Shaw see Brook Thomas, *Cross-Examinations of Law and Literature: Cooper, Hawthorne, Stowe, and Melville* (New York: Cambridge University Press, 1987), chaps. 9–10. On *Billy Budd* in relation to British naval legal protocol see C. B. Ives, "*Billy Budd* and the Articles of War," *American*

Literature 34, no. 1 (March 1962): 31–39; repr. in Milder, *Critical Essays*, 88–94; and Richard H. Weisberg, *The Failure of the Word: The Protagonist as Lawyer in Modern Fiction* (New Haven, CT: Yale University Press, 1984), chap. 8.

13. See Bucker F. Melton Jr., *A Hanging Offense: The Strange Affair of the Warship* Somers (New York: Free Press, 2003), chap. 5.

14. See Dillingham, *Melville and His Circle*, chap. 2. For a discussion of Schopenhauerian themes in *Moby-Dick*, raising the possibility of Melville's awareness of the philosopher's ideas in the early 1850s, see Greg Pritchard, "*Moby-Dick* and the Philosopher of Pessimism," *Australasian Journal of American Studies* 22, no. 1 (July 2003): 34–48.

15. See Olive Fite, "Billy Budd, Claggart, and Schopenhauer," *Nineteenth-Century Fiction* 23, no. 3 (December 1963): 336–43; Dillingham, *Melville and His Circle*, 61–62.

16. Schopenhauer, *Studies in Pessimism*, trans. T. Bailey Saunders (London: Sonnenschein, 1891), 24–25; Melville, *Piazza Tales*, 243.

17. Schopenhauer, *Religion: A Dialogue; and Other Essays*, trans. T. Bailey Saunders (London: Sonnenschein, 1891), 12. On Melville's markings in "Religion: A Dialogue" and in other essays in his copy see Steven Olsen-Smith and Peter Norberg, eds., *Melville's Marginalia Online*, at http://melvillesmarginalia.org.

18. Norman Vance, *Bible and Novel: Narrative Authority and the Death of God* (New York: Oxford University Press, 2013), quotation at 190.

Index

Adam (biblical), 44, 45, 47, 50, 117, 207, 209, 210, 214–16, 219
Adams, Henry, 28
Adams, John, 126
Adams, Samuel, 46
Adler, George, 15–17
Aeschylus, 174
Albany (New York), 6, 7
Albany Classical School, 6
Albany Evening Journal, 103
Albany Microscope (Munsell), 6, 7
Albany Young Men's Society for Mutual Improvement, 6
Alcott, Louisa May, 138
Alcott, William, vii
Alger, William Rounseville, 191
All Souls Unitarian Church, 170, 208
Allen, Ethan, 3, 122
Altick, Richard D., 25
American Revolution, 108, 112, 113, 123, 126, 128, 130
American Whig Review, 22
Anderson, Walter E., 59
Arnold, Matthew, 2, 170, 171, 178, 184; *Empedocles on Etna*, 170, 172, 177, 179, 184; "Stanzas on the Grande Chartreuse," 184; "Switzerland," 184
Astor, John Jacob, 33, 37–40, 55, 58
Ataraxia (tranquility), 9, 13
Athens, 28
Atlantic Monthly, 167

Bacheler, Origen, 4
Baker, Edward Dickinson, 146
Ball's Bluff, battle of, 145–46
Barbour, James, 102–4
Bard, The (Gray), 137
Bardowell, Matthew R., 64
Baron-Cohen, Simon, 212
Bayle, Pierre, ix, 10; *Historical and Critical Dictionary*, 10, 17, 171

Beach, Moses, 35
Beale, Thomas, 11
Beecher, Henry Ward, 138
Beecher, Lyman, 5, 66; *Lectures on Skepticism*, 5
Bellows, Henry W., 8
Bennett, Frederick Debell, 11
Berkeley, George, 192
Bible, vii, ix, xi, 1–3, 15, 19, 30, 31, 32, 37–41, 48, 57, 66, 71, 77, 84, 87, 89, 90, 93, 108, 113, 206–8, 211, 224
Bible, books of: Acts, vii, 39, 40, 48, 77, 110, 142, 201; 1 Corinthians, 9, 25, 39, 58, 59, 65, 66, 79, 80, 151, 155, 196, 208, 219, 221; 2 Corinthians, 57; Ecclesiastes, ix, xi, 19, 84, 107–11, 113, 115–28, 130, 191; Ephesians, 47, 49, 102, 186, 187; Exodus, 112, 113, 125, 128, 158, 200, 204; Galatians, 42, 182; Genesis, 10, 13, 50, 117, 123, 142, 148, 177, 193, 208, 215, 217, 220; Hebrews, 134; Isaiah, 9, 41, 52, 113, 145, 162, 200, 211, 215; James, 87, 191; Jeremiah, 113, 145, 148, 150; Job, ix, 33, 54, 84, 86, 87, 89, 90, 102–4, 146, 147, 151, 154, 177, 193, 211; Joel, 200; John, 33, 45, 48, 53, 54, 58, 136, 186, 189, 221; Joshua, 148, 200; 1 Kings, 186; 2 Kings, 221; Leviticus, 126; Luke, 33, 40, 45, 46, 47, 54, 55, 58, 65, 68, 78, 164, 165, 186, 193, 221; Mark, 38, 40, 46, 52, 54, 65, 193; Matthew, 32, 37, 38, 40–44, 46, 50, 54, 55, 65, 74, 79, 101, 113, 136, 138, 150, 166, 173, 186, 197, 203, 209, 220; Numbers, 125; 1 Peter, 221; 2 Peter, 162; Proverbs, ix, 118, 120, 179; Psalms, 145, 151, 154, 177, 186, 200; Revelation, 101–2, 138, 142, 145; Romans, 26, 51, 57, 66, 113, 189, 211, 218, 221; 1 Thessalonians, 58, 151–52, 165; 2 Thessalonians, 207, 213; 2 Timothy, 187

Ingram Content Group UK Ltd.
Milton Keynes UK
UKHW010612210723
425518UK00004B/25/J

9 781501 770968